HERE ON THE EDGE

How a small group

of World War II

conscientious objectors

took art and peace

from the margins to

the mainstream

HERE ON THE EDGE

Steve McQuiddy

OREGON STATE UNIVERSITY PRESS ▦ CORVALLIS

The paper in this book meets the guidelines for permanence and durability of the Committee on Production Guidelines for Book Longevity of the Council on Library Resources and the minimum requirements of the American National Standard for Permanence of Paper for Printed Library Materials Z39.48-1984.

Front cover images: Fine Arts members and associates at the Shore Pines Cottages across the highway from Camp #56. For identification of individuals, see page 67. (Bruce Reeves Collection, Lewis and Clark College.) Image at top: Detail from "Sea, Fish and Constellation" by Morris Graves. For full painting, see page 141. (Courtesy of Morris Graves Foundation.)

Library of Congress Cataloging-in-Publication Data

McQuiddy, Steve.
Here on the edge : How a Small Group of World War II Conscientious Objectors Took Art and Peace from the Margins to the Mainstream / Steve McQuiddy.
  p cm
Includes bibliographical references and index.
ISBN 978-0-87071-625-6 (alk. paper) — ISBN 978-0-87071-599-0 (e-book)
  1. Civilian Public Service. Camp #56 (Waldport, Or.) 2. World War, 1939-1945—Conscientious objectors—Oregon—Waldport. 3. Conscientious objectors—Oregon—Waldport—History—20th century. 4. Arts—Oregon—History—20th century. 5. Artists—Oregon—History—20th century. 6. Authors, American—Oregon—History—20th century. 7. Musicians—Oregon—History—20th century. 8. Oregon—Intellectual life. 9. World War, 1939-1945—Oregon—Waldport. I. Title. II. Title: How a Small Group of World War II Conscientious Objectors Took Art and Peace from the Margins to the Mainstream.
D810.C82.M37 2013
940.53'1620979533—dc23   2013013096

Oregon State University Press
121 The Valley Library
Corvallis OR 97331-4501
541-737-3166 • fax 541-737-3170
www.osupress.oregonstate.edu

Contents

Acknowledgments

I am neither a conscientious objector nor an authority on the subject. I am merely a writer who recognizes a good story when he sees one. Little did I know, however, that this story would launch me on a journey of nearly twenty years from idea to publication—a journey that would require immersion in the complicated topics of peace and war, and a willingness to question my assumptions about the role each of them plays in our society. Nor could I have guessed how much this book would rely on the many individuals who contributed time, energy, expertise, and more. It is impossible to credit everyone here, but some in particular are due special acknowledgment.

The late Brian Booth, dean of Oregon literature, introduced me to the rich literary history of my adopted state. Keith Richard, University of Oregon archivist emeritus, introduced me to the Fine Arts at Waldport. James Fox, director of Special Collections at the University of Oregon, put me in touch with Oregon State University Press. Doug Erickson, Paul Merchant, and Jeremy Skinner at Lewis and Clark College Special Collections provided extensive knowledge, feedback, and generous assistance. Tom Booth and the editorial team at Oregon State University Press offered steady direction and support. Camp Angel members Francis Barr, Charles Cooley, Warren Downs, Vladimir Dupre, Clayton James, and Bruce Reeves, as well as the late William Eshelman, James Gallaghan, and Kermit Sheets, generously shared their memories and personal materials. Thanks to my old mentor, Edward R. Beardsley, for teaching me how to think.

The directors and staffs of the museums and archives I visited were cordial and helpful. In particular, I would like to thank Terry Barkley, Virginia Harness, Keith Morphew, and the late Ken Shaffer at Brethren Historical Library and Archives; Bruce Tabb and Linda Long at University of Oregon Special Collections; Susan Garner at the Angell Job Corps Civilian Conservation Center; and Phyllis Steeves of the Siuslaw National Forest. John Hawk of the University of San Francisco, Scott Jacobs at the

Clark Library, UCLA, Stephen MacLeod of UC Irvine, and Jeanine Wine of Manchester University, Indiana went out of their way to provide copies of ephemeral publications and letters.

Another delight was visiting or otherwise getting to know the booksellers with interest or expertise in the Fine Arts at Waldport and the Untide Press: the late Peter Howard of Serendipity Books and Jeff Maser, Bookseller, in Berkeley; Phil Wikelund and John Henley of Great Northwest Bookstore in Portland, Oregon; Scott Givens of Browsers' Bookstore in Albany, Oregon; Bob Tibbets of Beechwold Books in Columbus, Ohio; Mark Wessel of Wessel and Lieberman Booksellers in Seattle; and Dan Gregory at Between the Covers Books in Gloucester City, New Jersey.

Thank you to the many copyright holders and libraries who have generously granted permission to use materials both published and unpublished. Names and credits are listed on page 277.

Thanks also to John H. Baker, Katrine Barber, Eliza Canty-Jones, Matt Empson, the late Orval Etter, Jude Everson, Lisa Law, Melissa Marshall, Kathleen McLaughlin, Erin Kirk New, Meg Partridge, Bill Rankin, Pat Rom, Kim Stafford, Maggie Wilder, and Robert Yarber.

Inevitably, with a story as complex and convoluted as this, some stones must be yet unturned, some voices yet unheard. Any errors of fact or omission are the sole responsibility of the author. I welcome corrections, additions, and insights and will do my best to incorporate them into any future editions.

Finally, to all the friends, family, and colleagues who offered encouragement in what sometimes must have seemed but a slice of arcana with a topping of eccentricity, my gratitude here is as long as the list of your names—too long for this page. And a closing thank you to Debby, Rosy, and Virgil for their patience, support, and understanding. I couldn't have done it without you.

HERE ON THE EDGE

CHAPTER 1

An Unusual Gathering

IN JANUARY 1943, a little more than a year after the Japanese attack on Pearl Harbor, Bill Everson boarded a bus in Fresno, California, headed for a camp in a place he'd never seen. His draft number had come up, and although he didn't want to go, he knew he must. He'd already missed the earlier call for his scheduled departure, lingering in the station with his wife, Edwa, as if they could somehow hold off their coming separation. When the next bus came, it was a scene like those played out all across America at the time—the hugs, the tears, the good-bye waves through windows grimy with exhaust and road dust—as the country mobilized to take on Hitler, Hirohito, and a world at war.

Except Bill Everson wasn't going to war. He was one of more than 50,000 men during World War II who were conferred status as conscientious objectors, or COs. About half of them were inducted into the armed forces to perform some manner of noncombatant work, nearly 14,000 were classified as unavailable due to medical or other conditions, and about 12,000 like Everson were classified 4-E, eligible to do "work of national importance under civilian direction."[1] Rather than fight or otherwise engage in war-related activities, Everson would spend his conscripted years at a CO work camp in Oregon—Camp #56 at Waldport, one of the eventual 150 scattered across the country for the Civilian Public Service (CPS) program, part of the Selective Training and Service Act of 1940. Some of the men in CPS were assigned to work in such places as mental hospitals, or volunteered as human guinea pigs for medical experiments. The majority, though, were sent to remote rural areas, where they did work similar to that done by the Civilian Conservation Corps (CCC) of the 1930s New Deal programs. Many of the CPS camps were, in fact, originally CCC camps. The camp spaces, work equipment, and job supervision were provided by the U.S. government; everything else, including room and board for the men, was handled by one of the three "historic peace churches"—the Brethren, Friends (or Quakers), and Mennonites. The COs would generally work eight-and-a-half-hour days, six days a week, with no pay beyond a $2.50 monthly allowance for basic needs such as toothpaste and shaving razors. They had Sundays and Christmas Day off, with furlough days available similar to their counterparts in the military. Their service term would last the duration of the war plus six months. Depending on a camp's location in the country, the work might be in forestry, soil conservation, agriculture, fish and wildlife management, or even weather research. Camp #56, just south of Waldport, on Oregon's central coastline in the heart of logging country, would focus on tree planting, road building, and firefighting.

The thirty-year-old Everson, raised in the hot, dry expanse of central California's San Joaquin valley, rode for two days—up through the farming towns to San Francisco, then over the Golden Gate and past the rolling hills and fields of the Mendocino country, into the timeless redwoods hugging California's northwest corner, and then two hundred miles through the slashing wind and rain of winter on the Oregon coast, along a route so curved and winding that bus drivers sometimes handed out paper bags in case the riders got sick.[2] Arriving behind schedule in Waldport, a town of some 630 people whose business was seafood, tourism, and work related to the adjacent Siuslaw National Forest, Everson got off the bus and realized he'd gone about four miles beyond the camp. He telephoned there for a ride, then waited under that peculiar small-town combination of curiosity and suspicion. "I must have stood there, being eyed, for almost two hours," he wrote Edwa, "when a closed-in pickup, the laundry-wagon type, came up. It was full of new arrivals being driven to the doctor, and I was taken along." After the standard intake medical examinations, the new men arrived at the camp just in time for supper; they were taken directly to the mess hall, where about one hundred other camp members were already seated. "It was certainly an unusual gathering," Everson wrote Edwa later that night. "The faces were largely of the plain, placid farm-boy type, with beards and off-style hairdos noticeable, but here and there a fine brow, or nose, or a sensitive mouth." A few appeared somewhat intellectual, but most were, he said, "the simple fervently religious."[3]

For the next three years, these would be his people. Everson was a poet, a published poet, and he fit the stereotype—tall and thin, with serious eyes behind large glasses, and an introspective tilt to his head. As a young man back in the San Joaquin valley, he'd worked in the vineyards, orchards, and industrial fruit canneries. During the Great Depression, he joined the CCC, clearing trails in Sequoia National Park. While a student at Fresno State College, he discovered the poems of Robinson Jeffers, prompting what he called "an intellectual awakening and a religious conversion in one."[4] The publication of Everson's work in *Poetry* magazine, followed by two thin collections printed in California, led to

The poet: William Everson, ca. 1943.

friendships with the influential UCLA librarian Lawrence Clark Powell and the iconoclastic author Henry Miller, whose notorious *Tropic of Cancer* had been banned from sale in the United States since its 1934 publication in France. In 1938, Everson married Edwa, his high school sweetheart, and spent the next few years balancing the agrarian and creative life—growing grapes for raisin companies, working seasonally at the Libby's fruit cannery, and submitting poetry to the literary journals. When the draft board called, he declared himself a pantheist, stating that America should pull out of the war so that "men of the future would say: here was finally a people in all the bloody past who loved peace too much to fight for it."[5]

Now, at Camp #56 in Waldport, he would walk with other poets and writers, artists, actors, musicians, creative types—and also with scholars and engineers, architects and philosophers, machinists, carpenters, accountants, welders, pipe fitters, religious absolutists, and those "plain, placid" farm boys whose convictions and curiosity were defined by what they had been taught from the Bible. It was an unusual gathering, indeed. Men from all regions of the country, all economic and social classes, with differences in age, race, prejudices, and understanding were thrown together with really only one thing in common: they refused to take up arms in the name of one nation against another.

They were also isolated. Like most CPS camps across the country, Camp #56 was chosen partly for its remote location, with the aim to keep contact between the unpopular COs and the general public at a minimum. The central Oregon coast did offer a kind of rugged tourist experience: stunning scenery, an escape from the interior valley heat in the summer, and marvelous crabbing and salmon fishing. But much of the year it was wracked by windstorms, battered by rain, or draped in fog. Driftwood, giant logs, the occasional fishing boat, and sometimes even a

ship or a whale were tossed like toys by the indifferent Pacific onto the strands of beach cut by rocky headlands and rivers tumbling out of the forested hills. Salal, huckleberry, and rhododendron often comprised a thick green wall between the coast road and the beaches, in some places so dense that the access path was actually a tunnel people had hacked through the brush. The ocean here, fed by currents from Alaska, was freezing and full of flotsam and heavy ropes of seaweed. And the rustic tourist cabin courts, built during boom times, had sat largely empty over the last decade of economic depression. As one CO put it many years later, "These camps were really just prisoner of war camps . . . just a place to keep us out of society."[6]

The camp itself was a recently constructed CCC compound, carved out of the woods at the edge of the national forest, just off the highway and down a short road informally called Quarry Drive. Set up in a quadrangle, one side was bordered by four dormitories, the long buildings stacked in a row with ends facing the open area. The opposite side was defined in a similar manner by buildings that housed camp offices and administrators' quarters, a library, an infirmary, and a chapel. The dining and recreation halls filled in the other two sides, a tall flagpole marked the center, and, as one camp member described it, "in between, mud."[7] A water tower on the bluff overlooking the camp and a few outbuildings at the periphery completed the picture. And this was home, to the extent such places can be. The buildings were portable shells, only the most rudimentary four walls, a floor, and a roof. Heavy storms in November and December had twice blown down the garage buildings; at one point telephone lines were severed and electrical wires damaged, making it impossible to pump water except by a gravity feed—creating the irony of a camp with limited potable water in a region drenched by rain.[8]

Rain or shine, the men worked their fifty-plus hours a week, with tasks divided into two main categories. "Overhead" was the camp work: administration, record keeping, cooking, cleaning, health care, and directing the various programs such as education and recreation. "Project" referred to outdoor labor, the "work of national importance" mandated by the federal draft law. At Camp #56, the focus was on tree planting in the winter and firefighting during the summer—with road building into the forests a major support effort, and wood cutting for fuel a daily necessity. The reforestation projects, under supervision of the U.S. Forest Service, were on a 12,000-acre tract southeast of camp, which had been heavily logged during World War I and in the 1930s scorched by forest fires. Work crews of sixty men planted an average of four hundred to five hundred seedlings a day, eight feet apart on what camp director Richard C. Mills called "the dreary hillsides." From October 1942 to the following April—what in Oregon is known as the "rain year"—they planted more than 1.25 million trees.[9]

Another group of men worked crushing rock. They gathered boulders, sometimes pounding them down to manageable sizes with sledgehammers,

"Gull's eye view" of Camp #56, looking east from the Pacific Ocean and Highway 101.

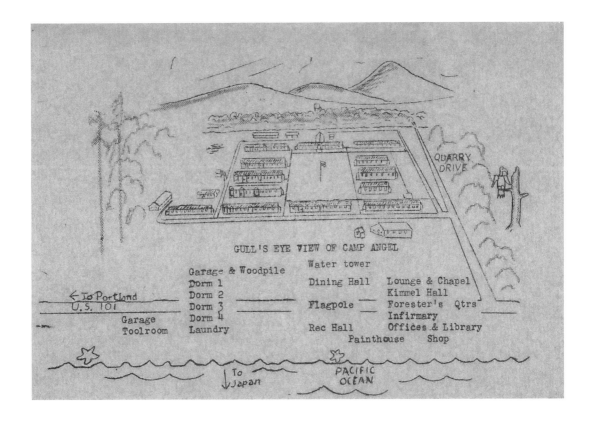

GULL'S EYE VIEW OF CAMP ANGEL

		Water tower	
Garage & Woodpile			
	Dorm 1	Dining Hall	Lounge & Chapel
	Dorm 2		Kimmel Hall
←To Portland	Dorm 3	Flagpole	Forester's Qtrs
U.S. 101	Dorm 4		Infirmary
Garage	Laundry	Rec Hall	Offices & Library
Toolroom		Painthouse	Shop

To Japan   PACIFIC OCEAN

"We live in a sea of mud." Camp #56 in winter.

and dumped them into bins that were hauled to a rock-crushing machine located on a hillside five miles from the camp. The aggregate was then spread along the muddy roads in an attempt to make them passable for the tree-planting operations during rainy season and to provide access to the vulnerable forests during the hot, dry fire season. Day after day, the men traveled a five-mile road that was so muddy it took them two hours to reach their destination, Mills wrote. "Month after month, the men poured tons of crushed rock onto the road leading to the planting area, only to have it disappear in the mucky ooze," he said. "It was not until spring came and the rains lessened that it was possible to travel the five miles' distance in the normal time of fifteen or twenty minutes."[10]

The men settled into the work, the daily toil of manual labor. Everson, although familiar with hard work from tending the vineyards and laying concrete irrigation pipe back home, noted to his librarian friend Larry Powell, "The work is quite hard; we are crushing rock for a road, and heap fragments on a truck to be hauled to the crusher. The weather is cold, an icy wind has persisted, and rain falls. These factors would make any exposure uncomfortable, and handling the heavy and ragged stones with icy hands becomes a kind of drudgery. I look through the hours to the evenings in the warm barracks."[11]

The source of that warmth was, of course, wood. The barracks and other buildings were heated by woodstoves, and the kitchen cooking was done with wood. The camp might burn three or four hundred cords per year, according to one member's recollection.[12] The woodcutters weren't indiscriminate loggers, though, clear-cutting hillsides and taking good trees. They went out with Forest Service rangers and felled snags—dead or dying trees usually damaged by lightning, fire, or windstorms, often with the top section missing and the remaining trunk beginning to hollow out. Once the wood was brought into camp, a crew of six to eight men spent their days cutting it into pieces small enough to fit the stoves. Not every camper on the detail felt that splitting wood was exactly work of national importance, but they generally accepted that, like the rock crushing and road building, it did support the work of planting trees. This was their job, and it had to be done. No one pretended that CPS work was supposed to be easy. But for a number of COs from drier climates, a winter on the Oregon coast must have seemed more like a sentence than an assignment.[13]

The Pacific Northwest's weather often originates in Alaska's Aleutian Islands, an archipelago sometimes referred to as the "Smokey Sea" because of the region's perpetual cloudiness.[14] The storms swirl up as if pulled from the ocean and are carried by the jet stream southeast along Canada's British Columbia coast, gathering water and power as they surge toward Washington's Olympic Peninsula and down to Oregon. About a hundred miles inland stand the Cascade Mountains, a string of volcanoes rising ten thousand feet and higher, running from southern Canada to northern California. These peaks give the eastbound storms a kind of gut punch, stalling them just long enough to dump a load of rain in the valleys and snow at higher elevations, thereby providing the Pacific Northwest its reputation as a dreary rainforest. Seattle, Portland,

Woodcutting operations fueled cooking and heating for the entire camp.

and Eugene receive their share of rain, but the coastline takes the brunt, with one hundred inches or more falling in some areas. Waldport, at twelve feet above sea level, has a generally moderate climate with average annual temperatures of 37 degrees for the low and 66 degrees for the high. It rarely snows, but the region gets more than seventy inches of rain each year, the bulk of it falling between October and April.[15]

"In the fall of 1942," Dick Mills wrote, "the rains began and descended in more than their usual precipitation."[16] Forrest Jackson, a new camp member from Kansas, was a touch more hyperbolic. "It rained sixty days from the time I got there . . . an inch a day! I tell you, it was muddy!"[17]

The lack of Vitamin D from the shortage of sun is enough to risk depression for even the most optimistic soul. But a life of wood cutting, rock crushing, and tree planting, all immersed in a steady rain, slippery mud, and the heaviness that attends a world that can never quite dry out, turns a mind almost inevitably inward. Introspection, reading, and reflection—and their offspring, creativity—can become not just a choice but also a matter of survival.

Mills wrote of attempting to forge a community spirit around what he determined were the three main groups of conscripts: those with strong authoritarian religious teaching, those who had formed personal convictions based on religious philosophy, and those who objected to what he called "the State's War Machine." The religious zealots, he said, refused to participate in anything that involved humor or voting. The others were encouraged to participate in holiday programs and special evening meals with short theater skits, humorous stunts, and group sing-alongs.[18]

Everson, not particularly inclined toward skits or stunts, battled homesickness and depression through conversation with two younger COs, Harold Hackett and Glen Coffield. Hackett, twenty-two years old and raised by missionary parents in Japan, had a bachelor's degree in literature and philosophy and shared Everson's enthusiasm for poetry and criticism. He was smart and idealistic with a sharp wit, even though he also possessed, Everson said, "an irritating sense of rebellion and irresponsibility." The two men quickly became friends.[19]

Coffield was, Everson observed, "a Missourian with a great beard and a fine, high-domed head." A photo of Coffield at the time shows him looking positively wild—like a kind of unwashed mendicant with shoulder-length, tangled hair and a thick, dark beard sticking out like an overused whisk broom—a bold presence even in this place where many beards could be found. His actions, too, set him apart. Coffield had no money and dressed in rags, but he worked as hard as anyone and never complained. Twenty-six years old, he'd earned a bachelor's degree and also played on a championship basketball team in college. He had been a greenhouse worker, professional entertainer, lab technician, high school teacher, hotel clerk, and switchboard operator. He'd invented an electric organ and performed on radio programs. After being drafted and classified as a CO, he walked the nearly three hundred miles from his home in Missouri to Camp #7 at Magnolia, Arkansas, rather than accept the services of bus transportation provided by the government. He was a true anarchist, right down to his hair and beard, which he was growing not out of laziness or deficient hygiene, but as a protest for peace. None of this, though, stopped him from enjoying life. He wrote ceaselessly, composing all manner of verse; he made up satirical songs, teaching them to others while on Project work. And when the camp put together an ad hoc basketball team to play against the Coast Guard one night in Waldport—without practice—Coffield apparently was a standout with his flying hair and beard, for a woman in the bleachers reportedly kept yelling, "Hurrah for Whiskers!"[20]

Shortly before Everson arrived, Hackett and Coffield and another CO, Larry Siemons, had begun publishing a satirical newsletter as a protest against the official camp publication, the *Tide.* Nearly every camp produced some manner of bulletin, paper, or magazine dedicated to the life and concerns of the men in CPS. The church administrators, as in many such organizations, viewed themselves as inclusive, tolerant, and supportive, open to a wide range of perspectives and attitudes. Yet the *Tide,* like so many officially sanctioned products, generally offered benign informational bits, overarching platitudes presented as inspiration, and the occasional opinion or creative statement. It never really provoked or dissented.[21]

The idealist: Harold Hackett, ca. 1943.

The anarchist: Glen Coffield, ca. 1943.

SLUG RACING

Not since the days of the immortal jumping frog of Ca-valveras County has a person-ality in the animal kingdom attracted such local atten--tion for physical prowess as has the lowly slug of the O-regon hills! Slug racing has become a classic innovation of a troubled day.

Last Wednesday was the day of the opener. Even Kermit the Hermit came out of re -tirement to collect a stable of four prize slugs: Marlene Dietrich--a honey of a slug, streamlined, with a quick take-off, and a brilliant spirit, but little stamina; City of Portland--one of the steadiest creatures ever dis-covered, and with a long cruising range, but not much sense of direction; Mae West--a bit sluggish, but fast; and Adolph Hitler--who had great possibilities but was too easily distracted by the ladies.

Then on the opening day (continued on page 7)

(continued on page 7)

- 1 -

The *Untide:* the Camp #56 weekly alternative paper, strong on humor and satire.

Hackett, Coffield, and Siemons unleashed the complete opposite, right down to the name of their rag: the *Untide*. The four-page, folded half-sheet, mimeographed pamphlet showed up surreptitiously on tables, bulletin boards, and desktop file baskets in the wee hours of each weekend. Beneath the title on its masthead, a motto proclaimed, "What is not Tide is Untide," and by way of explanation said the newsletter would "offer expression to the literary and artistic talents of the campers." It also intended to "expose in an impish way the failings of our society, to encourage discussion, to lead in action, to entertain." An editorial signed by "The Mole" was rich in metaphor and symbolism: "I am The Mole. I seldom come above ground. My claws are sharp for digging in soft dirt. People say I am blind, but I work with a purpose." The Mole doesn't state that purpose explicitly, but calls it "the same purpose that fills all of existence." Some want to trap him, he says, but "they forget that earth is my element, just as water is the element of fishes, and air is the element of birds." Subversion is never mentioned, but "I am very active—undermining, digging in under. I am seldom killed."[22]

Most of the material was light, poking fun at the bureaucratic system and the ironies of a life centered on crushing rocks into gravel that disappears in the mud, and planting trees so that they might later be cut down. One piece titled "99 Ways to Have Fun on Project" suggested taking part in pranks and games: mud fights on the tree-planting crews (including a clever use of saplings as catapults for the mud clods), sliding down riverbanks like otters by using a shovel blade as a sled, hiding in the trees and pelting unsuspecting co-workers with chunks of rotten wood. "Safety Suggestions" took satirical aim at ignorance and incompetence: "Always put 32 men in one truck and 12 in another so that one truck is not overloaded." And: "Always carry explosives and dynamite caps in the crew trucks. We can always get new crews." The Goldbricker Award went each week to whomever in the Mole's estimation took the art of work avoidance to newer and greater heights.

A lot of the stuff was downright cornball, full of inside jokes and sophomoric digs at fragile egos—and if that had been the entirety of it, the *Untide* would likely have found its rightful resting place in history's dustbin. The newsletter itself, Everson recalled decades later, never actually subverted anything. Its real value, he said, was that it got some creative minds working together outside the official camp channels.[23] Everson, already recognized as a serious poet of some repute, quickly aligned himself with the looser, anarchic *Untide* rather than the more conventional *Tide*. He contributed poems, particularly his new "War Elegies," which gave voice to the feelings of many COs, judging not only from reactions in Camp #56 but also responses that filtered back from other CPS camps that had received the *Untide* by mail.

This was an important detail. The CPS camps shared publications and communications of all kinds, official and otherwise. When the *Untide* showed up, it both literally and figuratively bucked the tide. For other COs across the country to see that some fellow conscripts not only felt as they did but were creatively addressing their condition provided the necessary sense of unity and purpose that inspires people to act and not just observe. And while there were many forces at work in this world consumed with war, and the vagaries of chance often play as strong a part in history as any calculated or conscious choice, something prompted Everson to sit down one evening, about six weeks after he'd arrived in the isolated sogginess of the Pacific Northwest woods, and pen the following piece for the March 13, 1943, issue of the *Untide:*

HERE ON THE EDGE

If you come by night you will see nothing. The camp, from the road, will be hooded and dark. It faces the sea, the western sea and the Eastern war, and the war imposes: puts blinds on our windows, darkens the lights of the creeping cars. The beach is patrolled.

But if you come from the hills to the east, our lights would be friendly, each window alive, its streaming shaft extending outward against the dark. That way lies home, the states and the nation, and the continent's breadth. The mountains are there, the tillable valleys and the distant towns we now do not know. Our people before us came out of the east, the rolling wave of colonization that poured out of Europe and crossed America, to break against this ultimate shore, and spread back on its course, filling the farms. That is the quarter we have known, and toward which we shall turn.

But at night in the camp we can hear the sea, stamping and beating upon the shore. We look out on that waste, and remember that Drake once travelled those waves, his lonely ship binding together an unknown world. But, looking, we are also made aware that what gathers there now, the vast event, is shaping the future as Drake could not shape it, pulling within its merciless orbit the millions of lives, and the subsequent order of half the globe.

Here on the edge we look east to the West, west to the East, and cannot resolve them. We can only watch; watch and prepare; and bide on the time when what we are, and that for which we have taken this stand, can be tangent again to the world.

Bill Everson carves out some reading and writing time at his cubbyhole desk in the dormitory. The men stacked their beds to make more room.

That time would come, another generation down the road. For now, the members of Camp #56 were literally and metaphorically "on the edge," talking about a world of peace during the greatest war civilization had ever known. They could hardly have anticipated how their words and actions would resonate far beyond the borders of this backwoods camp.

CHAPTER 2

The Cost of Conscience in America

IN THE FALL OF 1934, a book appeared in England and America titled *Peace with Honour*. Essentially an appeal to reason, it sets out a case for the renunciation of modern war—the industrial, massive destruction committed by humans and their machines. Political leaders declare that they do not want war, the author says, yet they apparently do not want to avoid it enough to keep it from breaking the peace. They gather their commissions and committees, they sign treaties and agreements, they speak of honor, prestige, and patriotism—and they, and the people of their nations, succumb again and again to the romantic view of war as "an affair of flashing swords and charging cavalry."[1]

It doesn't have to be this way, the author argues, offering case after case, historical and hypothetical, of the madness exhibited by otherwise reasonable human beings in the name of honor, prestige, and patriotism. For instance, he says, if our neighbor trampled our garden flowers, we would never throw a bomb to punish him, obliterating not only the offender but his wife and children—and perhaps other neighbors' wives and children. Yet we routinely bomb cities and villages, which may kill ten times the number of people we call enemy. Defenders of this practice say that until humans become saints, war will be inevitable. Rubbish, the author asserts. "We need not be saints. It will be enough if we stop being criminal lunatics."[2]

The book covers two hundred pages of point, counterpoint, analysis, and conclusion. This thing we call war is no longer war, the author says, but a monstrous activity of destruction and degradation. He makes his expected appeal to the political leaders, those who decide how and when a nation goes to war. But then he adds an appeal for "true peace," which will require not only an alternative choice, but an alternative way of thinking. "If you want Peace," he concludes, "then you must renounce the *idea* of War. If you do this, then the way to Peace is easy, and the vast majority of your people will follow you along it with thankfulness."[3] The message struck a chord with the reading public, enough so that the book went into multiple printings on both sides of the Atlantic and within a year was issued in a revised edition with a new preface by the author: A. A. Milne, the man who had given the world *Winnie-the-Pooh*.

History is full of artists' commentaries on war, so much so that one critic opined of Milne's book, "Here is another best-selling author writing a book to declaim against war."[4] But history has also shown that we need our artists and writers to bear proper witness to what repeatedly comes off as an appalling and ridiculous activity. From Francisco Goya's horrific *The Disasters of War* etchings of the early 1800s to Mark Twain's "The War Prayer," so provocative that it wasn't published until after his death, the artist's eye provides us a necessary reminder of human nature's capacity for cruelty and willful ignorance. Stephen Crane's *The Red Badge of Courage*, Picasso's *Guernica*, Pete Seeger's "The Big Muddy," and thousands more paintings, photographs, plays, songs, novels, poems, and all manner of art serve as the conscience of the people. And that theatrical masterpiece of protest, *Lysistrata*, in which the women of ancient Greece refuse to sleep with their men until they put an end to the long-running Peloponnesian War, thoroughly delineates the humorous and tragic elements of human folly.

The aftermath of World War I produced a number of novels realistically depicting the brutal industrial slaughter of that conflict. *A Farewell to Arms* by Ernest Hemingway, *Three Soldiers* by John Dos Passos, and Erich Maria Remarque's *All Quiet on the Western Front* saw their share of critical and public acclaim. Perhaps this time, so the thinking went, the cycle might be broken.

But an alternative way of acting requires more than imagination; it requires an environment that allows people to do more than respond to the immediate need at hand. As the 1930s ground its way through the poverty and despair of the Great Depression, societies worldwide teetered between unstable democracy and belligerent totalitarianism. The fascist dictatorships in Germany and Italy were making clear their military intentions, while on the other side of the globe Japan expanded its imperial conquest of east Asia and the Pacific Ocean. The idea of peace as a new world order gave way to harsh reality. Even A. A. Milne revised his hope for a worldwide revolution of the heart, and in 1940, as Adolf Hitler's war machine spread across Europe and prepared to strike England, Milne published a thirty-two-page pamphlet titled *War with Honour*. "If anybody reads *Peace with Honour* now," he wrote, "they must read it with that one word 'HITLER' scrawled across every page."[5]

Another war had come. Again.

■ ■ ■

As certain as America's eventual entry into the war may have seemed at the time, it was also certain that some Americans would refuse to fight it. This was the thinking that brought seven men to the White House in Washington, DC, in January 1940 to meet with President Franklin D. Roosevelt. They were leaders of the three historic peace churches (Society of Friends, the Mennonite Church, and the Church of the Brethren), so called for their long-standing traditions of nonresistance and belief that all war was wrong. They presented a letter thanking the president for his efforts to keep the United States neutral in the European hostilities, and noted their own ongoing efforts to help war victims and refugees in Spain, China, and Poland. Should war come, they said, they expected the need for relief services to increase both at home and abroad. They believed this work would be suitable for conscientious objectors—both the members of their churches and others who, for reasons of conscience, could not permit themselves to engage in or support military conflict. "Our desire is to cooperate in finding the best solution to the problem of the conscientious objector," they wrote, "and it is even more to render as loyal citizens the highest type of constructive service we can to our country and to the world."[6]

They added a memorandum of "concrete proposals," including the appointment of a civilian board to judge conscientious objectors' sincerity and assign them to service projects, and the creation of the peace churches' own organizations to run projects of war relief, forestry reclamation, community reconstruction, and health and farm services. They could not at that moment offer help for absolute objectors—those who refused to recognize military conscription of any kind and usually had been sentenced to prison—but their hope was that whatever agreement they worked out for their own church members could apply to any truly conscientious objector, regardless of religion.[7]

This proposal was not made in a vacuum. Conscientious objection is as old as war itself, and the history of war refusal in America goes back to colonial times. Friends, Mennonites, and Brethren arrived in the late seventeenth and early eighteenth centuries and maintained their nonresistance through suspicion, persecution, and worse. These people were generally honest, hardworking, and stalwart in virtually everything—including their refusal to engage in war. In 1672, a group of Friends in New York petitioned the governor that "we have behaved ourselves peaceable and quietly amongst our neighbors and are ready to be serviceable in anything which doth not infringe upon our tender consciences, but being in a measure redeemed of wars and stripes we cannot for conscience' sake be concerned in upholding things of that nature."[8]

During the American Revolution, the Friends of Pennsylvania stated, "We do not believe in revolutions and we do not believe in war. . . . We are out of the whole business and will give aid and comfort to neither party."[9] A petition jointly read by the Mennonites and Brethren to the Pennsylvania Assembly in November 1775 said, "It being our principle to feed the hungry and give the thirsty drink; we have dedicated ourselves to serve all men in every thing that can be helpful to the preservation of men's lives, but we find no freedom in giving, or doing, or assisting in any thing by which men's lives are destroyed or hurt."[10]

So strong was this commitment to nonviolence and renunciation of war that it caught the attention of the U.S. Congress as they considered the amendments to the Constitution that would come to be known as the Bill of Rights. In June 1789, James Madison, speaking to the House of Representatives, advised that one article might read, "The right of the people to keep and bear arms shall not be infringed; a well armed and well regulated militia being the best security of a free country: but no person religiously scrupulous of bearing arms shall be compelled to render military service in person."[11] In August of that year, the House adopted a clause to Article I that said, "the equal rights of conscience, the freedoms of speech or of the press, and the right of trial by jury in criminal cases, shall not be infringed by any State."[12] No reference to conscience survived into the final version.

Throughout the nineteenth century, as the United States expanded across the continent, various states' constitutions adopted language recognizing conscientious objection. Pennsylvania, Alabama, Texas, Illinois, Iowa, Kentucky, and Kansas all allowed some manner of exemption for the CO, usually in the form of alternative service or restitution paid to the state.[13]

When the United States invaded Mexico in the 1846–48 Mexican-American War, conscientious objection took on a more secular—but no less moral—expression, as in Henry David Thoreau's 1847 lecture, "Resistance to Civil Government" (which later became popular as "Civil Disobedience"). The United States had entered the war with Mexico, Thoreau said, due to a wealthy few manipulating the government to serve their desires for power and profit. The American people on the whole might prefer peace, he said, but when they give such a government power over their conscience, they should expect to be called to war. The mass of people, he charged, serve their government not as humans but as flesh-and-blood machines, exercising no judgment beyond their duty to the state. "They are the standing army, and the militia, jailers, constables, *posse comitatus*, etc." A few, he noted, "serve the state with their conscience also, and so necessarily resist it, for the most part; and they are commonly treated as enemies by it."[14]

When the Civil War brought the first national conscription order, the Enrollment Act of 1863, the law included an exemption for anyone who paid a three hundred dollar fee. This set off rioting in New York City, requiring two thousand policemen and five army regiments to disperse the crowds, angry at what was considered a "rich man's act." What came to be known as the New York Draft Riots, along with disturbances in other northern cities, took much-needed infantry and sometimes artillery away from the battlefield. According to one source, the Union army was so shorthanded because of this that when they defeated the Confederates at the pivotal Battle of Gettysburg, they did not have enough men to pursue General Robert E. Lee's forces retreating south.[15]

Congress was not ready to acknowledge secular COs in the Civil War, but in 1864 did provide a kind of parole for individuals who refused to either serve in the military or pay the exemption fee and who were also backed by their church. To some degree, the North's willingness to accommodate COs was a reflection of its leader; President Abraham Lincoln was sympathetic to the churches' beliefs, and in some cases offered parole or pardon. One report tells of a woman who came to see Lincoln about her son, a fifteen-year-old who had been lured into joining the army, but upon realizing his mistake had then deserted and was now sentenced to be shot. She implored the clerks to let her see the president, but was told he was busy in the War Office. "Wild with grief," she begged again, and her message was relayed to Lincoln, who responded, "That must not be, I must look into that case, before they shoot the boy." He telegraphed to suspend the order.[16]

Conscientious objectors in the Confederacy found somewhat different conditions. Conscription in the South began earlier (1862) in an effort to counter the population advantage of the North and contained a long list of exempt occupations that included journalists, lawyers, teachers, druggists, postmen, and more—but not religious objectors. Later that year, though, members of the peace churches were granted exemption, provided they found a substitute or paid a five hundred dollar tax—even if they were employed in one of the exempt occupations.[17]

Civil War documents also include written records of conscientious objectors suffering what can only be described as torture. One Union draftee, a Vermont Quaker named Cyrus Pringle, writes in his 1863 diary of being imprisoned and forced to march, fully loaded with war gear and a rifle hung about his neck, miles from one town to another, without water. He also was tied to the ground, his wrists and ankles lashed to stakes, limbs stretched into an X, exposed to the hot sun for hours— because he refused to carry a gun. "I wept," he said, "not so much from my own suffering as from sorrow that such things should be in our own country, where Justice and Freedom and Liberty of Conscience have been the annual boast of Fourth-of-July orators so many years."[18]

A southern Quaker, Himelius M. Hockett, writes of his treatment in North Carolina, which included imprisonment without food or water, hard labor in a military fort, and being tied with a ball and chain. He tells of deserters having the letter *D* branded on them, three inches across. "This was done in my presence with a hot iron," he said, "accompanied by the screams of the unhappy victims." A few days later, Hockett and another objector were ordered to unload railroad cars of weapons and ammunition—and warned that if they didn't, they would be "pierced four inches deep" with bayonets. They refused anyway, and Hockett was hung by his thumbs, his feet barely touching the ground, while his fellow CO was stabbed according to the order. When a corporal pointed out that the orders were for piercing and not hanging, Hockett was cut down and then stabbed, but not as deeply, he noted, "perhaps on account of having already suffered unauthorized punishment."[19]

One scene played out as a drama worthy of any story or film. It was 1863, at a Confederate camp near Petersburg, Virginia. Seth Laughlin, a Quaker, refused to serve. He was kept awake for thirty-six hours by a soldier prodding him with a bayonet whenever he dozed off. They tied him to the ground each day for a week and hung him by his thumbs. When he still refused to use a gun, they court-martialed him and ordered him shot. The time came, and the entire camp was called to witness the execution. Twelve soldiers formed the firing squad, none knowing if they were one of the six with live bullets in their rifle chamber. Laughlin stood calmly and asked if he might say a prayer before the order to shoot was given. He then spoke: "Father, forgive them, for they know not what they do." Hearing these familiar words, each man lowered his gun and refused to shoot, directly disobeying a military order. The officers, too, were shaken; they revoked the command.[20]

The Civil War seemed to have somewhat exhausted America's appetite for organized conflict, as the ensuing decades saw the nation expand across the continent, offering to many the American dream of individual freedom, prosperity, and peaceful living. The fulfillment of that dream, however, depended on one's perspective. As pointed out in the 1920s by Norman Thomas, a Presbyterian minister and co-founder of the organization that would become the American Civil Liberties Union (ACLU), "American pacifism was born of a sentimental rationalization and moralization of our fortunate geographical position. It had seldom interfered with the march of our own empire. We ruthlessly disposed of the Indian and took what we desired from Mexico; we continuously lynched Negroes, and carried on labor struggles with more bloodshed than England, France and Germany combined. This is not the record of a pacific people."[21]

Perhaps no one embodied this dichotomy more than Andrew Carnegie, a Scotsman who came to the United States as a child in 1848 and worked his way up from poverty to become one of the wealthiest men in the world. His ruthless and hard-nosed pursuit of riches came on the backs of factory laborers, many of them children, who worked unregulated hours at sometimes horrific jobs, with little reward beyond a subsistence living and an almost certain early death. Carnegie in later life turned his focus to philanthropy, as if he were attempting to somehow pay back those whose thankless toil had made him rich, and in 1910 he gave ten million dollars to establish the Carnegie Endowment for International Peace, with a charge to "hasten the abolition of international war, the foulest blot upon our civilization."[22]

When war broke out across Europe in 1914, many Americans were almost indignant about peace. The decades spanning the late 1800s and early 1900s had seen not only the unchecked capitalism that brought untold riches to the few, but also the emergence of organized labor, women's suffrage, and populist movements through Grange halls and other community organizations. Change was no longer necessarily a top-down affair, and, driven by emerging technologies such as the automobile and electricity came the social evolution of workers' rights, public education, and empowerment of the common people; organizations such as the Fellowship of Reconciliation (FOR), the Industrial Workers of the World (IWW), the Socialist Party, and the American Union Against Militarism (precursor to the ACLU) boasted memberships in the tens of thousands.

The people who actually fought the wars began to openly question the legitimacy of traveling long distances to fire bullets at people they'd never met who were firing bullets back at them—and being ordered to do so by people who had enough money and power to ensure that they would never be engaged in such actions themselves. As the European conflict in 1915 and 1916 slumped into a brutal stalemate of trench warfare on the blasted fields of France, U.S. President Woodrow Wilson was astute enough to run for reelection on the slogan, "He kept us out of war."

By 1917, however, mass communication techniques were improving, partly through a more scientific understanding of mass psychology, and the manipulation of American opinion through the use of emerging technologies was showing its power. That year, President Wilson authorized the Committee on Public Information, founded to garner support for American participation in the European war. Among the group's members was Edward Bernays, nephew of Sigmund Freud and the man who later invented the term "public relations." In his 1928 book, *Propaganda*, he summed it up succinctly:

> The conscious and intelligent manipulation of the organized habits and opinions of the masses is an important element in democratic society. Those who manipulate this unseen mechanism of society constitute an invisible government which is the true ruling power of our country.

We are governed, our minds are molded, our tastes formed, our ideas suggested, largely by men we have never heard of. This is a logical result of the way in which our democratic society is organized. Vast numbers of human beings must cooperate in this manner if they are to live together as a smoothly functioning society.[23]

This manipulation wasn't particularly difficult, wrote Norman Thomas in *The Conscientious Objector in America*. The rugged individualism so valued by Americans had passed into myth, he said. "Conformity is the social law in America. We wear the same sort of clothes, read the same sort of magazines, belong to the same sort of social organizations." He relates an anecdote about Lord Northcliffe, the powerful British newspaper publisher and director of propaganda for his government during World War I. On a visit to New York City in 1917, shortly before the United States' entry into the war, Northcliffe was talking with a reporter about how to influence Americans' views on war and the draft. They were in an office overlooking the busy streets; Northcliffe went to the window and pointed at the crowds rushing back and forth below. "Do you see these people?" he said. "They all wear the same kind of hats. They are the most docile people in the world."[24]

The sensationalism and hysteria that whipped America into World War I is well documented, with the tales of German soldiers butchering Belgian babies merely part of a long list of behavior prompts leading to April 6, 1917—Good Friday—when the United States declared war on Germany. A month later, Congress passed the Selective Service Act, which required men between twenty-one and thirty years old to register for military service. In June came the Espionage Act, later expanded into the Sedition Act of 1918, which, among other things, made it a crime to criticize the U.S. government.

The Selective Service Act did allow exemption from combat duty for conscientious objectors "of any well recognized religious sect or organization . . . whose existing creed or principles forbid its members to participate in war in any form." However, they were not exempt "from service in any capacity that the President shall declare to be noncombatant."[25] Ten months after the bill's passage, President Wilson named three classifications for noncombatant service: the Medical Corps, the Quartermaster Corps, and the Engineer Service.[26]

Of the 2.8 million men inducted into the armed forces during World War I, less than 65,000 claimed noncombatant status, and about 57,000 of those were determined valid by their local draft boards. From this number, less than 21,000 were actually inducted, and about 16,000 of them for various reasons gave up their noncombatant status. This left a little more than 4,000 true conscientious objectors. Many went into noncombatant service or were furloughed to work on farms. About five hundred men were court-martialed and sentenced to prison for anywhere from twenty-five years to life; seventeen men were condemned to death. Even though most of the heavier prison sentences were later reduced, and none of the death sentences carried out, the conscientious objectors of World War I clearly were not a force with any real power—and their treatment reflected it.

Norman Thomas acknowledges in *The Conscientious Objector* that the sufferings of the COs cannot be compared to the sufferings of soldiers on the battlefield. However, he notes, "something must be said on the subject for the sake of a true record of events." Conscientious objectors were kept in unsanitary and unheated cells without blankets in winter and forced to stand at attention in cold or heat. They were "beaten, pricked or stabbed with bayonets, jerked about with ropes round their necks, threatened with summary execution," and given the "water cure" by having their mouths held open beneath a water faucet. At least two men were dunked in latrines, one of them face down. The list of abuse and torture goes on, confirming that the more base elements of human nature hadn't changed significantly since the Civil War.[27]

Even so, something was evolving in American society, and hints can be found in a memoir by Wisconsin newspaperman Ernest L. Meyer. His story of being a conscientious objector, published in 1930 as *Hey! Yellowbacks!*, tracks Meyer's progress through military camps, where he suffers the usual verbal abuse and hard labor, and witnesses others receiving worse. Men were made to stand against searing hot walls in hundred-degree sunlight, they were barracked with soldiers suffering from terrible diseases, and some were placed in upright coffinlike cages so tight that they could not sit down or even turn around. Despite these varied yet unimaginative tortures, a new kind of CO was emerging, Meyer said. They were political dissenters who did not denounce violence, but objected to war in the name of the state. They were, Meyer observed, "a different breed that has borne the brunt of the torture: the socialists, I.W.W.'s and other political heretics. They are not meek, like the religionists; they do not turn the other cheek. They are upstanding, militant; they irk the fort commandant more than white-hot goads, and he has used everything short of murder to break their spirit."[28]

It was two years after the war ended before the last COs were released, and by then people in Europe and America were beginning to realize that their so-called victory in the Great War may not have been as complete as advertised. Meyer related the words of a British CO commenting on the attitudes of his fellow citizens in the 1920s. "They are awakening to the hypocrisy, the ghastly stupidity of the thing. Out of this war to end wars have come not merely poverty and famine and deranged economic life, but more wars and the seeds of more wars." The politicians repeated the same old phrases, but the people were finally seeing through it, he said. "Let another war come in our generation, and I warrant you the ranks of the objectors will swell a hundred-fold."[29]

The senseless slaughter of World War I also made people more amenable to the organized peace movements. The League of Nations, an international organization aimed at building world peace, convened in 1920 with forty-four member nations, although the United States never joined. The War Resisters League, a secular organization begun in 1923 as an American affiliate of the London-based War Resisters International, offered this credo for its members: "War is a crime against humanity. I am therefore determined not to support any kind of war, and to strive for the removal of all causes of war."[30] The Fellowship of Reconciliation, founded in 1915, continued its activities in support of pacifism and worked to facilitate interfaith understanding. In 1926, the "Anti-Conscription Manifesto" was published, signed by seventy-one world-renowned figures from fifteen countries, including Mahatma Gandhi, Albert Einstein, Bertrand Russell, and H. G. Wells.[31]

By 1935, though, the wheels of war were turning again. Germany and Italy were run by fascist dictators who made no secret of their militaristic aims. Japan was expanding its armed activities in Asia and had withdrawn from a multinational treaty limiting the size and scope of national naval forces. That same year, delegates from the Friends, Mennonites, and Brethren met in Newton, Kansas, for the Conference of Historic Peace Churches—the first time this designation was used.[32] "War is sin," they declared. "It is the complete denial of the Spirit, Christian love and all that Christ stands for. . . . We cannot support or engage in any war, or conflict between nations, classes, or groups."[33]

■ ■ ■

With the long history of conscientious objection in America and the sorry legacy of CO treatment during World War I at their backs, the seven men from the historic peace churches brought their "concrete proposals" to Franklin Roosevelt on the eve of World War II.[34] They also had nearly a decade of evolved national perception on their side. The Depression demonstrated that government could have a role not only in the nation's defense but also in the welfare of society as a whole. With the rescues of the failed banking system and the "alphabet soup" of federal agencies that comprised Roosevelt's New Deal, American society had undergone a systemic change and now functioned with a government as partner rather than nemesis. One of the most successful New Deal programs, the Civilian Conservation Corps, was seven years old, had employed half a million young men at its peak in 1935, and received the president's direct, personal interest.[35] The sight of government-sponsored crews working in the fields and forests of the country was a familiar one. Why not continue this work with men who were ready to serve their country but could not, for legitimate reasons of conscience, participate in its wars?[36]

The president greeted the delegates and invited them to stand around his desk for an open conversation. They'd been allotted three minutes, but stayed for thirty, and when the visit concluded, Roosevelt seemed pleased. "I am glad you have done it," he said in reference to their plan. "That's getting down to a practical basis. It shows us what the conscientious objectors can do without fighting. Excellent! Excellent!"[37]

But a single genial meeting with the chief executive proved no guarantee. After Congress passed the Selective Service and Training Act of 1940 with its "work of national importance" clause, the peace churches created an oversight organization called the National Service Board for Religious Objectors (NSBRO) and proposed that both government and private agencies administer the work done by COs. The government would cover costs and pay wages for their charges, and the church agencies would do the same for theirs. Clarence Dykstra, director of the Selective Service System, and Colonel Lewis B. Hershey (who would later play a significant role in the evolution of CPS) got behind the proposal, and Dykstra took it to the president. But this time, Roosevelt was not so pleased. He said the CCC camps would be too easy for the COs, and suggested they be drilled by army officers. Exactly what precipitated this change in the president's attitude from the earlier meeting with church leaders is not clear. It may be the church leaders had assumed the president understood their view of separate government and private agencies. Perhaps the president hadn't fully grasped their interpretation of what alternative service meant. Or possibly he had heard an opposing point of view that changed his mind. As it was, Dykstra called a special meeting with the NSBRO members and told them that wages for COs were impossible, and asked if they would agree to administer—and pay for—all upkeep of the COs. Otherwise, he said, CPS would require a funding appropriation from Congress, with all its attendant delays and restrictions. This was not what the church leaders had envisioned, but it was better than a purely government-run work program over which they would have no control of any kind. The NSBRO accepted the counterproposal, Roosevelt and his budget director agreed, and on February 6, 1941, the president signed Executive Order 8675, which would "establish or designate work of national importance under civilian direction for persons opposed to combatant and non-combatant service in the land or naval forces of the United States."[38]

The government took a very positive view of the agreement. Although Selective Service had to initially address and determine what to do with the COs, the problem of dealing with them would in effect be handed off to the peace churches. Dykstra later told church members that CPS was "an experiment in which the Government and voluntary groups share a responsibility and a burden in a very unique way. . . . It is going to be significant for many years to come." Lewis Hershey, promoted to general and, after Dykstra left for another position, appointed director of Selective Service, called CPS an "experiment in democracy," in which the United States would learn just how truly democratic its system of government was.[39]

The peace churches, while somewhat less sanguine, accepted the compromise as a step in the right direction, an opportunity to make real, concrete progress toward developing a society in which the teachings of the Sermon on the Mount were accorded more than Sunday lip service. A. J. Muste, executive secretary of the Fellowship of Reconciliation, said hopefully that CPS could provide "pacifist service, witness against war and conscription . . . and preparation for future volunteer services including nonviolent direct action to achieve basic social change." Frank Olmstead, chairman of the War Resisters League and later a critic of CPS, grudgingly called it "the most effective argument for pacifism which the anti-war forces of the country can offer."[40]

It truly was an amazing partnership of public and private enterprise. Selective Service draft boards determined CO status, the peace churches funded and ran the camps, and government agencies such as the Forest Service and Department of Agriculture oversaw the work. Nobody, however—not the government, not the churches, not the COs—really knew what they were getting into. "If we knew how many [were] coming in, we probably wouldn't have tried it," recalled M. R. Zigler, who chaired the NSBRO throughout the war. "It was a good thing we didn't know."[41]

CHAPTER 3

Shared Misery and Gallows Humor

WHEN THE FIRST CPS CAMP OPENED in May 1941 at Patapsco State Forest in Maryland just outside of Baltimore, twenty-six conscientious objectors arrived, accompanied by twice as many reporters and photographers. The United States was not yet at war, so the curiosity element was strong. Who were these people, where did they come from, and what were they doing here? There were all types of COs, said a *Saturday Evening Post* story on the Maryland camp. There was a Yale graduate whose father was building army camps, a Jehovah's Witness who said he didn't believe in war but would punch the first newsman who tried to take his picture, and an ex-boxer who retired from the sport because he "didn't want to hurt nobody and it ain't Christian." There were religious fundamentalists, highbrows and lowbrows, political radicals, beer drinkers, and vegetarians. "They come," the *Post* said, "like any other American group, in all sizes, shapes, colors and convictions." The challenge for camp administrators was in accommodating and directing groups that could number one hundred or more men whose only uniform quality was what they *didn't* believe in.[1]

The peace churches, of course, held in common the antiwar position as a fundamental element of their doctrines although they differed somewhat in how they carried it out. The Mennonites, named for the sixteenth-century Dutch reformer Menno Simons, came from the Anabaptist, or adult baptism, tradition and a strict interpretation of the New Testament. Obedience was important, but the affairs of the soul, they believed, were not the affairs of the state. Thus, they could have an authoritarian, patriarchal household yet reject larger societal politics and the forces that attend it.

The Brethren, known through history also as German Baptists and Dunkers (for their baptism rituals), were similar to the Mennonites, particularly in the importance of the New Testament. However, their sense of mission—to relieve suffering and spread peace—led them to become more engaged in civic matters.

The Friends, or Quakers (so named after founder George Fox's call that worshippers should "tremble at the word of the Lord"),[2] believed in the "Inner Light," the spirit of God working through the individual. Their interpretation of the Bible included viewing it as a confirmation of individual conscience. They also believed in civic administration and social activism—as exemplified in the work of American Quaker leader William Penn, for whom the state of Pennsylvania is named.

Even under such wholesale generalizations, we can imagine the challenges faced by those running the camps. Not only were there differences among the peace churches, but other Protestant denominations furnished COs as well. The Methodist Church issued a statement shortly before the Second World War that it "will not officially endorse support, or participate in war."[3] The Roman Catholic Church, with its determination of "just" and "unjust" war, chose not to condemn members who interpreted modern warfare as the latter.[4] The Jehovah's Witnesses, an evangelical movement founded in late 1800s America, believed there was only one war worth fighting—the "end days" of Armageddon; until then, they would preach their Gospel. They saw themselves as neither pacifists nor conscientious objectors, but ministers—and therefore exempt from military service. Other religious groups were numerous and varied: Christadelphians, Molokans, Seventh-Day Adventists, Assemblies of God, and various sects of the Church of Christ. Added to that, some non-pacifist churches stated that their members had a right to claim conscientious objection and that those claims should be honored. Department of Justice records for the roughly six years of the war era show that in a representative group of ten thousand COs, there was membership in 345 churches.[5]

Also for this war, Selective Service came up with twelve categories to identify types of objectors. Beyond the obvious *religious* objector, they identified the *moral or ethical* objector, who "considers war inconsistent with his moral philosophy and humanitarianism." Other categories ranged from *political* and *sociological* to *philosophical* and *personal*. There were even categories for physiological reasons: *naturalistic* ("based on an abhorrence of blood") and *neurotic* ("a phobia of war's atrocities").[6]

Exactly how and where someone claiming CO status fit into these categories, and which categories were considered legitimate by a draft board, depended literally on where the draftee lived. Local people, usually businessmen and ex-servicemen, filled positions on 6,700 Selective Service draft boards across the country. A draftee could fill out a questionnaire called DSS Form 47, in which he provided background on his religious training and beliefs, participation in organizations, and names of references. A classification of 1-A-O meant a noncombatant role in the military, such as a medical or support assignment. A full exemption (4-D) went to religious ministers, and the 4-E classification sent a man to CPS. If the local board refused an applicant CO status, the draftee could take his case to a regional board of appeals, and beyond that, qualified appeals could eventually make it to the president of the United States.

The fates of the COs were as varied as the individuals involved. The Boston poet Robert Lowell, who would later win the Pulitzer Prize, went to prison. Actor Lew Ayres, who gained fame for his starring role in the 1931 film version of *All Quiet on the Western Front,* applied for non-combatant status but instead was assigned to CPS Camp #21 at Cascade Locks, Oregon. According to one story, his local draft board in Hollywood tried to embarrass him by refusing him 1-A-O status.[7] Thomas Banyacya, a member of the Hopi Nation who later became known as a tireless advocate for environmental causes, remembered hearing President Roosevelt's call for conscription; he chose instead to follow the teachings of the tribal elders and his understanding of the Indian experience with the United States. He spent seven years in prison.[8] In one small midwestern town, all applicants for CO status were denied. A draft board in an Oklahoma town refused Mennonite and Brethren members who'd applied for farm deferments and sent them all to CPS camps.[9] Bill Everson, who admitted that he didn't know if his father's position as justice of the peace in his hometown of Selma had anything to do with his draft board's decision, pointed out the vagaries of the system. "It was notorious that in Berkeley you could live on one side of the street and be sent to camp, and on the other side of the street—if that was where the draft board district broke—and be sent to prison."[10]

The draft had begun in peacetime. In its first year through November 1941, about nine hundred thousand men were inducted into military service. Between the first CPS camp opening in May 1941 and the end of November, perhaps two thousand COs were interned in twenty-three camps. That would change almost overnight.[11]

■ ■ ■

The December 7, 1941 *Sunday Oregonian,* printed in the wee hours after midnight, contained an innocuous three-inch news item on page 20, titled "Trainee Flood to Begin Soon." Some 1,200 Oregon men would be called to service in January, the story said. There was no mention of readiness or other plans, only that this was the largest number of draftees yet. A few hours later, America was at war.

The entire West Coast went on high alert. Cities and towns ordered nightly blackouts; interceptor aircraft were sent to key points along the coast; the weather bureau ceased its summary reports of Pacific coast conditions; and citizens were warned that sabotage, bombings, and even invasion might come. New York Mayor Fiorello LaGuardia, also director of the newly formed Office of Civilian Defense, flew out to Los Angeles with Eleanor Roosevelt and declared that California could be attacked at any moment. All levels of civilian defense must be made ready immediately, he said. "Training must be intensified and we must have daily drills by the forces charged with defense protection."[12]

In Oregon, a newspaper story noted that the closest point to Japan in the continental United States was the mouth of the Columbia River, just seventy-five miles from Portland. Guards in that city were doubled at airport and military posts; all furloughs and leaves were canceled. Soldiers were sent to waterfront docks, sheriff's deputies to the county courthouse, and policemen to the city's bridges. Three officers were stationed at the Japanese consul's home and one at his office. Portland's mayor called civil defense leaders to a meeting; more than one hundred people showed up, five times the number expected. When informed of the overflow crowd outside, World War I general and former governor Charles H. Martin growled, "Well, it's a good idea—why in hell discourage it?" The chief of police reported that his officers were on guard at all critical locations, and the chief of detectives said an additional one thousand "utility police" would be available within ten days. Eight hundred firefighters were ready; six thousand Red Cross workers waited. The Teamsters union, the Longshoremen and Warehousemen, and the International Woodworkers of America all pledged support. Even the Oregon Congress of Parents and Teachers said its twenty-five thousand members could be rallied within twenty-four hours. Portland was shocked at the news but resolute about the future, *Oregonian* reporter Earl Pomeroy wrote. "There was no hysteria. There were no demonstrations. But there was emotion—a mounting anger born of the conditions under which the United States had been attacked, a gnawing kind of anger which found release in fervently expressed desire for full vengeance."[13]

On the coast, independent-minded residents took matters into their own hands, quickly marshalling into armed militia groups from Florence to Tillamook Bay, with names like the Siuslaw Rifles and the Newport Guerillas—and were quickly celebrated across the country as modern-day Minutemen. "The spirit behind the guerilla bands is typical of the spirit of the whole American people—still willing to fight hard for their liberties," said a coastal newspaper, "just as their ancestors did in 1776."[14]

As the apprehension of 1941 galvanized into the resolute purpose of 1942, the United States was at war with Germany and Italy as well as Japan. Throughout the year, another three million Americans were drafted as the United States made the transition from the internal focus of the Great Depression to the external emphasis of joining a world at

Three months after Pearl Harbor, Tillamook guerrillas on the Oregon Coast roar their readiness for any invaders.

war. Industrial production boomed as mobilization of and support for the military became the country's primary occupation. Scrap drives, price caps, and rationing went into effect as sacrifice for what was commonly called "the war effort" was made a national experience. In June, President Roosevelt ordered the establishment of an Office of War Information and an Office of Strategic Services, a forerunner to the CIA.

With the worries of a West Coast invasion, cultural paranoia took over, and more than 100,000 people of Japanese ancestry—more than half of them American citizens—were removed from their homes and businesses and sent to relocation camps inland. "Portland Soon to Be Clear of All Japs," announced a front-page headline of the *Oregon Daily Journal* afternoon edition on Wednesday, April 29. That day, about 350 people of Japanese descent were registered at two offices in the city and lodged in the Pacific International Livestock Exposition Center, following instructions in an "orderly and cooperative manner," according to Ernest Leonetti, manager of Oregon's wartime civil control administration. During the weekend, they would undergo medical examinations and then likely be sent to the Tule Lake Relocation Center near Klamath Falls, southeast of Crater Lake in southern Oregon, Leonetti said. "By noon Tuesday, Portland will be the first city in the nation completely evacuated of Japanese."[15]

By the end of 1942, the sheer volume of energy and resources pouring forth from America began to produce results. In Europe and Africa, Nazi Germany commenced the inevitable shift from invading other countries to defending its occupied territories. In the Pacific, the U.S. Navy went from being nearly demolished at Pearl Harbor to routing the Japanese fleet at Midway Island, in what is generally considered the turning point of the Pacific war. But the sacrifices were far from over. On the home-front, President Roosevelt ordered freezes on wages and salaries, controls on rental rates, and price caps expanded to include butter, eggs, and poultry. Even jitterbugging dancers were ordered to toe the line, as the War Production Board regulatory commission announced that the popular loose-fitting "zoot suit" nightclub outfit with a "rear pleat and a drape shape and stuff cuff, also a cleave sleeve, a free knee and a grip hip" was considered "unpatriotic" as a waste of cloth.[16] Humor was not extinct, though, as a United Press newswire story revealed that a 1920s automobile parked on a street in Detroit sported a sign requesting, "Do not collect this scrap; I still drive it."[17]

Navy airships patrolled the coastline on both defense and rescue missions.

Concern about attacks, sabotage, spying, and the other elements of war continued, particularly along the nation's coastlines. In the Pacific Northwest, the guerrilla groups had evolved into Oregon State Guard units, while the U.S. military activities included a fleet of blimps operating out of the Tillamook Naval Air Station on the north coast, the oval airships becoming a familiar sight as they patrolled the coastline and practiced search-and-rescue missions. Mobile radar stations were set up at intervals along the coast, including one at eight-hundred-foot-high Cape Perpetua, attended by an army unit based at Yachats (pronounced "Yah-hots") a couple miles to the north. Local lore included reports of an artillery gun installed at the top of the cape, in the stone lookout shelter built by the CCC in the 1930s, but most likely the story developed from speculation about the radar equipment, which was guarded as a classified military operation.[18]

The national civil defense plan involved an education and information network aimed at engaging citizens as active participants in the country's defense. People were urged to watch for suspicious behavior ranging from the obvious, like an enemy airplane overhead, to the subtle, such as a potential arsonist carrying a book of matches. "NO INFORMATION IS TOO INSIGNIFICANT to be turned in to the FBI," said the national weekly newspaper, *Civilian Front*. "You furnish the leads, FBI will establish the facts."[19] The fear of domestic saboteurs was strong enough that the Western Defense Command issued a plan for Oregon, Washington, and northern Idaho that featured a list of possible suspect types—including enemy agents or sympathizers disguised as refugees, people who had frequented or lived long periods in enemy countries, people susceptible to promises of money or power, and this catch-all category: "Fanatics, citizens or aliens, such as extreme radicals, pacifists, religious zealots, habitual criminals (especially arsonists), racketeers, and those in narcotic or other vice rings, and unbalanced, perverted, and thwarted individuals such as sadists, frustrated 'geniuses,' disgruntled failures and swindlers."[20]

While this kind of language might sound shrill and fear-mongering today, it wasn't entirely fabrication and propaganda at the time. A team of German saboteurs actually did land on New York's Long Island in June 1942, although they were quickly apprehended before they could do any damage. The West Coast sustained numerous attack scares and a few cases of actual bombardment by Japanese submarines off the Southern California shoreline and near the mouth of the Columbia River—although damage was minimal and the incidents were censored as much as possible.

The Coast Guard in the Pacific Northwest already had a shoreline defense system set up to some degree, with bases, lighthouses, and lookout points. From this beginning, they established control stations at twenty harbors and estuaries along the coasts of Oregon and Washington, where they checked every vessel entering and leaving those areas. But how to cover the huge spaces between? One early idea called for fencing off hundreds of miles of beach, but it was quickly dropped. In the late summer of 1942 a beach patrol program commenced, in which teams of men equipped with pistols, rifles (sometimes machine guns), and attack dogs would patrol sections of beach in four-hour shifts. Although there was no invasion of the mainland, and most of the challenges faced by the patrols revolved around the weather and the rugged landscape, there were occasional rescue operations, discoveries of drowned bodies, alerts regarding unidentified lights, and, in one vague mention, "an exchange of gunfire and pursuit, although none of the suspects was caught."[21]

Now that the war was on and young men went into the military instead of the Civilian Conservation Corps, that program's funding was discontinued in 1942, and more of the locations were shifted to CPS. Another forty-six of the CO camps were added that year, most of them in the eastern and midwestern states. West Coast camps included five in California and one in Washington. Camp #21, the first camp in Oregon, opened in November 1941 at Cascade Locks on the Columbia River, thirty miles east of Portland and adjacent to Mt. Hood National Forest. In the summer of 1942 Selective Service notified the Brethren Service Committee that a new camp would be opened near Klamath Falls. Harold Row, BSC national director, appointed sixty-year-old Charles Kimmel, who had experience at other CPS camps, to open and direct this new one. But at the last minute, Kimmel was told to head for an abandoned CCC camp on the central Oregon coast, a few miles south of Waldport. Perhaps the proposed Klamath Falls site was considered too close to the Tule Lake Relocation Center, where people of Japanese descent had been interned beginning in May. Or maybe it really was the reason given by

Camp #56 director Dick Mills (center) with COs George Trombley (L) and Norman Haskell, ca. 1943.

Selective Service when asking for volunteers to transfer from camps back East: COs were wanted to fight forest fires, and the Waldport site was a ready-made camp adjacent to national forests.[22]

In August, ten COs from Cascade Locks arrived at the CCC camp location on the coast and set up what was officially called at the time a "side camp," joined by some hired locals and a Forest Service project superintendent. Once the site was accorded official status as Camp #56, another crew of ten, with Richard C. Mills appointed assistant director, came down from Cascade Locks to help ready the site for occupancy.[23]

Thirty-four years old, Dick Mills had cut his administrative teeth before the war as a YMCA director in Los Angeles and honed his skills as public relations director at Cascade Locks. He hand-picked his group to set up the Waldport camp, bringing in an office manager, a foreman to supervise all the Overhead staff, two dieticians to plan menus and order food, and another supervisor to create and run a laundry service. Mills even brought in Maude Gregory, the mother of a Cascade Locks camper, who had served there as a kind of matron and stabilizing mother figure to the younger religious COs—some of whom had barely left the Midwest farms where they'd been born and raised. Having this "crackerjack crew" ready and the services running smoothly when the first campers arrived made a world of difference, Bill Everson recalled, crediting Mills with the leadership skills to make it happen. Mills also was one of the first directors who was a CO. For the first year of CPS, most directors had been older church officers of one sort or another, usually married, who may not have shared perspectives with the younger campers. Mills, on the other hand, was there for exactly the same reason as the other men, and he quickly established a reputation as a smart and forward-thinking director. Yet he was also ambitious, and this could sometimes manifest itself in a need to assert his control over a matter—most often behind the scenes.[24]

Maude Gregory, mother of a CO, was a stabilizing presence for many of the religious young men who had never traveled much beyond their farms, ca. 1943.

Meanwhile, a passenger train that included three Pullman sleeping cars assigned to COs made its way across the country, picking up men from camps in Pennsylvania, Indiana, Michigan, Arkansas, and California. Most of these transfer COs had volunteered, perhaps curious about life in the Pacific Northwest, or looking for more meaningful work than what they were doing in the eastern camps, such as cleaning out chicken coops or clearing brush on wealthy landowners' holdings. But for some it may have been similar to what drove a steady stream of people in the nineteenth century to load up their wagons and hit the Oregon Trail: a general dissatisfaction with their lives as they were and the hope that things might be different somewhere else.

Bob Hyslop, from Camp #42 in Wellston, Michigan, recalled a diverse assemblage of backgrounds and attitudes as the train collected its passengers and the men sat up talking while they rolled toward their future into the Great Plains night. "Thus, somewhere on the Wyoming prairie, groups from several camps were rapidly merging into a new camp," he said. "Past experience could only be a helpful guide for creative thinking, planning, or whatever may come."[25]

This train also carried a rarity: the wife of a CO. Elizabeth Meeks was heading west with her husband, unsure of exactly what they'd find at the end of the trail. Selective Service rules didn't allow her to travel with the men in their chartered Pullman cars, but she said she preferred it that way, for then she could hear what passengers in the other cars were saying. There were the expected comments, the standard digs about cowardice and manhood, she said. "Every CO knows the epithets likely to be applied to him." Nor did it help that the CPS men ate their meals separately and *before* everyone else on an overcrowded and late-running train. Meeks also knew that for most people, their only encounter with conscientious objection would be whatever they heard and saw from her—and the pressure to say and do the right things was great. But generally she found that the more informed people were, the more tolerant they were. She noted in particular that the most favorable thing the COs had, public relations-wise, was that the government wasn't paying their way. It was easier, she felt, for people to accept different points of view when their tax dollars weren't involved.[26]

Passenger trains did not run to Waldport, and the group transferred to buses in California. One camper wrote, "We've been in Sacramento all day. May pull out at 5:00 p.m. Moon was bright last night. Mountains beautiful so we sang old songs till late in the night." Another wrote the next day, "Calif. was bare till Dunsmuir [north central California], then mtns, tunnels, trees and streams. Moon was soft and bright again. Saw Mt. Shasta at 3 a.m. this morning. More mts along the coast. Our buses drive with only parking lights— 'Dim out' orders."[27]

Finally, the men arrived at the camp, somehow appropriately in the dark of night:

> Brakes applied!!! A flashlight puts forth its tiny rays into the dark night as the man bearing the light enters the bus to give the driver instructions as to where to go. Dim lights in many windows. The bus comes to a stop. Everybody makes their exit with arms loaded with baggage. Wet sand under foot. Bare campus. Beyond the grounds to the west—tall trees in the moonlight. On three sides low hills stand out bare but for here and there a tall gaunt memorial to fire razing a majestic forest. Well—in with your luggage—barracks two or three—and pick out a bunk.
>
> Wellston, Lagro, Walhalla, Magnolia, Kane, Cascade Locks, and Lyndhurst melted into Camp Albert Angell. . . . Now to the dining hall for a late but delicious meal before evening prayer and retiring.[28]

So it was that on October 24, 1942, Civilian Public Service Camp #56 (also referred to as Camp Waldport, Camp Angell, and Camp Angel)[29] in Lincoln County, a little more than halfway up the Oregon coast, four miles south of Waldport, two miles north of Yachats, and a couple hundred yards inland from the beach, officially opened with ninety-six members under the administration of the Brethren Service Committee and assigned to do work for the U.S. Forest Service—just in time for the fall rains. Crews were immediately put to work constructing more buildings to accommodate camp needs, only to see two of them flattened by a storm. The rain was incessant; the mud ubiquitous. The camp newsletter, the *Tide,* in its first issue, dated November 1942, observed, "Where there is smoke there is fire and in CPS 56, where there is rain there is mud and that is everywhere. Having removed the top soil when leveling an area for camp, no seeds were left in the exposed earth to start new

A portable shed at Camp #56, flattened into the mud by a late-autumn storm.

vegetation; hence, not a blade of grass, not even a dandelion, graces our campgrounds. . . . we live in a sea of mud." And no one knew how deep and boglike that mud might actually be. Another camper noted that it had rained every day so far, adding this wry note: "Thus far all trucks, tools, and men have been accounted for at the end of each day, but no one knows how long that will last."[30]

All told, however, the mood in the beginning was generally optimistic. Despite the weather, the men actually seemed to like the new camp, the *Tide* editor wrote. "Perhaps they have caught something of that indomitable, carefree, pioneering spirit of the west." There was indeed hope, another camper said. "Our staff shows promise, the fellows are fine, our equipment is of more recent vintage . . . and who knows? Perhaps grass will grow if we plant it!"[31]

The Brethren Service Committee didn't just throw the men into a pool of mud to dig out a life by themselves. On the first two days of camp operation, the church's peace education secretary, Dan West, was on hand to help set the tone with discussions on how CPS fit into the aims of the peace churches and pacifism. Nearly everyone at Waldport had experience in other CPS camps, and with Secretary West they created a seven-point list of goals for Camp Angel:

1. Eliminate paternalism in administration of the camps.
2. Build an efficient specialized education program.
3. Seek out the good in every camper and utilize it.
4. Build an attitude of respect for the obnoxious. (Tolerance)
5. Develop a community spirit.
6. Earn favorable public relations.
7. Develop a well-rounded religious program that will give opportunity for the expression of the religious beliefs of all.[32]

The men quickly set up a system for organizing and governing themselves. They created a camp council and drew up a constitution containing eight articles on governance and decision-making processes. They elected a president and secretary, instituted a Workers Committee and a Religious Committee, and added others that they named Public Relations, Education, Recreation, and Health. Chairmanship terms lasted three months with a second term possible, and representatives elected to camp council from each of the four housing units would serve three months also, with half the body up for election every six weeks alternating.[33]

Dick Mills went back East for a month of administrative training, and on his return took over as director from Charles Kimmel, who moved to assistant director, his role of providing an experienced face to the camp identity having been completed. Soon enough, the committees devised responses to the rain, mud, and isolation, Mills wrote. They came up with entertainment programs on holidays, as well as table-waiting service in the dining hall, a dishwashing crew and the free laundry service. One popular program was the birthday night, when camp members who'd had a birthday the previous month were honored with dinner at a special table, entertained with a vaudeville-type variety show, and encouraged to speak a few words about their background or interests. Camp administrators also chose a "family style" approach to governance, Mills said. Outside of the imposed Selective Service regulations, camp rules were made by the campers, not church administrators. The point was to place decision-making power with the individual and encourage him to consider the needs of the group, Mills said. He apparently did not mention that his idea of family-style governance placed him in a paternal, authoritative role.[34]

Whether these kinds of beliefs and statements were a matter of politics, hopefulness, naïveté, or that "indomitable pioneering spirit" is impossible to say. It's worth remembering, though, that this was a camp run by a church, and that for many of the men, religion was the predominant force in their lives. Daily prayers, Bible study, and sermon attendance were as fundamental as eating and sleeping. Some were so intense about saying grace at meals and reading their Bibles every night that it was like they were willing themselves into God's presence, Everson observed.[35] Yet, within their limitations the practices were diverse. In early 1943 nearly half of the roughly 120 campers were Church of the Brethren members, but the remaining men represented twenty-nine denominations, ranging from Methodists and Baptists to lesser-known groups like the Essenes and the Moody Bible Institute. About 10 percent were labeled "Unaffiliated"—which in this case included those practicing no religion.[36]

Other demographic groups were broad but with identifiable majorities. Age ran from twenty to forty-four, with most in their early twenties. About twenty states were represented, the bulk of the men hailing from California and Michigan. Race was overwhelmingly white, so much so that the monthly personnel reports didn't mention race at all. Occupation categories included professional and managerial, clerical, sales, service, farming, fishery, and forestry—with about a third in the skilled and semi-skilled trades, and about twenty of the men students. Education ranged from sixth grade to master's degrees, with most having completed high school and perhaps some college. Only twelve campers were married.[37]

Physically, camp life centered around a dozen buildings, with most activity focused on the four dormitories and the dining and recreation halls. In his letters to Edwa, Everson sent an almost daily record of the environment and events. He drew a rough sketch of the camp that included the compound, the beach, and on the bluff above it a "vacant

The scrapbook containing this photo says, "Camp Waldport 'inmates,' spring of 1943."

summer home" and a row of tourist cottages. A stand of trees partially hid the camp from the highway, and the back of the compound butted up against a hill, leaving the relatively enclosed quadrangle a clearly defined, perhaps in some ways claustrophobic, area. The men's living spaces were side by side, both within and without the buildings. If they wanted food, they stepped outside their dorm and took a diagonal course left to the dining hall. For recreation, they took an identical path to the right. To wash their clothes, they headed due right to the laundry room at the end of the dorms. Chapel was across the mud quadrangle, as were the camp offices and infirmary. The Project work equipment was in garages behind the dorms, and down a path from there toward the highway was the Forest Service building. The water tower squatted slightly above the camp, partly up the hillside, its ladder leading to a tiny platform that offered a view of the ocean and respite from too much public living. This was their world.

Everson's second sketch describes the dorm floor plan: thirty-eight beds, set side-by-side in pairs as if they were double beds and extending to a center aisle; next to each set of beds was a similarly paired set of lockers. Heat came from woodstoves at each end of the dorm. The bathroom was at the end of the building with an open row of sinks along one wall and a row of toilets opposite, with a row of showers through an open doorway.[38] While this was not much different than any other military or temporary group-living environment, the lack of bathroom privacy was so bothersome to Everson that he took to defecating out on Project, using a hollow stump for his commode.[39] One modern benefit of the bathrooms, though, was that they had flush toilets and hot-water showers—the latter a significant relief after a day's work in the muddy hills and freezing rain. And a nice touch was that part of the night watchman's duties was to stoke the fires beneath the hot-water tanks in the predawn hours so that when the men awoke they could wash up with hot water.

Responding to the climate was perhaps the most shocking adjustment for many of the men who came from the eastern and midwestern states, where rain usually postponed outdoor work. In Oregon, there was no such thing as a rain cancellation; people simply put on raincoats and boots and went about their business. With the constant cloud cover and frequent precipitation, the temperature rarely dropped below freezing, although it did tend to remain in the thirties and forties around the clock for days or even weeks at a time. It might be snowing just a few miles away at the higher elevations—five hundred or a thousand feet—and at a given stretch the men might find themselves working in a mixture of giant, fat raindrops and soggy half-snow with flakes more like wet leaves than ice crystals. For the most part, they simply trudged along and did what they could in an utterly waterlogged world.

Their work was pretty much what the CCC boys had done. Besides the rock crushing and road building, the COs were scheduled to plant 1.5 million trees and build a fire lookout tower. In areas that still had trees, they would thin and prune the sections to facilitate future logging throughout the Siuslaw, Willamette, and Siskiyou national forests—an area that covered just about the entire southwest quadrant of the state. They would also form disaster response crews and be trained for emergency relief work "to fight fire, combat flood damage and serve as emergency units in case of bombing or other casualties inflicted on the civilian population."[40]

Keith Utterback relaxes over the Christmas holiday, 1942, with decorated evergreens hanging from the ceiling. Note the adjacent bed for another CO.

A section of scorched hillside ready for planting.

For the first winter and spring their planting focused on the Blodgett Tract, the twelve thousand acres south of camp that had been logged of its spruce trees during World War I to make airplanes. Interestingly, much of that earlier work had been done by soldiers, many of them from the East Coast and with no forestry experience—not unlike their CO counterparts in World War II—and at least two had died in logging accidents. When the remaining timber was cut in 1935, the logging companies chopped down everything but took only the best logs, not even bothering to burn off the slash, and left a crumpled landscape behind. In the summer of 1936, one of the hottest and driest on record, fire swept through some ten thousand acres of the tract, turning the land into a moonscape with the burned tree trunks sticking up like charred witnesses to their own destruction.[41]

Fire is, of course, a natural part of the healthy forest life cycle; when the fire has burned out, the tree trunks and other organic matter remain as nutrients for the new soil. But clear-cut logging is exactly what it sounds like; the forest is completely cut down, and when fire sweeps through the slash and brush left behind, the raw material of regeneration simply isn't there. This, then, was the task for the COs: to put tree seedlings in the ground and start the forest anew.

Six days a week, they woke at 6:30 a.m. to the clanging of a metal rod beaten on hanging railroad irons. Half an hour later they were at breakfast, gobbling down the eggs, bacon, milk, and whatever fruit or vegetables might be available that day. Each man slated for Project work was issued an identical lunch: four sandwiches doled out as one meat, one cheese, and two peanut butter and jelly, along with a gallon of milk and sometimes a cookie or piece of pie.[42] By 8:00 they were packed in the back of a (sometimes) covered truck, lurching up the muddy roads into the hills; sometimes the vehicle reached the work site and sometimes the men had to hike in over particularly rough terrain. At the site, each crew of ten to sixteen men took their hoes—hand-held pickaxes with flat metal blades—and strapped to their belts a canvas bag of fifty or so six-inch fir and spruce seedlings that had been grown from seed in a Forest Service nursery. Then they lined up eight feet apart as directed by the crew leader, and started forward in unison. They took three steps, slammed the hoe into the ground and jerked it back to make a wedge-shaped hole, drew a seedling from their bag and slipped its root into the space, then pulled out the hoe, tamped down the earth, took three steps and did it again. It was back-breaking work that left no desire or even breath for conversation. They just bent to it and moved forward in a kind of hunchbacked dance. As Everson wrote Edwa, "You line up with the man on your left and keep even. And you go over the mountain. You go over rocks, stumps, logs, briars, gullys [sic], creeks, gulches, ravines, arroyos. You go over

Six tree planters all but
disappear on the bleak
hillsides.

Toasting sandwiches at lunch on
the trail. Everson in white shirt
at center.

anything and everything and by noon every bone, every muscle in your body is alive and crying."[43]

The tools were provided by the Forest Service, and later in the war men were issued a water-repellent jacket-and-pants outfit made of canvas so stiff that it was called a "tin suit." For the steep and uneven terrain, they also later would be given logger-style caulk (pronounced "cork") boots with spikes in the soles. In the early days, though, this equipment went only to those who had the money to buy it.[44]

At lunchtime they gathered around a fire and toasted their sandwiches by holding them over the flames with forked sticks cut from green wood, partly in an attempt to dry out the soggy bread. During the colder weather, they might climb inside burned-out, old growth tree stumps for protection from the worst of the wind and rain. One camper from Indiana recalled how an entire ten-man crew climbed inside a giant stump larger than anything he'd ever seen, built a campfire, then hunkered down together and ate their lunch.[45]

Most of the men, coming from conservative religious backgrounds, took an idealist approach to the work, doing it for what they considered the betterment of humanity. As Everson observed, "Most of them just plant trees and wish they were home." One of his new friends, Bob Scott, was a pianist and music teacher with no physical affinity for the work, yet he toiled away with philosophical acceptance. "Furiously he goes on tree planting," Everson said, "which will without a doubt kill him." The young rebels, Harold Hackett and Larry Siemons, took advantage of the directive that Forest Service bosses could only tell them where and how to work, and couldn't actually make them do anything. Hackett would work when he felt like it, stating that he was against the Project labor itself as a matter of principle. Siemons was a goldbricker of the highest order, with a whole catalogue of tricks to keep from doing anything required of him. Glen Coffield, ever following his own star, worked in his ragged clothes, with pants so torn he had to wear pajamas beneath them. He couldn't afford rain gear, yet he refused all help and slogged along, Everson said, "day after day in the interminable rain, drenched, shivering and sore."[46]

Beneath all this was an underlying suspicion that the work was really just something to keep the men busy, that government officials had not actually thought out what constituted work of national importance, and that many in the chain of command would just as soon have the men digging holes and filling them in somewhere out of sight for the duration of the war. In some cases, particularly with the so-called road building, this seemed almost literally true, as the *Untide* reported sharply in early February. "Govt. Project Complete," the headline said, with an accompanying cartoon showing trucks foundering in the mud. The subtitle and story dripped with sarcasm:

ROAD TO QUARRY IS FINISHED: SO ARE MOST OF THE CREW

On Wednesday morning, February 3, [Forest Service supervisors] Rice, Aufterhide and McLaughlin officially opened the new scenic drive to the rock quarry. Over the flats, across the Saddle, and around the Hairpin the pickup sped in low gear, conveyed by two crew trucks and two dumps filled with C.O.s and garbage.

A comment on winter work at Camp #56, not entirely in jest.

While the pickup sat axle-deep in a mud hole McLaughlin, in an exclusive interview, declared, "This road is in 1-A condition. We are now ready for the tourist trade."[47]

Progress:.. . . . . November, December, January

ROAD TO QUARRY IS FINISHED: SO ARE MOST OF THE CREW

Another *Untide* editorial, titled "Trees—4F" (a reference to the draft category designating someone as unfit for military duty), blasted the Forest Service for apparently having the men plant diseased seedlings. "Consider, toilers, what it is we do," the unsigned opinion piece exhorted its readers. "With every bend of our backs, with every whack of our hoes, we place in the ground some miserable runt that may never mature." Even the seedlings that made it thus far could not survive the coming disease, flooding, drought, and grazing wildlife, the writer said. "Comrades, to what end do we labor? Shall we sow and reap not? Must the sweat of our brows be poured on the earth and no good come out of it? Those sickly specimens that we plant are foredoomed!"[48]

Yet through it all, in that odd camaraderie born of shared misery, the men found a way to abide, and developed their own brand of gallows humor. Along with the jokes from the *Untide*—about bombing each other with mud clods on Project, dangerously cramming men into the backs of trucks, traveling with dynamite and blasting caps packed together, poking fun at administrators' egos—other reports revealed a creativity, willingness, and even optimism that better times may come. In the long tradition of responses to work crews, chain gangs, and compulsory labor, the men came up with all manner of songs to help them through the day. The *Tide* in April printed a page commending Glen Coffield, "Scotty" Walker, Jim Ragland, "Jay" Williams, and Don Kimmel, who changed the words from popular tunes to fit local conditions. They sang everything from opera to swing, they sang while the trucks bounced over the bone-wracking roads, they sang while scrambling over stumps and logs in the wind and rain. And to the delight of many, the men reprised their songs for nighttime entertainment in the dining hall. During a particularly rain-soaked week, one group calling themselves Crew Five did a skit satirizing a full day of Project work, described later as "pantomiming, contorting, adding sound effects and individual lines as appropriate." They sat astride benches and simulated the bumpy ride in the back of the trucks, then gathered in a line to act out the tree-planting dance.

> Hiking to the planting, [doing] the planting; all was there, all
> in unison, as rhythmic as the Rockettes, "One two three, plant
> a tree," down went the hazel hoes to the floor, "One two three,
> plant a tree," a pause and Crew Five broke out with,
>> "High ho, High ho, it's off to work we go,
>> To plant a tree, for Forestry,
>> High ho, high ho, high ho, etc."[49]

Bill Everson joined in the singing, offering a bit he called "The Monkey Song," which made reference to a kind of reverse-evolution, something to do with climbing trees, and that the *Tide* said "will outlive

Sketch of the "dead stump" that is actually full of life.

CPS." He also, according to one camper, would remove his clothes at lunchtime during the more mild days on Project and lie naked on the rocks, to the consternation of the more religious men. And, in a kind of precursor to the beatnik jazz poetry of the 1950s, he stood up at the birthday night celebration for his month and announced, "I was conceived in Bakersfield, born in Sacramento, married in Fresno, and died in Waldport."[50]

Not to be outdone, Coffield took his songs into the music recording room—just a closet with a microphone and a tape machine—where he chanted and sang original and contemporary poetry. It was a good recording, Everson reported to Edwa, although he added that Coffield "murdered" one of his poems.[51]

Other campers made recordings, too. Keith Utterback took a recorder down to the beach and sang "Danny Boy" with backup from the ocean waves. Ray Long laid down a version of "Ol' Man River." Art Brown pulled out his guitar to record some blues standards, then was joined by Utterback for a duet of "Red River Valley."[52]

And Larry Siemons, while perhaps a goldbricker on Project, penned an ecological observation thirty years ahead of its time:

A QUESTION OF LIFE AND DEATH

Have you noticed the life struggling out of the charred stumps on the hillsides? A crown of green [salal] with gangling alder and fir trees rising in little spires; delicate mushrooms among the mosses and ferns, nourished by the roots; huge gnarled fungi with their horny backs and soft white bellies clutching the sides. Within, the wet brown wood is tunneled by the boring of worms. Glistening green slugs lie in their dark winter sleep; beside them the shiny beetles eat their way to maturity and the grey outside world. And as we work *planting* trees, we guide by "that dead stump."[53]

Camp #56 was mixing a strange brew of tree planting and rock crushing, misery, music, humor, and imagination. From the traditional and conforming ways of the religious conservatives to the rebellious poet sunbathing on the rocks, from the pious Camp Angel chorus recording Charles Gounod's "Nazareth" to the unshaven anarchist Coffield singing a cappella into a recording microphone, "I love an onion / in a pot of stew / I love an onion / more than you," from Hackett and Siemons goldbricking on the job to staying up until 4:00 a.m. to finish mimeographing copies of the *Untide*, this soggy outpost between the mountains and the sea was beginning to show signs that something more could happen here, that it contained the necessary ingredients to achieve a critical mass.

They could laugh at their condition, as two transfers from Camp Lagro in Indiana, observed: "At present our main project is tree planting, but even that is different than it was in the East. Here we plant on the sides of mountains and often we have to climb the last tree we planted in order to plant the next one."[54] But they were soon to be reminded that this was no game, and that the consequences of ignorance or carelessness were quite real.

The dangerous beauty of the Oregon coast. Rock outcroppings make it easy to walk right up to the unpredictable waves.

CHAPTER 4

Community, Cooperation, and Sacrifice

AS THE CALENDAR TURNED to January 1943, the camp addressed the routine matters of day-to-day living and how they might abide the circumstances of their conscription. The *Tide* featured a front-page graphic of a dock piling extended into a cross and a full-page prayer that began, "Dear God Most High, in these times of chaos incurred by our own indifference and wandering from Thy way, we are again brought to our knees in humble, heart sick prayer because we have believed we are self-sufficient to the exclusion of Thy will. . . . Oh God, may we live in closer communion with Thee, that our lives might be instruments in Thy hands to again calm time's troubled tide. May we then follow Thee at as great a sacrifice and even greater than those we are now giving in the present war effort."[1]

This issue also reported on the latest birthday night event. The evening of January 1, a special table was set for the guests of honor; the camp cook, "Capable Carl" Rutledge, was master of ceremonies, and entertainment was provided by John "Red Dog" Dellinger, Glen "Whiskers" Coffield, Charlie Draper, and Art Brown, who offered folk songs and other musical numbers. Then Coffield, Kermit Sheets, and Charles Homig contributed some humorous and dramatic readings, and Keith George played piano to finish out the program. It was good old-fashioned fun to help the men relax and forget homesickness for a bit. "And so goes the evening," the story concluded. "And so—goodnite."[2]

The next day the first camp member died.

It was a sadly familiar scene to anyone who knew the Oregon coast. On the afternoon of January 2, Denton Darrow, an Idaho boy and temporary transfer from Cascade Locks, was swept into the ocean near Yachats and drowned. He'd volunteered for a twenty-man team that was searching the shoreline for signs of seven crew members lost when a navy seaplane crashed in the ocean during a recent storm. It was low tide, and Darrow's group was on a rock outcropping. As a wave receded, Darrow stepped onto a low point but was caught from behind by a sudden wave that threw him into the channel. Other men were nearby, but trying to swim these channels between the rocks would be like jumping into a blender, and they could only watch as he bobbed and floated further and further away, apparently knocked unconscious from the fall—for, although an excellent swimmer, he made no visible attempt to move. The Coast Guard arrived with its men and equipment, but the unforgiving currents had already done their work; Darrow's body was swept out to sea. The search for the missing navy men continued for several days, a local newspaper reported, "but three life jackets, a rubber life raft, and a silk scarf [were] all that could be found."[3]

Eight days after Darrow disappeared, men at Cascade Locks, Camp Waldport, and the CPS camp at Fort Steilacoom in Washington paused for thirty minutes, the *Tide* reported, "in memory of their colleague and dear friend, Denton Darrow, who lost his life in service to his fellow man."[4]

Aside from the moment of silence, there wasn't much more. The Civilian Public Service handbook, or "CPS Bible," dictated that in event of a CO's death nine steps were to be followed, including family notifications, undertaking services (not to exceed $100 locally and $50 in the deceased's hometown), and transportation for the body, with all appropriate forms completed in duplicate or triplicate. No insurance settlement, no help for dependents. Just a body delivered—under whatever conditions $150 afforded. In the extant Camp Waldport "Bible" files, a note is typed under the category "Responsibility—Accidents," dated January 13, 1943. "In regards to responsibility, it seems to us that neither SS [Selective Service] nor the BSC can be held responsible for this accident, inasmuch as Denton Darrow volunteered his services. On the same basis, I do not see how the Coast Guard can be held responsible unless undue negligence can be proved."[5]

One unexpected result of Darrow's death was an educational talk about one of America's opponents in the war. The Methodist minister from Darrow's hometown in Idaho, a Dr. Shaeffer—who accompanied Darrow's father to the camp—spent twenty years as a missionary in Korea and Japan. During Shaeffer's three-day visit, he gave a talk on the history of Japan, providing insight into the religious and political aims of that country, and joined informal conversations after meals. "Scheduled speakers are few enough out here," said the *Tide*, "but to have a well-informed and interesting speaker come among us unannounced and in the simple guise of a visitor was a yet rarer piece of luck."[6]

This kind of curiosity and inquisitiveness was a hallmark of life at many CPS camps. For a fair number of campers, a primary goal was to find and nurture common interests beyond their shared fundamental objection to war. Generally speaking, the "free time" activities beyond work and daily chores fell into three categories: religion, education, and recreation. For many COs, their religious life in camp was simply an extension of their previous experience. Men quickly fell into association with those of like beliefs and organized their own Bible studies, church services, prayer meetings, and daily devotionals. Some of the more strictly religious COs were supported by their communities back home, who paid for their wives and children to join them and live in the various tourist cottages along the highway. One group set up Sunday school classes for the kids and welcomed others in the area to attend.

The Religious Life Committee, formed in part to facilitate understanding and interaction among the faiths, followed its constitutional dictum to "provide a religious program to serve the needs of all the camp" by setting up a schedule for Sunday services to be led on a rotating basis by members of the different denominations. Vigorous discussion often followed the lectures, which is no surprise, considering the diversity of viewpoints and participants in such a small and isolated locale. Around thirty denominations were represented in camp, and services might be run by campers, their wives, or outside visitors. They might be Jewish, Quaker, or Jehovah's Witness. A Roman Catholic priest might speak one week and a group of Mormon elders the next. A college professor or university president may come. The service might be a written text, panel discussion, communion, or meditation; attendance could range from little more than a dozen to upwards of eighty. Sunday evening meetings featured anything from traditional hymn singing and readings from the *Life of Saint Francis* to inspirational music accompanied by slideshows of the nearby natural beauty, or holding vesper services on the beach. Some groups preferred to gather independently of others, such as the Jehovah's Witnesses, who held Bible study and classes on their *Watchtower* texts just about every other night of the week. The evangelicals attended midweek services, and early risers kept a pre-breakfast meditation.[7]

While this diversity might seem positive on the surface, in some ways it also separated the men. Perhaps a Presbyterian or Baptist might be curious about a Quaker service, and vice versa, but generally people tended to circulate with those of their own faith. Additionally, the camp community was very different than the world most members had left. Back home, the men went to church not only for worship but to meet friends, or perhaps to hear a particular minister. At camp, however, worship seemed to be almost the sole presiding reason anyone attended, with only about half the campers regularly taking part in religious services and activities. Granted, about 10 percent of the men identified themselves as atheist or agnostic, but that still left 40 percent at best only partially involved in religion at a camp run by a church. One activity related to religion, though, reaped great dividends both within the camp and in relations with the surrounding coastal communities. In "deputations" sent out to area churches, campers sang in choruses, quartets, duets, and even solos at religious services. This kind of ambassadorship promoted understanding and acceptance of the pacifists' views in ways that no amount of public education or legislative petitioning could hope to achieve. And, not surprisingly, this universal language — music — would continue to bring disparate groups together.[8]

The campers' backgrounds, interests and abilities beyond religion were even more diverse. The Education Committee, headed by Don Brumbaugh, took a survey of residents' preferences in classes and activities. The majority, of course, preferred Bible study; other strong topics included cooperative and community living, music, and foreign languages. General interest was expressed in first aid, public speaking, postwar reconstruction, subsistence farming, typing, dietetics, and celestial navigation. Eight men signed their name to the literature and art category, and half a dozen went for nonviolent direct action. Write-in topics included craft work, vocational guidance, parliamentary law, and math. One camper wrote a single word: "girls."

The first thing the committee did was to build a library. They had Frank Allen, an architectural draftsman before the war, draw up plans for a space adjacent to the camp offices in the southwest corner of the quadrangle, near the entrance to the camp. They collected scrap wood from around the site, then took some hammers and crowbars down to an earlier CCC camp location that had been abandoned near Cape Perpetua and dismantled the remains of the buildings there. They hauled everything back to Camp Angel, then Allen, Dick Brown, and Pius Gibble put their carpentry skills to work, constructing bookshelves, reading tables, and a built-in office desk. Comfort and accessibility were priorities: reading tables were spaced in two stacked rows, indirect lighting helped eliminate shadows, murals were painted on the walls above the shelves, and, in a nod to abstract design, an irregularly shaped low table dubbed "the Amoeba" was situated in a corner with a modern chromed chair.

More than a thousand books were gathered through a combination of loans from camp members and a special three-month borrowing privilege from the Oregon State Library in Salem. As might be expected, reading was widespread in the camp; along with the fifty or so volumes loaned for the three-month period, the state library might receive orders for another fifteen or so books per month. There was no favorite author or book type; representative titles ranged from *Spotlight on Peace Plans* and *America's Role in Asia* to *The Screwtape Letters, Language in Action, Art and Freedom,* and *Brothers under the Skin.* Magazines were very popular, including *Christian Century, Musical Quarterly, Popular Mechanics, Popular Photography, Harper's, Collier's,* the *Nation, Time,*

Camp #56 library. A portion of the "amoeba" table can be seen at lower left.

Monthly Survey of Race Relations, Common Sense, Consumer Reports, the *New Yorker,* and the *Federal Council of Churches Information Service.* The daily news came via the *Oregonian* from Portland. "The use of the library has been spontaneous and wide," wrote education director Brumbaugh, adding that he felt it was partly due to the choices made in its design and construction.[9]

Group activities and classes quickly followed—not as an external requirement imposed on the men but as a natural extension of their thoughts and interactions. Talk in the tree-planting hillsides and night-time "bull sessions" in the dorms grew into official forums, sometimes with guest speakers. Even though Camp Waldport's isolation could make it difficult for people to travel there, they were able to host the occasional visiting CPS leader, university professors, church officials, or peace organization members, who covered topics generally related to religious and social questions. Professor Robert Dann of Oregon State College spoke on psychology; Raymond Peters, the young people's director of the Church of the Brethren, dashed through the area one night and, between scheduled bus arrivals and departures, delivered a talk titled "We Must Learn to Live Together!" Mary Farquharson, former Washington state senator and now secretary of the Fellowship of Reconciliation, spoke of a case regarding Gordon Hirabayashi, an American citizen from Seattle, of Japanese ancestry but also a Quaker conscientious objector, who was on trial for refusing relocation to a government internment camp. Helen Topping, former secretary to the Japanese Christian missionary Toyohiko Kagawa and at that time employed at the Tule Lake Relocation Center, discussed her work in building cooperative education movements in Hawaii, Australia, and the Philippines. The east-Asian societies had a much longer history with intercultural understanding—and the West could learn from them, she said. "For the present that may mean working together in isolation [with] Japanese-Americans, sharing their liability as refugees until it becomes an asset to us all." And Kirby Page, a Disciples of Christ minister known for his energetic speaking and passionate advocacy for world peace, astounded everyone who attended, including one camp intellectual who commented, "He is the first man I have ever heard who has made Christianity seem reasonable."[10]

Interests were progressive and broad enough to include consideration of a talk by Ralph Borsodi, a pioneer of organic agriculture and self-sufficient or "decentralized" communities, as carried out by his School of Living, which he'd founded in rural Pennsylvania in 1934. His forty-two-page seminar proposal included a sharp assessment of American culture that was decades ahead of mainstream thinking in this country:

> Some of the items of faulty ideology which people are taught include: reliance on doctors and hospitals, eating what advertisers suggest, including large quantities of cereals, and sugared drinks, and 150 pounds of sugar per capita per year, muscle meat, fruit and vegetables harvested green and grown in chemically fertilized soils as far from the consumer as possible. In clothing they are taught to discard clothes as often as fashion dictates, to wear high heeled shoes which misshape the feet; to live in buildings at high temperatures; to live always in crowds and to compete in study and games, to listen to exciting radio stories; to marry late, to do repetitive work for money, to spend leisure hours watching others, to look as young as possible, to spend old-age sitting in an institution, to depend on sanatoriums and psycho-analysis, to bear as few children as possible, and never, if possible to avoid it, breast-feed a child. People are taught to live abnormally—and unless differently taught this set of ideas will prevail.[11]

While there is no record of Borsodi actually coming to Waldport, his thinking was indicative of the larger ideas being considered across the camp. They kept his proposal on file.

Camp members also took it upon themselves to foster an atmosphere of shared inquiry and thoughtful examination. Each night after dinner, Dick Mills offered a summary of the day's official communications and relevant information. Musicians Carl Rutledge, Keith Utterback, Bob Carlson, and Hugh Merrick gave concerts. Everson began informal lectures on modern poetry—but he also really wanted to talk about jazz. He was the only one at camp who had any knowledge in this music, he wrote Edwa not long after his arrival, and he sent lists of jazz records he hoped she could either bring with her on a visit or have shipped to the camp. In the meantime, the COs held Saturday night "record concerts" hosted by Bob Scott, the piano teacher, focusing mostly on classical music. Everson participated as a listener here—and a very active one. Sometimes he became so involved in the music that he began waving his arms and stomping his feet, disrupting the others so much that Scott had to tell him to stop.[12]

Participation in most classes was initially small, but those who did attend generally found it worthwhile. The key to success here was in working within limits, and the Education Committee adapted to their circumstances by building a program that employed the basic tools of progressive education. For those with limited academic background, they set up individual study sessions aimed at addressing each student's interests and goals. The more advanced students, some of them taking correspondence courses, also received tutoring and support according to their needs. The foundation of this approach rested on one important rule: regardless of demand, they would not attempt to offer classes beyond the availability of qualified people to teach them.

It wasn't all teaching and discipline. Nobody was required to take any classes, and there were plenty of recreational activities lined up. Sports were big. The COs were generally healthy young men, and while the fifty hours of manual labor was hard work, many of the fit became fitter; as long as their food was sufficient and nutritious, they had energy enough. Team sports included softball and volleyball on the beach, and badminton was offered (although its availability might be affected by the regular heavy winds). Indoor games included ping-pong, chess and checkers, as well as card games—including a game called rook, similar to bridge and an alternative for people whose religion forbade them from using a standard deck of gambling cards. For visual entertainment they brought in religious, documentary, and popular films of the day. And early on, camper Frank Allen presented an evening of his color slides from a prewar trip to Europe. The education director's report treated it as a highlight, perhaps underscoring that many of the men were not particularly well traveled.[13]

As life settled into the daily and weekly routines, the men adapted and the camp developed its personality. Everson had written Edwa when he first arrived that in the camp there were few restrictions. "We may smoke in the barracks if we wish. Everything here is moderate, and left up to the individual." As a smoker, Everson no doubt appreciated this openness and tolerance, yet he saw—or rather heard—the other side of tolerance when a couple weeks later he recounted his difficulties with writing in the mornings when the dorm was full of fellow campers playing guitars and practicing yodeling. He considered leaving Dorm 1 and moving to Dorm 4, the intellectual hub of the camp and home to a nascent communal living experiment, but he opted for more privacy and eventually got his bed assignment moved to the end of the dorm, where his space was bordered on one side at least by the wall. There was a flip side to that as well, with the noisy showers just through the wall, he noted, "but when I weigh the differences—."[14]

Privacy was cast aside in the Dorm 4 communal living plan. Stemming from a desire to understand the roots of war, members determined that much conflict could be traced to society's focus on personal property. Americans, they said, had long been taught that possession means ownership. But they also claimed that possession alone does not provide security; the only real security comes through concern for others and the resultant social cooperation. Dorm 4 residents therefore decided that all possessions there would be considered community property, and they outlined their program in the *Tide*. "We start by sharing our clothes as we see needs arising. We double-decked our beds to make room for a sort of living room for reading, writing, and lounging. Some in the group pooled their cash for each to spend according to need." All were invited to join, they said—individuals or groups.[15]

Other communities were less defined by space. One group called themselves the "Christian Service Unit" simply because they shared an attitude that working hard on Project was for the betterment of humanity, and that it could be fun to engage in friendly competition such as seeing who could plant the most trees in a day. Another group began a "silent meditation" practice, rising at 5:15 each morning before the usual 6:30 camp reveille. One CO proposed taking the cooperative living idea beyond the camp and creating a national network of pacifist-minded "Hospitality Centers" modeled after the European youth hostels that were popular before the war.[16]

Still another community was taking shape across the highway on a bluff overlooking the beach, in the tourist cabins owned by a couple who were sympathetic to the secular as well as religious CO perspective. The business was officially named Shore Pines Cottages, but the driveway entrance was unmistakably marked by a sixty-foot whale skeleton—the remains of a carcass that had washed up on nearby Tillicum Beach some years earlier, had then been cleaned and cured, and was now mounted on blocks and advertised as "Tillie the Whale," which became the place's popular name. With gas rationing and other wartime privations, the tourist trade was almost nonexistent, so the cottage owners rented cabins to the campers' families and friends at bargain rates, where a wife or girlfriend might stay a few days, a week, a month, or longer. There were about a dozen cabins, most of them two-room affairs with bare wooden floors, simple furniture, a flat-topped woodstove, and a large window facing the ocean. Over time, the renters treated these vacation quarters more like homes and decorated them with driftwood, shells,

"Tillie the Whale" skeleton on the highway advertised shoreline cottages where CO couples stayed.

and the colored glass floats that had become detached from fishermen's nets and carried by the currents across the ocean from, ironically, Japan. Creative-minded renters took discarded burlap potato sacks from the camp kitchen, bleached and dyed them, and hung them as wallpaper. One person visited the kitchen for another reason: to gather plucked chicken feathers and make large lounging pillows.[17]

Accommodations were made for wives and family members to eat meals at the camp—although they were generally expected to pay a share of the expenses. How people came up with this money seemed as varied as their backgrounds: some had savings, some were sent money from their families or hometown churches, some picked up enough local work to get by, and some lived on the goodwill of others. After all, in a camp run by a national church whose fundamental beliefs included charity for those less fortunate, it seemed unlikely that people should be left to starve. There was also the basic code of rural people, a generosity grounded in the understanding that self-sufficiency in the country is tenuous at best, and a kindness extended today would be reciprocated when the roles were reversed. Occasionally, a CO might be released for a temporary work assignment away from the camp, usually to help a farmer with harvest or related needs. Mary Kessler, who lived with her husband, Warren, as he worked on a dairy farm in the Coquille River region south of camp, remembered how they survived when she was pregnant and recovering from a burst appendix. Living in a small house along the river bottom, set on eight-foot stilts against the flood tides, she recalled waking one morning to find a side of deer laid at the top of the front porch steps. Other times they woke to discover a string of ducks. "It was like whoever was doing it didn't want us to know," she said. "But it was nice."[18]

With military and Coast Guard units on the coast requiring food and living staples, and wartime rationing imposing limits on what was available, the camp was compelled to start its own farm. They rented three pieces of land nearby—about four acres total—even though this strip between the ocean and forested hillsides was hardly prime agricultural property. They cleared the land and planted root crops like potatoes and turnips, which tended to tolerate the foggy summers. They also acquired about a dozen hogs, feeding them mainly garbage from the camp kitchen, and kept chickens and rabbits as other meat sources. They couldn't afford the grain to feed any dairy cows, but the local sources of milk were reliable.

The relationships with suppliers went generally well, as the camp was a steady source of income for businesses that had spent the previous decade mired in the Great Depression. The following letter from one Marion Stern (presumably a grocer or distributor as well as a church member, judging from the salutation) gives the flavor of trade in 1943 on the Oregon coast. He writes from Myrtle Point, about one hundred miles south of Waldport and a dozen more inland.

> Business Manager
> C.P.S. Camp 56
> Waldport, Oregon
>
> Dear Bro.
>
> Writing to you again about produce. I'm sorry but the beef which I told you about, priced at 14¢ - lb. is not available. I do however have in mind one which this same man can get for us at around 18¢. He didn't say how large it is.
>
> We can also get dried beans for you—any amount up to 250-300 lbs. These were quoted to me at 10¢ per lb. And the potatoes which I told you about are fairly good. . . . They are in the bins as field run potatoes. Most of them are No. 1s, but there are also some not worth moving. A sort of blight or dry rot. Now if you could come sort them yourselves they would cost $1.75 per hundred or if you had them sorted by the man himself he said he would want $2.00. He doesn't feel that he has the time to do it. You would need to bring as many of your own sacks as possible. There might also be some carrots. I haven't found out for sure.

It also helped that the camp had something to offer beyond cash for goods sold. In this case, Mr. Stern makes a reference to the singing quartet from the camp, which traveled to various communities and sang at their church services:

Now would it be possible for you or Dick Mills to come down or the Quartet, say on Sunday afternoon, have charge of our evening service here, then Monday we could load you up for your return trip. If you are interested in the produce, that would be the easiest way to get it all there at once, provided you have a large enough truck.

A reply from the camp—presumably notes for a telephone conversation—is scribbled after the letter:

get us the beef—to be butchered by Mon. noon
we will sort potatoes on Mon. 25 sacks or more
will furnish a Sun. eve program
could use a couple of hogs also
can use a few crates of carrots[19]

A little perspective on how 2,500 potatoes and more than a thousand pounds of beef were doled out comes from an accounting of the camp's food consumption for January, printed in the *Tide*. In a single month, the men devoured 1,100 pounds of meat, one ton of potatoes, 1,350 loaves of bread, 1,900 eggs, 170 pounds of butter, and 1,200 gallons of milk—along with 140 pounds of cheese, 60 quarts of salad dressing, 200 pounds of raisins, 190 pounds of fish, and literally thousands of oranges and apples. Per man, this equaled approximately eleven pounds of meat, twelve and a half loaves of bread, eighteen eggs, three and a half pounds of butter, and eleven gallons of milk. The five cooks and five service staff members would continue doing their best with what they had, the kitchen writer said, but with ongoing rationing the campers should expect less: "More meat substitutes will be used, oleo in place of butter, and dehydrated grass added to the vegetables."[20]

The meat substitutes were not a concern for everyone, as about one quarter of the campers were vegetarian—for religious, ethical, or other reasons—but the dehydrated grass was another matter. Part of a program exploring alternative sources of nutrition for the millions in devastated countries who would need food assistance after the war, boxes of the experimental food were distributed to CPS camps. Tips of rye, wheat, and barley were dried and pressed into pellets, which could be "sprinkled on salad . . . put in soup, or tossed down like salted peanuts," said an announcement in a government newsletter. "Its chief drawback is the odor and taste."[21]

Fish and other seafood were available, but only inasmuch as the locals could provide them. The camp administration was continually looking for ways to become self-sufficient, so when member Dick Brown expressed interest in building a fishing boat to help procure food, support

Box label from "Gras-Tips," an experimental dried-grass food tried at various CPS camps.

was there. He worked nights and Sundays through the winter of 1942–43, but by March food supplies were precarious enough that his time on the boat construction was added to the Overhead budget so that he might be excused from Project work and finish the vessel sooner.[22]

The boat was completed in May—about thirty feet long with a twelve-foot mast and an outrigger pontoon. This kind of craft was native to the South Pacific, but also was considered unsinkable and good for speed and adjusting to the waves. On a calm spring day with the tide low, a group of eight or so campers gathered on the beach to launch it. Everson was there—at first just to watch, but then he was asked to help—and he described the scene in a letter to Edwa. The men dragged the boat into the water, then stripped down naked on the deserted beach. In the shallow water the craft was light and easy to maneuver, but as they waded deeper their leverage lessened against the breakers of the incoming tide. Each time a wave hit, they clung to the boat until it passed, then pushed forward through the trough until the next one came. As the six-foot-four Everson reached water up to his chest, he looked back and noticed that he was the only one left pushing on his side of the craft. He figured he never intended to go in the water anyway, so he let go and headed back to join the others watching. But this left only the three men pushing the outrigger pontoon with no counterbalance on the other side. The breakers quickly turned the boat broadside and pushed it toward the shore. The group gathered again and finally dragged the boat back on the beach and began to put on their clothes. Suddenly, they heard a police whistle and three Coast Guard officers approached, armed and angry about the men launching a boat without notifying the authorities. Dick Mills, who was reputed to have a penchant for nude sunbathing, was still naked, as was the camp clerk, and as they stood there arguing in the buff, the officers added indecent exposure to the complaint. Once the authorities realized the men were from the CO camp and not enemy saboteurs, they left the beach and the campers figured that was the end. A few days later, though, the officers drove into camp and arrested Mills and the clerk on the charge of indecent exposure—which could cost them as much as sixty dollars or ninety days in jail. They were taken before a judge, fined thirty dollars each, and set free. "It looks as if the Coast Guard is really hounding us," Everson wrote. "No one was within a mile of us."[23]

Mindful of the needs in public relations, education director Brumbaugh in his report to the Brethren Service Committee related the episode a bit more optimistically: "One of the exciting events of the month was the launching of Dick Brown's boat, a twenty-eight foot out-rigger to be used for fishing. The attempts to launch the *Friendship* through the surf failed because of the breakers and insufficient wind, but the boat was finally hauled into town and set into the water off the town dock. Brown will use the boat to catch fish for the camp, and he has promised to give lessons in navigation to as many men as he can handle."[24]

There is no further record of a South Pacific outrigger plying the waters of the Oregon coast, although the May education report also noted, "Jim Gallaghan is building a thirty-six foot sloop, has the keel laid, and the plans complete for a project that may take two years." Then Brumbaugh added a final comment on boat building: "An earlier attempt of a camper to build a thirty foot dugout canoe failed when an ignorant wood crew cut the boat up for firewood."

May 1943 also brought thirty-seven transfers from two camps in Pennsylvania. The Camp Angel administration, aware that its system of committees and shared governance was not necessarily shared by the eastern camps, set up a thorough orientation session featuring talks by the director, activities coordinator, and Overhead staff, followed by a trip to the top of Blodgett Peak where the Forest Service foreman explained both the geographical territory and the nature of the Project work. The aim of all this was to introduce and engage the new men in the life and operations of the camp. It seemed to work—by the end of the month the percentage of new men participating in the group activities was nearly equal to the number for longer-term campers.[25]

The men influenced their physical environment as well. As the spring rains subsided and the earth began to dry out somewhat, they set to work landscaping the grounds, employing both practical and aesthetic considerations. The center quadrangle—that sea of mud—was made passable by rerouting a small creek along the edge and building a rustic bridge across it. Cement walks were laid across the quad in graceful curves; a fish pond was dug near the dorms and decorated with plantings; a drinking water fountain was built. A group interested in the sciences built a rammed-earth laboratory, where they planned to conduct experiments in biology, chemistry, geology, and physics—another harbinger of the ecology movement that would come a generation later. And an outdoor stage was constructed in front of the dining hall, with a drama group beginning rehearsals for an excerpt of a Shakespeare play.

Attention continued on preparation for the postwar world, building around the central theme of how to establish communities not just dedicated to but actually carrying out the tenets of peaceful living. Plans were drawn up to offer courses in nonviolent actions and principles, and to offer leadership training in health, recreation, religion, teaching, and work projects. Recognizing that group identity can be used for educational purposes, Brumbaugh noted the spontaneous nature of how men got together for activities ranging from photography and crafts to concerts, team sports, and card games. There was energy to be channeled there.[26]

Landscaping included this drinking fountain next to the flagpole at center of camp. Dorms are in background.

There were, of course, challenges, including the ongoing problem of how to accommodate the vast differences in educational background of men who might enroll in a course or activity. The further challenge of the upcoming fire season was an unknown. With the men split into side camps and mobile firefighting crews for two months or more, how could they maintain any consistency and cohesion in educational pursuits? Brumbaugh took the broad view in his reports, suggesting that the restrictions and obstacles faced by the men in CPS provided an opportunity to explore the depth and sincerity of their convictions. "By contact with each other, through personality conflicts; by observing others, their domineering traits and submissive weaknesses; by implication and direct appeal, by smile and by frown, by forwardness and reticence, by act and word, all have become learners and teachers." Within the five acres of land that made up the camp, he concluded, what they had was a laboratory filled with human beings, all with something to gain and share. "Is it too much to expect that from that laboratory there may come new life which will permeate all society with the love of brotherhood, equality in justice and a challenge for right living?"[27]

Circumstances too often thwart noble intentions, and in the June report education director pro tem Glen Coffield, filling in while Brumbaugh was away on furlough, put it bluntly: "Our educational program is beset with problems." First, he said, there's too much light—as in daylight. Waldport, at 44 degrees latitude and with a western horizon at sea level, doesn't get fully dark in the peak summer months until nearly ten o'clock at night. The men were not inclined to go inside for meetings while it was still light outside, Coffield said, and by then it was nearly time for bed. The directors knew better than to fight this, so they simply let the men wear themselves out playing volleyball and softball on the beach.[28]

The second problem was morale. The very nature of CPS fostered a feeling of impotence. The men's basic food and shelter needs were covered, yet they had no power to do anything beyond the camp. They might try to fill their time with projects and discussion, but they had no hope of earning money, no chance to meet women, and no compelling reason to change their condition. Some men had begun going into town and eyeing the young girls leaving Sunday school, Coffield said. "Their religious zeal is definitely apparent, but of a peculiar nature." In camp, they "mope around like beaten dogs," he said, "with no light in their eyes." The committee hoped to address this at least partly by sponsoring visits for college girls from Corvallis and Portland, and by having a dozen young women from the Fellowship of Reconciliation come for a Fourth of July program featuring a concert and square dancing. At the moment, however, Coffield wrote, "I have no suggestion other than a general notion that the teaching of non-violence and pacifistic ideals needs the virility of a more dramatic approach."[29]

The inevitable cliques had formed also, he reported. The religious purists who opposed anything secular—even education to some degree—had organized themselves into a separate group. The Jehovah's Witnesses continued to have no interests beyond their specific religion, although Coffield noted they were friendly enough to outsiders. The secular COs and religious liberals tended to dominate the cultural activities, leaving the conservative ones feeling marginalized. The Overhead men were resented by the Project men, partly because the former didn't have to work outside in the rain. The group members scowled or made remarks when they passed, and in one case it literally came to blows when a Project worker accused an Overhead assignee of being a "company man" who bowed to authority for personal gain.[30]

The problems were so fundamental, the challenges so critical, that the education committee had begun a kind of stealth program to help identify and promote common interests between the cliques. The informal "bull session" was the natural form of communication in camp, Coffield said, so they planned an intervention. "An interested group of tongue-waggers [is] going to inhabit the places where the men hang out, and when the opportunity arises, direct the talk into channels of vital topics. They will then prepare written summaries of the conclusions for publication or for posting on the bulletin board." Other creative ideas included a whistling choir. This "daring organization" arranged a whistled version of the second movement of Haydn's Surprise Symphony, providing, Coffield said, "a democratic service for classical music by proving that even a symphony is something that can be whistled."[31]

There was also the play. On the newly built outdoor stage in front of the dining hall, Camp Angel saw its first dramatic production, the play-within-a-play scene from Shakespeare's *A Midsummer Night's Dream*, billed here as "The Comical Tragedy of Pyramus and Thisby." On one of those subliminally disorienting high-overcast Oregon afternoons, the players, in costumes fashioned from sheets and pajamas, put on their play in a stiff wind for an audience seated on wooden benches and fruit crates. During the breaks, music by Mendelssohn floated across the camp from a loudspeaker above the stage.[32]

The context of the camp was external—a force outside the men's control had put them there. But the choice of how to respond to those conditions was internal. And the tension between the individual and the collective, between the personal and the political, the moral and practical, the short and long term, permeated every facet of life. Added to the problems described by Coffield were the ongoing tensions within the work crews. Although the Forest Service supervisors were technically

A Midsummer Night's Dream performed on stage in 1943. Costumes were made from pajamas and bed sheets.

Audience sat on boards laid across crates in the sandy soil.

only advisors and could not force the men to work, they could report someone's refusal to do so, as when Larry Siemons one day on Project simply threw down his hoe, said he wasn't planting trees anymore, and walked back to camp. The Forest Service man swore at Siemons and marked him AWOL. The Workers Committee, chaired by Earl Kosbab, a thirty-six-year-old factory foreman from Michigan, negotiated a "sub-foreman" system, whereby each crew elected one of its own members to act as a liaison with the Forest Service employees. On paper it probably seemed a reasonable and even productive move, but whether it could overcome personality conflicts remained to be seen.[33]

When the Forest Service announced plans to build a forty-foot-high fire lookout tower on Blodgett Peak in the tract where the COs had been planting trees, the project made sense as a preventive measure to protect the freshly planted seedlings. But it also tied in with the government use of fire lookouts for the Air Warning Service (AWS), a civilian defense program in which observers, usually volunteers, would occupy the look-out and report all airplanes they spotted in the area. This was considered war-related work by the COs, and most of them would have nothing to do with it. However, they had just planted more than a million trees, which would reclaim forests ravaged from previous war work and could therefore be considered worth saving.

Complicating the problem was the fact that some members of Camp Angel felt their conscience *could* permit them to both watch for fires and spot planes—and the BSC policy was to never interfere with an indi-vidual's decisions of conscience. Hackett, whom Everson described as an "intellectual idealist plus a temperamental anarchist," was incensed. He fired off an editorial for the *Untide* on a Saturday night and asked Everson to edit it for the next day's edition. This particular Saturday eve-ning happened to feature the monthly birthday night and a talk by a visit-ing speaker, followed by a discussion facilitated to some extent by beer. The *Untide* crew finally got to work around midnight, hammering out the issue through dawn, then distributing it across the camp. As usual, the *Untide* editorial was credited to the invisible Mole. "It has been sug-gested that we of C.P.S. #56 are faced with a dilemma," the piece began. "When 'acceptable' fire-spotting is combined with 'unacceptable' plane-spotting; when a fire-tower needed to protect a plantation representing months of our labor is, in all probability, to be used also as a direct aid to the military, what can we do?" To do nothing would invite com-promise and further chip away at whatever gains they'd made regard-ing work conditions, said the Mole. Therefore, make the terms of work clear: "If conservation is so important, and a new fire-tower is in such imminent demand, let it be guaranteed that such a tower will be used for no other purpose. If smoke-spotting is so urgent, let it be disassociated from plane-spotting." The CPS and camp authorities do have power, the

Untide cartoon shows flames licking at a fire lookout tower while its occupant searches for enemy airplanes.

Mole conceded, but the men had power also—the power of their labor. If they used that power, the Mole said, they could determine the conditions under which they shall or shall not work.[34]

The editorial didn't directly alter work assignments on the fire tower, but with Earl Kosbab heading the Workers Committee and Everson now a member, they worked out a deal that once the tower was built, it would be manned by someone from the camp whose job would be to spot fires. If the CO *volunteered* to spot airplanes as well, that would be his choice, but no one would require him to do so. It was a compromise, exactly what Hackett had bridled against.

The chances for tense encounters in the community increased as more soldiers were sent to the region. Detachments from military camps in the Willamette Valley were sometimes sent to the coast for training, and the Coast Guard beach patrols continued through 1943. On occasion, a CO might be hiking on the beach or walking back to camp from Waldport, and the Coast Guard patrol would pick him up just before he reached camp. They might haul him back to headquarters in town on the pretense of checking his papers, then tell him he was free to go—and he'd have to walk the four miles of highway again. But this was not common. One night, though, authorities picked up a CO walking along the road with a flashlight, which technically could be interpreted as a violation of dim-out orders. They brought him into camp and spoke to Dick Mills. When they found out the men could leave camp during off-work hours simply by signing out, they were flabbergasted. Mills patiently explained how CPS was different than the military, how it was run by a church. He'd already cultivated a generally positive relationship with the area residents, aided by weekly visits from the local doctor, who came out to perform health inspections and assured town citizens that all was well at the camp. But the Coast Guard was military, and the newer members not necessarily from the region. They saw themselves as having a job to do, and part of that job was picking up people they thought looked suspicious. "Coast Guard now patrol the beach with police dogs at night," Everson wrote Edwa. "Vicious brutes. We expect things to get worse."[35]

Adding to it all was the uncertainty surrounding CPS itself—with questions about funding and support from Congress—which fed further questioning and rumors. Would everyone show up for work? Would they be called upon to do work they couldn't in good conscience accept? Would someone refuse to work and be sent to jail? Would CPS be disbanded and *everyone* sent to jail? Dick Mills continued his nightly dinner reports of the latest news, but he wasn't always helpful because he tended to present information in ways that reinforced his control over a situation rather than facilitating a democratic process. For example, he might report on a standard communication from BSC headquarters or Selective Service, then add that he felt there was something worrisome behind it, but not offer any further insight or information, leaving the men feeling power-less and eventually resentful. So, when a sudden announcement came up that all furloughs were indefinitely canceled, it fostered unrest rather than trust in leadership, and inclined men more to take matters into their own hands. Some filed grievances through the Workers Committee; some claimed they were sick and headed for the infirmary, where the attendant, Bruce Reeves, had made clear that he would accept anyone who said they were not feeling well. Reeves noted that he was no doctor, and whether a CO's ailment was physical, mental, or other wasn't his place to decide. "There were a lot of fellows sent out on the job who shouldn't have been out there," he recalled. "I figured it helped to ease their pain once in a while to rest, or just lie back and listen to the radio.[36]

Some left camp entirely, in an action becoming known across CPS as a "walkout." A CO might decide, for whatever reason, that he no longer could stay in the program. He would not be physically forced to remain in camp, although he would be considered AWOL, with the expected consequence that eventually he would be taken into custody by the FBI. Many felt clear in their conscience about walking out and openly broadcast their intentions. In early March 1943, Arthur P. Brown, a staunch religious objector, announced that he was returning home to Virginia. His father was ill and could no longer support himself, he said, then quoted from the Bible: "But if any provide not for his own, and especially for those of his own house, he hath denied the faith, and is worse than an infidel" (1 Timothy 5:8). His fellow campers took up a collection and netted twenty dollars to help him get across the country. Another CO, Jim Sulek, a twenty-four-year-old from Iowa who considered himself selectively both fundamentalist and secular, had more personal reasons for leaving. Based on his inability to perform manual labor due to bad cartilage in his knee, he'd applied for release in the past but to no avail. Finally, he'd had enough and simply left, declaring that he did not believe in conscription, that CPS was slave labor, and that no one at Camp Angel could understand his particular beliefs.[37]

On Project sites, Hackett pushed rebellion as far as he could. One day in April, working down a steep canyon in the rain, Hackett and three other men trailed far behind the others. The Forest Service fore-man, a gung-ho fellow named Murray Lieper, had been watching Hackett for a while and decided this was too much; he declared the four men "refused to work" (RTW) and ordered them off the site and back to camp. Hackett challenged him, saying Lieper had no power to order him anywhere, that the Forest Service was only a technical advisor, and that any disciplinary action was the province of the Workers Committee. The incident quickly ballooned into a test of power between the Forest Service and the Workers Committee (and to some degree between Hackett and

Dick Mills, whom Hackett disliked as a camp director). After a complicated series of negotiations, Mills suspended the Workers Committee role as liaison between the COs and the Forest Service, and Lieper took this as an assertion of his power, goading Hackett and others even harder on Project. Finally, Everson approached Lieper at a lunch break and asked if he would leave them alone as long as Hackett promised to work and the crew promised to make sure he did. Lieper agreed, and the case was closed. But trust—and all its components—was damaged. "Poor Hackett is finally beginning to see that even JUSTICE does not always reap its soothing rewards," Everson wrote. "For himself, he doesn't give a damn . . . but when he sees the Workers Committee, the crew, and in fact, the entire project, jeopardized just because he blatted off at the mouth, it's beginning to sink in."[38]

Between the COs themselves, a certain level of daily tension was unavoidable—as is the case when any group of people live together over time. No doubt there was the usual garden variety of complaints regarding personal habits, communication styles, and consideration of others. But Larry Siemons appeared to be a lightning rod for conflict. For one thing, he rarely bathed. In close quarters for sleeping and eating, particularly after a day's hard work in the woods, this was a problem—even in a group known for its eccentric behavior. Within the even smaller *Untide* group, Siemons pushed some sensitive buttons. One evening in March, after working all day in the muck and rain, the crew gathered in the warmth of the laundry room for an editorial meeting on the next *Untide*. Siemons made a crack about one of Coffield's stories, and the Missourian exploded, Everson said—"his whiskers bristled all over the room!" The others in the group smoothed things out, but the pressure was still there.[39]

One aspect of life, as old as life itself, must certainly have been a source of frustration and tension—yet it is hardly mentioned in the records. Or perhaps those filling out the reports felt it was described enough in that one-word answer to the survey question on campers' interests: girls. Now, these were men whose convictions were strong enough that they chose punishment over military service, so one might expect they possessed a certain element of discipline. Still, they were generally healthy young men, and their commitment to pacifism did not make them necessarily celibate. The men whose wives lived in the cottages across the highway presumably continued their normal marital behaviors, and it stands to reason that furlough trips to the cities provided some alternatives for the others. But the town of Waldport and the village of Yachats were likely too small to accommodate professional services, and the camp itself offered virtually no privacy of any kind. Groups of young women from the inland colleges did come to visit, but their focus was specifically sociological or religious. To cap off these serious discussions they might have folk dancing or singing or games—all heavily chaperoned. There is, however, one brief mention in the education report for April 1943. Summarizing a visit by "18 non-pacifist girls" from Oregon State College in Corvallis, the writer noted that discussions about CPS and its justification compelled some of the men to reconsider why they'd come to the camp—and perhaps some of the women questioned their views as well. The writer then added a parenthetical note that in his opinion whatever "understanding was made mutual" occurred "not in the discussion groups but in the twosomes and threesomes that viewed the beach or overlooked the forest." Who could say, he concluded, that the questions and discussion were not continued there?[40]

To call yourself a pacifist in 1940s America easily invited assumptions of homosexuality. Yet it is only briefly acknowledged, and apparently exclusively in personal letters, not camp records or reports. Everson writes to Edwa shortly after his arrival, "There seem to be several homo's [sic] here, but all inactive. I just speculate. But the womanish element is certainly pronounced." He also described an evening's entertainment, part of a birthday night celebration, that included a dance by a female impersonator. When the dancer was announced and the door swung open to reveal a figure in the shadows, Everson initially thought they had really brought in a woman. The impersonator was, he said, "perfectly made up, with a white satin gown, and showed a tantalizing bit of thigh." The only thing giving the dancer away was the short hair showing under a wig. "I had never seen anything quite like it. 'She' was so completely at home in the garb it's a pity 'she' couldn't adopt the mode permanently." It was quite a show for those who knew what was really going on, he said, but for most of the naïve farm boys it was simply a very good impersonation.[41]

That's as far as Everson goes on reporting the activities of others. Ever self-reflective, though, he covers to an almost exhausting level of analysis his own episode of sex and longing and love, one that certainly affected others beyond the immediate players. He had written Edwa from the beginning of his attraction to Harold Hackett, nearly ten years his junior and full of energy and ideas. With his poet's eye, Everson did comment on campers' physiques and appearances from time to time, but with Hackett, he was most descriptive. In one letter, he almost gushes: "His hair is getting longish, and is a deep reddish brown, and he has a small reddish beard, and tonight as we talked he looked so stately and fine, a really beautiful head at times." When Everson learned Hackett was taking a furlough to Los Angeles in May, he insisted his friend visit Edwa in Selma, which was on the highway that linked central California to the metropolis in the south. "Do you think it would be scandalous if he stopped over for the night?" Everson wrote his wife. "He's a swell egg, and wouldn't lay a hand on you (!) but the neighbors don't know that."

A summer 1943 visit by Edwa Everson brought out some key personnel. L-R seated: Earl Kosbab, Robert Walker, Larry Siemons. Standing: Jim Gallaghan, Dick Brown, Harold Hackett, Jim Harman, Glen Coffield, Edwa Everson, Bill Everson.

Edwa wrote back that she was anxious to meet Hackett and that he could stay as long as he wished. Apparently in reference to their modest furnishings, and, according to one account, Everson's suggestion that they share the bed, she answered, "He may have half the bed of course and to hell with the neighbors." Then she added a coquettish note—"Are you sure you trust me?"—followed by a disclaimer. "But that's just by way of a feeble joke—I await next week impatiently."[42]

Something must have been communicated between the lines, because Hackett and Edwa shared more than just the bed—and apparently with Everson's blessing. When the younger man returned to Waldport, he spoke so highly of Edwa that Everson was bursting with pride. Maybe it was a quirk in the poet's personality, or the consequences of extended separation, or some combination of both. But his next letter to Edwa was full of appreciation. Hackett, he wrote, "told me how the first night you took him into the big bed beside you, insisting that those were my explicit instructions! . . . That was what really got him, the utter ease with which you took him in. You're a marvelous woman. All lips proclaim it, including mine, who have so much to be thankful for."[43]

But the happiness quickly soured. The letters, talks, and self-analysis that followed were not significantly different from any other love triangle through the ages. Whatever Everson's complexes might have contributed to the episode, once it settled in that Hackett had indeed slept with his wife, the relationship between the two men changed, as did the energy and attention being put into their joint creative efforts. When Edwa visited

Waldport for about six weeks in the summer, she made friends with many campers and left a lasting impression by sculpting a head from a chunk of myrtlewood, which was displayed in the library and admired by all. Hackett avoided her, however, and she stayed with Everson in a rented room at a nearby farmhouse and later in the Tillie the Whale cottages across the highway. When she left, a fair amount of the issue had been discussed intellectually, but emotionally everything was up in the air.[44]

No doubt there were similar yet less well-documented stories at the camp and throughout CPS. The "Dear John" letter is a heartbreaking staple of every war, and the idiosyncratic passions of artists and the challenges to their partners are common enough in all places and times to be considered cliché. But this was a small group; they could ill afford to lose even one or two members and hope to continue their work successfully—and they probably knew it. At any rate, the focus of the handful of COs doing creative work began turning more toward a larger purpose beyond the immediate challenges and tensions. What were they doing here? And what effect could their actions have after they were done?

In some ways, these kinds of questions were also part of the national conversation. Already in 1943, newspaper articles mentioned the massive reconstruction projects countries would require after the war. It seemed nobody questioned the eventual outcome—it was only a matter of how long it would take. The nation had officially been at war less than two years, but the machinery of war had been working steadily since 1940. The popular newspaper columnist Ernie Pyle, after covering the Allies' campaign against the Nazis in North Africa in late 1942, admitted that early in the war he hadn't been sure how things would ultimately turn out. However, after months of watching not just the soldiers but also the entire chain of supply and support at work, he summed it up succinctly:

> We are producing at home and we are hardening overseas. Apparently it takes a country like America about two years to become wholly at war. We had to go through that transition period of letting loose of life as it was, and then live the new war life so long that it finally became the normal life to us . . . and if I am at all correct we have about changed our character and become a war nation. I can't yet see when we shall win, or over what route geographically, or by which of the many means of warfare. But no longer do I have any doubts at all that we shall win.[45]

President Roosevelt, in his State of the Union address in January, had assured as much. "The Axis powers knew that they must win the war in 1942—or eventually lose everything," he said. Now, with American factories producing at previously unimaginable rates, the Allied assaults would be heavy and relentless. "Day in and day out we shall heap tons upon tons of explosives on their war factories and utilities and seaports," Roosevelt said. "The Nazis and fascists have asked for it—and they are going to get it."[46]

The outcome may have been certain, but how civilization would emerge from this war was another question. The lessons learned here, and the ability to avoid future wars, might decide the very survival of the species. What, then, was a person of conscience to do about it?

Some approached the issue on a personal level. Conscientious objectors who felt their work in forestry or soil conservation wasn't truly work of national importance answered calls for volunteers to be subjects in medical experiments—including being infested with lice to check for typhus, being inoculated with malaria, drinking throat washings or body wastes from patients with hepatitis or pneumonia, living on saltwater, being exposed to extreme heat and cold, or spending months on a starvation diet.[47]

Some of the more religious COs chose to follow the "second mile" dictum from the Sermon on the Mount: "And whosoever shall compel thee to go a mile, go with him twain," and attempted to take on double the work required of them. One camper showed up one morning wearing a backpack as they boarded the work truck to plant trees. The Forest Service crew leaders asked him what he was doing with a pack. "Well," he replied, "I was reading the Bible and [it said] if somebody compels you to work, you should work double time for him. So, I'm going to stay out there in the woods and work sixteen instead of eight." The Forest Service men decided to keep him in camp.[48]

The CPS leadership looked for more structured answers that might best employ their young charges' talents and abilities. A number of special "schools" were established at particular camps, often with a governing body and director, with modest funding for administrative needs. Announcements for the schools were sent out through CPS memos and newsletters, telling interested men that they could request transfer to those locations. Among the Brethren camps were the School of Co-operative Living at Camp Walhalla and later Camp Wellston, both in Michigan; the School of Pacifist Living at Cascade Locks, Oregon; the School of Race Relations at Camp Kane, Pennsylvania; and the School of Foods Management at Lyndhurst, Virginia. Camp Angel had brief flirtations with possibly hosting schools in forestry and then political economics. But through a combination of practical need, personal preference, and perhaps plain blind luck, the future for many at Waldport pointed in a different direction.

CHAPTER 5

Against Them the Creative Act

THE FOUNDATIONS FOR CREATIVE WORK at Camp Angel were there from its inception. The more-or-less monthly *Tide* newsletter, even with its stamp of officialdom, tried to accommodate the artistic urges of its contributors—although the poetry tended toward doggerel, and the artwork was simple line drawings. The *Untide* wasn't any more accomplished artistically, but its looser, somewhat anarchic style and weekly immediacy better captured what Everson called "the intellectual ferment of the camp."[1]

The two publications did share a kind of cross-pollination. Harold Hackett began as associate editor of the *Tide,* and Glen Coffield published poems and prose in it—and both founded the *Untide*. Their other co-founder, Larry Siemons, later became art editor of the *Tide*. Kemper Nomland, a twenty-three-year-old architecture school graduate who had come with the temporary crews from Cascade Locks, did illustrations for both journals. Everson published poems in both as well. None of this was particularly unusual, in that members of a creative group often break away to start a new venture when they feel their editorial interests and ideas are limited by the one.

So the *Tide* ran its monthly reports, announcements, and observations, and the *Untide* put out its weekly satire, criticism, and sharp humor—and both were cranked out on the hand-powered mimeograph machine with its inked rotary drum and waxed stencils. Starting in February 1943, the *Untide* included installments of Everson's "War Elegies," poems he had written between the beginning of the Selective Service Act of 1940 and his internment at Waldport. Totaling ten in number, they were typed into the mimeograph stencils with hand-lettered titling and surrealist illustrations by Nomland, then mimeographed onto tan-colored paper, cut into half-sheets, and placed each week in the *Untide*. Kemper was prolific with sketches, cartoons, drawings, and paintings, and at first Everson felt that he approached art as more entertainment than serious endeavor. But the poet's respect for the artist grew as the project developed, and by the time the last elegy had been printed he wrote to Larry Powell in Los Angeles that although Kemper was returning to Cascade Locks, Everson hoped to work with him again. "His last designs I feel are quite good—exactly what is required."[2]

Through March, as the steady winter rains gave way to the intermittent spring rains, the small but energetic *Untide* crew spent Saturday nights in the blackout-shaded dorms, working to publish their answer to authority and conformity. When positive words came back on the *War Elegies* from both within the camp and other units that received the *Untide* by mail, the group prepared to staple the poems together and issue them as a book. The idea came from Larry Siemons, Everson wrote later, calling him "a natural born promoter of impervious confidence." They ran off 250 copies and priced them at ten cents apiece. The *Untide* ran an advertisement, Larry Powell ordered 50 copies and seeded the library trade, and orders came rolling in. Everson had originally predicted they'd need no more than 100 copies, but Siemons had insisted otherwise, the poet recalled, and he "chortled as we went through impression after impression on the mimeograph."[3]

The whole thing was a catch-as-catch-can operation. The book itself was a thin pamphlet—twenty pages of those half-sheets stapled together near the top and bottom, with a blue construction-paper cover folded over and the text block glued in at the crease. The cover art was the title and author's name silkscreened in black and yellow. The opening page featured the title written by hand, with the author's name and illustration credits to Nomland typed in. No copyright—just the publisher, address, and date in lowercase type: "untide press, camp angel, waldport, oregon, 1943."

Taken alone, and by today's standards, the booklet may not appear impressive. But it was created in a time when everything from gasoline and metal to coffee and paper was being rationed, published in a place so isolated that the camp telephone number was simply "89," and printed during so-called spare time after the men had spent fifty-plus hours working in the woods. Under these conditions, the book was an indisputable success.

As word spread and orders continued for the *Elegies*, Everson began to be considered a spokesperson for the CO experience, and Camp Angel a place where creative things were happening.[4] *Pacifica Views*, a smartly produced weekly newsletter published by members of Camp #76 at Glendora, California (an agricultural town twenty miles east of Los Angeles), put out a call in June for more creative work from CPS members. What the present-day pacifism needed, they said, was a whole army of Thomas Paines to show readers the necessary way to a real and lasting peace. Letters to friends and family are fine, but the greater need was for quality pamphlets and papers that showed a real grasp of the issues. The readers are out there, *Pacifica Views* said, "but where is the material?"[5]

Silk-screened cover of *Ten War Elegies*, in yellow and black on blue construction paper.

The *Untide* group sent down a copy of the *Elegies,* and four weeks later a review came out. The California sheet stressed that they were not a literary journal and as a policy did not print poetry. However, they said, this occasion demanded special treatment. They quoted from "Elegy III," a poem that lays out the bitter truth of generations of war and urges conscientious objectors to reach for the core of their beliefs:

> . . . let him . . . , turning to the past,
> Seek out the iron rib of conviction
> Beaming beneath the steep thought of all times,
> The unbending belief of man holding to truth
> Through wave upon wave of unreason and doubt.
> Let him be like those dreaming infrangible Jews
> Fronting their centuries;
> Let him build program for action based on repose,
> The tough and resilient mind
> Gazing from out of its central strength,
> Rock-like, the beam of morality
> Holding it up against terror, oppression,
> The howling fronts of revolution and hate.
> Let him dare that;
> And let him know in his daring
> He had all any man ever had.

In this case, *Pacifica Views* said, the *Elegies* "are not simply good pacifist poetry; they are exceptionally fine poetry which rises above the special pleas of pacifist doctrine, yet is profoundly pacifist."[6]

This was precisely what Everson had hoped—that readers would see the poetry not as pacifist propaganda, but as poetry that communicated the ideals of pacifism; the aesthetic over the political, art transcending activism. After a similarly positive review in the *Conscientious Objector* magazine helped bring in a single-day order for more than twenty copies, Everson wrote to Edwa, "My dear, it looks as if your husband is rapidly becoming *the* pacifist poet of these good United States!"[7]

By the end of the summer, the United States had fully transformed itself into the war nation that Ernie Pyle had described. Allied military forces across the Atlantic retook North Africa, jumped to Sicily, and moved up the mainland peninsula of Italy, prompting that country to surrender. In the Pacific, the U.S. Air Force destroyed or damaged three hundred Japanese planes and killed fifteen hundred pilots and support crew at a strategic air base in New Guinea. Americans recaptured the Alaskan island of Attu—the westernmost point of the Aleutian chain, and the only American territory occupied by Japanese forces. At home, Victory Gardens and scrap drives continued, two million women were employed in war-related work, and the Supreme Court ruled that state laws could not require schoolchildren to salute the flag.[8] At Camp Angel they'd spent the year planting trees, building roads, fighting forest fires, and coming to terms with what they were doing there. Camp membership was fragmented by assignment to side camps and mobile firefighting crews, and this, along with the daily grind of hard manual labor for no pay far away from home, took its toll on extracurricular activities. The *Tide* ceased publication with a final issue in July. The *Untide* had lasted just twelve intense weeks, but its name lived on through that casual mention on the title page of the *War Elegies*. And, as the handmade booklet of poems garnered further reviews in *Poetry* magazine and the *New Republic*, orders came in and the men kept grinding out edition after edition on the mimeograph, eventually producing one thousand copies. Whether this creative-minded group knew it yet or not, the Untide Press was born.[9]

▓ ▓ ▓

Everson was certainly not the only one writing, and the Untide Press was hardly the work of only one man. Other creative projects also left an impression as individuals across camp wrote down their thoughts and published as they were inspired. Glenn Miller produced *The Holy Apple and Others,* a thin volume of "war poems, erotic poems and poems on social reconstruction," offered for sale at five cents.[10] A broadsheet titled "Good News," with commentary and quotes from the Bible, was put out by members of the Religious Life group; an anthology of the material was stapled together as *Remember Now Thy Creator.*[11] The various committees printed their reports, summaries, and messages; individuals penned their letters and diary entries. But it was Glen Coffield, the bearded eccentric, who constantly fed the creative fires. Not only had he co-founded the *Untide,* but also, during his time as educational director in June, he'd sent copies of the *War Elegies* to Brethren Service Committee education secretary Morris Keeton and other CPS leaders, calling the poems "an inherent part of what is perhaps the greatest pacifist movement yet apparent in history."[12] He wrote a treatise on noncompulsory education and published two versions nearly simultaneously—one in the *Tide* and a longer one in *Pacifica Views.*

Known to write dozens of poems a day and to fill up the space between his bed and the wall with crumpled sheets of discarded drafts, he set to work in the summer of 1943 and produced the second book to come from the Untide Press. While other campers slouched through the dog days of August, Coffield single-handedly produced his entire book—writing, illustrating, stencil-cutting, mimeograph cranking, and stapling—a series of ten experimental poems under the title *Ultimatum*. He made only fifty copies of this work, in which he employed his "scientific method" that he said would "test combinations of experience that cannot be tested in life." One such test was to combine words that normally would not appear together. A short opening piece, titled "The Argument," set the stage:

Rawboned reality, scandalous though sugared,
tangles a torture with tyrannous ugliness;
erroneous ferity-glamour is in the prohibitory
index—
the nucleus opens to the particulars.[13]

Reactions were mixed. One reader from the East Coast commented that use of the scientific method in poetry could launch a creative revolution. Others flatly disliked the book, using adjectives of varying strength. Coffield was unmoved, promising further experimentation in his methods of writing poetry—unless, he confided to a friend, he dropped art entirely and turned his attention to society's problems. For now, he noted, they had a table-top printing press in camp, they expected to print books by half a dozen or more CPS poets, and the future was literally wide open. "We don't know just what we can do," he concluded, "but we are going to find out."[14]

Acquisition of that table-top press was pure serendipity. For a number of the men, after the daily monotony of campground maintenance and building roads, the arts were like a tonic. "Waldport was a beehive of activity after hours," recalled Charles Davis, who arrived at camp in the summer of 1943. The son of a minister in Southern California, Davis had helped his father turn out religious tracts on a small table-top printing press, called a Kelsey. Seeing the heavy use of the mimeograph at Waldport, Davis remembered the old Kelsey, which his father no longer used. "Why don't we print this stuff?" he said to his fellow campers, and they agreed. Davis wrote to his father, and the printer was sent.[15]

The Kelsey was truly a small press—a hand-operated affair with a five-by-eight-inch printing area that could accommodate only one sheet at a time. They made a surface for prepress work (a "stone" in printing nomenclature) from the slate of an old pool table and bought a small sampling of type from the only supplier in Portland who answered their query. However, nobody had real experience as a printer. Davis had done only basic work back home, and Everson had watched his father run a small job-printing operation when he was growing up. But it was mostly a matter of learning through experience.

As summer turned to fall and the fire season ended and the COs battened down the camp for the winter rains, the Untide Press crew—

Detail from the
letterpress printed
cover of Coffield's
Horned Moon.

"When asked for a
photograph, Mr.
Coffield submitted one;
we match his audacity
by printing it."

Everson, Coffield, Hackett, and Siemons (with trouble-shooting help from Davis)—began work on their first book that would come from an actual press. It was another collection of Coffield poems, titled *The Horned Moon*.[16] Everyone worked on this one, putting in their spare-time hours printing, folding, and sewing the thirty-two-page pamphlet in a run of 520 copies—printed one page at a time. The design was simple by necessity. The dark tan cardstock cover was blank, a plain brown dust jacket wrapped around it and held in place by folded flaps. In the lower right front corner, printed in black, was: *THE HORNED MOON / BY GLEN COFFIELD*, and stamped over that in red was the outline of a crescent moon. The poems were less experimental than the author's first book, although he noted in the foreword that his reason for writing the poems was to discover a mode for expressing what he had to say, and that each poem was "a kind of individual experiment complete in itself." Whether or not the experiments fully succeed in their aims, the reader can decide. But anyone who has stood on the desolate beach of the Oregon coast and looked out at the ocean and then back at the woods rising up those rugged headlands can understand to some extent the book's final poem, "The Breakers."

> The breakers shouting on the rocks,
> The fall of civilization,
> Are not as loud as grief;
> Grief is the blood-beating breast,
> A holocaust of sound.
>
> The clouds, the ragged pine,
> Grey towers that jut the coast,
> Are silent, even as stars,
> Even as apprehension,
> Or an open grave.
>
> But silence is a paradox;
> A deaf man cannot hear
> The breakers roaring to the open sea.

This writer clearly understands grief, understands emptiness and loss. According to one account, Coffield had spent some time during the Great Depression teaching school in the poorest parts of Missouri, deep in the Ozark Mountains. There, the story went, he lost his home, wife, and children in an unexplained fire, after which he took to the road and never settled down.[17]

But when you first open the book, it's the photo that gets your attention. The third page contains a black and white photograph of the author, with his full head of tangled hair over the collar of his jacket and a wild mass of untrimmed whiskers maybe six months old. He looks down and away from the camera lens, his head tilted in a kind of distracted stare. He might be an unkempt genius, he might be a bum, he might be nuts, or he might be something else. The dust jacket blurb, presumably written by Everson, sums it up succinctly. "When asked for a photograph, Mr. Coffield submitted one; we match his audacity by printing it."

Putting it all in context, the inside rear flap provided the background of the press, mentioning the *Elegies* and *Ultimatum,* and their plans for more. "We solicit your interest and your orders—if nothing more, your curiosity," it said, and then concluded with a mission statement on the role of art in society, as clear as any ever uttered: "As to our purpose, it is simple enough. These are the years of destruction; we offer against them the creative act."

■ ■ ■

Meanwhile, another literary venture was begun at Cascade Locks by two of the men who had come to Waldport in the temporary work crews during the fall and winter. Kemper Nomland, the architect whose graphic design and illustration work was in the *Untide* and Everson's *War Elegies,* was joined by Kermit Sheets, a drama teacher from central California who possessed a considerable creative talent, a passion for theater, a sharp intellect and a keen, almost impish wit. The two first met at Cascade Locks in early 1942; they worked on the camp newsletter there, but had wanted for some time to collaborate on a more creative journal. When they returned from Waldport with ideas inspired by the energy and passion of the Untide Press crew, they knew it was time. In spring 1943, they joined with compatriots Don Baker, Hugh Merrick, Harry Prochaska, and Bill Webb to produce the *Illiterati,* which they described in their pun-loving manner as a "journal of creative excretion."[18] It was a literary cousin to the now-defunct *Untide,* a collection of mostly poetry, with some short prose pieces (largely satirical) and even a musical score, all fit into eighteen sheets of legal-sized paper, folded in half to make thirty-six pages. The silk-screened cover featured a hand with a large circle filling the palm—some with a yellow hand and red circle, some with the opposite color combination.[19]

The issue included two of Everson's *War Elegies,* helping to further circulate his name, and two Coffield poems. It was profusely illustrated with Kemper's drawings, which provided a kind of surrealistic backdrop to the printed words—reminiscent of Salvador Dali, and in some places perhaps evoking hints of Goya's antiwar sketches. Overall, the blend of abstraction, satire, and double entendre would be enough to give pause to even the generally educated reader familiar with CPS. And one might

Cover of *Illiterati #1*. Some copies showed a yellow hand with a red circle; others had opposite colors.

think the full-page line drawing of an anatomically correct male nude would raise a few 1943 eyebrows. Or perhaps the erotic, disguised homosexual poem, "Love Cycle," signed anonymously as "Thy Slave," could possibly spark a scandal. But it was none of these. Instead, it was a small line sketch of a female nude that upset the censors: a reclining woman with breasts exposed and legs slightly apart, as if sunning herself on a sand dune, with an apparently dreamy expression on her face and one hand resting very high up on her inner thigh. "This copy, the whole edition, was closed down because of that drawing," Kermit Sheets recalled sixty years later, when he was nearly ninety years old. It was all about the placement of her hand, he said, "down there in her snatch."[20]

The post office solicitor wasn't quite as direct in his choice of words, writing in the tone of bureaucratic communication, "The ruling to the postmaster at Cascade Locks, Oregon, was necessitated by the presence in your publication of a figure of a nude female, which was regarded as being of an obscene, lewd, lascivious and indecent character. This ruling was issued under authority of Section 598, P. L. & R., 1940 (18 U.S. Code, Section 334)."[21]

Few actions excite interest in something more than declaring it forbidden. The *Illiterati* crew never found out how many copies of the journal were destroyed beyond "all of the last large mailing" as described by the post office.[22] When they put out *Illiterati* number 2 in summer 1943, they told readers they didn't know whose orders of the first number had gotten through before the censor's eye fell upon the drawing they now called Agnes ("the chaste, pure one"). Those who never received the first issue would "simply have to content themselves with whatever picture their own more or less fertile imaginations dream up."[23]

It happened that "Agnes" had been placed on a page illustrating Coffield's poem, "The Breakers" (from his *Horned Moon* book), and he wrote to Brethren Service Committee headquarters in Elgin that he'd played no part in the magazine's design. The illustration placed with his poem, he said, "went way beyond my concept and almost shocked even my callous modesty." But, he added, the men producing the *Illiterati* could hardly be branded pornographers, for they approached their work as art and saw themselves as no more obscene than the sculptor of the Venus de Milo.[24]

As if to test this point, *Illiterati* number 2 also featured a nude woman in a similar pose as the original Agnes—but in a less languid attitude and with a painful grimace on her face, her right hand held open and away from her body. There is no record of this issue being withheld from the mails.

While the Waldport group was printing Coffield's *Horned Moon* on the tiny Kelsey press, they came upon another, larger press more suited to their vision of producing substantial and lasting works. It was fifty years old, worn out, dirty, and crusted with ink from printing untold numbers of newspapers and other items; it now sat covered with dust

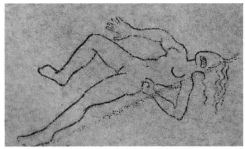

Two faces of "Agnes" featured in the *Illiterati*. First version was declared obscene and destroyed by post office. Second version brought no reaction.

in a Waldport secondhand shop. The owner, Doc Workman, was an old radical and sympathetic to the CO position; he sold them the press for sixty dollars. This was a huge sum of money to the CPS men, but they'd been selling hundreds of the *War Elegies* and were able to offer twenty dollars as down payment. Workman agreed to accept the balance on an installment plan, and on a cold day in January 1944 the men drove a Forest Service truck down to Workman's shop, loaded up the giant press, and moved it into a corner of the Camp Angel recreation building. To pay off the balance in the following months, they managed to pick up some outside work at nearby farms and put in some time installing septic tanks, work Everson had done back in California.

They called the big press "The Challenge"—partly because it was the Challenge Gordon brand, and partly because it needed work before it could run. But an experienced pressman, Joe Kallal, who had transferred to Waldport, looked the contraption over and pronounced it fundamentally sound, so they set to work fixing it up, beginning with replacing the "trucks"—the steel wheels that propelled the rollers across the ink plate and the type. Bill Eshelman, a Southern California college student who'd arrived in December and promptly joined the Untide group, wrote the Challenge company, asking the dimensions of the trucks on their Gordon press. They wrote back that the Challenge Gordon hadn't been made in thirty years, and that no records were available. So the Waldport group came up with their own solution of rubber rings and metal plates,

Bill Everson works the "Challenge" press with a foot treadle as experienced printer Joe Kallal watches.

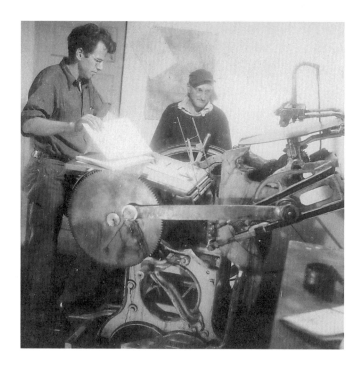

wherein the rollers could be adjusted to accommodate for worn pieces. The printing surface, at 14½ x 22 inches, was nearly three times the size of the Kelsey, and it would allow them to print four pages at a time—a huge leap in efficiency for projects limited to spare time after a fifty-hour work week. They rigged up a foot treadle to run the machine and printed the wrappers for Coffield's *Horned Moon.*[25]

As 1944 moved into Camp Angel's second full year of existence and another tree-planting season on the soaked and miserable hillsides, a vision was coming into focus for better articulating what had been and could be accomplished through art. The first Untide Press book was sold out through multiple printings, the second one was completed and being distributed both for sale and as a gift to subscribers of the *Illiterati,* and the men now turned their attention to how the time and energy they'd invested might yield something larger and more lasting. "Above all, I want to continue the Untide Press," Everson wrote to Larry Powell in January. His aim was to marry poetry and pacifism, to get the word out not through propaganda but by simply presenting the two together. The world would soon enough be facing problems greater than after the first global war, he said, and he wanted to be in a position where his work could relate to those larger, long-term challenges. "I have that in pacifism. I do not intend to let it drop."[26]

■ ■ ■

Simultaneous to this, another idea was taking shape. As far back as June 1943, hints had appeared that there might be a place in CPS for a group focused on the arts. Morris Keeton, education secretary for the Brethren Service Committee and a key figure in establishing the handful of specialized schools at various camps, wrote to Coffield about the monthly educational report he'd submitted in May. Keeton praised Coffield for the camp's focus and creative approach in their educational activities, adding that he hoped they could keep it up.[27]

When Don Brumbaugh returned from furlough to resume duties as education director, his July and August report featured an accounting of the many and varied creative activities. Despite the camp membership being riddled by transfers and assignments to side camps and firefighting crews, the mood was upbeat. Cooking and nutrition classes were taught by a woman who ran an ice cream parlor in Newport while her husband was in the air force in Europe. More than half the camp attended lectures by a forester who spoke on selective-cut logging, range management, watershed control, and conservation. Two campers' wives, who had visited for part of the summer and mended many of the men's clothes, gave a class in "clothing repair" with lessons on making shirts and swimming trunks. The whistling choir disbanded after only one show, but the concert series continued, with Art Snell, a Brethren church member from Southern California, offering a vocal program and the music teacher, Bob Scott, giving a piano recital, during which he also spoke about the background of the works played, the composers, and musical trends of the period.

The crafts room in the recreation hall was going full steam, with work being done in clay and plaster, wood carving, silk screening, molding and casting. It became a meeting place as well, hosting gatherings by a group that went by the various names of The Royal Order of the Descendents [sic] of the Mole, The Midnight Coffee Club, The Ultra-Liberals, and Associated Agnostic-Atheists. "Whether its basic purpose is gestopoic [sic], or an underground for the liberation of CPS from the throes of religion, or be it the champion of a democratic regime through revolution of the benevolent dictator—any guess would be hazardous," Brumbaugh wrote. "But who would venture to say it hasn't been educational?"[28]

Not long after the Brethren Service Committee leadership had invited suggestions for special-focus schools in the camps, BSC director Harold Row visited Camp Angel, where, along with covering general administrative chores, he wanted to meet the poet whose *War Elegies* were reaching so many in CPS and beyond. At dinner, Row had Everson and Coffield sit with him so that he could inquire after their activities. Everson was initially unimpressed with Row, describing him as "the palsy walsy type" with little understanding of poetry. But when the conversation turned to the possibility of a camp devoted to the fine arts, Row told the two COs that if they could show justification for it, one might be established. Everson argued that a culture lives on through its art, that everything else ultimately decays. Civilian Public Service and even the memory of it will fade away, he said, if they did not find some way to preserve the work being done already, and nurture the work to come. Row replied that he would think about it.[29]

When the director got back to Brethren headquarters in Elgin, he learned of even more interest. Kermit Sheets had written from Cascade Locks that the group there for some time had felt that work in the fine arts could play a powerful role in communicating the ideals of pacifism. With the painting, writing, and other creative work already being done across CPS, they should organize these activities in a single camp, he said. Row assigned the project to Morris Keeton, who wrote back to Kermit that setting up a fine arts school would take four to eight months in arranging for administration, equipment, training, and transfers. If the men at Cascade Locks and elsewhere really wanted to make a fine arts school happen, he said, they should draw up a solid proposal—something that he and Harold Row could take to the Brethren Service Committee.[30]

Letters, plans, and rumors flew among the camps. Kemper and Kermit traded ideas with Everson and Coffield. A memo went out to all

L-R: Kemper
Nomland, Don Baker,
Kermit Sheets at
Camp #21, Cascade
Locks, ca. 1942.

of CPS, signed by men from Cascade Locks, Waldport, and Glendora, California, that the best location for a school of fine arts would be Camp #36 at Santa Barbara. The area's cultural opportunities and proximity to Los Angeles would make for a stimulating and productive creative environment, they said—and then invited any interested CPS men to both apply for the as-yet-nonexistent school and urge the BSC to launch it at Santa Barbara. As the calendar turned toward fall and the fire season bounced the Oregon men around side camps throughout the Mt. Hood and Siuslaw National Forests, Kermit and Kemper kept the pressure on Keeton. *Pacifica Views,* the weekly newsletter out of the Glendora camp, voiced its support. A young Kansas poet named Bill Stafford, whose work had appeared in the second *Illiterati,* signed on for the choice of Santa Barbara, where he was already stationed. A CO named Tom Polk Miller wrote from Camp #27 at Crestview, Florida, what was likely a common view for many: "I haven't been able to visualize very much of what might materialize in the actual camp," he said. Even so, he added, "I think it's something I'd like to have a chance at eventually."[31]

Keeton told the fellows at Cascade Locks that Santa Barbara wasn't looking so good after all—plans were being made there for a school of religious living. The best bet for the fine arts, he said, might be a joint sponsorship with camps run by the American Friends Service Committee, and that they would discuss it at an October meeting of the CPS executive camp directors and educational secretaries in Washington, DC.

Everson, who'd gone on furlough in September back to Selma so he could harvest his raisin grapes, wrote to Kermit when he returned to Waldport late in the month that he thought the chances for an arts group at Santa Barbara were pretty slim—mainly because the director there was against it, and they'd need everyone on board to make it succeed. Most importantly, he said, they needed the right people in place. "If there were someone able and willing to take hold, someone of organizational capacity, intelligence, and creative sensibility, who could make such a thing work, I'm all for it." Optimally, he said, it should just flow freely from within, like the *Illiterati* and Untide Press groups. "What I can't see is organized classes with pedantic lectures and charts by ex-high school teachers, and I'm afraid that's apt to be the Church conception of a special interest camp."[32]

Two days later, he added further thoughts, based on information relayed to him about happenings in Santa Barbara. It seemed support for the fine arts there was strong, but the director remained so dead-set against it that he'd come up with the school of religious living idea to counter it. This led the Santa Barbara men to float the idea of something called a creative living and arts camp, prompting Everson to wonder if a broader coalition of artists and non-artists might work to their advantage. "With these boys as a base," he said, "I'm beginning to think we can swing it."[33]

A week after that, Kermit sent Keeton a page-and-a-half proposal for a school of fine arts. It stated that the school should integrate the creative arts as part of creative living, that members could be working artists or those interested in the arts no matter what their ability, that academic trappings and limitations were to be avoided at all costs, and that the school should develop organically from within. They could begin, he proposed, with interested parties each writing a paper on how they saw the creative arts being integrated with creative living.[34]

The proposal didn't get to Keeton before his October executive meeting, but it didn't matter, for the AFSC reported that they'd found in their organization "virtual unanimity" in opposition to creating a school of fine arts, and offered a somewhat disingenuous explanation that moving all the artists to one location would "drain the artistic talent" from the rest of the camps. Everson heard this and snorted in disgust, "How about draining all the cooks to a cooking school? Shit."[35]

A letter-writing campaign to locate the school in Santa Barbara prompted the BSC leadership to consider sponsoring it without the Friends' participation. But, as usual, the devil was in the details—and by the end of the month Keeton reported that the fine arts school would not be allowed at Santa Barbara and that the men should explore other plans. He suggested that all interested in the fine arts might transfer en masse to a children's or mental hospital, where their creative work could be used in teaching or occupational therapy. Kemper and Kermit separately asked why the school was refused at Santa Barbara, but no specific reasons were officially given. Everson concluded that the administrators simply didn't want to risk having "a bunch of crackpot artists" in the same place—a sentiment echoed by Bill Eshelman, who recalled hearing that the Santa Barbara director had exclaimed, "You're talking about getting all the troublemakers together!"[36]

As the summer fire season gave way to fall rains and tree planting, the core trio—Kermit, Kemper, and Everson—told Keeton that the next best place for the fine arts was Waldport. The camp already had an active printing press and an artistic reputation, stemming largely from the Untide Press and the response to the *War Elegies*. There were likely other reasons in play, although not officially stated. For one, Waldport was isolated, very isolated—and the fact that this was *not* the most opportune environment for an artistic community to interact with metropolitan America perhaps somewhat assuaged the fears of nervous administrators.

By December, it was becoming apparent that Waldport would be the place. All they really needed was, as Everson had said, the right people—or person—to make it happen. Whether he did it unconsciously or not, Everson had already made a compelling case for himself as director when he wrote an animated letter to Kermit and Kemper in October. In what amounted to an exhortation for the fine arts—even the beginnings of a manifesto—he outlined his belief in and vision for the creative arts as a compelling force in the cause of pacifism. "I've been talking it over with Coffield," he wrote, "and this thing has been coiling in my head for a long time . . . the tie-in between aesthetic creativity and pacifism." There was a basic need for a certain type of cultural expression, a marriage of politics and art, he said, and it hadn't been met in American society. The British were beginning to do it with their young pacifist poets; the communist painters in 1930s Mexico had done it. But America simply talked about it, he said. "That's all the American movements ever do—holler about culture and produce none." The opportunity was now, the place was here, and they just might be the right people, he implied. They could plant the seed, form the nucleus of a movement that would be ready to be heard after the war. They'd begun with the *Illiterati* and the Untide Press, he said. Build on that; produce a series of works by pacifist poets; maybe hook up with the British writers; go beyond poetry, too. They could print the *Illiterati* on the Waldport press rather than a mimeograph, make it so attractive and reasonably priced that people couldn't afford *not* to buy it. Do that with all their works. "We've got the whole future at our hands," he said. "What do you think? Sure, I'm steamed up!"[37]

It was more than steam. A month earlier, heading south on his furlough to Selma, and accompanied by Jim Harman, a fellow artistically inclined CO who'd offered to help with the grape harvest, Everson experienced an encounter that could have dampened his enthusiasm, yet instead perhaps leavened it. In early September, the two men took the bus that ran from Portland down the coast to San Francisco. Buses at the time were supposed to travel no faster than thirty-five miles per hour in order to reduce wear on the rubber tires, Everson remembered. But they also stopped at nearly every town of any size, and often the drivers, he said, "went like hell between stops and waited at the next depot for time to catch up."[38] Not long after the two men boarded the crowded coach, Everson looked around and said to Harman, "Why, there's Theodore Dreiser," indicating a tall, heavy man with white hair who was traveling with a younger red-headed woman in a black dress. He wrote to Larry Powell in Los Angeles about the trip:

> Every piss-stop down the coast I'd pass the old boy and become more and more convinced it was Dreiser. Finally at lunch in Gold Beach he went back to the crapper and we followed him in. He was taking a leak at the piss trough and Harman said: — "Are we correct in assuming that you are Theodore Dreiser?"
>
> He hunched there a moment, shaking his whang and replied: "That happens to be the case — yes."
>
> "We're a couple of young writers," I said, "coming down from a C.O. camp. We're interested in writing, and presume that to be sufficient to accost you like this — " or some such damned fool thing. A mistake, anyway, he hunched around, hobbled over the wash-basin and began washing his hands. "Well," he said, "that's interesting, I suppose, but so what?"
>
> Caught, I grinned like a cat in a slop pail and muttered a lame — "Nothing at all."
>
> He went on: "The country is full of writers. I know schools that have as high as 150 poets alone — and all trying to shock the world." He turned to go out. There was nothing more to say.
>
> Having rebuffed us, he softened a bit, permitted a friendlier gleam to enter his eye, and said in conclusion — "But I wish you luck."[39]

Warnings came from other quarters as well. Everson's literary correspondents spoke of their experience with artists' colonies and warned of the challenges seemingly built into such endeavors. "Same old stuff about artists not getting along," Everson reported to Edwa. But, he added, "I think our 'camp' could escape that."[40]

The November weather brought its usual gloom as the daily tree-planting work slogged along, exacerbated by a particularly difficult plot in the hills above Yachats that required a jolting ride packed together in the truck bed (no heat, of course) and a three-mile hike just to get there. As if to hammer home a final point on their pitiable condition, the men were forced to work on Thanksgiving Day. Everson wrote Edwa that their lunchtime routine of toasting sandwiches at the campfire was particularly depressing. Out in the wind and rain and mud, he said, "trying

to make a sandwich on a stick seem like a turkey drumstick was a bit desolate."[41]

A shot of energy came as the Christmas holidays approached, and a new group of transfers and inductees came in—among them Warren Downs, an eighteen-year-old cello player from Salem, the state capital just a hundred miles away in the middle of the Willamette Valley. He quickly caught the attention of Bob Scott, who saw a chance to broaden his piano repertoire by playing with a real string musician. Even though Downs was quiet, almost taciturn, he excited further interest when he had a trunk-load of some seventy record albums shipped over from his home. Not long after, Bill Eshelman arrived, having just completed his studies at Chapman College, a Disciples of Christ school in Los Angeles. Twenty-two years old and filled with ideas from his college pacifist group under the tutelage of a charismatic philosophy professor, Eshelman quickly became interested in the creative activities, particularly the printing, where he learned to set type and run the press. Things were looking the best they had since last spring, Everson noted. "The intellectual activity is more pronounced, more vigorous. The new men have brought with them a new focus, that has stimulated us all."[42]

The Untide Press received another boost when a literary-minded buyer ordered ten copies of the *War Elegies* to send as Christmas presents. This inspired the press crew to mail out a promotional card inviting similar orders, and in a five-day period they put together 130 copies of the book. "It's been one mad round of mimeographing, printing, silk screening, assembling, gluing, make out addresses, signing names, cashing checks, buying, ordering, swearing and praying," Everson wrote Edwa. And all this was done *after* they'd spent an entire day laboring on the water-logged hillsides. "Oh my God," he said, "why did we ever start this?"[43]

Serious cracks appeared in the group after a letter came from a pacifist in New York who wanted to print a thousand copies of the *Elegies* and distribute them in the United States and England. Everson called a meeting of the six main Untide Press members to discuss it, and the fireworks between strong personalities erupted again. Larry Siemons was dead-set against the offer; they had a real press now, with the future wide open—why would they give away their best seller? Jim Harman, Hackett, and Coffield were all for it; a printing like this would be good for the *Elegies,* and it would free up the Untide crew to do other works. Davis, the printer, was noncommittal. He'd brought his Kelsey up specifically because of the *Elegies*—but he could certainly see this being good for Everson. The clash of opinions brought up older unresolved conflicts, and the meeting broke down into finger pointing and countercharges regarding creative responsibility, distribution of menial chores, and even personal hygiene. "Everyone accused everybody of everything," Everson wrote later. Harman got mad and left. Then Hackett did the same, leaving the four remaining men to slug it out. It must have seemed like an amateur play rehearsal when Harman returned and apologized, then Siemons apologized, and Hackett came back as well. "Upshot of it was we write the man for more dope," Everson concluded. "Less consequential upshots were that Harman and Hackett would do a bit more of the tedium and that Larry would agree to take an occasional bath. Ah me."[44]

One way or another, things were going to change.

■ ■ ■

Morris Keeton visited Waldport in December, and he was ready to talk. He spoke with camp members and learned that enough were interested in a fine arts school, but only if Everson was director. Everson said he was no administrator and couldn't do the job. But when some of the artistically inclined campers came to him and said they didn't want an outsider taking over what had originally been his idea, and that they wouldn't support a fine arts program unless he ran it, Everson agreed. The first meeting of the fine arts school committee was held the day after Christmas in 1943, and the minutes recorded, "The committee unanimously elected Bill Everson temporary chairman. He will act in this capacity until the school opens officially and more members will be able to select a more permanent director."[45]

Everson lost no time in looking for someone to run the show. In what was either a potential stroke of genius or an exercise in astounding idealism, he wrote to Henry Miller, with whom he had been corresponding since they'd met in 1941 through their mutual friendship with Larry Powell. Miller, fifty-two years old and living in Big Sur after ten years in France, was arguably America's most controversial writer. His *Tropic of*

Cancer and two related books, written of his time during the 1930s in Paris, were widely praised by critics and literary people, coveted by collectors, yet labeled obscene and banned from sale in the United States and Great Britain, ostensibly because they used four-letter words and spoke of sex without reservation or shame. His extensive number of essays and commentaries, collected in a handful of books able to pass the postal inspector's eye, gave blunt treatment to the shortcomings and hypocrisies of modern-day civilization. Forced by the war in Europe to return to the United States in 1940, Miller spent a year traveling and observing the country, publishing his account as *The Air-Conditioned Nightmare.* Of his native land he wrote, "We are accustomed to think of ourselves as an emancipated people; we say that we are democratic, liberty-loving, free of prejudice and hatred. This is the melting-pot, the seat of a great human experiment." When in fact, he said, the opposite is true. "Actually we are a vulgar, pushing mob whose passions are easily mobilized by demagogues, newspaper men, religious quacks, agitators and such like. . . . What have we to offer the world besides the superabundant loot which we recklessly plunder from the earth under the maniacal delusion that this insane activity represents progress and enlightenment?" Like any good polemicist, Miller knew how to offer a note of optimism. "Some people think that a declaration of war changes everything. If only that were true! . . . Yet, for good or ill, war can bring about a change in the spirit of the people. And that is what I am vitally interested in—a change of heart, a conversion."[46] Miller was an undeniable and disconcerting creative force, a writer of formidable talent with a personality that offered no excuses and expected none in return. He was brilliant, original, unapologetic, somewhat mercurial, and, to mainstream America, scary as hell.

Everson wrote to him two days after the first fine arts committee meeting and got right to the point. "I know this is the wrong time . . . but I at least want to approach you, and see if perhaps a blow cannot be struck for pacifism and the arts. Bluntly:—*will you come to Waldport and serve as director for a pacifist School of Fine Arts?*" He explained what the school was, what they hoped to accomplish, and why they needed Miller. "It seems to me we can really contribute, and we need the help and affirmation of you few people out there who have seen through the bloody scum, and have no use for it." All Miller needed to do was be there, Everson said; the administration and headaches would be handled by others. His days would be free, with the campers out on Project work, and nights would be open for conversation and camaraderie. He'd receive eighty dollars per month, with room and board covered—and the food was good. "Can you let me know your reaction?" Everson asked. "It would mean a hell of a lot to us, Henry, if you could say yes."[47]

Miller replied that he was flattered—and he seemed genuinely so. But he had too many things going on, he said, big projects that demanded his time and attention. Besides, he added, he was no good with groups or bosses. "I would soon prove to be a thorn in everyone's side." He saluted Everson's enthusiasm and said he felt they would find a capable person. "I regret not being available," he said in closing. "You are one man I would go out of the way to do something for. But, as I said, it's just impossible now. I hope you understand."[48]

The conservative faction of COs at Camp Angel had no idea how close they had come to facing their own local judgment day—never mind the larger community of Waldport. Miller would have exposed their hypocrisies like the morning sun shining on a garbage heap.

Dick Mills also dodged a reckoning from Miller's sharp, critical eye. He hoped to move up the administrative ladder and perhaps be offered a position of real power after the war—and that ambition eventually worked against him. His pattern of public liberalism and behind-the-scenes manipulation was so well known, even from his time at Cascade Locks, that the first *Illiterati* had featured a cartoon with a man clearly resembling Mills standing in a prayerful attitude and saying, "And God, guide us to unanimity of thought so everyone will think as I do."

On top of that, Mills's penchant for nudity had brought him a bit of trouble beyond the brush with local authorities when launching the outrigger boat earlier that year. Within the camp, speculations about his sexual orientation were fed by his possession of a photograph album containing pictures of men in camp—sunbathing and posing nude. When someone got into his office, stole the album, and threatened blackmail, Mills was incensed, nearly tearing up the camp in his efforts to locate the book and discover who had taken it. Desperate, he called together a group of the more influential campers and explained that his interests were purely aesthetic, a matter of appreciating the male body. He also told Everson separately that he'd collected the pictures of the men *sans* clothing so that they wouldn't be embarrassed in later years seeing themselves wearing outdated fashions. Both explanations probably seemed more creative than plausible—and neither was accepted by the conservative religious men, who held prayer meetings that their wayward director might eventually find the right path.[49]

Whatever his personal proclivities, Mills was an astute enough politician to know it was in his best interest to support the fine arts school, and it didn't take much for Keeton to secure his agreement. As the calendar moved into 1944—the second year of Camp Angel and the third year of the war—the core group at Waldport, along with Kermit and Kemper at Cascade Locks, perhaps Bill Stafford and others at Santa Barbara, and who knew how many more out there in CPS, had something tentatively called the School of Fine Arts. All they had to do now was to figure out exactly what it was and how to make it work.

CHAPTER 6

Democratic Sausage Making

"ATTENTION PORTLAND NEWSPAPERS! Contact editor of Waldport paper for information concerning activity of conscientious objectors there!" So came this warning from national radio commentator and newspaper columnist Walter Winchell during his popular weekly program in January 1944. Winchell was huge, heard by millions across the country every Sunday evening, and on that week's program went on a bit of a nationalist tear. Talking about sabotage and sedition, he segued neatly into the note about Waldport—a place that meant little to a national audience other than that it was somewhere on the Pacific coast and therefore vulnerable to Japan. The exact nature of the CO "activity" wasn't made clear, nor did it need to be, as innuendo alone is often sufficient to incite suspicion during times of uncertainty and fear. Winchell had gotten the story from Dave Hall, editor of the *Lincoln County Times,* Waldport's four-page weekly newspaper. It had been a shot in the dark scoring a mention on the Winchell show, and Hall was ecstatic about his small-town journalism coup, greeting townspeople the next day with, "Did you hear my story break on Winchell's program?"[1]

Context is everything in cases like this, and Hall's context apparently was that these "conchies" south of town were up to no good. He had recently published some editorials in his paper, quoting from Everson's *War Elegies* and implying that they were unpatriotic. After the mention on the Winchell program Hall commented on the *Tide,* which he described as "published by three or four conscientious objectors at Camp Angel near here." Never mind that this had been the official camp newsletter with a dozen people involved in its production, that it was no longer being published, that the article he mentioned was six months old, and that he'd had it in his possession the entire time. He pulled a single paragraph from a five-page story on how propaganda is used to demonize the enemy and rhetorically asked, "Why is this rot being published???" The attacks continued into February, generally along the lines that anyone who didn't unquestionably support the war was not just un-American but an enemy.

"All these so called Pacifist Movements are the result of warped minds and cockeyed thinking, or they are Nazi-inspired," Hall wrote. "They are anti-American and should be silenced in war-time."[2]

The newspaper attacks were at first surprising to the camp members. Hall had been friendly with the camp, but something changed after the Untide group bought the old Challenge Gordon press. It turned out that the *Lincoln County Times* had once used this press in a partnership, Dick Mills said. But when Hall's partner felt he'd been shorted some money by the editor, he took full ownership of the printing press and put it up for sale on consignment at Doc Workman's secondhand store—and told Workman he could sell it to anybody except Dave Hall. Once Hall learned the press had been sold to the COs, he launched his attacks, Mills said, stressing that the newspaper had possessed copies of the *War Elegies* and the *Tide* since the previous summer. "Neither of these publications contained news until Dave had an axe to grind." And, Mills added, he'd learned that one of the Portland newspapers had told Hall they would pay "a goodly sum for all well-documented stories of subversive activities" at Camp Angel.[3]

By today's standards, this was pretty lightweight stuff. But in 1944, in a village of some six hundred people, it couldn't be left unanswered—particularly with the Winchell announcement's ability to feed fear and suspicion well beyond the specific region. In March, the camp sent out a letter to the community with the salutation, "To Our Friends and Neighbors." A short paragraph summarized how the men came to be in the camp, and then came a listing of what they had accomplished while there:

> Since October 1942 these men have devoted 8½ hours a day for 6 days a week to work of National Importance under the direction of the Siuslaw National Forest officials. The work has resulted in the planting of 2½ million trees on the 9,000 acres in the [Blodgett] Tract, the construction of 9 miles of gravel roads, the building of 3½ miles of fire trail, the crushing of nearly 10,000 tons of rock for road surfacing, the maintaining of 37 acres in 6 Forest Service Parks, and the assistance in the suppression of 7 fires in Oregon and Washington. Furthermore, they constructed a look-out tower on [Blodgett] Peak and have built 6 new buildings on the camp site.

This was followed by a statement describing finances:

> The men have received no pay for any of this work. Neither has the government made any provision to care for the families dependent upon many men in camp. Food for the men is provided by the Church of the Brethren with headquarters in Elgin,

Illinois. Many men with savings are contributing to their own support. Church of the Brethren members throughout the nation are raising $35,000 annually for the operation of this camp. . . . Monthly this camp spends over $1,000 in Waldport. The government's total expense in the operation of the camp is the salary of the project work supervisors and the cost of operating work trucks and machinery.

The letter then gave a brief accounting of how many men had come and gone, and under what circumstances, then finished with a reiteration of the peace churches' four-hundred-year opposition to war of any sort, and the assurance that they'd upheld their part of the bargain with the U.S. government to provide basic necessities for the men in the camp.[4]

One relatively positive aspect of Camp Angel's particular brand of isolation was that the townspeople knew them—and most of the local population were not moved by Hall's attacks. Generally the Waldport people remained friendly, Mills assured the campers. The justice of the peace had recently come for dinner, and the school superintendent and others were showing more interest in the camp. Overall, Mills said, the newspaper dust-up had been good practice in putting theories of nonviolence into action. Everson, buried in work with the Untide Press and in getting the School of Fine Arts going, dashed off a note to Powell. "Local editor is after us for publishing. Even got Winchell to attack us over NBC. . . . We don't expect a witch hunt—yet."[5]

No witch hunt ever materialized, but in late February a small act of vandalism reminded the men that there would always be those who disapproved of the camp and what it represented. The large wooden sign at the entrance, announcing CAMP ANGEL, C.P.S. CAMP 56, BRETHREN SERVICE COMMITTEE, WALDPORT, OREGON was attacked one night with red paint. The word "Angel" had been crossed out and "Coward" painted over it. Warren Downs, who had been recording events in a diary he'd gotten for Christmas, noted, "The job, by the workmanship, looks like a high school kid stunt. Why, they didn't even have the sense to use yellow paint. Wouldn't be surprised though if Hall was somewhere behind it."[6]

In an odd way, Hall may have intuitively grasped what was happening down the road from his town; he just couldn't articulate it effectively. All art is subversive—and art was now the focus at Camp Angel. Everson was the director of the School of Fine Arts whether he liked it or not, and he wrote up a prospectus, bringing to bear all the ideas and perceptions about art and pacifism developed through his conversations and letters over the past year. They printed it up and ran off copies on the old mimeograph, eight pages printed on legal-sized paper, folded over and stapled into a booklet titled simply *The Fine Arts at Waldport*, with its lone graphic a symbol resembling an upside-down "4" superimposed over a line drawing of the myrtlewood head that Edwa had sculpted the summer before.[7]

"Almost everyone sufficiently enlightened to perform the act of reading recognizes the validity of art as a universal experience," it began, positing that art is fundamental to the intellectual development of a society, even if it sometimes takes another generation to recognize its value. Accomplished art, when joined with a compelling idea, can be a powerful force for change, Everson said—and this was the opportunity to give a new voice to pacifism. There was no longer a need for the pacifism

Title page from the Fine Arts prospectus sent out to all CPS camps, 1944.

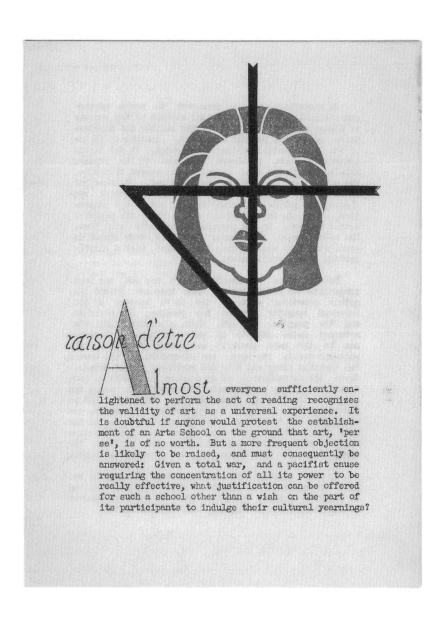

raison d'etre

Almost everyone sufficiently enlightened to perform the act of reading recognizes the validity of art as a universal experience. It is doubtful if anyone would protest the establishment of an Arts School on the ground that art, 'per se', is of no worth. But a more frequent objection is likely to be raised, and must consequently be answered: Given a total war, and a pacifist cause requiring the concentration of all its power to be really effective, what justification can be offered for such a school other than a wish on the part of its participants to indulge their cultural yearnings?

of simple refusal, or the poetry of disillusionment that so shockingly revealed the horrors of the First World War. The peace movement needed to be more active after this war, and now was the time to forge its voices: "Pacifism can be the most powerful motivating factor in the post-war world; its seeds are everywhere in the unrest, the terrible agony and fear and weariness of the people. Given the articulation of an earnest and serious artistic movement, a movement that could make whole and poignant the longing of the people, what might not be accomplished?"[8]

The prospectus included an invitation to artists and those interested in art to transfer to Waldport. Here, they would engage in the practice and production of literary, musical, visual, or spoken arts and related crafts. The members would have an active role in developing the program, the different arts groups would intermingle, and they would present their work through exhibits, concerts, and publications. Facilities included a few small rooms for arts and activities; the chapel, which could also be used for theater productions; and a library with two thousand books. Arts equipment included a record player and amplifier, more than sixty record albums, the Challenge printing press, a mimeograph and several typewriters, along with a silk-screen setup and two photography darkrooms. They expected a piano soon and were designing a kiln for sculpture and ceramics. They had the Untide Press members and were expecting to be joined by the *Illiterati* editors from Cascade Locks. They had a core group of musicians and the beginnings of a theater troupe; a sculptor and a painter were waiting to transfer. They hoped for more photographers and painters—visual artists—and noted that one of the most attractive "facilities" of the camp was the Pacific Ocean, just two hundred yards away, "with its superb beach, its ever-changing expanse, and a nearby shoreline of cliffs, rocks, and headlands rivaling anything on the western coast."[9]

They acknowledged the pros and cons—a liberal camp government and generally important work such as firefighting, but also the seemingly interminable rain and the inescapable isolation. Crowds of people would *not* be traveling fifty or a hundred miles through slashing rain over winding mountain roads or washed-out coastal highways to view the CO paintings or hear their concerts. Some also might say artists' colonies never survive, that the pettiness and ego rivalries of those sensitive and creative types doom such projects from the start. But this was different, Everson wrote. They had an overarching principle—pacifism—that they believed could unify the group beyond any disruption. If this makes sense to you, he concluded, put in your application for transfer. "The need is apparent; given the insight and the will, the returns can be memorable."[10]

The pieces—and the people—were coming into place. The Fine Arts was official; they would be accorded a space in the camp and funding from BSC headquarters of one hundred dollars a month for materials and administrative costs. At the end of six months the program would be reviewed and a decision made regarding continuation. They had a printing press and a core group using it. Everson, Coffield, Hackett, Harman, and Seimons had been there from the beginning; Bill Eshelman had enthusiastically signed on since he'd arrived in December, and Charles Davis remained available for technical help. Glenn Evans, who majored in sculpture and crafts at the University of Wisconsin, had arrived in November and was working with clay and other materials. The multi-talented Kermit Sheets and architect-artist Kemper Nomland were back in Cascade Locks but expected to transfer as soon as possible. Bob Scott on piano and Warren Downs on cello made up the music contingent, and Everson was hopeful they could attract a violinist, or even two. For theater, according to one account, a seminal moment had come in January when "tall, lean, sardonic" Jim Harman leaped onto a giant stump at the tree-planting site, flung down his hoe, and launched into the "To be or not to be" soliloquy from *Hamlet,* shaking his hands at the sky, his seedlings bag hanging from his belt. Dark humor and absurd behavior is a staple of any sustained arduous labor, and Harman's speech was hardly the sole spark of inspiration for the Fine Arts theater productions. But the spark was certainly there.[11]

Glenn Evans working on the potter's wheel in the Fine Arts workshop.

Letters of interest came in—from both new and familiar names. Everson had been working on the assumption that permanent transfers for Kermit and Kemper were a given. "I wish to hell you could get here," he wrote Kermit. "We need both you and Nomland badly—you to help with plans, Nomland to work on the art." From the beginning, however, getting people actually approved for the Fine Arts was a challenge. Maybe it was part of that "troublemakers" reputation so many creative types carried with them—justified or not. Maybe it was simply the glacial pace of bureaucratic motion. Or maybe it was some combination of those inexplicable and maddening forces that attend anything related to real and lasting change. It was February 1944 when Kermit and Kemper finally had formal requests filed for transfer to Waldport. Part of the problem was in keeping a population parity between the camps. Each of the peace churches separately paid for the room and board of campers in their charge, and oftentimes a transfer request to a given camp would not be approved unless someone already there was willing to transfer out. Everson told Kermit he thought they might be able to make an even trade between the Fine Arts and the School of Pacifist Living at Cascade Locks. "One guy here has put in—another probable," he wrote. "This exchange may help get you here."[12]

Another person Everson had been corresponding with was Martin Ponch, who was currently at the Friends-administered Camp #108 in Gatlinburg, Tennessee, where he also edited the *Compass,* an all-CPS magazine featuring journalism, essays, and some creative work. Originally conceived as a bimonthly publication but turning into something closer to semiannual, the forty-eight-page, letter-sized magazine enjoyed competent production with strong visual elements, including photographs. Ponch, who had helped begin the journal in late 1942 when he was at Camp #32 in West Campton, New Hampshire, had known about Waldport since he had received a copy of the *War Elegies* in 1943. When the call came for the Fine Arts, he was ready to move, magazine and all. He explained his decision in a lengthy letter to the Friends camp in Gatlinburg, addressing it, "From: Martin Ponch. To: Anyone Concerned About Him." Equating his departure from Gatlinburg to a walkout, he stated his reasons for leaving, included a list of grievances about the camp and CPS in general—not the least of which was its disregard for creative thinking and expression—and concluded that "while some opportunity for creativity exists in CPS it is not only to our advantage but the world's advantage that we make the most of it." This is what he hoped for in Waldport.[13]

An intriguing response came from Vladimir Dupre, writing from Camp #121 at Bedford in the Blue Ridge Mountains of Virginia. Declaring that he had no talent in the arts but plenty of interest, Dupre said the real benefit of his transfer would be his fiancé, Ibby (Elizabeth), who had been a top actress in the theater at Oberlin College in Ohio. "They knew I was going to be married to this actress," Dupre recalled of his correspondence with the Fine Arts. "I sort of traded on her."[14]

Other answers to the prospectus came from painters Clayton James and Harold Steers, both in Camp #46, at Big Flats in central New York State. In response to their apparent inquiry about time to paint, noise disturbances, and the weather, committee member Bill Eshelman wrote that the schedule at Waldport was the same as at all camps and that Overhead work as a special consideration for artists was "highly improbable." As to noise, they might hear the printing press (now powered by an electric motor), which was located next to the crafts room, and the recreation space with its ping-pong table was nearby. The weather was rainy, Eshelman noted, but if they wanted subject matter in nature, this was the place. "If you are interested in landscapes, ocean scenes, or hauntingly beautiful windblown trees," he said, "you will never regret your decision to transfer here."[15]

Everyone filed their papers and waited.

■ ■ ■

By spring 1944, life in camp had passed through its cycles a few times. Tree planting, trail clearing, road building and wood cutting governed the daily rhythms; religion, recreation, and art were the dominant after-hours activities. The workload wasn't nearly as intense this season, with only half as many trees slated for planting, and none scheduled for January. Bill Eshelman pulled night watchman duty, making his rounds from 9:00 p.m. to 6:00 a.m., stoking the woodstoves in the dorms and running general safety and security checks. It was a dream job, he wrote to a friend— as far as jobs went at the camp. He was on his own, no one giving orders or asking questions. As long as he completed his work, how he spent the remaining time was up to him. "All this," he said, "and quiet too!"[16]

The evening "bull session" in the dorms maintained its prominent position in the camp culture and sometimes carried over from the night into the next day. Everson in particular was known for his tendency to expound philosophically as the crews toiled through the tree planting. While hiking back to the truck after Project work one day, he and Coffield sparred about the meaning of thought itself. "There is no true philosophy," Coffield said, "because man can only think with or in terms of analogies." Because there are no true analogies, he continued, "there can be no true philosophy." As might be expected, the word "relativity" came up, moving into talk of Einstein's theories, which opened the discussion to all manner of conjecture and possibility—while the men hiked down the soggy, logged-off hillsides.[17]

In this intellectual environment, an overall sense of participatory democracy prevailed, nurtured also by the various committees, shared educational programs, ongoing monthly birthday banquets and the occasional softball game on the quad or ping-pong tournament in the rec hall. A discussion about smoking during meals was brought up at Camp Council; the group decided that smokers should voluntarily refrain from lighting up while others were eating—an acknowledgment of the consequences of individual action within a group. The record concerts continued, featuring Beethoven, Brahms, Handel, Schubert, and what Downs called some "pretty rugged jazz." Hackett and Eshelman gave a talk in the chapel on race relations, using records for sound effects. The co-op store stumbled along, encountering the usual difficulties of attempting to apply an equally shared venture to a diverse group of individuals with different ideas of what constituted an honor system based on need. Side camps at Mary's Peak (in the Coast Range about halfway between Waldport and Corvallis), Mapleton (just east of Florence, thirty miles to the south), and Hebo (fifty miles up the coast, below Tillamook) established their own subcultures, even hosting the various CPS guest speakers whenever circumstances made travel reasonable.[18]

The work assignment for the directorship of the Fine Arts, however, uncovered some issues that had apparently been simmering for some time. Generally, about 20 percent of the hundred or so campers were assigned to Overhead work—whether it be administration, kitchen and laundry duty, mechanical work in the machine shop and garage, or sign painting for the various Forest Service–maintained campgrounds and trails. So far, the system of generally matching men's assignments to their talents had sufficed; when questions came up, Mills and the Workers Committee would address the problem and hammer out a solution. Although some might occasionally grumble when they headed out to plant trees or crush rock on yet another cold, wet morning while others stayed inside a warm kitchen or dry office, it often boiled down to who had earned the respect of the campers. There was no apparent objection when Mills suggested that Everson—who clearly held the respect of many at Camp Angel—be reassigned to Overhead work as director of the Fine Arts. The problem was that one more on Overhead meant one less on Project. Mills proposed a solution whereby different Overhead members could rotate part-time into Project work, sharing the duty. The education director could go out one day, the office secretary the next, and so on. With the expected transfer later that spring of some twenty or thirty men to Waldport, Mills said, there would be enough Project workers to justify adding to Overhead.[19]

This was democratic sausage making at its most fundamental level. The Fine Arts had been approved, its director was a well-respected member of camp, and making room for him on Overhead was not a major issue. Yet it brought up the larger question of rotating *anyone* into an Overhead position, and how policy so far had been largely determined by personality. This in turn brought attention to how long some campers had already been in Overhead positions—and not all of them having gained their position by earning the respect of others. This led to debate and then a recommendation by the Workers Committee that *all* Overhead positions be filled on a rotating basis, which further lifted the lid on simmering resentments and mistrust. So far, the majority of camp had steadily supported the Workers Committee as the decision-making facilitator between administration and the campers; after all, that was their stated purpose for existing. A minority, however, had sometimes gone directly to the managers—for reasons ranging from personality conflicts to ideological values—and this time some were more vocal in their opposition to the Workers Committee decision. This opened up a Pandora's box of deeper issues. For one, there had already been tension around how to deal with "goldbricking," the practice of only pretending to work; the Workers Committee had directed that when a CO crew leader saw someone loafing on the job or otherwise avoiding work, they should take it to the committee and not to the Forest Service officials. But some campers felt this undermined the basic principles of discipline and authority, and for some of the more conservative individuals it called into question the very foundations of society. The more liberal members felt that what they saw as a blind obedience to authority stifled democracy—supposedly the very thing for which the country was fighting. Once again, the rift showed between the religious and the more secular objectors. During the discussion, for example, one camper asked, "Is the Workers Committee recognized by Selective Service?"—effectively framing the legitimacy of a democratic group within the context of a hierarchical institution. This prompted Warren Downs to later remark in his diary, "Such questions indicate quite a minority psychopathically want and need to be told what to do."[20]

In short, the question of Overhead rotation as recommended by the Workers Committee implied a vote of confidence on the committee itself. A secret ballot was held, and Downs reported to his diary the results. "Voting on support or non-support of workers committee revealed this: 49 yes, 12 blank, 2 disqualified, 8 no." Most of the nonvoters, he said, were Jehovah's Witnesses, who didn't participate in such things. However, one member confided to Downs that they unanimously supported the committee. Democracy had done its work.[21]

■ ■ ■

The outside world was in many respects far away. The nighttime black-outs and beach restrictions had been eased, and only the most tenacious worriers could have feared a Japanese invasion on the West Coast. By the end of February, U.S. forces were some five thousand miles away in Micronesia, where they continued their "island-hopping" strategy of bypassing certain islands and blockading the Japanese forces there, who were then weakened by hunger and lack of supplies. In Europe, General Dwight D. Eisenhower took over as Supreme Commander as the Allies pushed up the Italian peninsula to drive the Germans from Rome, and the U.S. Air Force launched its first bombing raid on Berlin. Everyone knew the invasion of Europe was coming, that it would be bloody, and that it would take time to vanquish the German military machine. Looking ahead, President Roosevelt signed an executive order creating the War Refugee Board, and the U.S. Congress authorized up to $1.35 billion for the United Nations Relief and Rehabilitation Agency.[22] The question of who would win this war, in both Europe and the Pacific, had clearly been answered. The questions regarding what to do with the devastated countries and their residents had only begun.

For some COs, particularly the more religious ones, postwar relief work perfectly matched their sense of mission, and they continued their classes in languages, first aid, and cultural geography. Even though they were currently forbidden by Congress to actually go overseas and do anything, the men were willing to prepare themselves and bide their time until the need for their skills would be urgent enough to overcome the prejudices of the decision makers.[23] For others, the continued refusal of government officials to recognize that COs could make a productive contribution was getting harder to bear. As a U.S. victory in the war became a certainty, more COs questioned the usefulness of CPS, and the percentage of walkouts, refusals to work (RTW) and work slowdowns increased.[24] Further concern centered around hints that Selective Service was considering tightening its rules, that as a result of this interference the peace churches were considering giving up their management of CPS, and that the government would be taking over the camps—all of this reported by Dick Mills in his after-dinner talks, further stoking uncertainty and fear. The men weren't necessarily afraid of the government—with their conscientious objection they had already established that—but they did worry about their ability to stay true to their conscience in a government-run camp. A common subject in the nighttime bull sessions was whether or not to openly break the law by simply refusing to work at all or walking out of camp and possibly going to prison. For some, this course of action was about as true to conscience as one could get. "Bill Eshelman talked with me tonight about going to prison—he and Smith," Downs wrote in his diary. "He seemed to favor it." The men also talked about how they might respond if the government took over the camps, with some feeling that might be a good time for a mass walk-out, Downs said. "Brumbaugh suggested to someone that we should all fast then."[25]

Although the end of the war might have seemed apparent, it was not yet in sight. The COs knew that their views would someday, as Everson had written a year before, "be tangent again to the world," but there was much to do meantime. Those in the Fine Arts, before diving into the work of influencing how the world thought about war and peace, needed to take care of some practical matters—such as exactly where in the camp they would operate. The committee thought about dedicating one of the four dorms to the school, combining the living and working space for its members. This, however, could invite separation from the rest of the camp, and the group did not want to risk being perceived as elitist. Yet the dorm residents had already arranged themselves somewhat through self-selection, with the strongly religious campers bunking together, the more liberal and politically minded COs gathering on their own, and the Jehovah's Witnesses establishing their own orbit. The Fine Arts members ended up sharing Dorm 4, nearest to the rec hall and the laundry room, with the Jehovah's Witnesses. The two groups fashioned bunk beds with curtains as a kind of dividing wall between each half of the long, narrow dorm; they weren't necessarily in sight of each other, but could certainly hear the louder conversations. The artists played their jazz records and debated politics and philosophy, and caught no complaints from the other end of the dorm. The Jehovah's Witnesses, largely ranch workers from eastern Oregon, smoked and played cards and swore at each other. Sometimes even during their Bible study in the close quarters, someone might shout in exasperation, "Jesus Christ!" or, "Fuck you!" On the other side of the room divider, the Fine Arts bohemians smiled.[26]

Another concern was the Fine Arts name. In politics and social dynamics, perception is often reality, and the group thought hard about not only who they were but also who they should be. While the original name, School of Fine Arts, followed the same style as the other CPS "schools," Everson insisted that the Fine Arts was not a school with formal classes and teacher-student relationships. Referring to a paper he had drafted for the Brethren Service Committee, Everson told Morris Keeton that he'd specifically avoided any reference to the Fine Arts as a school. "It ain't and must not be considered as such," he wrote. "Don't insert that word into my paper."[27] Keeton acknowledged the objection and asked, "Would you like to substitute some other word in the official title of the group? How would 'Colony' do? Or would 'Fine Arts Workshop' be better?"[28]

The group of men meeting as the Fine Arts decided that's exactly what they were—a group, and Everson passed this on to Keeton. "We have decided that the word 'group' best explains our status, despite the unsatisfactory euphemistic characteristics," he wrote, noting their awareness of the consequential acronym, FAG. "Our title is still the Fine Arts at Waldport," he said, "but in refering [*sic*] to us you may do so as The Fine Arts Group."[29]

Whenever a particular group is given singular attention or recognition, a certain amount of grumbling from the larger population can be expected. The fundamentalist "Holy Joes," as they were sometimes called, naturally viewed the Fine Arts liberals with some suspicion. The farm boys and mechanically inclined campers, conditioned to hard physical work and a straightforward logic, found it sometimes difficult to accommodate the softer, more intellectual artists, particularly on Project. When some of the more politically minded Fine Arts members engaged in work slow-downs, some of the conservative religious men with the "second mile" philosophy of doing twice the amount of assigned work attempted to take up the slack, perhaps not always without resentment. And Jim Gallaghan, the boat-building, blunt-talking welder from Oakland—who

L-R: Larry Siemons and Vlad Dupre examine some writing while Bill Eshelman changes a record in what is likely the Fine Arts dorm.

also loved opera, sang arias from treetops, and sometimes walked the camp quad at night roaring out expletives in Italian specifically to irritate the Holy Joes studying their Bibles—referred to the artists as the "Fine Farts," although he professed a personal admiration for some members, particularly Everson and Coffield.[30]

The truly creative ones poured their energy into the work, Everson said. But some in the Fine Arts could be temperamental and difficult, he admitted, and the ingredients for trouble were always there. Hackett, Harman, and Siemons were impossible when together, Everson said; the others tried to keep clear, but it was unavoidable at times. "I've never heard so much bitching and back-biting in my life," he wrote Edwa. And the older poet, much as he had worked to analyze with his intellect the unresolved triangle between himself, his wife, and Hackett, couldn't resist voicing his feelings about the younger man. "I would not, and I'm saying every word deliberately, consign any woman, much less my own wife, to a life with that man Hackett for anything. My God, such a guy! Absolutely undependable; totally careless of other people's feelings, and often so. Bah! It angers me."[31]

The tension grew also between Coffield and Siemons, who had never gotten along very well. Coffield was the loner, a true eccentric, almost pure in his convictions. Siemons was the operator, a manipulator who tried to ingratiate himself to people. While he certainly could light a fire to get a project going, such as with the original *War Elegies* book, he didn't always see things through, and was generally not considered trustworthy. Whether it was a single thing Siemons did or the accumulation of his actions over time was never made clear, but Coffield finally had enough. In March, he put in for a transfer to leave Camp Angel and enroll in the School of Pacifist Living at Cascade Locks. While changes in personnel were hardly anything new for the camp, the impending loss of Coffield was a terrible blow. He'd been a significant force in the creative energy of the camp, co-founding the *Untide* and helping launch the Untide Press. As camp education director he had tirelessly promoted Everson's *War Elegies* and the creative educational programs. Now he was leaving, ostensibly because of Larry Siemons—who the other men felt should be sent to a psychiatrist. Everson in particular was crushed; Coffield had been one of his closest allies, a true comrade in the arts. "Everson came in with the most hurt miserable expression to tell us that Coffield, unable to endure Simons [*sic*] any longer, was applying for transfer to Cascade Locks," Warren Downs wrote in his diary. "This may be the death knell of the fine arts school, for no telling how it may appear to [Morris] Keeton."[32]

Although we'll never know for certain, perhaps Coffield had a larger purpose in mind. The shifting and transferring of men between camps demanded a constant balancing act for administration. Each new member's arrival required consideration for not only food, shelter, work assignment, and other basic needs but also where a CO's talents, abilities, and inclinations might best fit into the camp environment and culture. Every request for a transfer to the Fine Arts required a give and take between the affected camps, the headquarters of the peace churches involved, the government agency that oversaw that particular camp's work assignments, and Selective Service. A question, hesitation, or personal bias at any point in the sequence, including each organization's internal chains of command, could delay the process for a day, a week, or indefinitely — and all of this existed within the construct of a massive national bureaucracy, with its forms, regulations, power struggles, and petty details. As the number of Selective Service draftees fluctuated and some CPS camps worked out better than others, the peace churches' administrators sought to balance camp membership throughout the system. With the Waldport roster full, for someone to transfer into the Fine Arts, someone from within the camp had to leave. It may be that Coffield, feeling his presence there was no longer productive, decided to make room for some new blood.[33]

Later in March, Morris Keeton wrote to Everson about the ongoing delay in approving the transfer requests for Kermit and Kemper. It was probably at the federal government level, Keeton said; he suspected it had something to do with the general reduction in numbers at the Friends' camps, and that Selective Service had put all transfer approvals on hold until that was sorted out. He closed with what he thought was a hopeful note: all requests for transfers to the Cascade Locks School of Pacifist Living, including Coffield's, had been approved. "Or maybe you don't regard that as hopeful," he noted. "Depends, doesn't it, upon whether you look at the fact we got transfers this month or at the number of months it took to get them!"[34] Perhaps he didn't realize how much it mattered to Everson and the others exactly who *wasn't* transferring in — and exactly who *was* transferring out.

CHAPTER 7

No Use for War

SHORTLY AFTER THE FINE ARTS SCHOOL officially opened in March 1944, they were joined by Waldo Chase, a largely self-taught artist and craftsman from Washington's Olympic Peninsula, as their first visiting artist-in-residence. Chase, a forty-five-year-old pacifist who followed a simple and cooperative lifestyle, quickly gained popularity with his classes in drawing, color woodblock printing, and weaving with a loom. His beginning drawing class brought in some twenty participants representing every disparate group in the camp. They met three days a week over a two- to three-week period, first drawing simple objects like blocks of wood, chairs, hands, and feet; then they progressed to drawing live models, using pencil and charcoal. The works may not have been particularly accomplished, but the classes were an excellent introduction for those unfamiliar with the arts, and invited at least interest and perhaps participation in the new school.[1]

Within its first month, the Fine Arts presented an exhibit of paintings and sketches in the dining hall, and also presented their first concert and recital in the chapel. The Friday night show featured Glen Coffield (in apparently his last Waldport performance) chanting a long poem titled "The Chinese Nightingale" by the troubadour poet Vachel Lindsay, a duet of Handel's "G Minor Sonata" with Warren Downs on cello and Bob Scott on piano, and a dramatic reading by Everson, Hackett, and Jim Harman adapted from Thomas Wolfe's novel, *Look Homeward, Angel.* Part of the Fine Arts mission was to treat the work as professionally as possible, no matter when or where it was presented, so they mimeographed a program titled "The Fine Arts at Waldport: First Showing" and included a list of the players and works being performed. They also couldn't resist taking a swipe at government bureaucracy, offering a short summary of the Fine Arts so far, in which they referred to Washington, DC, as a "Morass" and a "Labyrinth." It had been a month since the Fine Arts officially opened, yet no transfers had been approved, they said. So the current artists would have to do. "But look," they asserted, "here

is what we do have: the tongue, the ear, the discerning eye. Let us foster the act that awakes them."[2]

Warren Downs noted in his diary the next day, "Concert or recital or exhibition of 'The Fine Arts at Waldport' was adequately successful. Glen was fine. His sing-song tremulous voice was hypnotic in its conveyance of the antiquity, patience and wisdom of old China." Hackett and Harman and Everson were fine, too, he said. "It was rather deep though."[3]

A more ambitious show followed in April, with interested campers joining the cast. Norman Haskell gave a reading from iconic Russian poet Alexander Pushkin, followed by Art Snell's vocal performance of works by Debussy and Verdi accompanied by Downs and Scott on cello and piano. The final act was a synthesis of readings from John Dos Passos's *U.S.A.*, a trilogy of novels published throughout the 1930s that employ a combination of cinematic description, internal monologue, biography, and multiple-plot narrative to convey the increasingly complex and contradictory elements of life in America during the first three decades of the twentieth century. Edwa Everson, on a recent visit to the camp, had designed a backdrop for the show—a collage of bold images featuring an American flag pennant, the British Union Jack, a portrait of Woodrow Wilson, a hand holding a giant bag of money, an airplane dropping bombs, Christian crosses, a burning candle, and a heavily muscled working man—all connected by abstract ribbons of color, like a river—or maybe blood—flowing behind the symbols. Jim Harman, Everson, and Bill Eshelman sat in simple chairs before the scene, portraying different

An early Fine Arts show: dramatic reading from *U.S.A.* by John Dos Passos. L-R: Harold Hackett, Jim Harman, Bill Everson, Bill Eshelman.

characters—sometimes reading slowly and deliberately, and other times jumping up and shouting their lines—as Hackett narrated from a podium to the side.[4]

Downs duly reported in his diary that Haskell gave a "sensitive reading" of Pushkin, and that the *U.S.A.* presentation was a "smoother performance" than the previous month's interpretation of the Thomas Wolfe novel. He was characteristically self-effacing in describing his own performance on the cello: "It went all right except for the tricky ending, where I sneaked, and not too secretively, home about a beat too late." He also noted that the new Forest Service supervisor, Orville Richman, attended the concert. "I realize his family isn't here and he has nothing much to do, but it still is encouraging to see a supervisor take part in camp activities."[5]

Later that month came a performance of Everson's *The Masculine Dead,* which had been published in 1942 as a long poem. Originally written as a radio play, the story takes place in a world where all the men have been killed off, represented here by a chorus of "the masculine dead." All the other voices are female: an old woman, a girl, a widow, and a wife. The stage for the show, done by Glenn Evans and Larry Siemons, featured a backdrop with abstract drawings and sketches of men, run on rollers in the style of old panorama screens; lighting effects were done with jagged pieces of cardboard moved by hand over spotlights set on small tables. The speakers were behind the curtain, with the intention to evoke the feel of listening to a radio play. Particularly intriguing was that the cast included not only Everson, Hackett, and Harman as the male chorus, but also female voices played by five young women visiting from Oregon State College in Corvallis. The audience, too, included women from the college, who sat silently through the play and barely applauded at the end; some said later that the subject seemed too serious for applause. Everson thought perhaps the erotic sections of the poem had offended the women, but his worries were unfounded. "Later they came around and asked if *they* could put it on at their 'club' at school," Downs wrote in his diary. "So Bill is sending the scripts and paintings."[6]

A few days later, Warren Downs and Bob Scott gave a recital of classical pieces by Vivaldi, Beethoven, Debussy, and others. It was apparently well received, as Downs was called out for an encore, where he performed a work composed by his sister, Flavia Downs Olson, who'd been inspired by Bach. Low-key as ever, Downs wrote in his diary that "pieces didn't go too badly. Much encouraged."[7]

Everson was more enthusiastic. "Downs gave his cello recital, probably our most imposing musical production of the year," he wrote Morris Keeton back at Brethren headquarters in Elgin. "Guests from all over

Five women from Oregon State College in Corvallis as guest readers for *The Masculine Dead* with (L-R) Harold Hackett, Bill Everson, Jim Harman.

Warren Downs on cello and Bob Scott on piano perform in the chapel. Myrtlewood head sculpture on post done by Edwa Everson.

Oregon and the townspeople well represented. Damned good." Keeton fired off his approval in a memo: "If you keep this propaganda up we will be moving out to live with you."[8]

The same weekend as *The Masculine Dead* performance saw the first arrivals of Fine Arts transfers from other camps, including Clayton James and Harold Steers. The two men, who had taken the train from Big Flats in New York across the country to Corvallis and then hitchhiked and walked the remaining forty miles to Waldport, each brought their own brand of personality. Steers, a thirty-two-year-old gruff-talking nursery-man and Jehovah's Witness from western Pennsylvania, had been classi-fied as a political objector. When his induction notice came, he said he had no use for the politics in Washington any more than the politics in Berlin. He made ten trips before his draft board until finally one day he walked in, slapped a dollar bill down on the table and told the board, "Go buy a shell. I'll go outside and stand against the building and you can shoot me. It'll be a hell of a lot cheaper and better for everyone." They sent him to Big Flats, where, as a professional nurseryman, he was assigned to attend forty acres of Russian dandelions. He knew his plants, so he inquired as to why they were growing that species. He learned that they were being used to create latex for the war effort, as the nation's rub-ber supply in Southeast Asia had been cut off by the Japanese conquests. Steers called a strike at the camp, and as he remembered it, about 180 men walked off the job. But it didn't take, he said, and shortly after, he was sent to Waldport.[9]

James, in his early twenties and a graduate of the Rhode Island School of Design, had bounced around four CPS camps already, strug-gling to balance his time between the required camp labor and his per-sonal need to paint. The Fine Arts seemed a perfect solution, and when he came to Oregon he was inspired by the magnificent trees and opulent greenery. Yet he was overwhelmed by the raw beauty of the coast. "The ocean was so strong and powerful that I couldn't paint," he remem-bered, acknowledging that part of it may have stemmed from his strong Methodist background."[10]

James was soon joined by his girlfriend from art school, Barbara Straker, also a painter. They quickly married, one day hitchhiking the twenty miles up to Newport, then another half dozen inland to the lum-ber mill town of Toledo, where they found the justice of the peace and recited their vows. Back at Camp Angel, they rented one of the Tillie the Whale cabins across the highway, on the bluff overlooking the beach, and lived a sparse life centered on painting and each other's company. Clayton simply refused to do Project work, so camp administration put him in the kitchen, where he baked bread and prepared meals, which provided him some free time to paint. Barbara painted also, and did some

Clayton James painting in the Fine Arts studio.

weaving on a loom that Clayton built. They sold a small piece or two, allowing them to eke out a subsistence by hitchhiking for transportation and having their meals at the camp.[11]

Everson took immediately to Clayton, declaring him one of the most important figures in camp. He had a fascinating manner, Everson said, with features like a Picasso painting—and his own work was impressive in its wildness and abstraction. He could make considerable contributions, the poet said, if he didn't exhaust himself fighting the CPS bureaucracy.[12]

Right behind Clayton and Steers came Martin Ponch, bringing with him the *Compass* magazine and its subscription list, along with a knack for getting people involved. Within two days he had a crew signed on to produce the *Compass*, surprising even himself with his success.[13]

Ponch's real interest, though, was in theater. Born in Germany of Jewish parentage and raised in New York City, he studied theater at New York University and later visited at the Hedgerow Theatre, an innovative repertory company founded by Jasper Deeter outside Philadelphia in 1923. Hedgerow's approach to theater as a cooperative venture that focused on artistic growth rather than financial profit appealed to Ponch, and he wrote in the *Compass* that a truly "legitimate theatre" should strike a balance between the practical matter of earning a living and the artistic examination of the individual in society. At present, he said, both the amateur and professional theaters were based on the capitalist system of competition for personal profit. Whether it be local thespians hogging the spotlight or a Broadway star expecting special treatment, whether it be a two-year run of a play that after two months no longer challenges the artists, or a quickly closed production that leaves the actors seeking instead of doing work, the results more often reduced rather than enhanced the theater experience—for everyone from the stage crew and performers to the audience. The answer to these problems, Ponch said, could be found in pacifism, which already accepted the cooperative ideal in business and life. Once all agree to share the total theater experience—to do the stage work, take the minor role, become part of something larger than themselves rather than serving personal ambitions—the benefits can be substantial. Continuity in employment, variety in creative experience, and a group whose members feel trusted and respected serves the entire theater community, he wrote. "And, of course, the regular audience at such a theatre, like the customer-shareholder in a cooperative grocery, receives values and advantages unobtainable elsewhere." It wasn't like this had never been done before, he concluded. The Greeks did it. Companies in Shakespeare's and Molière's times did it. More recently, the Provincetown Playhouse and Washington Square Players in New York City—producing works by Eugene O'Neill, Theodore Dreiser, George Bernard Shaw, Anton Chekhov, and Henrik Ibsen—were founded on a cooperative model that influenced the Greenwich Village bohemian scene of the 1920s. Then there was the Hedgerow Theatre, Ponch added, which for twenty years had operated pretty much as the ideal cooperative theater. Interestingly, Ponch noted, at least six members of Hedgerow registered as COs in the war. Although he had no way of knowing it at the time, two of those members would have significant influence on the Fine Arts at Waldport.[14]

Not long after his arrival, Ponch joined with Jim Harman (of the Hamlet stump speech) to perform "A Morality Play for the Leisure Class," a short allegorical piece on heaven and hell, published in the 1920s and featuring only two characters. Backstage work included a set designed by Edwa Everson, costume design by Barbara James, and help with sewing from Maude Gregory, who continued her quiet presence as camp matron. The only surviving response to the show is a single sentence from Warren Downs in his diary: "Harman was fairly good and I think shows possibility of becoming much better, since he's had so little experience."[15]

Then the first Hedgerow man arrived. David Jackson, a Pennsylvanian in his mid-twenties, brought both drama and literary experience, and he helped launch a play-reading series intended to broaden campers' awareness of recent and established works. In what appears to have been a truly participatory program, interested persons signed up to rehearse and "perform" parts in the chosen work by taking on a role and reading from the script before an audience. A surviving copy of the sign-up list for the first play, Thornton Wilder's *Our Town*, evokes images of the names signed on the Declaration of Independence, with the first a bold, flowing signature of "Norman M. Haskell" followed by ten others, also written large.[16]

Compared to the months of preparation and waiting, the Fine Arts were now racing along. "Things travel on here, time spinning under the gears like mad," Everson wrote to Kermit. "Almost the first of June. When the hell are you coming?" The Challenge press was rolling, producing book pages as well as programs for the shows, he said. Clayton James was painting wonderful pictures. Hackett had been away at the Hebo side camp but was now returned, which brought the original group back together—all except Coffield. "I think about him constantly, wishing him back," Everson said. "I'd never have started this thing here, knowing him gone." But a week later, he wrote that it looked like the red tape binding up the transfer orders for Kermit and Kemper was nearly untangled. He added that he was sending a memo to the other camps, asking for photographers interested in transferring. Clayton had told him of two friends from Big Flats—a painter and a musician—who were interested in Waldport. Things were looking up, Everson said. "Come a runnin'."[17]

Printing had gone apace for the shows, done in the tradition of "ephemera"—small press runs of a single or folded sheet set up for a particular occasion and then the type distributed (taken apart and replaced in the case). One piece of ephemera, though, aimed for a larger purpose: a full broadside protest. It came about in response to a seemingly innocuous call for submissions to a proposed anthology of antiwar poetry, to be sponsored by the War Resisters League (WRL). "Here is a delicate commission for you," began a letter signed by WRL membership secretary Frances Rose Ransom. "For some time we have wondered if it might be possible to assemble for publication the best of the pacifist poetry from CPS." Ransom asked each camp to organize a poetry committee, collect submissions, and forward the five best poems to the WRL, whose own committee would then select their preferences and send those to an appointed editor, who in turn would have the final say.[18]

Taken at face value, this seemed logical enough. The WRL's mission had always been political—as the name said, to resist war—and they were asking for antiwar poetry. But it apparently pricked some sensitive egos in the Fine Arts, whose members perhaps considered themselves more qualified to select and publish such poetry. As if to prove as much, they set their response in letterpress type, produced a fine-looking seven-by-nineteen-inch broadside, and sent it across the CPS network:

An Indelicate Commission

We of the Fine Arts At Waldport, a venture of C.P.S. writers, artists, actors and musicians devoted to the furtherance of pacifist creative expression, are appalled. There is an issue at hand. We've been facing issues, as pacifists, ever since we came to the camps. We have not often faced them as artists. This one, then, is unique. We are not letting it by.

We are protesting the sponsorship, by the W.R.L., of the anti-war anthology of verse announced in its recent under-the-table circular. There has long been need of a collection of creative pacifist expression, and we will be the first to champion one, but the present venture is so limited in conception, so questionable in method, and placed in such inadequate hands for selection, that we consider its value not only negligible, but of actual danger to the incipient creative movement forming in American pacifism.

They spelled out their reasons for protest, and did acknowledge that their reaction might appear extreme. But, like any group of young artists struggling for recognition, they considered their mission profound:

Many will say this is taken too seriously, that we make a tempest in a teapot, that we are presumptuous and arrogant. But it is because we hold these things in too high regard to see them made cheap, the carry-all drudge of every program (even our own!) that hits the times, our statement is made. The arts can be among the most effective mediums pacifism has—but not by such means as these.[19]

It was indeed an excessive reaction. And its excessiveness was perhaps partly because the Untide Press crew felt a sense of ownership for the idea—they had, after all, been talking off and on about producing an anthology for the past year. Various friends and allies applauded them on the sharp, critical response. Morris Keeton, always a fan, sent a memo congratulating the Fine Arts on a "vigorous, yes, delightful, attack."[20] But a more objective view came from someone named Alan Harvey, who appeared to have had experience with the WRL. In reply to Everson's request for his opinion, he said he agreed in principle with the Fine Arts members, but felt that they might be attaching too much importance to the item. He suggested that the WRL was hardly an arbiter of artistic merit, and they were in all likelihood simply trying to expand the voices for war resistance. "You fellows are the artistic avant-garde of

CPS—whether you like it or not," he said. "Better take my advice and do your own anthology and trust that the WRL book won't be too bad; if it is, rest assured that it will carry its own death warrant."[21]

The group, acting either on Harvey's advice or of their own accord, printed up a similar-looking but less bombastic sheet, titled "An Importunate Proposition," in which they apologized for their earlier blast, confirmed that there was no ill will between the WRL and them, and then proposed that the Fine Arts serve as a center for creative work produced in CPS. This way, they said, they could eventually publish a worthy collection.[22]

Throughout the spring, guest speakers continued to fill the slates. April brought Katharine Whiteside Taylor, a pioneer in cooperative education in early childhood. William O. Mendenhall, who had resigned as president of Quaker-founded Whittier College in 1943 when they considered offering training programs for military groups, spoke of his personal vision of religion, frankly acknowledging that he could not prove God existed although he felt such a presence within himself. Ruth Suckow, a successful Iowa novelist with whom Everson had corresponded over the last year, gave popular talks titled "Poetry of Soldiers & Conscientious Objectors" and "Violence in Literature." But she preferred informal discussions over lectures, meeting in smaller groups to talk about writing and art. This was what the Fine Arts needed, Everson wrote to BSC headquarters, this interaction with artists already accomplished in their field. What Suckow brought was of vital importance: "The sense of dedication to the highest ideals of her art in a time when the written word has been debased by commercialism and political expediency."[23]

Even the *Tide* returned. Bill Eshelman took over the camp newsletter, dormant since the previous summer, and churned out a new edition on the old, battered mimeograph. It featured summaries of the Fine Arts and the Untide Press, reports on the early-spring sketching class with Waldo Chase, a recap of the weekend with the women visitors from Oregon State College, and a book review of Lillian Smith's *Strange Fruit*, the provocative novel of interracial romance and its consequences in the Deep South. Smith's book had already earned the dual badges of bestseller and "banned in Boston," but the *Tide* reviewer, Fine Arts member Glenn Evans, an African-American from Texas, already knew the subject well. "There is nothing new or sensational about the plot of *Strange Fruit*," Evans wrote. "This novel deals with characters and incidents that may be observed anywhere in the South." Evans acknowledged that Smith was a white woman from Georgia who had been denouncing segregation and bluntly challenging the deep racism of her region for years. But even she gave the most powerful scene in her book—a lynching—treatment at arm's length, Evans said. Citing his memory of a case in which a pregnant

African-American woman had been publicly hanged during World War I, he concluded, "One wonders if even Lillian Smith may not be reluctant to tell the horrible truth."[24]

Less serious but no less sharp was a front page satire of Dave Hall's *Lincoln County Times* column, "Ramblin' Around," in which he had earlier attacked the COs and Camp Angel. Titled "Rumblin' Around" by "Nave Haul," the *Tide* column took full liberties with Hall's typographical idiosyncrasies, including extended ellipses and spelling errors, while also poking fun at various campers in a manner reminiscent of the *Untide*. In fact, Eshelman—who had written more than half of the six-page newsletter—worried that it might be too much like the original *Untide*, in that nearly every story had some element of double meaning or side-handed commentary. "Did I go overboard on the side of satire and sarcasm?" he wondered. "Is the *Tide* too closely allied with the *Untide*?"[25]

Whether or not that was his overriding concern, Eshelman did not produce another *Tide*, nor did anyone else. Most likely, the reason was the same as for all the other projects that fell to the wayside: lack of time and energy. In Eshelman's case, he was simply spread too thin. Along with the assigned camp work, he was treasurer of both the Fine Arts and the Untide Press, as well as editor of the *Tide*. Something had to go, he wrote a friend, and then made clear his priorities: "The real contribution we are doing here will prove to be the Untide Press."[26]

The printing and other arts activities were certainly the focus of the camp, and they found their way into previously unlikely places. The monthly camp summary of statistics noting age, marital status, occupation, home states, religion, and education levels was now prepared by Eshelman as camp clerk. He created bar charts in color mimeograph, prompting education committee co-directors Glenn Evans and Bob Stevens to note in their monthly report to BSC headquarters, "A large number of these attractive summaries . . . are available to campers, guests and for official use." Perhaps this attitude rubbed off on others, as Evans and Stevens described widespread interest and activity through the spring and into the summer months. The reading series, with its opening of *Our Town* that included performers from both the Fine Arts and the greater camp membership, fostered a spirit of inclusiveness that carried into later readings. Presentations of George Bernard Shaw's *Androcles and the Lion*, Thornton Wilder's *The Woman of Andros*, Kurt Weill's *Johnny Johnson*, Stravinsky's *Petrouchka*, and *High Tor* by Maxwell Anderson were well represented and well attended. "These productions have probably done as much as any other single activity in cementing favorable relationships between the Fine Arts Group and the rest of the camp," the co-directors said.[27]

The crafts, too, offered a strong commonality. A large purchase of Oregon myrtle, that rare wood known for its burls and intricate grains,

Bruce Reeves took many of the Camp Angel photos with his Rolleicord camera.

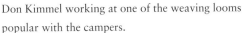

Don Kimmel working at one of the weaving looms popular with the campers.

sent camp members of all stripes into the wood shop, keeping the two lathes in constant use, turning out bowls and other items. They also constructed a kiln for ceramics and sent out samples of local clay for testing at the University of Oregon, which found the material suitable for the work. Weaving became very popular; after the purchase of a large loom introduced the men to this practical craft, they built seven smaller ones, even sending one to a side camp. Leather work was available, and some campers were learning block printing and creating personal letterheads for stationery. Bruce Reeves, a twenty-five-year-old Brethren who had come to Waldport in February, documented many activities with his Rolleicord camera, an affordable model popular with amateur photographers. "I wasn't what I'd call an artist," he said, "but I was very eager to make sure the artists could do what they needed to do and had time to do it."[28]

They were taking it outside the camp as well. Evans, also crafts director for the Fine Arts, spent a week in Portland teaching crafts at a community center, which led to similar invitations from the Oregon Baptists and a group in Seattle. "Such trips as these," the co-directors wrote, "are just tiny opportunities to render the type of 'Civilian Public Service' which many c.o.'s might be rendering day by day were they not held in securely and inconspicuously under the heel of Selective Service."[29]

Reading was, not surprisingly, stronger than at most CPS camps as the men at Waldport continued their regular monthly borrowing from the Oregon State Library in Salem (on top of their own library holdings), bought books and pamphlets from Portland booksellers, and added subscriptions to magazines such as *Bread and Butter, Free World,* the *New*

Republic, Etude, South Today, and *Pacifica Views* to their already sizable list. The co-op experienced a resurgence, a Spanish interest group was started, and discussion sessions began on how to reform the camp government to accommodate changing needs. The education committee approved "skills-interest" meetings for people interested in typing, auto mechanics, truck driving, radio, archery, and aeronautics. They weren't worried about formal classes, they said. "In a group with such varied interests and such little opportunity for desirable contact with the outside world, the more spontaneous the activities in 'our world' the better."[30]

There was something else at work—what Everson called the "all-pervasive Waldport equanimity." Men who had come from other camps reported having been told what time they should go to bed, when they should rise, and when they were to change their sheets. Martin Ponch had a long list of complaints from his time at a Friends' camp, and Clayton James and Harold Steers had nothing good to add about their experience at Big Flats, also run by the Friends. It didn't seem to matter what church was running a camp, however. A group recently transferred from Camp #42 in Wellston, Michigan—a Brethren camp—were "disillusioned, embittered, disgruntled CPSers," Everson said. But as the Waldport environment did its calming work, one Wellston transfer exclaimed, "The only trouble with this camp is that the morale is too high!" Certainly the men at Waldport had complaints, but when they came up, the new transfers laughed and said, "You don't know when you're well off!"[31]

Some comments, though, stung more than others. Hoping to increase visibility for the Fine Arts and related projects, Everson asked Henry Miller to submit something for the *Illiterati*. Miller sent his essay, "Of Art and the Future," declaring, "Nobody will agree with my views. It's a prophetic piece—and I go whole hog for the next thousand years, and beyond." Miller's essay went the same route as the other submissions, handed off from reader to reader at both Waldport and Cascade Locks, sometimes sent on the shuttle trucks along with food, work tools, and other gear to side camps where a member of the loosely assembled editorial board might be stationed.

And the *Illiterati* rejected Henry Miller. When Everson heard of this, he sent an apology to Miller, stating that he was not part of the *Illiterati* board. He also attempted to explain the conditions under which the men worked, and how what they accepted for publication must be something that spoke to them strongly enough that they could devote their energy and attention to printing it after doing manual labor for more than fifty hours a week.

Miller told Everson not to worry, that rejection didn't bother him. Besides, he said, the piece was already being published in three other countries—just not in America, which still banned most of his other writing. However, he added, he didn't understand exactly what their objections were. "The joke is, that here these lads are prisoners—because of their ideas!—and they haven't the tolerance to let a man, who is a friend of theirs and not an enemy, express his ideas freely. Don't they see the irony of that, I wonder?" Good thing he hadn't come up to direct the Fine Arts after all, he said. "They would have kicked me out in a few weeks, if not sooner." Then he tacked on a comment which in some respects was certainly true, but which also struck a raw nerve with COs nearly every time some version of it was uttered. "You really are sitting pretty," he wrote. "You're *protected*. And in a way, lucky, because under another regime (Republican, for instance) you would be dragging a ball and chain around." Never mind about the work and boredom and isolation, he said. "You had that when you were free, too. You can still dream."[32]

Maybe it was that raw nerve. Maybe Everson had had a bad day on Project, maybe he'd been reading some of Miller's books and was pricked by the rebellious spirit, or maybe he was simply tired. But something was stirred inside him, for Everson picked up his pen and took the master polemicist head-on. "Dear Henry," he wrote, "You've got us all wrong. It's wonderful here. Surely you've jumped to conclusions. Why, we love it." In two pages of tightly spaced typing, in the thickest sarcasm he'd perhaps ever written, he spelled out his "reasons" why CPS was so marvelous. First, he said, was the fact that one was never alone. Getting out of bed, at mealtimes, in the barracks listening to some "good brother" singing hymns or playing the radio, day or night, night or day, they were never, ever, left to the emptiness of being completely on their own. Of women, he said, "We simply don't have to bother with it anymore." Sure, there were those spells of "diabolical rut" when the hills "become female. The dead snags strain their white phalluses at the heaving clouds. The semen pours down the canyons. The ocean pants in its vast erotic mumble." But that was merely a physical problem, he said. They also avoided the evils of money. "Since there is none, it cannot taint us. We simply coast along in a kind of relaxed acceptance and take things as they come." So what if some family member has to work and send money for things like shoes or a pair of pants? "After all," he wrote, "the Good Book says: *ask, and ye shall receive*. A wonderful teaching, that." The best part of all, he said, was the work. "We thrust manfully about the hills with axes and hoes. . . . We sweat in the sunlight or trudge through the rain. . . . The rocks aren't really heavy, not when you love your work." He noted that the men in CPS had done nearly twenty-five million dollars' worth of work yet hadn't been paid a penny. This could be a model for other marginalized groups, he suggested—racial and cultural minorities, those who didn't fit the mainstream look and behaviors.

"Just like us c.o.'s," he said. "We're showing the way." He concluded by restating Miller's comment about being protected. "That's exactly right," he said. "Protected from all the humdrum trivia that used to trouble our days. Protected from the freedom of movement, the necessity of pay, the bother of marriage, the worry of earning a living." He invited Miller to come up to Waldport and give the conscripted life a try. "You really can't make a fair test in less than a year," he ended, "but you'll love it."[33]

A copy of the letter circulated around camp, if not raising morale at least providing some amusement and consolation. Miller, for his part, was unfazed. He'd blasted—and been blasted by—society enough times that he took literally nothing personally. He wrote back that he didn't mean to sound indifferent; surely Everson must know that he, Miller, had always felt that much of modern life was a kind of self-imposed incarceration. His timing for such a reminder was likely not very good, he said, and asked forgiveness. But make the most of it while you can, he added; to have any creative freedom at all is a rarity of the highest order—and that is worth more than anything. "There is so damned little freedom in the world, and yet so much, once one truly accepts the situation. It is all paradoxical, and at times the highest words on the subject have a ring of mockery." But it's true, he said, closing with a note that not long ago he had been offered everything he needed by a patron—and for a moment he'd felt complete freedom. "It was as if God had offered to make any dream come true," he said. "What happens then? O, a very wonderful thing. You realize that you need almost nothing."[34]

■ ■ ■

What the Fine Arts needed most right now was time. Even with help from the likes of Joe Kallal, the experienced pressman who'd come with the last transfers from Michigan, rolling up his sleeves and digging in each night, the men knew they couldn't keep up their pace and level of production without some sort of change. When Kermit and Kemper finally arrived at the end of June, there was so much going on that there was no time for celebration; they simply jumped into the mix as if they had never been away. This brought back together most of the founding group, Everson reported to Keeton. "They have set to work in their various ways on what we are beginning."[35]

Meanwhile, another Fine Arts member had quietly been making himself useful as he learned the ins and outs of the program. Vladimir Dupre, who had sweetened his transfer request with the note about his future wife's acting ability, arrived in March and joined the crews on Project, planting trees and cutting trails. An East Coaster who had spent time working with the War Resisters League in New York City, he found forestry work demanding and at times dangerous—although in places like Cape Perpetua, with its eight-hundred-foot-high promontory, the scenery was spectacular. And you never knew who you might meet, he remembered years later with a laugh, then told of working on a trail and finding himself suddenly face to face with a black bear. "We both turned around and ran in opposite directions!"[36]

After a short stint of firefighting—during which the men were stuck in the woods for a week when a self-set training fire got out of control—Dupre was rotated to night watchman duty, the same as Eshelman had been earlier that year. His fiancé was still back East, so he had no problem with the nighttime schedule, making his rounds through the dorms and other buildings. He got to know not only the physical camp but also the denizens of the night—the bakers in the kitchen, preparing their countless loaves of bread; a fellow or two in sick quarters who might be awake; the occasional bull session that carried on later than usual. The Fine Arts members, too, were hard at work—Everson, Eshelman, and sometimes Hackett and Harman in the rec hall, hunched over their type cases or feeding paper into the press. Once the theater program got going, Martin Ponch, David Jackson, Kermit, and others held play rehearsals in the chapel, the performers with scripts in hand, practicing memorization, intonation, blocking, pacing, and cues—and sometimes Bob Scott sat at the nearby piano, practicing and composing in his individual way. In the wee hours, Dupre recalled, once everyone had gone to sleep, he could hear the ocean through the trees and across the empty highway, like a neighbor keeping him company as he quietly made his rounds.[37]

Dupre earned a reputation as a reliable and committed Fine Arts member, often helping with the tedious chores that others shunned; when it became clear the directorship was too much for one person to handle, Everson approached Dupre about picking up the office administration duties. While Dupre was not technically an artist, his competence and enthusiasm were "a joy to behold," Everson wrote to Morris Keeton. They decided that Everson would retain the director title; Dupre would assume the Overhead time allotment and do the administrative work as executive secretary. Everson handed over the office with relief, telling Keeton he could expect far better record keeping and concrete evidence of what they accomplished.[38]

His first day on the job, Dupre fired off a letter to Keeton, outlining plans to more effectively communicate the Fine Arts work and mission to other CPS camps. They'd review past accomplishments, current activities, and plans for the future, he said, then offered as an example their idea to provide a complete portfolio of every theater production, including notes on direction along with the script and pictures of the set. These could be sent singularly to other camps, or even made into a catalogue, he said.

"Many more ideas are in the process of formation and as they develop, I shall send them along." He signed it, "Vladimir Dupre, Executive Sec."[39]

Interestingly, in all this activity and correspondence, there is no mention of D-Day. The largest military invasion in the history of the world garners no mention in Warren Downs's diary, Everson's letters to Powell, Eshelman's letters to his friends, the Fine Arts meetings minutes, or even the Camp Angel records. The event was probably noted somewhere, but Downs's entry for June 6, 1944, speaks only of a visit by Forest Service officials from Washington, DC, who talked about the difficulty of finding work for COs that matched their skills and abilities. His entry for June 7 covers not the Allied landings in Europe but another kind of invasion much closer to home: "Last night at 1:30, Bruce Reeves and Vladimir Dupre burst into the dorm and went tearing up and down the length of the hall, swearing, shouting about fires, roughing up Scott and Mac (just a little) and generally making fools of themselves." They were drunk, having spent the evening at a party in the cabin across the highway rented by Clayton and Barbara James. Downs adds that Jim Harman, who perhaps enjoyed drink a bit too much, couldn't be roused for work call the next morning. The cellist ends the day's entry not in comment on the world conflagration but with a note about a talented violinist, who had been playing since the age of three, thinking of coming to Waldport and bringing a friend who also played. "The first violinist's ambition is to form a string quartet in CPS," Downs wrote. "Man, what a boon that would be to the drear existence here."[40]

War? These people literally had no use for it.

■ ■ ■

When Clayton James arrived in April, he and Everson easily fell into their own late-night bull sessions as they sorted through some difficult fundamental beliefs. Clayton was seeking something beyond the Methodist Church, and Everson was attempting to understand his very soul. "Clayton James is a great man," Everson wrote to Powell. "A terrific, natural, simple person. A man capable of enormous, sudden concentration. A religious man, batting his head out on the physical restrictions that keep him from God. His paintings are one prolonged search."[41]

After Barbara Straker arrived and became Barbara Straker James, and the newlywed couple took the cabin across the highway, Everson would come over for "long philosophical discussions" about religion and art and the meaning of life, Clayton recalled decades later. "That was the basic thing; that was our big subject matter." Barbara added, "We were searching for the absolute. We tried to reduce everything to one—one solution, one creator, and in Clayton's painting, one simple element or symbol."[42]

Everson was so impressed with Clayton that he asked him to illustrate his next book, which would be the second Untide Press work done on a letterpress and the first one done completely on the large Challenge Gordon machine. Everson had been writing a series on his CPS experience, which he called, appropriately enough, *The Waldport Poems*. Clayton didn't much care for the title, and Everson considered an alternative—*Infertile Flower*, alluding to the frustration and pointlessness many found in the work at CPS—but the original title eventually prevailed. The eleven numbered poems were, Everson wrote in the preface, "an attempt to render whole the emotional implications of a kind of life that has become almost universal; the life of the camp, the life of enforced confinement, individual repression, sexual segregation." Such places were everywhere—huge, temporary centers holding millions, he wrote: "conscription camps, concentration camps, prison camps, internment camps, labor camps." The scars from these places lasted for generations, he said, and what he hoped to do with *The Waldport Poems* was to address the deeper consequences of war—none of which was more universal than separation. He'd seen its consequences in the lives of others, and in his own disintegrating marriage. In this oft-quoted stanza, from poem number 8, he aims to strip bare his emotions and reveal the bone:

The man struck from the woman—
That is the crime.
As the armies grow so gathers the guilt,
So bloom the perversions,
So flower the fears,
So breed the deep cruelties
And the secretive hurts.
And each, the man and the woman,
Too much alone,
Age and grow cold.

Clayton had been focusing on painting, but for the poems he created four linoleum cuts, simple abstract images exploring the relationship between dark and light. He also designed the book, placing one image on the cover and the remaining three opposite particular poems, striving to communicate through that "one simple element or symbol." It was clearly the most accomplished work yet produced by the Untide Press, and when the book came out late in the summer, reviewers responded accordingly. *Pacifica Views* saw it as a statement not just from Everson and Camp Angel but one for all conscientious objectors. It was, they said, "an expression of poetic insight joined with craftsman's skill of which we may all be proud." *Accent* magazine called it "beautifully printed." *Poetry* deemed it a "shrewd and aware . . . voice in the wilderness." Glen Coffield also weighed in from Cascade Locks, declaring that the book

THE
WALDPORT
POEMS

WILLIAM
EVERSON

"this, then, is our world . . ." a record of the conscripted
life. . . . . block prints by Clayton James . . . . printed in
two colors on Linweave paper . . . . twenty-five cents
UNTIDE PRESS, CAMP ANGEL, WALDPORT, OREGON

exceeded all expectations in both design and content. He added further
approval about another decision: "I can't tell you how damn glad I am
that you changed the title. *Infertile Flower* sounds too much like an editorial opinion. Not only that—it would be a tacit admission that even the
poems were no good since they came out of C.P.S." *The Waldport Poems*
had the right sound, he said. "I always did like that name Waldport."[43]

Everson, working now with a real press and an officially recognized
group of artists, raised the bar on his own work and the expectations for
others. Since Clayton James came on the scene, he wrote to Powell, "I
have slowly altered my attitude toward art and illustration."[44]

Sharing space in the printing room was the third issue of the *Illiterati*,
which Kermit and Kemper had been assembling at Cascade Locks and
now brought to Waldport. In the summer of 1944, they put out the
issue as a combination of mimeographed and letterpress printed pages.
It featured what could be called the usual suspects—Kermit, Kemper,
Everson, and Coffield, along with Don Baker and Harry Prochaska from
Cascade Locks—and also included artwork by Clayton James. A "Choral
Prelude" for organ filled three pages of musical transcription composed by
William Henderson, a CO cellist in Washington State who also played in
the Tacoma Symphony. The center spread was a poem by Everson, titled
"Though Lying with Woman," decorated with Kemper's surrealistic art-
work, including one more nude woman reclining—but this one with arms
completely outstretched, no facial features at all, and legs fading into a
gray quadrilateral image. "Agnes" had dissolved into abstraction.

Another poem was set up sideways in a long vertical spread across
two pages with its title running at an angle like a steep slope, a concrete
representation of the title: "Contemplation of My Navel on the Slope
of Mt. Hood." Written by Del Vaniman, a young CO from California
and stationed at Cascade Locks, it began with a light-hearted, literal

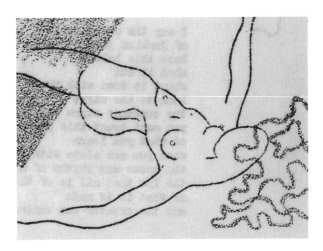

description of the title: "Oh you small round circular dent, / Crevassed and sprouting with hair, / What deep significance do you / Conceal in the hidden valleys of your nature?" But five more stanzas have the reader wondering if maybe he's not kidding after all, as he heads into a series of questions about humanity's achievements and the meaning of life, concluding, "Must I seek solace in the fact that / Seventy years is all the grace given to man? / It would be hard to find in a time such as this."[45]

The poet Bill Stafford, now at Camp #134 in Belden, in the mountains east of California's Sacramento Valley, offered a two-page prose meditation titled "So Long, Chimes" about a fellow with this unique name. "I remember coming down from Little Pine Mountain in a truckload of men with Chimes," Stafford wrote. "We were packed in, prisoners from the war camp, rolling along in the open air, singing and talking." In the story a fellow named Yogi Ed talked with Chimes about their work of cutting down trees:

> "I don't see why we should do it," Yogi Ed was saying. "We've got no right. They belong here. . . . Yes, I think all things trying deserve our respect." A hawk rested on the sun-shaft air; and, watching directly, coldly, I thought about these two men, prisoners in a world at war, talking along, happy with benevolence, wondering if it is right to cut down a tree.[46]

Kermit contributed a two-page rumination titled "Pilgrimage to Henry Miller," which recounted a visit he, Kemper, and Don Baker made while on furlough to the author's home in Big Sur (with no mention of Miller's earlier rejected manuscript). It opens with a stream-of-consciousness rush: "Kathie and Junior whispered to me that they didn't want to go in, and I whispered back that I didn't either—it was mostly Don and Kemper's idea—but we might as well, so they said ok and we all piled out of Brunnhilde and trooped up to the door." Then it moves through a phantasmagoria of images and commentary, a wild collage of their moment in the house with the famous author and assorted characters, ending with the line, "It all seems like a hop-head's dream."[47]

Near the end of the issue is another photo of Coffield—rather, a photo of a painting of Coffield, done by Kemper and accompanied by a poem that just might have had its genesis in that discussion on "true philosophy" he'd had months ago with Everson, one afternoon out on Project:

THE ONLY ABSOLUTES ARE THOSE MEN DREAM ABOUT

A mountain stands by more than definition;
More than all words can speak about,
Is physical condition.
Proof needs the case left out.

Yet, love is more than everyday illusion,
More than just an act—
A crystal of confusion,
Unverifiable fact.[48]

Waldport now had three printing projects: the Untide Press, the *Illiterati,* and the *Compass* (for which Martin Ponch was planning a full section on the Fine Arts). Although each was officially a separate entity— and none were under the aegis of the Fine Arts—their memberships, materials, and equipment overlapped; sometimes they even borrowed money from one another. It was an intense concentration of literary and publishing activity, certainly the largest in the country in relation to CPS and pacifism. They also had the beginnings of a cooperative theater, with people experienced in repertory, classical, and modern approaches. They had highly competent musicians giving top-notch recitals, and the likelihood of some extraordinary talent on the way. Their painters and photographers enjoyed the inspiration of both nature and community, with inquiries going out to accomplished artists, inviting them to spend a residency. The crafts program aimed to engage campers and their wives who perhaps didn't consider themselves specifically artists but who could produce weavings, carvings, and pottery for exhibit, use, and perhaps even sale.[49]

It was all coming together. Young men and women with energy and talent. Big ideas with institutional backing. A chance to do something more than bide their time. The forces that had put them here were now channeled into something productive. Literature, art, theater, music, crafts—all out here at the end of the continent, here on the edge of nowhere.

CHAPTER 8

As Close as It Gets to a School

NOT LONG AFTER Kermit and Kemper arrived, they were joined by their good friend, a woman who came to occupy a unique place in the Fine Arts. Manche Langley, twenty-six years old and single, came from Portland, where her father had been a district attorney and her aunt one of the city's first female lawyers.[1] Surrounded by academics and intellectuals, Manche developed a curiosity and confidence that sometimes took her beyond the accepted norms for a young woman in 1930s mainstream society, reading George Bernard Shaw and deciding to start a pacifist club at her Catholic school. "I was totally unfearful," she remembered, "most unusually so." After high school, she hit the road (more literally, the water), spending time in Hawaii and then San Francisco, where she lived among the artists and radicals in the jazz clubs and "crash pads" of that city's North Beach neighborhood. From a communal apartment on Telegraph Hill, they'd walk down to places like the Black Cat, a popular bohemian hangout sometimes visited by authors William Saroyan and John Steinbeck. "The only career I wanted was to get on a tramp steamer and go around the world," she said.[2]

When Pearl Harbor hit, she was in Los Angeles, working as an office proofreader. Up until this time, the antiwar mood in America was still strong, she recalled, but after the attack even the peace advocates supported calls for war. The military bases went on high alert, and the planes swooping low over the city made her sick, she said. "I was born a pacifist; I can't stand conflict." She headed back to Portland, but found generally the same attitudes there. "There was no one in Portland that felt the way I did," she remembered. "No friends, no family, no anybody."[3]

In spring 1942 she took a job with a railroad company, walking the yards and inspecting the cars. Talking at lunch one day with another young woman, she learned about a conscientious objectors' camp up the Columbia River at Cascade Locks, and jumped at the invitation to attend a barn dance there. She met Kermit and Kemper and other creative people from the camp, people who felt the same way she did, who shared the

Manche Langley at Cascade Locks, ca. 1942.

same values and convictions about peace and war and art and life, people who were outsiders just like her. "It was like coming home," she said.[4]

She regularly visited the main camp and side camps in the region, sometimes staying over and helping out wherever she could. When Kermit and Kemper transferred to Waldport and suggested she come assist with the Fine Arts, she said she liked the idea, but they'd better have some real work for her to do. "I don't want to just languish down there," she wrote. "It drives me buggy and I start feeling horribly useless."[5]

Shortly thereafter, she quit her job in Portland and made a final visit to Cascade Locks, writing an account of her weekend that reads like an episode from the frantic adventures of the Beat Generation wanderers, who were yet a decade away from the national spotlight. She kayaked across the Columbia River one night; the next evening she was at a side camp in the tiny mountain town of Zigzag, watching a movie with the COs, who were on forest-fire alert:

> It was all mad—among other things—in the midst of the movie, a fire was announced—everyone rushed out. I went to the highway to hitch-hike back home. [Two camp members] came by on their way to the fire—I got in. Everyone returned from the fire—which wasn't—more movie. And then 12 of us and luggage layered ourselves into the camp car and headed [to Cascade Locks]. I got out at Gresham [southeast of Portland] at about 12 and rapidly found there was no bus for 1 hour. As I moaned and groaned on the street corner, a novel creature in an ancient Model A churned along, asked if I'd like a ride to Portland and I jumped in, but quick. He soon resolved himself into a wonderful character—used to break horses in Southern Utah. AND he worked just a skip and a jump from 1505 [her home], so I got a ride to the door. If it hadn't been for the lovely man, I'd probably still be leaning against a telephone pole in Gresham.[6]

A week later she was at Camp Angel, bunking in a cubbyhole room in Kimmel Hall, the guest house at the corner of the camp where Maude Gregory the camp matron lived. Manche helped out as a secretary for the Fine Arts, typing correspondence and handling other office duties. The early days were "a really nice time," she said. She'd wake in the morning and go down to the dining hall after the men had left for Project work, and someone in the kitchen (usually Kermit, who'd established himself as a conscientious and quality chef) would fix her breakfast and maybe sit with her while she ate. She would then meet Vlad Dupre at the Fine Arts office, adjacent to the printing press room in the recreation hall, and dive into the paperwork. "I am still astonished at how much work we were able to turn out," she remembered. "Vlad and I worked hard. And we worked regularly; it was a routine."[7]

They'd work until lunchtime, then head up to the dining hall for a bite, after which Vlad would retire to the dorm and Manche went to her room for half an hour to read or take a short nap. Then they worked until the dinner hour, when all the campers returned. After dinner, she said, "is when the real work began."[8]

They would head back to the rec hall and into the press room. Setting type was intricate and painstaking labor, and Manche felt she was better at larger tasks, such as running the press. Doing that work properly required a particular combination of speed and coordination, she later recalled. The paper had to be inserted into the press and pulled out after printing, and each one set on an adjacent flat surface with a blank sheet slipped in between so that the ink wouldn't smudge—and all this done in rhythm with the machine. "I was the only one who could do that and smoke a cigarette at the same time."[9]

She was more than just another worker, though. She was smart and tough, which made her one of the gang. She was also a single woman—a rare creature in the CO environment—*and* she could buy liquor. Oregon's laws at the time were such that only state residents could buy liquor; they applied for and then were issued a card. So, when a party or gathering was lined up, usually at the Tillie the Whale cabin communally rented by the Fine Arts, they'd collect the money, then Manche would go to Waldport and procure the liquor. The townspeople would stare at her when she came in, Manche recalled. One time, she was walking down

Vlad Dupre and Manche Langley working on Fine Arts correspondence. Painting on wall is by Kemper Nomland.

the street and a pair of large women blocked her way. "Why don't you join the WACs?" they said. "I don't want to," she replied. The women couldn't seem to find a response to that, and they let her pass.[10]

Manche didn't let episodes like this get her down. "I was happy-go-lucky always," she said, "always good-natured." It was easy enough for a camper to become depressed, she added. "The guys didn't want to be there. So I was good at keeping their spirits up."[11]

As word got out and the Fine Arts took shape, members focused more on recruiting others whose contributions might help fulfill their mission. Not long after Clayton James arrived from Big Flats, he'd told Everson about two men back there—both violinists. Broadus "Bus" Erle had been playing since he was three years old; he had studied at the Curtis Institute in Philadelphia, played in classical string quartets and vaudeville, and done live radio with the NBC orchestra just before the war. His wife, Hildegarde, was a pianist also trained in composition, and Erle was adamant that she and their two-year-old daughter, Robin, be allowed to accompany him wherever he may be transferred. Hildegarde's music background would perhaps fit into the Fine Arts program, he suggested, and he also had an idea for child care for Robin—a cooperative living arrangement with the other possible Big Flats transferee, Bob Harvey and his wife, Joyce.[12]

Harvey was a multitalented artist with the temperament to match. He could paint and write and play the violin—and do all three quite competently. He was enthusiastic, handsome, charismatic, curious, and opinionated. In a word, mercurial. Born of a wealthy family in upstate New York, he graduated cum laude from Phillips Andover Academy in Massachusetts, where he'd dismayed his fellow students by refusing to play sports although he was built like a fullback. He went to Dartmouth, riled sensibilities there and got kicked out, then went to study art in New York City, where he met and married Joyce Lancaster, also an artist. Seeking an unconventional life, they went to the Catskills and tried subsistence farming, but with little success. When Harvey's draft call came, the twenty-nine-year-old artist applied for CO status, citing a Quaker background in his family, and was sent to Big Flats, a few hours from where he was living.[13]

At the Friends-administered camp, Bus Erle and Harvey quickly connected through their shared interest in music. With their added nonconformity, they soon enough irritated camp administrators—so when the invitation came from Waldport, a transfer made sense in more ways than one. The musicians sent a letter to Dick Mills, stating that they had no money and asking if the camp could board their wives for a month or two until the women might find work and afford a place to live. Mills shared this information with the Fine Arts office, and Dupre wrote back that, while the camp administration said they couldn't support some campers' wives and refuse others, perhaps the Fine Arts could arrange something. "We are exceedingly anxious for you to come and we will do all in our power to ease any difficult situation," Dupre said, "for we are launching an extensive program and we need your contributions."[14]

The Brethren Service Committee, however, didn't share the enthusiasm of the Fine Arts. The same day Vlad Dupre was penning his positive thoughts from Waldport to Erle and Harvey, BSC secretary W. M. Hammond in Elgin wrote a reply to the American Friends Service Committee (AFSC), who had requested clearance for the men to be transferred from the Big Flats camp. "We are sorry that we feel compelled to tell you that we cannot at this time accept the above two men at any Brethren camp," Hammond said. Apparently Erle and Harvey had requested work in the kitchen or elsewhere on the camp grounds, what Hammond termed "special berths" in assignment. They needed men at Waldport, he said, but only men who would do Project work. Referring to the men's ratings of suitability for CPS provided by the AFSC administrators, Hammond said, "All indications are that these two men have not been sufficiently 'oriented' to get them out of the 'highly doubtful' class. This is particularly true of Robert Harvey."[15]

When Clayton heard about this evaluation, he was livid. He sent a letter to Harvey, expressing his anger and exasperation; Harvey replied that he was mystified by the administrators' reticence to release Erle and him if they were as bad as described. It was, he said, ultimately a matter of being caught in the bureaucratic web. "The people who hold the reins are, as you know, small-minded bigots," he wrote. "They are tangled in a maze of proper forms and office routine that pretty well smothers the purely human issues to death. And to bore through this dense wall of beurocracy [sic] and callousness takes—well, words fail me." But they weren't going to give up, he said, and then promised, "If I by some chance do not get this transfer I am going to make life at Big Flats a fucking nightmare. I'll probably only succeed in landing myself in the guardhouse or in some spike camp in the Great Basin Desert, but I'm going to have some fun first."[16]

Everson, too, was incensed. He felt strongly that the Fine Arts, not the disinterested administrators, should be choosing the people they wanted to accept in the program—but he knew that only a measured response with a tone of inquiry would stand a chance of accomplishing anything. "The past several days have brought developments indicating a general lack of clarity in regard to transfer procedure to the Fine Arts," he wrote Hammond. Recent approvals of transfer for people entirely unknown to the Fine Arts, and rejections for people the Fine Arts had requested (such as Erle and Harvey), did not consider the group's specific needs, he said.

"It would seem well to devise, for the future, some method by which we could indicate any man's acceptability for a specific arts group transfer, unless this is a privilege not granted to other specialized schools."[17]

The wheels of the system slowly creaked along.

■ ■ ■

July signaled legitimate summer and the beginning of the heavy fire season in the Northwest. As men headed out to side camps, fire lookout towers and other dry-season assignments, the main camp population was reduced so much that when the Fine Arts gave its first public reading of *Our Town*, the readers outnumbered the audience.[18] But this didn't stop them from doing another show, *The Mikado in CPS*, a parody by Kermit Sheets adapted from Gilbert and Sullivan's long-popular *Mikado*, itself a satire of British government in the 1890s. The COs had performed the show back in February at Cascade Locks to an enthusiastic reception. With only three actors available for the ten parts—and a chorus—Kermit and company tailored the show to Waldport circumstances, turning a sharp eye and pen to the absurdities and hypocrisies of CPS, not entirely unlike the *Untide* had done the previous year. A particularly hilarious skewering came in the song, "I've Got a Little List," in which the acting assistant director rattles off the identities of the COs who would be reclassified as 1-A-O and sent to noncombatant military duty:

> There's the cheerful riser in the dorm who sings a merry note,
> At six a.m. he grins so gay, you'd like to slit his throat;
> The cook who makes the lunches you consume out in the rain
> of sandwich one and two and three—I'd just as soon abstain;
> The guy prolonging meetings, of all talk monopolist—
> They'd none of 'em be missed, they'd none of 'em be missed.[19]

Writing the parody didn't take long, Kermit recalled, and there was apparently never another performance of what he termed a "stupid little skit." But enough requests for the lyrics came that he eventually printed up a script on the letterpress, complete with color line drawings and abstract graphics very much in the manner of the *Illiterati*—enough so that it was designated an *Illiterati* publication. Of the piece's origin, the preface stated, "In the finale, the phrase—'we merrily sing to keep face'—wryly expresses the spirit which prompted writing this parody." It was also how Kermit learned to set type, deepening his experience and relationships with others in the Fine Arts.[20]

The Fine Arts theater group had officially formed in June when David Jackson, Martin Ponch, and Kermit sat down and outlined the reading series. Now that regular shows had commenced, they drew up a statement of purpose describing their reasoning and objectives—agreeing heavily with Ponch's "Towards a Legitimate Theatre" (which Kermit had read and admired) and the principles of community theaters like Hedgerow, from where Jackson had recently come. The focus was on a fulfilling experience for both the participants and audience. They wanted to allow room for experimental and educational projects that might not fit within the overall Fine Arts intentions, but on one thing they were adamant: quality. "Plays are to be chosen because they are good plays, rather than because they have literary merit alone, or good scene design possibilities alone, or any other single aspect which is only part of the finished production as seen by an audience." Their interest was in cooperative, not amateur, theater.[21]

With this in mind, they chose for their first production *Aria da Capo*, an antiwar verse play by Edna St. Vincent Millay, the popular poet known for her sonnets and who had connections to the Provincetown Players. First produced in late 1919, just one year after the end of World War I, the play juxtaposed tragedy and farce, bringing into sharp relief the decadence of modern society and the consequences of its horrifically destructive ways—the right combination of serious art and pacifist philosophy sought by the Fine Arts. David Jackson took the reins as director and lined up the five-member cast. Manche would play Columbine, the sole female role; Kermit would be her counterpart, Pierrot, in the farcical play-within-a-play. Bill Eshelman and Enoch Crumpton (who had come to Waldport in February) would play the tragic shepherds, Corydon and Thursis. Vlad Dupre—although he'd said he possessed no artistic talent—would be Cothurnus, the "Masque of Tragedy," who oversaw the action. However, duty called people away for the summer work and fire season. It would be two months before the curtain rose on *Aria da Capo*.

■ ■ ■

Meanwhile, Adrian Wilson arrived. An optimistic and idealistic young student from Wesleyan University in Connecticut, the kind of fellow you immediately call by his first name, Adrian had already experienced three CPS assignments before Waldport. At Big Flats, run by the American Friends Service Committee, he cleared land as a stump puller and broke up concrete floors in old barns as part of an air-hammer crew. He was intensely self-conscious about meeting the demands of the job even though the COs there knew it was make-work labor, something to keep them out of the public eye. "I am consciously trying to throw everything into a task," Adrian wrote his parents. "And secondly I am trying to *run*, not walk, the second mile for Selective Service and the A.F.S.C., trying to *turn* the other cheek, not just let them hit it.[22]

He took that attitude to Camp #94 at Trenton, North Dakota, where he dug ditches and did farm work. At the height of his idealism, he embarked on a life of "voluntary poverty" and posted a "Denial of Ownership" statement on the camp bulletin board, announcing that he had placed all his possessions in public-use areas, "in hope that they will be used freely and without hesitation by all campers and staff members who so desire."[23]

This was followed by a stint as a guinea pig in medical experiments at the University of Minnesota. While not one of the thirty-six test subjects in what came to be known infamously as the Minnesota starvation experiment, Adrian did take part in studies involving extended inactivity, spending two weeks lying as still as possible in bed. At one point in the experiment, the doctor realized that even allowing the men to lean over and flip the phonograph records they listened to might throw off the results, and volunteers were brought in to handle that chore. He was allowed to write, though, and his extended idleness provided time for much thought and reflection on various topics, including the nature of freedom. To be completely free, he felt, he would have to walk out of CPS—whereupon he would be picked up, sent to jail, and no longer be free. But even in jail, he believed, if he lived purely according to his convictions, he would be spiritually free. "I should not have a moment's doubt that I will be left completely free, especially if I justify that freedom with a more significant life than I am living here." Always inclined toward the arts, already an accomplished clarinetist and with ambitions to be a writer, he noted, "Of course I realize that real freedom comes only in the individual creative experience."[24] Two months later he saw a flyer for something called the School of Fine Arts at a camp in Oregon, and by the end of July he was in Waldport.

"The Fine Arts already!" he wrote to his family while listening to Stravinsky in the dorm his first night in camp. He was impressed by the music room with its built-in record player and speakers, by the auditorium and its stage, by the successful honor system of the self-service co-op store, by the camp guest house with its "cozy living-room supervised by gray-haired Mrs. Gregory," and, after his time in the arid North Dakota camp, perhaps impressed most of all by the flush toilets.[25]

The arts were clearly a presence, although he noted the oft-asked question, "Are you a fine arts man?" seemed to indicate that to some campers the group was separate and even exclusive. Of the Fine Arts members, he found Everson "not the suave artist I had expected but a gawky, tousled-black-haired dreamer" and Vlad Dupre sporting "the most abundant of beards in a place where beards are very abundant." He attended a prayer meeting his first night, but didn't care for the kneeling, hymn-singing and testimonials—particularly from one fellow who swore that God had saved him from a truck accident that very afternoon.[26]

A few nights later were more to his liking, when he met most of the Fine Arts members at a party across the highway in their Tillie the Whale cabin. There, aided by the ambiance of the nearby surf, the crackling logs in the fireplace, and a couple glasses of scotch and soda, he took in this group he'd traveled to the edge of the continent to join:

> It was cozy to the point of congestion and smelled like the Goodyear but the talk was highly spiritual, Everson leading on the methods of writing or being creative, why we feel inspired or obsessed, and the relationship between the artist and the mystic. I took the point of view of the straight mechanist; he left room for the freedom of will and God. The others, including Manche Langley, the camp's "U.S.O." girl, and Barbara James, Clayton's pretty wife, introduced objections, illustrations, and confusion. It broke up about two with Jim Harmon [sic], getting slightly high, reading a criticism by an unschooled pulp writer who couldn't understand why Leonardo da Vinci's men didn't have balls. Everybody thought this was very funny.

As far as he could tell, Adrian said, "this is as close as the School of Fine Arts gets to school. The rest of it is individual creation and mutual stimulation. Occasionally they work together on publications and on the weekly play readings."[27]

New transfers to the camp were given a period to acclimate before being assigned to Project work, and Adrian began by sweeping the barracks. His first day on the job he met Martin Ponch, also pushing a broom, who told him about the *Compass* magazine and recruited his help even though Adrian knew nothing of typesetting or publishing. But he never got started, because a week later he was sent out on Project, chopping away at Forest Service fire-access roads, and was then assigned to the Mary's Peak side camp, where twenty men would spend two weeks bushwhacking trails and maintaining roads while on constant fire alert. He was impressed with being issued a pair of brand-new, eighteen-dollar caulk boots such as loggers wear, but he expressed surprise that he was being sent away from the main camp—when he had transferred specifically to join the Fine Arts. Even so, Adrian found plenty to be positive about up on Mary's Peak, including the impressive forest and breathtaking views. He even got to bring his clarinet, and his second night there he took part in a jam session with a Jehovah's Witness who had an accordion—and who, Adrian declared, played his instrument better than Adrian played his own.[28]

During the days, as they hiked through the brush, clearing tree limbs along miles of telephone lines connecting the ranger stations, he observed the beauty and breadth of the great Pacific Northwest forests:

> Yesterday was the finest I have ever had on project. Carroll McMillen and I started out in the clear blue morning on the

Fine Arts core members heading for the beach. L-R: Adrian Wilson, Clayton James, Vlad Dupre, Bill Everson.

east side of the Coast Range in the "Corvallis Watershed, No Trespassing." Immediately we were in thick forest and before we had tramped half a mile we began to encounter big trees, mostly aged Douglas firs. For the rest of the day we were in a cathedral walking on the soft needled floor through arches a hundred or more feet high. . . . Whenever we would come to an especially beautiful grove we would stop and browse around looking up the strong straight trunks into the mossy branches as if these firs were great leatherbound volumes in some ancient library.[29]

All was not peace and poignancy, though. The road from Waldport to Corvallis, rising to summit the Coast Range at 1,400 feet and then winding and twisting down hairpin curves to the hundred-mile-long Willamette Valley, was the main line for the truckers driving furiously to carry out the timber from the seemingly endless forests. "Over this tortuous ribbon the logging trucks grind all day long," Adrian wrote, "fairly grunting under two, three, or four fir logs two or three and a half feet thick, and occasionally one really big one four to seven feet in diameter, all thirty-two feet in length so that they will yield two batches of sixteen-foot boards." The trucks huffed and puffed to the summit, then, with a clashing of gears roared down to the valley, screeching on the curves and leaving a trail of steam from their water-cooled brakes. Once unloaded, the two-piece trailer was decoupled at the halfway point and the back half lifted with a crane and placed piggyback on the front half, with the beam protruding over the cab. The drivers then raced back up over the hill for their next load. They were paid according to how much they hauled, and could make forty dollars a day pushing so hard that they wore out a truck after just three months. "It is a frightening industry," Adrian wrote, "this ruthless plundering of the forests and noisy hauling of the fat logs, full of the power, wealth, and immensity of the Northwest."[30]

While the summer fire season practically emptied out the camp—at one point in early August nearly all Project men were at side camps or on fire detail—the men in Overhead positions remained on site. True, Adrian was on Mary's Peak, Warren Downs had gone to a fire lookout tower, and others like Kemper and Jim Harman were scattered here and there. But a working core group of Fine Arts men were together in the camp. Kermit and Clayton were in the kitchen. Vlad Dupre was now on Overhead as the Fine Arts director (or executive secretary, depending on the stationery), and Manche was officially employed as the Fine Arts secretary, paid through the program's monthly allotment from BSC headquarters. Bill Eshelman had moved to camp clerk. David Jackson was in the office, too, and Everson, while not working in the Fine Arts office anymore, continued more or less directing the show.[31]

With the *Waldport Poems* finished, Everson and Kemper went to work on a typeset version of the *War Elegies*, something they'd wanted to complete since a real printing press had become available. It would bring a kind of closure to the period of early, raw, and somewhat undisciplined activity. They'd been the loosely connected group that put out the *Untide,* the *Illiterati,* and some mimeographed books. Now they were the Fine Arts at Waldport, a destination for talent and energy, attracting accomplished artists committed to their work.

■ ■ ■

One afternoon at the end of July, a letter came addressed to Everson and Clayton. Dated merely "Sunday," it read:

> Wm Everson, Clayton James: I have had a very fine journey down the coast—Have taken a cabin at Waldport.—Would like a few days to feel further toward the informing-essence of this coast country.
>
> I realize this (via letter) is now a very indirect way to communicate with you—I hope you will forgive it.
>
> I did not look you up today not because I do not accept your generous offer to supply a place for me at the camp—it is, I must confess, that I have not yet disciplined myself to learn to retain a certain necessary balance (for painting) when sharing with others a diagram of space—. However, I do fully believe that the cross currents, the individual rhythms, must be far less opposing at Camp Angle [*sic*] than elsewhere where men are under conscription. —I confess further—camping + removed from Camp Angle [*sic*] is not an avoidance of the reasonably varying rhythms—it is attempting to use my present freedom to live within the consciousness of another realm-of-law.
>
> I will come see you in a very few days.
>
> With best wishes
>
> Morris Graves

The mystic painter from the rainforests of Washington's Olympic Peninsula, who was just a few years away from international fame, had arrived.

Graves was a Pacific Northwest original if ever there was one. Born into a large Methodist family in the high desert sage country of eastern Oregon, then growing up in Seattle from the age of one, he dropped out of high school and signed on to a merchant ship. Visiting the Philippines, China, and Japan, he was particularly affected by the aesthetic and cultural approach to life in the Far East. He finished high school at age twenty, impressing teachers and students alike with his obvious artistic talent and eccentric behavior. He traveled to New York, the Virgin Islands, and back to the Pacific Northwest, where he divided his time between Seattle and an isolated island on Puget Sound. There, he built a home on a bluff, constructed in harmony with its surroundings and which he named The Rock. It was there, during the thick summer nights redolent with the whispers of the forest canopy and eerie bird calls, and during the long, bleak winters of endless gray, the incessant pounding of the surf and the steady drip, drip, drip of the rain, that he developed the works he called the Inner Eye series—using birds as symbols of spiritual enlightenment and yearning. A Seattle art dealer sent them to the New York Museum of Modern Art, where they were snapped up and included in a 1942 exhibit—where Clayton James, then an art student, had seen them and been profoundly moved. "The images seen within the space of the inner eye are as clear as 'seeing stars' before your eyes if you get up suddenly," Graves said of these works. "It is certain they are subjective, yet there is the absolute feeling that they are outside around your head."[32]

When his draft number was called, Graves registered as a conscientious objector, but a series of misunderstandings put him at the induction center. Realizing too late that he could not leave, he resorted to his last defense and refused to recite the oath of allegiance. He was sent to a military stockade, where he spent nearly a year fighting the system, and enduring hard labor and depression, until a psychiatrist determined that he would never adapt to military service. He was released with an honorable discharge, which he also refused to acknowledge. Graves had done his time the hardest way possible, Everson commented years later. Going to the induction center and refusing to take the oath was a direct challenge to military authority, leaving in their eyes no choice but to do everything they could to break the will of the objector.[33]

It was not entirely surprising, then, that the man who had built a one-room cabin on a cliff with no electricity or running water (save for the constant rain), a man who prized solitude and spiritual harmony so highly, and who had endured the punishment of military imprisonment, might be a touch shy and would send a letter by way of greeting when he was no more than a few miles up the road. In a way, though, he had already been introduced to the camp. When Everson had first contacted Graves at the urging of Clayton, offering simply an expenses-paid visit to a camp of like-minded artists, Graves replied by sending six paintings with return postage and a request that they be mailed back in a week. "The paintings may, in their way, serve as communication until I answer you more specifically," he signed off.[34]

Everson wrote back, making no secret of his excitement in finding a kindred spirit. "It is this kind of spontaneous and wholly generous gesture that speaks more clearly of the essential character of a man than anything he could say," Everson wrote, "and as such your donation of these paintings is very nearly in the category of your being here personally." The paintings went up for a week and elicited great comment from camp members, many of whom had little experience with sophisticated art. For the creative people in the Fine Arts, it was some of the most exciting work they had ever seen.[35]

After announcing his presence in Waldport through his letter, Graves scouted out the camp, the beach and surrounding area, and apparently found the environment to his satisfaction. He chose a space near the beach, overlooking a lagoon at the mouth of what the locals called Big Creek, and built a lean-to out of driftwood, covering it with wooden shingles obtained from a nearby lumber yard. Then one day he walked into camp and introduced himself.[36]

Over the next six weeks, Graves's studio-camp functioned as a kind of Camp Angel outpost. He set up his canvases and paints and brushes, and furnished the place with more driftwood and beach artifacts. His bed was wooden planks covered with moss, which he shared with three dachshunds he'd brought along in the old Ford Model A he'd driven

Morris Graves exhibit at Camp Angel, July 1944. Paintings were priced from $10 to $20. They later sold in the thousands.

Morris Graves in
his natural element.
Photo by Imogen
Cunningham.

down from Washington. A small campfire warmed a pot of water for
tea, served in round Japanese-style cups. While he had come to paint,
and his privacy was important to him, he also welcomed the Fine Arts
members when they visited, often staying up well into the night discussing religion, art, philosophy and politics, sometimes fueled by the alcohol
that Manche could buy with her Oregon liquor license. He wandered
the area as a kind of enigmatic master, perhaps reminiscent of a mendicant monk. He would come in from his campsite with an old camera
around his neck, a tall, thin man with a long stride and intriguing face,
Manche recalled, "ugly to the point of being beautiful." He might stop
and talk for a moment, always cordial yet oddly removed, she said. Then
he would move on to take pictures around the camp, as Manche stood
and watched him go, fascinated by the way he simply walked.[37]

At his outdoor studio, Graves laid his canvases on the ground and
painted leaning over them. This way, he told Bill Eshelman, he could "get
a freer swing and a more flowing curve by using all the muscles of the
torso instead of using only the upper arm and forearm." It also afforded
him speed; in one case, he finished a painting in ten minutes.[38]

He painted and painted and painted. The COs came by and admired
his work. Everson, who along with Clayton forged a strong bond with
the mystic, remembered that among his subjects was a dead seabird "in
various stages of disintegration, as if it were passing into another incar-
nation." There was also talk that Graves might do the illustrations for
Everson's next book, after he'd made two paintings of skeletal fish to
accompany a line from *The Masculine Dead* that read, "Under the grinding rivers of earth."[39]

The camp held an exhibit of his new work, hung in the Fine Arts gallery, with prices in the ten- to twenty-dollar range, a little something to help the artist continue living in his frugal ways. There is no record of sales although it's possible that some works may have been bought by locals. The COs, with their $2.50 monthly allowance, could not afford any—although the investment would have been a good one. A decade later, the paintings were selling at prices of four and five figures.[40]

Graves also did some of his darker paintings of ocean waves during this time, and there is a reason these works are so menacing, Everson said. In fact, he remembered, we almost might never have seen these paintings—or heard another word from Morris Graves or Clayton James. The two artists had gone to the beach one afternoon and taken some inner tubes out through the surf. But the unforgiving Pacific carried them into a pocket of pounding waves from which they couldn't escape. A wave would come over them and they'd hold their breath, then surface and barely catch a gulp of air before the next wave buried them. They held onto the inner tubes, unable to do anything but hope they wouldn't drown. Finally, the ocean cast them ashore about three-quarters of a mile from where they'd gone in. When Everson visited the lean-to that afternoon, he found the artists considerably shaken—and no doubt harboring an increased respect for the forces attending this violently beautiful shoreline.[41]

A later incident on the beach brought reminders of another power, second perhaps only to nature. One evening, Everson and Clayton were visiting Graves at his camp, sitting by the fire and drinking tea from the small oriental cups. The blackout orders in the region had long been

Morris Graves painting, "Sea, Fish and Constellation," perhaps reminiscent of the waves in which he almost drowned.

lifted, but the Coast Guard still patrolled the beach. Even though they knew about the CO camp, the authorities would sometimes stop and investigate men outside the compound. As the three artists sat talking by the lean-to, a Jeep pulled up and an officer jumped out, followed by two assistants. This was a time of clean-shaven faces and close-cropped hair, a military crispness and uniformity. And here was Clayton with a full beard, Everson with hair to his shoulders, and Graves—well, he'd been mysterious all his life. The GIs looked at the artists like they'd stumbled onto a nest of lunatics, Everson remembered. "Their mouths were draped open; their eyes had that kind of fixed look."

"Who's in charge here?" the officer barked.

Graves slowly stood up, with his mysterious air. "I am," he said.

"Let me see your papers," the officer said.

"Yes, sir," Graves replied. "Would you care for some tea?"

"No," the officer said. Then he added, perhaps a touch uncertainly, "No, thank you."

Graves turned to the two assistants. "Would you like to have some tea?"

They stared. "No."

"This is my friend William Everson and my friend Clayton James," Graves continued. "Are you sure that you would not join us for a cup of tea?"

"No," the officer insisted. "Let me see your papers!"

Graves handed over his papers, which said plainly, "Psychiatric Release."

The officer handed them back, then turned to Clayton and Everson. "Are you from the camp here?"

"Yes," Everson replied. "We don't have to have papers."

The officer appraised the men: their long hair and beards, the lean-to with its campfire, the tiny oriental teacups, the three dachshunds, and who knows what other manner of artist's gear and beach ephemera completing the scene. The artists appraised back: the sharp military dress, the fixed stares, the unquestioning commitment to authority. The GI assistants stared, waiting.

The officer turned and got back in the Jeep, the assistants followed, and they roared off in a cloud of sand and dust.

Graves watched them go, then slowly sat down. "Whewwwww," he said, "after those months in the stockade."[42]

Whether or not this incident influenced his next move, we'll never know. But not long after, Graves was gone, leaving behind his little camp, the lean-to with its moss bed, seashells and driftwood—and that sense of emptiness that follows the departure of those with a strong spiritual presence.

As the summer of 1944 waned and the war dragged on and the drain continued on church finances, general resources, and everyone's patience, cracks developed into fissures and possibly worse. Civilian Public Service by now had shown its strengths and flaws; in more and more camps the "work of national importance" dwindled, and the days turned more and more into a waiting game. As before, the conservative religious men tended to accept their burden and find solace and direction in the Bible. And, as before, the more secular and politically minded men talked of work slowdowns, walkouts, or even going to prison. Jim Harman was becoming edgy, threatening to take a furlough and never return; Larry Siemons was, too.

The tree-planting work had largely given way to trail maintenance, part of which involved snag-felling—cutting down the half-dead trees that had been struck by lightning, broken by windstorms, weakened by disease, or otherwise compromised. The reasoning was that these trees could fall over at any time—blocking access roads, bridging fire breaks and posing a danger to loggers and forest workers. Snag-felling was dangerous work, something even experienced loggers were reluctant to do. "It's not like falling a live tree," recalled Victor McLane, a Methodist from California who sometimes played piano with the Fine Arts. "You never know where a snag's going to fall; you never know what part of it's rotten down beneath and what part of it's solid." Snags, he said matter-of-factly, kill people.[43]

It didn't help that the Forest Service appeared to be merely searching for any kind of work the men could do. Bill Eshelman remembered being sent on a tree-planting crew out to the Blodgett Tract where one of the men recognized a hillside they'd planted the year before. "We just planted this," the CO said. "What are we doing?"

"Well, we made a mistake," the Forest Service foreman said apologetically, then offered a dubious justification regarding the seedling species. "What you planted last year won't grow on this side of the hill."

The men muttered and grumbled but did the work anyway. One camper, however, made his statement by planting his seedlings upside down, with the roots in the air. The Forest Service men were apoplectic, Eshelman said, but because the fellow doing it was also one of the camp's best tree planters, they went light on his punishment, dunning him two days of furlough.[44]

It was also becoming harder for the Forest Service to get new or proper equipment as rationing and the ever-expanding war effort took their toll. As most of the COs piled into trucks each morning, in their worn-out boots and secondhand work clothes, heading off to labor in the woods at work they felt was of no real importance to anyone, much less the nation, they saw others stay behind in the comfort of the camp—many of them belonging to that arts group. The roots of envy and suspicion spread, and the vines of discontent grew into what became known as "the kitchen problem."[45]

It began, Dick Mills said, when complaints came in about the quality of the food and service, stemming partly from the departure of accomplished cooks, and partly from the rotation of men into kitchen duty who may not have been the best ones suited for it. Meetings were called and comments went back and forth, ranging from denial of a problem at all to blaming the poor quality on the condition of the food when it was acquired. This led to comments that perhaps the issue wasn't so much about food as it was resentment that some Fine Arts members in the kitchen didn't take their responsibilities seriously enough. Maybe, one camper implied, the kitchen management was to blame for not being strong enough to run a cohesive crew. No, other campers insisted, this *was* about the Fine Arts people; these self-styled bohemians were more of a clique than the stodgy fundamentalists! Someone else pointed out that the Fine Arts made a rather convenient scapegoat for the current problems. No one had a solution.[46]

Underneath it all was a pet project pushed by Dick Mills, which may not have been the root cause of the conflict but in some ways could have served as a catalyst. Mills, ever mindful of the camp's standing in community perception (as well as his own standing in the BSC hierarchy), wanted to build a portable canning operation that not only provided for CPS needs throughout the winter but also supported the local and regional farming economy. The camp produce buyer had in the past arranged with Brethren women in the heavily agricultural Willamette Valley to can several thousand quarts of produce such as tomatoes, corn, and beans. The new idea, Mills said, was to set up a full canning operation with a boiler, pressure cooker, and sealing equipment, all mounted on a trailer. This way, the camp men could travel from place to place, buying the farmers' vegetables and working with local church women to preserve food for the CPS camps at Waldport, Cascade Locks, and Camp #59 at Elkton, in the Coast Range foothills outside of Roseburg. The challenge was to find men who could operate the portable cannery, which would require volunteers (or assignees) to work fifty or a hundred miles away for an extended period. The most likely candidates were the kitchen crew, made up largely of Fine Arts men. But they had come here to remain close to the main camp, and had no interest in the portable cannery. Compounding the problem was how the cannery positions would be funded; after all, this wasn't Forest Service work and so couldn't be considered Project labor. As Mills sought ways to manipulate administrative protocols, the Fine Arts members remained wary.

Into this mix came Jerry Rubin, a twenty-eight-year-old Jewish social-ist drafted out of San Francisco and sent to Waldport that summer. Rubin had been raised an old-school socialist in working-class Milwaukee, Wisconsin, surrounded by labor activists and radicals. He'd majored in labor economics at the University of Wisconsin, then spent a year in law school. In 1939, he went to California to help organize farm workers in the San Joaquin Valley, home of the state's massive agricultural indus-try—right about the time John Steinbeck's *Grapes of Wrath* was shocking the country. In the presidential election of 1940, he was the California campaign manager for Norman Thomas, the socialist stalwart making his fourth run for the office. During this time, Rubin met his future wife, Jan, at a socialist meeting. Jan was diabetic, and in that era child-bearing in her condition was considered too risky, so they knew they would be spending the rest of their lives committed to working for social justice. When the call came for Jerry to report for CPS duty in Waldport, Jan came along—as did their dog, Jimmy Higgins, named after a dedicated union worker in an Upton Sinclair novel.[47]

Rubin was apparently a known entity, for he was sent to the sign-painting shop, in a building away from the others, ostensibly so that his influence would be lessened. According to one account, he had regu-lar visitors anyway and, besides lecturing on labor issues, demonstrated his method of work slowdown by very, *very* carefully painting the let-ters on a sign—one letter per day. He also, naturally, joined the Workers Committee and immediately advocated for the workers' side on issues in a more direct way than Mills or the Forest Service men had been accus-tomed to seeing.

Everson, looking back decades later, chalked the whole kitchen issue up to poor decision making. Mills had originally set up an excellent kitchen crew, he said, and when the Workers Committee insisted the Overhead assignments be rotated equally, regardless of a camper's ability, the better cooks left the kitchen and the quality of the meals dropped. Whether or not the Fine Arts members were specifically responsible for the unhappiness, there were certainly more of them in the kitchen than had been there before. "The morale of the camp started to sag on the issue of bad food," Everson said. "Fine Arts got the blame."[48]

Everson also placed some of the blame on himself, alluding to when he had turned over the Fine Arts management to Vlad Dupre—who handled the administrative duties marvelously but did not possess the political clout that Everson had across the camp. "I should have hung in there and spent my time pacifying the various tension-points, trouble-shooting, etc.," he said, "which I could do, but Vlad could not. They called me the 'Great White Father.'"[49]

Whether it was Everson escaping his leadership obligations, Jerry Rubin with his history of labor organizing, Jim Harman's increasing agitation and drinking, or Larry Siemons and his constantly suspicious nature, the record doesn't make clear. But one day in August, Harman and Mills had a blow-up while clearing tables at dinner. Mills threatened to have Harman thrown in jail, Harman threatened Mills with bodily harm, and Mills retorted that it would make no difference because he was resigning, effective the first of November.[50]

Something like this had been a long time in coming, although precisely who was responsible for what was difficult to discern. In a way, it was a matter of the chickens coming home to roost for Mills. He had long expounded on the importance of trust and democratic processes, putting forth the face of open cooperation. Yet he had difficulty delegating responsibility, and sometimes attempted to manipulate outcomes from behind the scenes. It was inevitable, then, that assumptions would be made and suspicions arise. Over time, the incidents piled up: the portable cannery, the kitchen assignments, the ongoing tensions with the Workers Committee. Now, dealing with volatile personalities such as Harman and Siemons added even more pressure, bringing out the camp director's own vulnerabilities and shortcomings—which seemed to include an ongoing sense of insecurity. In short, Mills believed he was facing a crisis of confidence within the camp, and he decided to take it head-on in dramatic fashion. He wrote up a memo and survey questions for distribution. "Since I have been placed in the embarrassing situation of determining whether my work is acceptable to the men in camp, I seem to have no recourse except to ask for an opinion from each man regarding his feelings as to a change of Directors," he wrote. "If the group feels that I should go in the near future, such plans will be made and cleared with Elgin. If the camp feels that I should serve longer, that too, will be registered in Elgin and plans worked out in accordance with all the facts at hand." He offered an explanation of how the results of the survey might affect dates of his departure and possible replacement, then concluded in a kind of bureaucratic self-conscious sincerity, "It will help me to do the best job of which I am capable if every man in camp will indicate his opinion on the survey form which has been prepared."[51]

A week later, the Fine Arts group was meeting to discuss their own future. They had originally been approved for six months with one hundred dollars per month funding, which would expire the first of September unless extended after review by BSC headquarters. The Fine Arts had accomplished much, but they hadn't had any sustained period in which the entire group was able to interact in a fully cooperative manner—even though this had been stated in the beginning as one of their primary aims. They'd been rehearsing their first full-length play for most of the summer, yet it hadn't been produced. Manche had finally been officially made secretary of the Fine Arts, but if the funding was cut off they wouldn't be able to pay her. They'd reached out to the greater camp membership through crafts workshops and the reading series, yet they were still dealing with accusations of elitism stemming from the kitchen assignments. They had a talented cellist, a handful of piano players, a clarinetist, and classical singers—yet they couldn't get the transfer approved for a world-class violinist whose stated goal was to create a CPS string quartet.

Against untold challenges, they'd persevered and succeeded. Morris Graves had produced work unlike anything most campers had imagined, much less seen. Adrian Wilson had been there barely a month—and gone on side camp for half that time—but now he was enthusiastically practicing for musical performances, doing stage work for the upcoming play, and helping with typesetting and layout for the *Compass*. The *Illiterati* had arrived. *The Waldport Poems* was completed and already selling rapidly. Yet here they were on an August evening, unsure if the Fine Arts would continue. They knew Morris Keeton was supportive, and that as the Brethren Service Committee education director his influence was considerable. But it was Harold Row, not Keeton, making the final decision—and there was no telling what manner of forces were tugging at the BSC director's concerns. There had been many triumphs yet almost constant disappointments—and those who had worked so hard to make the Fine Arts work couldn't be blamed if they were feeling a touch of despair. Was the adage really true? Was it impossible for any group of creative artists to build a fully democratic and sustainable community?[52]

CHAPTER 9

The Revolution Begins

THE DAY AFTER the Fine Arts meeting about their uncertain future, Everson burst into the Untide Press room, Adrian wrote, "turning cartwheels and waving a stool over his head."[1] His *Waldport Poems* would be reprinted, in its entirety, in an upcoming edition of *New Directions*, the anthology of experimental writing edited each year by James Laughlin, a wealthy young publisher interested in printing the work of otherwise marginalized writers and artists. *New Directions* had already brought attention to authors such as Henry Miller, Dylan Thomas, and William Carlos Williams; Everson's publication in their company would make the Fine Arts more visible in the New York literary scene. The Untide Press booklets were already somewhat known through sales at the Gotham Book Mart and other New York bookstores catering to the literary and cultural avant-garde. In fact, by the middle of September—just two months after publication—the entire 975-copy run of *The Waldport Poems* had sold out. Unlike the earlier mimeographed runs of *X War Elegies*, though, they couldn't print a second edition. They had only so much type, and after they'd run just one sheet of four pages, they had to distribute the type back into the box and begin again with the next sheet.[2]

They were already typesetting the new edition of the *War Elegies*, with other writers from the pacifist and anarchist circles in the queue. In fact, the correspondence and submissions had grown to the point that the Untide Press had instituted editorial meetings on Friday nights, in which they reviewed and discussed manuscripts and made plans for further publications, in the fashion of a full-time literary press. They had a sheaf of poems by George Woodcock, the British writer and editor of *Now,* a literary anarchist journal he published from London and featuring the work of Herbert Read, e. e. cummings, and Henry Miller. They had plans for a book by Jacob Sloan, whom Martin Ponch had known at CPS camps back East and who had written poems about his time working in a mental hospital. They'd also entered into correspondence with Kenneth Patchen, the fiery antiwar poet with half a dozen books already published. His reputation as an iconoclast was borne out when, in answer to an invitation from Kemper to submit for the *Illiterati,* he proposed bringing together under one cover his antiwar poems—and added the startling recommendation that he receive no royalties. Any profits should go back into the press, he said; it was more important that they focus on providing a platform for voices against war.[3]

The Fine Arts got their next boost of confidence when word came from Brethren Service Committee headquarters that funding was approved for another three months, at which time it would again be reviewed.[4] Plans were made, aims adapted, discussions continued. Photography should be added, they decided, as a way to increase participation; Everson suggested they might hold monthly exhibits of the best pictures. Bob Scott, the pianist, was also on the Religious Life Committee; he thought there was opportunity for cooperative activities there. Adrian wanted more attention paid to music—more performances, more informal discussions, as ways to stimulate interaction and creativity. The crafts were a little more complicated in that there were two such groups in camp. One was connected to the Fine Arts, and had used money allocated for the group to build a kiln. The other craft group made items with the intent to sell them, and so came up with a separate name—Angelcraft—for accounting purposes. Because they used tools (such as the kiln) that had been bought by the Fine Arts, they were charged a small fee. With all the overlap and sharing among the different members and specific groups, completely accurate and detailed record keeping was surely a nightmare and perhaps impossible. In all likelihood, people probably did the work they were compelled to do, and, as long as their use of time and equipment remained reasonable, there wasn't a problem.

This cooperative spirit showed itself in a number of ways—one certainly being the production of the *Compass.* Martin Ponch pulled together twenty-two people in getting out the forty-eight-page Summer–Fall 1944 issue, the first one to come from Waldport. He had Vlad Dupre as associate editor, and Kemper doing layout. Kermit contributed artwork; Glenn Evans did the cover. Manche, Adrian, Bill Eshelman, and Jerry Rubin were involved. Bill Jadiker, a mechanically inclined fellow who'd been active in the crafts group, chipped in with business chores, and his wife, Gertrude, helped with production. Bruce Reeves contributed some of his pictures. Ponch even got some artwork from Waldo Chase, who'd been teaching his drawing and print-making classes in CPS camps across the country after he'd left Waldport earlier that year. For the magazine design, they took a modernist approach, running the table of contents inside the *back* cover. Inside the front, they ran excerpts from the 1940 Selective Training and Service Act regarding the "work of national importance" clause, and 1943's Public Law 135 about the issue of pay for COs, and then made their editorial statement by printing these quotes and statistics:

Cover of the *Compass*, Summer-Fall 1944. Artwork by Glenn Evans.

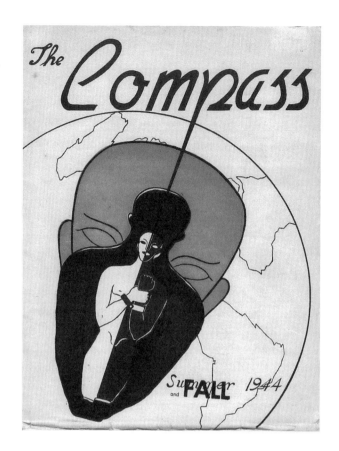

"*Some* work done by c.o.'s *is* nationally important: The estimated value to the country of all work done to date is more than $25,000,000. . . . from a document which some of the religious groups have sent me. . . ."—Eleanor Roosevelt.

Amount paid by the government to c.o.'s for salary, dependency needs, accident compensation: $0.00.

On the first page, they reiterated the purpose of the *Compass:* showing the directions of change. Between the world wars, they admitted, pacifists had not done a very good job of building a platform for lasting peace. But that did not negate the pacifist's ongoing job, they countered, which was through word and action to direct the changes of society away from common destruction and toward the common good: "As Civilian Public Service falters into its fourth year under conscription, COMPASS—no less subject to its restrictions—finds somewhere the assurance to attempt a charting of the directions in which those who are conscientious cooperators are going, or would like to be allowed to go. Directions they pursue not in the vain hope of finding some utopian and conflict-less future, but to create a future in which mature and civilized patterns of resolving conflicts will be discovered, tried and adhered to."

The issue featured articles on cooperative living, peace education, and CPS work in mental hospitals and earthquake relief in Mexico. Glenn Evans, in an essay titled "CPS and the Race Problem," listed activities in various CPS camps across the South that resulted in greatly improved understanding and relationships between races, yet noted the hypocrisy of the peace churches' top administrations by their general acceptance of the same segregation policies employed by the U.S. military. "Pacifists are constantly aware of the inconsistencies of military leaders who boast of forcing the Four Freedoms on all peoples, with an army that spreads the shadow of Jim Crow to the four corners of the earth," he wrote. "Do not some of these same pacifists who support CPS find themselves rather hard pressed for an answer to people of color who question the consistency of professing a philosophy of brotherhood and equality while participating in a system which, in practice, denies that ethical philosophy?"[5]

While this was not a literary issue, it did include three poems (one by Everson, of course) and a section of book reviews (one on Everson's *Waldport Poems,* of course). A four-page supplement reprinted recent pieces from *Pacifica Views,* and a marvelous couple of pages included contributors' photos and somewhat irreverent bios. Bill Jadiker, for instance, wrote that he was a "plumber by trade," that in CPS he "acted as a plumber," and that his postwar plans included "plumbing." Vlad Dupre wrote, "Major concern: getting married in October." Glenn Evans, again taking on advocacy for racial concerns, included in his summary of growing up in Texas, "rebellion against poverty, ignorance and black-boy-enter-the-back-door white supremacy."[6]

The Fine Arts got star treatment, in an eight-page section featuring a "double truck" title running across the opening spread, and large photos on every page. The section opened with an excerpt from the earlier Fine Arts prospectus, and then Everson introduced the program, noting the date of his writing as that infamous June 6: "This is D Day. In the narrow slit between the continent of Europe and the island of England, tens of thousands of men are hurling eastward in the final assault upon a civilization. Here in the West, on this shelf of earth and stone that forms the Pacific scarp, what can be said about art, that will be taken by the millions who watch that denouement as more than idle prattle? And yet, if it cannot be said on D Day, it should not be said at all."[7]

The rest of the statement was a revised and clarified version of all Everson and the Fine Arts had developed and articulated so far: A cooperative community was beneficial, even necessary, to art; they were pacifists but they were not propagandists; and it was through creative expression that concrete actions could emerge. Summaries of the program's elements included Martin Ponch on theater, Bill Eshelman on writing, and Clayton James on painting. Bob Scott covered the music element, stressing the universality of the medium. Everson wrote on the Untide Press, and also about crafts, noting its accessibility to a wider group and how the wives of Waldport campers were creating items specifically to sell.

They were new, they were small, and thus far their intentions were greater than their accomplishments, Everson wrote. "This is not a program that can be brought to maturity in a six months space." But they had to try, he said. "And at the very least we hope to show, when the camps have been folded up and stowed away, that of all this effort, of all this money, and of all this time, the things of the imagination have not been forgotten."[8]

Another prominent example of cooperation showed itself when the theater group's production of *Aria da Capo* finally hit the boards on September 22, a Friday night. David Jackson and his cast of Kermit, Manche, Eshelman, Enoch Crumpton, and Vlad Dupre had survived the summer season separations and coordinated with the backstage crew, who brought their own brand of creativity. Kemper Nomland, the architect, designed the set as well as the programs. Manche and Kermit were joined by camp matron Maude Gregory in sewing the costumes. Adrian jumped in with a nineteen-year-old Louisiana boy named James Siple and took care of the set construction, agreeing to build a curtain puller and also run the record player during the show.[9] Francis Barr, another nineteen-year-old who worked in the sign shop, applied his unique talents to the lighting. Always interested in mechanical projects and electronics, he'd heard somewhere in his past that light-dimmer switches could be made using salt water. When he told David Jackson about it, the director asked, "Could you do that?"

The Untide Press at work. L-R: Vlad Dupre feeds the press, Bill Eshelman sets type, and Bill Everson calculates.

"Well," Barr replied, "I could give it a try."

He collected some five-gallon metal canisters and filled them with salt water, then constructed a switch device from a wooden handle attached to a piece of tin that could be lowered into and raised out of the water. He then rigged it up to the lights built into a proscenium arch in front of Adrian's stage curtain. "I knew that salt water made a good conductor," Barr remembered. "The more tin you put in the salt water, why, the brighter the lights got. The more you pulled it out, the dimmer it got." Jackson, who had no understanding of electronics, was amazed, Barr said. "He thought it was some kind of black magic."[10]

But when opening night came, the forest-fire siren went off an hour before curtain time, and the firefighting crews were sent away—including Barr and Adrian. In holding to the theater creed, the show did go on as Bob Scott and David Jackson took over the lights and music. The audience was impressed with the show, Dupre wrote to Everson, who was on two-week furlough in California. After the second night's show, the crew threw a party at the Fine Arts cabin across the highway. There was apparently plenty to drink, for Dupre reported that he kept falling over, so the others put him to bed and took off for a midnight swim. When he woke up alone in the dark, he said, "I was so mad that I stumbled over to the James's and went to sleep on their bed in the front room."

Dupre added some camp news as well. Hackett, back from side camp duty, was shipping out to work at a mental hospital in Chicago. Harman was on furlough and had indicated that he may not return. Siemons, who now had a girlfriend in Portland, was ready to walk out, too. With Everson gone, Dupre said he now relied on Clayton and Barbara James for intellectual company—and they were heading out on furlough soon themselves.[11]

When the firefighting crews returned, they added another performance of *Aria da Capo*, then took it on the road for a show at Cascade Locks. They packed the lighting, set materials, costumes, and ten people into a half-ton panel truck. It was a tight fit made less so when Manche pulled out a quart of rum, and they passed around goblets used as props in the play and relaxed for the rest of the ride into the evening.[12]

It seemed people always arrived at the camps late at night, and this time was no different. It was a homecoming of sorts for Kermit, Kemper, and Manche, so the Cascade Locks crew broke open their "wine cellar" and uncorked some homemade elderberry wine. While the cast and crew caroused until the early morning hours, director Jackson, too serious to relax the night before a show, methodically ironed out the dyed sheets they would use for background in place of stage flats. Everyone else woke late the next day, but they got the set constructed, patching it all together with extension cords, multiple-head electrical sockets, and safety pins to hold the sheets together—and the curtain rose on schedule.

Kermit Sheets in
Aria da Capo.

Manche Langley as
Kermit's counterpart.

One Cascade Locks member reported that the acting was done fairly well and that Manche was superb. "She dignified her role with the requisite amount of illusion, and appeared simply marvelously in her make-up and costume."[13] Kermit, he added, was not at his best, but after the previous evening's "bacchanalian debauch" he could be forgiven. It was apparently good enough—or maybe everyone was simply happy to see Kermit, Kemper, and Manche—for they struck the set and then headed up the mountain, built a bonfire, and closed the night with another party, even though their refreshments were down to just beer, bread, and cheese. Reflecting later on the excitement with which they'd been received, Eshelman wrote that Waldport would be lost without the Fine Arts. "The spirit, or rather the lack of it at the Locks shows how much they miss something of the sort."[14]

It was all about the people involved and how they interacted. "Jesus, Everson, it isn't so damn good here without you and the Jameses," Dupre wrote in late September with Everson still on furlough and the artist couple now gone as well. "No solidity. No inspiration," he said, adding that he'd taken to going to the Fine Arts cabin alone and reading at night.[15] Warren Downs, recently returned from his two-month stint in the fire lookout tower, was struck by the animosity between Dick Mills and some campers. The conflicts around the kitchen assignments, the uncertainties of the portable cannery project, suspicions of favoritism, and the resulting overall degradation of morale fragmented the camp into factions that tended to either support or oppose administration—and specifically the way Mills handled things. "If I were pro-Mills or anti-Mills, things would be simple," Downs wrote, "but being in between and seeing so many different views and arguments, I am rather depressed by the complexity of camp life." Jim Harman in particular, he felt, was on the edge of a breakdown. Although Harman had threatened to "walk out" on furloughs, he always returned to camp, voicing his dissatisfaction and causing problems—so much so that over time, more and more of the Fine Arts members were finding it difficult to tolerate his mercurial personality. Now he had taken to wandering aimlessly around camp in a long black coat, nervous and thin, while others from the group avoided him. Each night he checked into the infirmary, complaining of exhaustion or some other ailment. It seemed Downs was the only one who would talk to him, and he confided to the cellist that next time he was definitely walking out—going on furlough and not coming back. The whole thing seemed pathetic, Downs wrote. "He's just plain cracking up and doesn't seem to care."[16]

At least the night watchman duty still offered its respite, this time for Adrian, who, like the others, hadn't realized how much he valued his privacy until he was actually alone. As he made his rounds checking the fires in the quiet buildings, he had time for real reflection. One night in late September, in that way that only someone who lives in the place can understand, he noted the depth and multifaceted meaning of the changes in Oregon weather. "And off and on during the night the rain pattered on the tarpaper roofs tapping out in a code I thought I understood, the end of the fire season."[17]

He also got to meet "the famous Glen Coffield," who returned briefly from Cascade Locks on a temporary exchange with a Waldport camper. As prolific and enigmatic as ever, Coffield had recently knocked out three books in a two-week period, and in recognition Everson read selections to the Untide Press group at their Friday night editorial meeting. "I was positively amazed at Coffield's genius," Adrian wrote. "His rhyming particularly is miraculous. He is the first poet I have met who writes systematically." But it wasn't just the poetry; Coffield sometimes had an effect on people by his presence alone. He had, Adrian observed, taken the conditions imposed on him by CPS and used them to explore and expand both his mind and creative activities. "I kick myself for not doing likewise."[18]

Adrian and the rest of the Fine Arts did receive a shot in the arm when the two violinists, Broadus "Bus" Erle and Bob Harvey, finally arrived from the Big Flats camp in New York. "They sure can play," Vlad Dupre wrote to Everson, adding that even Bob Scott, the pianist who often stayed aloof with his religious and conservative manner, seemed pleased. "I think you will like them," Dupre said.[19]

 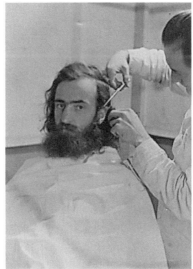 

Glen Coffield gets a haircut and shave. He'd grown his hair for a year as a protest for peace.

Broadus "Bus" Erle,
ca. 1946.

Warren Downs was initially cool, finding Erle "a queer duck"—short, dark-haired, and pale with an East Coast edginess. Harvey was more likable, a big, red-headed fellow, he said. But when they practiced as a trio the next day, doing some Beethoven and Mozart, Downs had trouble keeping up with Erle, who read the music at a blistering pace and got it right the first time. That's what happens when you play in a radio orchestra, Harvey said, referring to Erle's time with the NBC stations, which played the shows live. "They only rehearse an hour before each broadcast. That's all they get."[20]

Adrian was immediately impressed by both musicians: "Broadus (Bus) Erle and Bob Harvey have arrived from Big Flats. Any musical reasons for my going back to Minneapolis are eliminated. They are terrific, especially Erle, a radio studio orchestra player who last night played trios by Beethoven and Mozart perfect at sight. We are all so enthused about their performance we wonder what we have done to be so blessed. We should have some really good chamber music here before the winter is over."[21]

It kept getting better. Adrian had been practicing with Warren Downs and Bob Scott, but now with Erle and Harvey hammering out their Beethoven, he commented that it was like playing at Juilliard. Both men took to the Fine Arts easily, and at a party over at the cabins, Harvey shared his experiences with subsistence farming, relating with great humor his trials and failures. He had the place rolling in laughter with a story about why he hated chickens, Adrian wrote. "Harvey is suddenly one of the most popular guys in the group." A deeper connection was revealed when the two men discovered that the fellow who had hosted Harvey's wedding party back in Connecticut was also Adrian's best friend—and that Harvey and his new wife, Joyce, had even one day given Adrian's mother a ride home. With Harvey's easy camaraderie and Bus Erle's astounding talent and cosmopolitan character, right down to the brooding countenance and chain-smoking, Adrian was bordering on the ecstatic. Thinking of the music, the theater, and his burgeoning interest in printing, he wrote, "Every day . . . I feel more a part of this dynamic group until I am beginning to think that *this* is perhaps the community I envision and wanted to set up. What a stroke of luck! What a transformation!"[22]

They scheduled a concert featuring works by Bach, Beethoven, Schumann, and Ernest Bloch, the Swiss-born violinist and composer who, after emigrating to the United States, wrote his 1927 award-winning symphony, *America*. And, in what must surely rank as one of the more highly unusual chains of coincidence, Adrian just happened to sit at the vegetarian table one night in the dining hall because the kitchen was serving liver, and he just happened to hear Bill Jadiker's wife, Gertrude, talking about her job at the grocery store in Newport, twenty miles up the coast. She told of an interesting older gentleman who came into the store each day—and his name just happened to be Ernest Bloch. Everything Gertrude described—"long white hair, big nose, French accent, teaching in Berkeley"—matched what the pianist Bob Scott knew about him, and the COs were certain this must be the composer. Adrian wanted to write him immediately, sending a program and invitation for their upcoming show. Surely the coincidence of serious musicians performing his work just down the road would intrigue him. But Scott and Erle, who would be playing Bloch's *Baal Shem* for violin and piano, demurred. "They pointed out that the great are tired of being pursued," Adrian said, "undoubtedly the reason why Bloch lives in a no-place like Newport." The show would go on without the famous man's attention.[23]

The five musicians—Downs on cello, Erle and Harvey on violins, Bob Scott on piano, and Adrian on clarinet—practiced when they could get away from work. Adrian, Erle, and Harvey were in the kitchen, and Scott was in the office. Downs, though, was sent out to fight forest fires, where he caught a cinder in his eye and had to work with an eye patch. He was then moved to snag-felling work, running a drag saw—a ten-foot-long motorized device that cut the giant logs into manageable sections after they'd been downed. It was back-breaking, arm-numbing work and at the end of the day his hands shook so badly that he had difficulty playing the cello. When he asked Harvey what he could do about his shaking hands, the violinist deadpanned that he should "lay off the liquor and morphine." Still, he practiced diligently with the others. "The first movement is so far lousy," he wrote three days before the show. "I've got to practice that!"[24]

The concert took place on a Saturday night in late October, in the chapel building on a rounded stage meant to mimic a chamber—the base made of boards set on bent metal piping, a background of thick hanging cloth, and a ceiling constructed of the blue and purple painted flats left over from the *Aria da Capo* set. A floor lamp with an overturned clay crock for a pedestal and a spotlight so the musicians could read their scores completed the scene. Half an hour before the show, Downs met his brother, who he knew was coming over from Salem. But he was surprised to see also his father, his grade-school music teacher, and two of his music professors from Willamette University; they helped make up a standing-room-only audience, which Everson counted at seventy-four. Bus Erle ripped through the Bloch piece, impressing everyone; then Adrian, Bob Scott, and Warren Downs went through the Beethoven with sharpness and delight. They were mobbed backstage, Everson grabbing everyone and gushing, "Gee, fellows, that was great," and the two music professors striding through and exclaiming, "Splendid performance, great work, amazing!" Later, standing side-by-side at the urinals in the dorm, Everson told Adrian that he thought it was the finest music performance ever given in CPS. Warren Downs acknowledged in his diary, "Gave recital which seemed to go off fairly successfully."[25]

The performing mood continued at the post-show party in the cabins across the road. Whether alcohol played a part, no record reveals—but one member of the group certainly needed no prompt. Coffield was still in camp, and as usual, doing his own thing in his own way. Adrian reported: "We were in on a new departure in poetry last night, a fusion of the cerebral and the primitive. Coffield chanted a number of poems he has written here. Sometimes they were tunes like those you make up doing work, formless, repetitive, but definitely conveying a mood. Really it is something to be in on these revolutions when they start."[26]

■ ■ ■

As October's Indian summer settled across America, all eyes were on the future. In Europe, Allied forces had liberated Paris and just weeks later crossed the German border. In the Pacific, Americans continued their island-hopping campaign and launched an assault on Leyte Island in the Philippines, bringing to fruition General Douglas MacArthur's promise, "I shall return." But the war was clearly not over, and the need for fresh bodies dug deeper into the world's population pool.[27]

This also meant more COs were being shipped to the camps, some better qualified for the work than others. The snag-felling continued although all were aware of the dangers. The trees were often on steep hills, or the trunks so thick at ground level that the men had to create a platform so they could reach high enough to make a manageable cut, sometimes six feet wide. They followed the classic logging practice of cutting notches at about shoulder height on opposing sides of the tree, then driving long, narrow boards end-first into the trunk, making a "springboard," a kind of gangplank on which they could stand while swinging axes or sliding a two-handled saw. In the old-growth forests, the ground was thick with centuries of fallen trees, and the men walked on the downed trunks through tangled blackberry vines and other underbrush to their positions.

Russell Eisenbise, a Brethren CO from Kansas, remembered hiking in one time through thick brush and fallen timber to take down a snag with Wes DeCoursey, another Brethren from Idaho. According to Forest Service directions, they were supposed to cut to the point of breakage—when the tree began to "talk" with crackling sounds as the last strands of its vascular wood gave way—then step back a certain distance, call out "Tim-ber!" and watch it fall. The two COs did as they'd been told, and the tree came down. But when Eisenbise turned to find DeCoursey, the other man was gone. It turned out they were about eight feet above the ground and had walked in on the spine of a fallen tree. When Eisenbise stepped back from the falling snag, he stayed on the tree. But DeCoursey had stepped backwards off the giant log and plunged through the blackberries. He climbed out with only a few scratches, and the two men had a good laugh.[28]

Another report, from the Hebo side camp up the coast, told of a closer brush with mortality when a falling snag jumped sideways and hit a CO in the chest. "Man fells tree; tree fells man. Starring Ken Leedy," the *Tide* headline said. "He took the count, is somewhat sore about the midriff, but is otherwise uninjured."[29]

When Adrian and Francis Barr had been called away from the *Aria da Capo* performance to fight the late-September fire, they'd joined Warren Downs for their first snag-felling attempt as part of the work in creating a fire break. The snag was a "whopper," Adrian said; it appeared to be leaning uphill, so they decided to fell it in that direction. "Actually it was an optical illusion," he wrote, "the gray hulk finally went crashing like thunder downhill." After it landed, Adrian examined the cut and counted the growth rings, twice—getting 467 the first time and 454 the second. "If I had wanted to count some more I could have arrived at a figure that would have placed its birth in 1492," he said. "God, what dynamic things have happened on this continent while the tree I sawed down yesterday morning was quietly growing."[30]

It was interesting that Adrian mentioned the year 1492, because some three weeks after he wrote this, on Columbus Day 1944, the odds caught up with the snag-felling crews at Camp Angel. George Watkins, a thirty-year-old railroad man from Whitefish, Montana, was cutting a two-foot diameter hemlock with Prince de Bourbon, a twenty-year-old factory worker from Oklahoma. Warren Downs, who wasn't there but

Axemen stood on "springboards" to reach a diameter in the trunk that could be cut.

knew the area well, recorded the story in his diary: The two men aimed the tree to fall downhill and made their cut. As the tree began to "talk," the younger de Bourbon ran behind a debris pile while the more experienced and confident Watkins stepped to the side. But the falling tree caught between two others downhill, creating a fulcrum point, and the resulting force caused the butt of the snag to shoot ten feet sideways, striking Watkins at his shoulders and head. Watkins went down, and the tree crushed his skull against a log. The government would pay only $100 of the $175 total funeral expenses, Downs wrote, so the campers chipped in and donated the rest. The Brethren *CPS Bulletin* announced the death, gave Watkins's age and background, and noted that he was married with no children. The *Directory of Civilian Public Service*, compiled after the war, lists under his name simply, "left CPS: 10/12/44."[31]

With barely a hiccup, the wheels of life continued turning. Tensions between Mills and the camp simmered even though Harman was finally gone and Siemons had left on furlough, announcing after dinner one evening that he would not return. The work and recreation habits of some Fine Arts members still bothered some non-Fine Arts campers, and their complaints made their way to the higher levels, eventually bringing in the regional superintendent for the BSC, who'd been told that Brethren church members did not approve of the Fine Arts' drinking habits. Furthermore, Forest Service superintendent Orville Richman had told Selective Service he felt the Fine Arts transfers were not suitable for Project work. While it was true that some campers were uncooperative on Project, and some were also Fine Arts members, you couldn't hold an entire group responsible for the actions of a few individuals, Adrian wrote his family. "One thing is to be made clear," he said, "we are individuals, individualists in fact, and are only a 'group' or 'specialized school' while the B.S.C. underwrites the values for which we stand."[32]

This kind of individualism within a functioning group may have been what irked Dick Mills as his November 1, 1944, resignation loomed. He certainly did not like it when things weren't going his way—and even less so when he felt he had lost his power to influence their direction. He had apparently concluded by this time that not only had he lost control of the Waldport camp, but that the Brethren church had lost control of their original vision for CPS. In a six-page, tightly spaced report he titled "The Impact of the Resentful Individual upon CPS Camps," he called for a reckoning with the shortcomings of CPS and proposed fundamental changes to how the camps were run. The bulk of the report was steeped in psychoanalysis and group psychology; he categorized the COs into four groups: The "forward-looking" individuals had inquiring minds and confidence in their beliefs. The "resentful" individuals were generally smart and talented but rebelled against authority. The "unadventurous" were followers, usually guided by an authoritative religion. And the "alternating" were the back-and-forth types, wanting to do good but susceptible to coercion.

The resentful ones were the artists, Mills said. Conscripted into a camp against their will, denied the recognition they felt they deserved, these frustrated creative types turned their energies and talents toward destructive rather than constructive ends—doing so with great cunning and skill. "The presence," Mills wrote, "of a concentration of ego-thwarted individuals in a CPS camp tends to result in a mild form of unarmed conflict." The larger result, he said, is a "group psychosis" in which the resentful ones bridle against the administrators and declare themselves anarchists. Because these resentful ones are intelligent and talented, they are able to coerce the unadventurous and alternating ones into rejecting or at least questioning authority and the motives people may have for asserting it.[33]

On page five he got personal. The resentful individual is destroying CPS, he said, and a concentration of this type can be found at Waldport. Even though the Fine Arts offered a creative release for the thwarted egos, he added, their art was a far cry from an expression of the pacifist causes embraced by the church: "It is safe to say that so far there have appeared no paintings designed to arouse in people an awareness of the folly of war; so far, there have been no essays or stories written to help the average citizen understand the forces at work in the world that bring about wars. And to date, there have been no poems published that champion man's struggle to attain a peaceful world." He concluded with a call that the church must face the facts of the anarchistic forces at work in their camps and either turn administration over to the government or reassign the COs to camps according to personality type. "The Church must not wash its hands completely of CPS," he said, "but it must make the kind of adjustments which will help men rather than hinder them in their stand for peace."[34]

Mills sent the report to BSC leaders and prepared to leave for a camp directors' conference in Elgin; no one at Waldport was quite sure if he would return. Then, the weekend before he was scheduled to leave, things started unraveling. Saturday night, word came that the portable cannery on the trailer had wrecked in a ditch—that same canning unit of which Mills had been so proud and the kitchen crew had disdained. Right behind this, on Sunday evening, Jerry Rubin brought a proposal from the Workers Committee regarding rotation policy for Overhead assignments. They'd been negotiating this for some time, and Rubin's proposal was different enough from Mills's position that the director lost his temper. He accused Rubin of trying to get his friends into the less-demanding Overhead jobs, and reacted predictably by alluding to his connections with greater authority. He said that Orville Richman and the Forest Service wanted to shut down the Fine Arts completely; he warned that Victor Olson, the Selective Service field secretary due to visit the camp for inspection, would set them all straight, right down to making the kitchen help shave off their beards. These threats were made harder to dismiss when Larry Siemons, who dropped in at this time during his fugitive travels, said he'd been in Chicago and had heard from a "reputable source" that the National Service Board for Religious Objectors, which oversaw all of CPS, was going to bypass Brethren Service Committee national director Harold Row, close the camp, and disband the Fine Arts. The men called an ad hoc meeting in the Jadikers' cabin across the highway to cool down and set a course of action for Selective Service secretary Olson's visit. They knew that Mills was an emotional wreck and determined that if they appeared calm while Mills was unstable, Olson would naturally be inclined to question the director's accusations. They decided it was best to do nothing while Mills was still in camp.[35]

Then, in the wee hours of the day before Halloween, the lid blew off. More specifically, the kitchen caught fire. It was literally a dark and stormy night, the wind howling through the trees, the rain driving hard in from the sea, a classic coastal storm. As the men slept in their dorm cots, Hal Pottenger, twenty-two years old, Methodist, and an accounting student from Indiana, made his rounds as night watchman. He had to light nearly thirty fires in the wood stoves that night, and timing was important—particularly on the cold and wet nights, as the men would need plenty of hot water when they woke up and took their showers. He'd light the fires in the mess hall first so that the cooks, who rose earlier than everyone else, would have a warm work space. From there he'd move to the infirmary, the camp offices, the rec hall, and then the dorms, waking the cooks just before finishing his rounds.

At the dining hall in the predawn, Pottenger saw another camper, who was having trouble sleeping through the wind and rain. They talked a while, then Pottenger went to the end of the hall and into the kitchen and lit the fires there. He returned shortly, they chatted a bit more, and the other camper decided he'd go back to bed and try to get some sleep. Pottenger continued on his rounds through the other buildings.

Sometime later, after Pottenger had awakened the cooks and they'd headed to the kitchen, the fire bell clanged. Men ran from the dorms through the rain to find the dining hall on fire, flames licking out from under the eaves. Everson rushed across the highway to the beach cabins, for Clayton was camp dietician at the time. "Clayton!" he called through the storm, "Clayyy-ton! Clayyy-ton! The kitchen's on fire!"

The COs broke out a couple windows and leveled fire extinguishers at the flames, but for some reason they didn't work. Bill Eshelman brought another fire extinguisher, then ran up the slick hillside behind the camp to the water tower, checking the reservoir level as the other men hooked up hoses. Dick Mills arrived at the scene, running from one door to another but finding the handles too hot to open; he then called for a car to be brought up and the headlights turned toward the building. Once they got the hoses on the source—the heating stove that Pottenger had earlier lit—the blaze was quickly extinguished. The smoke, however, was a problem, for the synthetic insulation smoldered horribly. By the time they could see well enough to inspect the damage, it was nearly daybreak. They'd saved the dining hall, but the entire inside was blackened. The heat had been so intense that the paint was blistered all the way down at the other end of the fifty-foot building. Anything susceptible to heat was melted: the solder on the baking scales had dissolved, and the lightbulbs in the ceiling dripped down like icicles. "In five more minutes," Everson later commented, "she would have broken loose and gone up like a torch."

Mills lost his temper. He stormed up to Jerry Rubin and announced that Pottenger was immediately fired as night watchman, then demanded a list of prospective replacements. Rubin replied that Mills couldn't just dismiss someone without some sort of hearing. Mills turned away and ordered his office clerk to find a trainee replacement who could join Pottenger on rounds the next evening. For his part, Pottenger recalled decades later that Mills had accused him—in front of everyone—of setting the fire on purpose. He'd been happy at his first camp in Michigan, Pottenger said, and he'd made sure that Mills knew of his displeasure at being sent to Waldport. He figured Mills had labeled him a troublemaker and simply assumed that Pottenger had set the fire on purpose. But the night watchman had a witness—the camper he'd met in the dining hall—and he let Mills know that he'd fight any charges of arson.

According to the Forest Service property damage report, the likely cause of the fire was from cans of varnish that had been used to refinish the dining room tables the day before; the empty cans had been left in cardboard boxes and placed on a wooden rack near the stove, apparently unnoticed by the night watchman when he lit that evening's fire.[36]

This was more than Mills could stand. He was resigning his position, the camp was descending into anarchy, and, on the eve of his final BSC directors' conference, the lasting impression of his tenure would be a building engulfed in fire. That night after dinner (presumably in an alternative location, probably the rec hall), he stood up and announced in a quavering voice that he was dissolving the Workers Committee and assuming full authority of the camp. It was an embarrassing scene, Everson remembered, and everyone there—including Forest Service supervisor Orville Richman—could see that Mills was not thinking clearly. To cap it off, Jerry Rubin, perhaps unable to deny his labor activist heritage, got up and excoriated Mills, just as if he was giving a soap-box speech on a Milwaukee street corner.[37]

Thus ended the Mills era at Camp Angel. Two days later, he left and never returned—but he did fire a parting shot. The day of his departure, he posted another letter to Elgin, specifically to Harold Row, this time blaming all the camp problems on the Fine Arts group, which he said also influenced the Workers Committee with anarchist ideas. The campers knew better, of course, but they had no way of knowing if Row would believe Mills or not. "Ah, me!" Eshelman wrote a friend. "If worst comes to worst, though, all we will have lost in fact will be the money we are now getting from Elgin. And we can carry on without that."[38]

■ ■ ■

Sometimes it's fortunate that the wheels of change in large institutions move very slowly. On his way to Chicago, Mills had stopped in Portland and met with Selective Service secretary Victor Olson, giving him an assessment of conditions at Camp Angel. Olson then came to Waldport ready to bring in a new director and set the camp straight. But after meeting with Everson, who gave him a full report on the events and personalities involved, Olson concluded that maybe things weren't so bad after all. Some concerns still needed to be addressed, such as Richman's objection to certain Fine Arts men working on Project and his disapproval of their "bohemian" attitudes. But Olson assured the men that the camp and the Fine Arts could continue.[39]

The word from Elgin also was positive. Vlad Dupre, fresh back from furlough and with his new wife, Ibby, had visited in Elgin with Morris Keeton. The BSC education director thought the Fine Arts was the best thing being done in CPS, Dupre said, and if the camp was broken up before the war ended, Keeton would do all he could to keep the group intact and the monthly operating funds coming. Dupre also reported that the Brethren administration overall approved of the Fine Arts, and that members of the advisory council felt that a democratic approach to camp government was not only preferable but necessary. It appeared that the letters Mills had sent did not have their desired effect.[40]

Next were the ongoing issues between the Fine Arts and other campers. Don Brumbaugh, former education director, stepped in as the camp's acting director until more definite word came from Elgin; he'd always got on well with the Fine Arts, and he let them work things out in their own way. The group felt that improved communication across the camp could help clear up misunderstandings, so they set out to answer issues concerning privilege in work assignments, tolerance for other perspectives, attitudes of elitism, and more transparency regarding finances and operations. "It was generally felt that we should be more politic in our politics," the Fine Arts meeting minutes read. "We seem to be too aggressive—the method of our procedure causes friction." They decided to take a poll.[41]

Simultaneous to all this, individual ideas percolated. Adrian, who had been pondering his plans and positions for some time, was in high mental gear. American society was divorced from what was really happening in the world, he felt, citing as evidence the popular magazines such as *Life:* "First you get the war, then a magnificent article on Colorado, then some cheesecake, and finally a chuckle over the Roosevelt days before the war. What a hodge-podge." Art was the only viable way to counter this, he said, and outlined his dream of producing *A Soldier's Tale,* a stage play with music and dance, written by Igor Stravinsky and featuring violin, clarinet, cello, horns, bass fiddle, and drums—complete with a conductor—and four actors. "We would go on a two-week tour of the western C.P.S. units with the play," he wrote. "The vision!"[42]

On a more immediate level, he came up with a protest idea one afternoon while clearing ditches along a Forest Service road in the slashing rain. Finding this work hardly of national importance, he decided he would make his own work important. Like a number of his peers, he would leave CPS, he would walk out—but rather than abandon the camp entirely, he would walk *out* from forestry work and walk *in* to the Fine Arts. That is, he would remain in camp and continue with chores and maintenance obligations as did any other camper. Rather than go on Project, he would instead devote his time to the Fine Arts. Technically, he would be AWOL although physically present in camp. When the government agents came to investigate, they would find him doing work just like anyone else, except it would be work that *he* had decided was of national importance. If he were then arrested and sent to prison, it would confirm that the government was interested less in the actual work of the COs and more in controlling them through forced labor. "It would be a test case demonstrating whether this government is democratic or fascist," he declared. But when he presented the idea to acting director Don Brumbaugh, he learned of consequences he hadn't considered, such as taking camp maintenance work away from others who'd been fairly assigned those tasks. They decided together that Adrian should take the eight days of furlough he'd accumulated up to this point and stay in camp according to his plan. If he decided to continue that way when the furlough was completed, he'd then be listed as AWOL or RTW (refused to work), and they'd see what happened next.[43]

He poured his energy into the printing projects, helping with Untide Press correspondence and working on the *Compass.* One weekend, they set up a production line of ten people to print and prepare the magazine covers for shipping, he wrote, "five people loading in the cardboard liner-uppers I had invented, another passing to Bill, who slipped them into the press at 850 an hour, another pulling them out, one unloading the cards and slip-sheeting (putting used sheets in between each print to prevent off-set) and another handing the cards to loaders." Other

Compass pages had been done by linotype in Portland, then sent back to Waldport, where Adrian helped Kemper cut the sections and paste up the pages onto large double sheets that would be returned to Portland for industry-standard offset printing. Adrian even found time to cut linoleum blocks for Bob Hyslop, who was putting together a book of religious quotes, titled *Remember Now Thy Creator.* "I am always working for someone else instead of using my talent for writing and for other forms of self-expression," Adrian lamented. "But perhaps the odd-jobs I do with friendship as a goal are my medium of creativity and I will never go beyond into purer art."[44]

These kinds of friendships actually served the Fine Arts well. In fact, the connection to the religious elements of the camp was stronger than some had surmised. The Religious Life Committee had struggled through the summer, drained of any sustained energy by the same problems facing the other groups: transfers, firefighting calls, and assignments to side camps. Also, their own version of separation and exclusivity had been underscored back in May, when Eshelman wrote a short blurb for the *Tide:* "Over a column of space was reserved for the activities of the Christian Service Group. Apparently they had nothing to say."[45] A low point was reached later in the summer when a call for nominations of Religious Committee chair came up empty. They suspended operations and began a series of soul-searching meetings—and decided the model they should use was the one employed by the Fine Arts: build programs that meet the needs of its members but always invite greater participation and strive for overall approval. They even changed their name to the Religious Interest Group.[46]

Helped along by Bob Scott's attendance in both the Fine Arts and the reconstituted religious group, cooperation and shared participation increased. Scott and others from the religious group were joined by Fine Arts members Kermit, Adrian, Bill Eshelman, David Jackson, and Martin Ponch in providing music, recordings, and Scripture readings for a Sunday evening chapel service. Collaboration in the ongoing reading series brought five consecutive Sunday readings from Laurence Housman's *Little Plays of St. Francis,* co-sponsored by the Fine Arts and the Religious Interest Group. The education committee director's report for October praised everyone involved, Scott in particular, for facilitating the events. "This type of creative and cooperative effort between groups of widely differing interests and points of view," he said, "is certainly a step in the direction in which we need to be going."[47]

Another project in the works promised further positive relations with religious group members. Martin Ponch was adapting a transcript from a recent trial in Tennessee, where a group of devoutly religious African-Americans were charged with draft resistance, and their pastor accused of helping them. Ponch was calling the play *Tennessee Justice,* and he hoped to enlist a number of Brethren church members and other religious campers who might be interested in the subject's theme. His intention, he said later, was not only to get the so-called "Holy Joes" interested in seeing the play but also to have them involved in it.[48]

Furthermore, when a new crop of men arrived at Waldport in early November, the Fine Arts quickly met with them and explained the group's purpose, role, and standing in camp—emphasizing that the funding came directly from BSC headquarters and in no way was subtracted from the camp budget. They underscored also that the printing operations—the Untide Press, the *Illiterati,* and the *Compass*—were entirely self-supporting and separate from the Fine Arts, and therefore received no funding from the BSC. They stressed that all were invited to participate in the various activities sponsored by the group.[49]

The Fine Arts even censored themselves—or at least engaged in tactful presentation of controversial subjects. When a traveling art exhibit came to Waldport, they refrained from posting two nudes with the rest of the exhibit in the dining hall, choosing instead to hang them in the group's office in the rec hall, where they still could be seen but were not forced upon unwilling viewers.[50]

It shouldn't have been entirely surprising, then, when the results of the Fine Arts poll (sent out as a questionnaire) came in generally positive. Regarding whether or not the group should continue, the vote was overwhelmingly in favor. There was some concern expressed about certain personalities, privileges, and politics—prompting an observation from a CO who had been with Adrian at the North Dakota camp and was visiting Waldport just then. This man had been in CPS since it began in 1941, and he pointed out that the charges against the Fine Arts were the same as those leveled at a communal living group organized in North Dakota. "There will always be a certain faction opposed to what specialized groups are trying to do," Adrian wrote his family. "Wherever you go in C.P.S. the pattern is the same, old events with new names."[51]

Further complicating matters, the day before the Fine Arts poll was counted up a note appeared unexpectedly on the camp bulletin board:

> To Whom It May Concern:
>
> This note is to indicate that beginning with the third fiscal term of the Fine Arts Group on November 15, I no longer desire to be considered a member of the Group; and that I am not available for participation in any program or activity with which the Fine Arts Group has any official connection.
>
> Robert Scott[52]

Scott had always followed his conservative religious path, functioning as a somewhat arms-length member of the Fine Arts. Even though heavily involved in the music, constantly playing piano in the group performances and giving erudite, occasionally passionate talks at record concerts, he rarely got involved in the bull sessions and apparently never came to the gatherings in the cabins, especially when drinking was going on. He had been the Forest Service secretary for some time, and with supervisor Richman now so negative on the Fine Arts, it was generally felt that Scott's primary concern was to save his job by severing relations with these alleged troublemakers. Bill Eshelman acknowledged how some might feel Scott was acting in self-interest, but he believed it was self-sacrifice, stemming from what he saw as Scott's sense of fairness. While filling out the work reports for the Forest Service, Scott had noticed the large number of Fine Arts members assigned to Overhead positions—and he knew this was a point of tension across the camp. Scott quit the group so that less Fine Arts members would be on Overhead, said Eshelman, who also believed it was a real sacrifice because Scott loved teaching and playing music so much.[53] Warren Downs, who had played music with Scott for nearly a year, felt it was something more. Scott probably was concerned about keeping his position, he said, but mostly it was due to a conflict of personalities in the Fine Arts—and Scott's was one of the more difficult ones to accommodate.[54]

Whatever the reason, the resignation of a long-active member did not reflect well on the Fine Arts. No matter how many carefully outlined explanations, no matter how many clearly articulated arguments, the perception of the group as a kind of catch-all cause of the camp's problems just wouldn't go away. "Certainly we've made mistakes," Everson wrote to Morris Keeton in late November. "But we're trying to learn. We *have* learned." Along with the errors, they'd also had some bad luck, he said. Dick Mills losing control of the camp—and perhaps his senses—was the result of much more than his tensions with the Fine Arts. Orville Richman turning sour on the group was an unfortunate consequence of a few people being difficult. The dining hall fire was a poorly timed accident. All the other problems then seemed to coalesce so that the Fine Arts had become an easy scapegoat. The most surprising part was how quickly it happened, Everson said. "Two months ago things were fairly smooth."[55]

He included in the letter a sample sheet of the questionnaire and results of the camp survey on the Fine Arts. While the majority vote on whether the Fine Arts should continue was affirmative, the responses to questions about the group's influence on the camp were mixed. Regarding the "general effect of Fine Arts on camp," the vote of good over bad was twenty-five to fourteen, with eight voting "neither" and three saying "both." But the next question, "Do you think the bad outweighs the good?" came in at twenty-three "yes" and seventeen "no," with eleven voting "balances." Beneath that, respondents could choose reasons for this "bad" effect, which included personalities, influence on camp policies, snobbery, cliquishness, special privileges, unwillingness to work in side camps, and too many Fine Arts members on Overhead (such as kitchen and office). The final item, though, spoke volumes: "presence of Fine Arts Secretary, Miss Langley." Out of the fifty-six respondents at the main camp, thirteen said this was a reason for the bad effects. At the Hebo side camp, eight out of nine respondents checked this box—reflecting perhaps more an attitude than actual experience, as Manche was not present in Hebo, fifty miles up the coast.[56]

Manche. The single woman who worked for those artists. Who bought them liquor and hung out at their cabin across the road—sometimes late into the night, maybe all night long. Who smoked and swore and ran the printer like any old journeyman. She certainly did not fit the Holy Joes' image of a woman, if the group up at Hebo had any say in it. "While Manche is a very good influence here," Adrian wrote his family, "I am beginning to see that she isn't completely good." Early in her stay at Waldport, she wouldn't take part in any off-color conversation, Adrian said. "She used to protest when someone yelled a long drawn out, 'Shiiiit,' but now she says it." With her Oregon liquor license, she was the group's steady conduit to booze, but that was getting to be a problem with the Fine Arts under scrutiny, Everson told Adrian. They'd worked so hard to get her accepted as part of the program—and then she not only supplies the liquor but drinks up her share as well, he said. And when Adrian expressed amazement that Manche hadn't become intimate with any of the men, Everson looked over his glasses at the younger man and said, "Oh, but don't think she hasn't."[57]

There it was again: sex. In a conservative environment, be it a small town or a church-administered work camp, all it takes is one time, or the belief that something happened one time, to unleash the wagging tongues and disapproving stares. Manche was no prude, nor was she alone. The Fine Arts used their communally rented cabin for artistic work retreats, quiet time, raucous parties, and whatever else suited their moods and needs. Male, female, married, unmarried—pacifist does not mean dispassionate; it does not mean celibate. The Fine Arts was no hotbed of depravity, but there were affairs and sexual liaisons. These were creative people, subject to all the passions, desires, and diverse character traits that attend any such group. They were forced together in a period of great upheaval and uncertainty; that they reached out to one another for comfort should hardly be surprising. It wasn't just the Fine Arts, either. Suffice it to say the members of Camp Angel were human.[58]

Oddly enough, the perception of the Fine Arts as bohemian eccentrics led to a well-paying if short-lived music gig in which Adrian, Bus Erle, and Vic McLane, a piano player, substituted in a dance band in Florence, twenty-five miles down the coast. Getting there was a challenge, but Bill Eshelman procured some gas-rationing tickets assigned to the

Untide Press for cleaning purposes, and drove them down in the camp panel truck. They pulled up on Main Street at the Rainbow Room, a spacious hall decorated with streamers and a low stage for the band. They went in and met the three musicians, Adrian recalled: "the drummer in his snappy Coast Guard uniform," the singer, "a tall homely country girl," and a young saxophone player—all thanking them profusely and ready to play. "It took only four choruses of 'Blue Skies' to show us that our tastes in jazz were similar and that we made a pretty fair Dixieland band." It turned out, however, that the drummer was a madman, Adrian said, whooping and yelling and smashing the kit so hard that at one point he knocked the snare drum off its stand. When the slow numbers came up, he got a friend to sit in and then danced with the girls himself. No alcohol was openly available in town—and a good thing, too, Adrian noted. "It took two sets to bring him back to the stand after the intermission." Bus Erle, a professional musician accustomed to the usual complimentary drinks, wasn't too happy about the dearth of alcohol, but the good news was that they got ten dollars each, plus money for gas. Even Eshelman, as the driver, picked up $2.50 and got into the dance for free.

The following week they were joined by Vlad and Ibby Dupre, Manche, Kemper, and Bob Harvey—and this time they managed to bring down a couple cases of beer, which they visited in the panel truck during the breaks. This evening, however, brought in a fellow CO named Johnny Welch, who had been temporarily hired out to work at a sawmill in Mapleton, a few miles inland from Florence. Welch was a Jehovah's Witness, no teetotaler pacifist; he came into Florence, located some alcohol and got rip-roaring drunk, then pulled a knife on someone and was thrown in jail. The police said they wouldn't pursue charges if the other campers got Welch out of town that night, which they did. All seemed to blow over until the following week, when they received a letter from the band's saxophone player, who said they were canceling all dances. After the knife-pulling incident of the week before, the whole town was out for the COs, he said. "It would be foolish to try to give a dance."[59]

As if there weren't enough troubles in camp already, a new issue of the *Untide* suddenly appeared on December 7, the third anniversary of Pearl Harbor. It wasn't put out by the original crew—Coffield, Hackett, and Siemons were gone. Nor did the Fine Arts have anything to do with it officially. Instead, this independent effort came from Kemper Nomland and Henry Wolff, a twenty-year-old telephone clerk from New York State. No reason was given for the paper's resurrection. Maybe Wolff, who wasn't in Waldport when the *Untide* had its day, wanted to make his own mark. And maybe Kemper, who'd always enjoyed a good prank, couldn't resist the opportunity one more time. At any rate, the rag showed up with an editorial lambasting Bob Scott for his very public withdrawal from the

Fine Arts. They compared him to a little boy who wouldn't play with other children because his parents (in this case, the Forest Service) disapproved. Scott, who did not suffer criticism well, swore he'd never have anything to do with the Fine Arts again. It was a cheap shot, to be sure—and even some of the Fine Arts members expressed their disapproval.[60]

The front-page story caused more concern. Under the title "Memo #54,000,000,000,000" the piece satirized BSC director Harold Row's many messages regarding camp administration and policy. The appearance of this must have seemed incredible to some, for Row had recently arrived in Waldport to personally mediate between the Fine Arts and other groups in the camp. Luckily, Row possessed a somewhat thicker skin than Scott, and apparently didn't spend any time worrying about the *Untide*. Instead, he focused on helping the camp factions communicate with each other, first calling a meeting of any interested campers *not* involved with the Fine Arts and hearing them out. He then put together an advisory council of eight people, half from the Fine Arts and half from outside the group. They drew up a set of conditions under which the Fine Arts would continue, addressing the campers' concerns about special privileges and the Fine Arts' concerns about the entire group being held responsible for the behavior of just a few individuals. "Row came, saw, and conquered," Everson wrote to Morris Keeton. "The man's ability to get things straightened out by a combination of insight, cajolery and kidding is amazing." The advisory council in particular was marvelous in its simplicity, he said. "It gives people a focal point instead of running around like a bunch of coyotes howling at the moon. Now the beefs can be aired, conclusions arrived at, and action taken. Good."[61]

As 1944 neared its end, the sense of accomplishment was tempered by a bit of weariness. The printing had gone well: *The Waldport Poems* was sold out, and a new letterpress edition of the *War Elegies* was done. The third *Illiterati* had gone out, and a fourth number—to be done entirely on the press—was in the works. The *Compass* was out, with plans for another art and literary issue. Jacob Sloan's book of poetry, *Generation of Journey*, with illustrations by Barbara Straker James, was ready to go, waiting only on delivery of the paper. They had Kenneth Patchen's antiwar poems in hand, and while there were challenges ahead for this book, it would be their biggest-name project by far. Submissions for the proposed CPS anthology also trickled in.

Two more Fine Arts transfers had arrived. Tom Polk Miller, who'd earlier expressed interest from Camp #27 back in Tallahassee, Florida, came at the end of November. He was a "tanned, high cheek-boned, brown-eyed architect, pianist, and poet from Houston, Texas," Adrian wrote; they quickly became friends.[62] Joe Gistirak, another Hedgerow Theatre alum, had transferred from Big Flats and was setting up a

Drawing for "War Elegy V" letterpress version.

production of Henrik Ibsen's *Ghosts*. Also, word was that Bob Harvey's wife, Joyce, would arrive after the holidays and play one of the two female roles in *Ghosts;* Ibby Dupre would play the other. The readings series of plays, stories, and poems had resulted in twenty performances over a twenty-week span, including the five-week collaboration with the Religious Interest Group for the *St. Francis* readings.

The music program had a world-class violinist and other talented string and woodwind players. Although they'd lost Bob Scott and his competence on piano, consequently having to drop some elements of their shows, the rehearsals were less tense, Adrian said. "We all regret Scott's withdrawal but I am seeing it a little more as his own error."

The crafts continued as a popular activity, with myrtlewood carving, loom weaving, and ceramic potting. Waldo Chase returned to offer his popular classes in drawing and block printing, but this time around some of the Fine Arts members felt his folk-art approach didn't meet their expectations of quality, and they insisted that Chase be officially sponsored by the Education Committee rather than the Fine Arts. It came off more as snobbery than anything else, and Adrian expressed his regret after Chase left the camp. "I felt very sorry for him—the way he was snubbed—for he is a very good-hearted fellow," Adrian wrote. "He left me with a wood block and lots of paper to go ahead with color printing, but if I do it, it will only be for him, the lonely one."[63]

The camp had weathered large changes in personnel, the inevitable jealousies and conflicts, a breakdown of its governing system, the resignation of its director, and a vote on the continuation of its most visible and viable program. There were personal losses, too. In late November, Vlad Dupre learned that his brother, serving in the medical corps, had been killed in the Philippines. In early December, Edwa Everson came to visit one more time; she stayed a week, then left, and Everson announced they were separating.

As Christmas approached, the lifestyle differences yawned like a chasm between the conservative campers and the Fine Arts. The religious groups gathered at Kimmel Hall to sing carols while the artists clustered in the Tillie the Whale cabins across the highway, drinking and debating the usual topics in art, politics, and philosophy. Manche still slept at Kimmel Hall, in her cubbyhole space off the hallway, and one night she overheard a Christadelphian wife telling a Brethren wife that she and her husband didn't watch motion pictures because when Christ returned to earth for his second coming, they didn't want to be caught sitting in a movie house. The Fine Arts' comment on holiday festivities was to hang an undecorated spruce tree upside down from the ceiling in their office.

It was now like a small colony across the road with cottages rented by Clayton and Barbara James, Vlad and Ibby Dupre, Bill and Gertrude Jadiker, Jerry and Jan Rubin, and Isabel Mount (currently single but who would later marry Tom Polk Miller), in addition to the communally rented Fine Arts cabin. On Christmas Eve, as midnight approached and the artists lounged with their requisite drinks, they suddenly heard "Hark! The Herald Angels Sing" coming from some carolers outside—the religious conservatives, who had finished their worship services. "Everybody hid his glass of booze so that we could acknowledge the singing of the Holy Joes," Adrian wrote. Fortunately, he added, all the liquor was gone by noon on Christmas Day, and Erle and Harvey as part of the kitchen crew were able to serve the holiday dinner relatively sober and play music that evening.[64]

In the week leading up to New Year's Eve, the winter gales came through, the rain slashing across the rooftops and peppering the windowpanes. In between the storms, the campers could see the next one coming from far out on the water, the clouds bunching together as if gathering strength to throw the next blast of biting rain or hail against the land. With a replenished liquor supply, the Fine Arts crew livened up their debates as well, and one night Bob Harvey came back from watching the waves pounding the beach and declared that all government should be abolished, leaving everyone alone to cooperate as they liked or not. "But that would be chaos," someone said, "and people would die." Very well, Harvey retorted. "Give me chaos, give me complete anarchy, but by Christ, it would be a hell of a lot better and a hell of a lot fewer people would die than in this [world] where we're organized to kill!" As if to drive the point home, right before New Year's the infamous Johnny Welch, now slated for transfer to a government camp, drank too much again and went on a rampage, slowing down only long enough to vomit into the printing room stove. He eventually wore out as the year's clock ticked down, but not before deciding that Erle and Harvey were evil personified, and threatening to kill them with his knife.[65]

Everson retreated to a quiet space before midnight and penned a letter to Larry Powell. "I write from the tip of the year," he said. "It fades out in squalls and thunders. Right now the sky is clear, the moon full; the stainless stars sharp in their sky." He'd passed through a portal in both his personal and professional life—like so many others throughout the camp, throughout the country and the world, each in their own way. The war in the Pacific wore on, a step-by-step affair as it became clear the Japanese would not surrender but must be beaten, perhaps to the last. In Europe, the Nazis had launched their desperate assault on Allied lines in Belgium and France, in what came to be known as the Battle of the Bulge, raising concerns that perhaps the Germans would not surrender, either. "The war will drag through forty-five, forty-six, we'll be here till forty-seven," Everson wrote. "But that's little. The circumstances mean little any longer. Strange, how when the past collapses, you lose your fears. Like being reborn. A whole new fresh vigorous life opens out."[66]

CHAPTER 10

Be Cheerful, Keep Smiling

WHILE NEW YEAR'S WEEKEND at Camp Angel invited reflection and some degree of indulgence, the central coast communities were anticipating an overall lively time. "The Waldport Chamber of Commerce Inc., are sponsoring a Big New Year's Eve Dance Dec. 30th, at Cap's with all the proceeds going to the P.T.A.," announced the *Lincoln County Times* in its idiosyncratic typesetting style. "Bob Howe's Band will play with Its All-Star line up of Helen Marks 'The Wizard of the Keys' and George 'Paul Whiteman' Williamson on the drums. A Great Crowd is expected to be in attendance."[1]

One week later the story was very different, as a column headlined "The Act Has a Nasty Odor!!!" heralded another Dave Hall editorial attack on Camp Angel. "Last Saturday night a party of Conscientious Objectors and their wives or lady friends lined up before the bar for a Considerable time and later put on a Jitterbug Contest on the Crowded dance floor," Hall wrote. "This demonstration of the Art of Jitterbug dancing together with the elbow tipping episode must have given the people who witnessed this a very repulsive sensation in the pit of their stomachs." Hall tempered his criticism a touch with an acknowledgment that not all COs were bad—particularly the Quakers and Brethren. But American soldiers were dying in Europe and the South Pacific, he said. "So WHY are these Conscientious Objectors with the JITTERBUG COMPLEX allowed to go out, drink and publicly flount [*sic*] their draft status in front of hundreds of people who have Dear Ones in The Uniform of These United States? Let THESE Conscientious Jitterbugs stay in camp—Their Act Smells!"[2]

Bill Jadiker and his wife Gertrude were two of those "conscientious jitterbugs." Jadiker recalled years later that there were older people at the dance, and the music was jazz from the 1930s. When a lively number began, he and Gertrude started dancing. It was natural to do the jitterbug, he said, adding that they were rather good at it. As they were dancing, Jadiker noticed people talking to each other and pointing at them. He didn't know precisely what it meant, but he told his wife they should probably leave, and they did. Jadiker didn't hear anything more that night or in the days following, so he figured that was it. He was shocked when Hall's editorial came out.[3]

Enoch Crumpton, who sometimes worked with the Fine Arts, had assumed the acting director position at Camp Angel, and he sent a report to Harold Row, attempting to present the incident in a neutral light. Three married couples and two single men, he wrote, went as goodwill ambassadors for the camp. The dance hall, Cap's Beach Resort, had a large dance floor, a bar serving soft drinks and beer, and a small store. During the evening any of the campers might have stood at the bar, Crumpton said, and some of them probably had a beer. However, he added, they could have ordered a soft drink and still been at the bar, which he supposed technically fit under Hall's "elbow-tipping" description. As to the dancing, he said, "I am informed by the persons there that the only dancing that could be anywhere nearly described as 'jitterbug' was during one extra fast piece of music which required extra energy to follow the rapid tempo of the music. One couple was able to keep in time longer than the others and for that reason drew a small amount of attention." Nobody, he said, felt there had been an incident worthy of comment.[4]

The Forest Service also made their investigations and the regional supervisor submitted detailed reports, which boiled the incident down to this: Some COs went to the dance with some women. The proprietor knew them and had no concerns about their presence. He served them beer but did not feel they were drunk. Some of the couples did the jitterbug, and one couple got attention; some people thought they might even be professional dancers. The problems began when some COs danced with some of the local women, which upset some of the local men. When told they'd been dancing with pacifists, the women acted surprised, but not all the men believed them. Also, one of the women was Dave Hall's sister-in-law.[5]

Given Hall's adventures into editorial hyperbole regarding "subversive activities" at Camp Angel the previous year, this one should have blown over like the regular squalls that came in from the ocean and scudded across the hills to the inland valleys. But some of these "older" people tended toward the conservative margins—and some of them were World War I veterans, members of the American Legion. A letter from one "Geo. B. Williamson, Adjutant" sent to the Oregon director of Selective Service, set off a chain of controversy that made it all the way to national director General Lewis B. Hershey. Williamson's letter described yet another version of the New Year's dance, relating from his "eyewitness" experience that COs attended the dance "with their women in a noticably [sic] intoxicated condition," that some "conducted themselves in a most disagreeable manner, jitterbugging all over the floor and bumping into people," and that several COs "went so far as to ask for dances with the girls from Waldport who distinctly resent such advances from them." But this was about more than jitterbugging. Williamson stressed that Waldport was a decent, upstanding community and they didn't want any trouble with the COs. But, he warned, they could make no guarantees if an episode like the one on New Year's weekend occurred again. With that position made clear, he said the local American Legion post would like answers to the following questions:

What pay does the U.S. give a conchie and what for?

What religious creed or creeds sponsor Camp 56?

What hours are they confined to camp?

Are women permitted to eat their meals regularly there?

Are women permitted to roam promiscuously at the camp?

Are the personel [*sic*] permitted to live with their women away from camp overnight?[6]

This was a potential public relations nightmare; if there was one group Selective Service did not want to offend with regard to CPS, it was American Legion veterans and their families and friends. A letter from Colonel Lewis F. Kosch, Selective Service assistant director for camp operations, gave detailed answers to the questions requesting hard information about pay, religion, hours, and meals; he could not offer much in response to the ones that were less questions than veiled requests for confirmation of prejudices.[7]

More letters made the rounds: from regional and national headquarters of the Brethren Service Committee to offices of the National Service Board for Religious Objectors (the CPS oversight organization), and back to Camp Angel, where Enoch Crumpton was simply hoping the whole thing would go away. The immediate result was that the lid was tightened on rules regarding behavior in and outside of camp: the men were advised to stay away from Cap's dance hall for the time being, and they were urged to follow not only the letter but the spirit and intent of the Selective Service regulations for visitors and overnight leave—including the rule that a CO assigned to camp barracks could not live with his wife and family off the compound. Whether or not these rules were fully enforced, the record doesn't say. But Bill Eshelman did write to a former Waldport CO that "Crumpton has shown himself remarkably blind when he wishes."[8]

As with most such incidents, someone's head had to roll. According to one source, Manche had been at the New Year's dance; besides that, the issue of some campers' discomfort with her presence on the grounds had never been resolved. Now this latest accusation from the American

Legion, bringing up women who "roam promiscuously" in camp, forced Crumpton to follow up more literally on a quiet agreement made in December that Manche would move toward ending her official relationship with the group. As of February 1, she was no longer Fine Arts secretary, had moved out of her cubbyhole in Kimmel Hall, and was living in one of the Tillie the Whale cabins across the road. Maybe this official severance would be enough to placate the unhappy ones.[9]

In some ways, Manche's move across the highway concentrated the energy even more. Six of the other cabins were rented by Fine Arts members, and the Dupres were in a small house called the Jenny Wren just across the path to the beach. When Bob Harvey's wife Joyce arrived, there were actually more women than men living in the cabins, and their contributions were influential to the environment. Isabel Mount, Tom Miller's Texas girlfriend, decorated her home with dyed burlap curtains and painted the floors blue. When she spattered some red and yellow paint by accident, she continued the process by dribbling the colors throughout the room. A January open house at her cabin brought in all the gang, along with local guests Doc Workman and his wife, the secondhand store proprietors who had sold the Challenge press to the Fine Arts on credit. As the night wore on and the drink flowed freely, Workman told stories of his earlier days as a union radical, an orthopedic doctor, and a designer of celebrities' tombs. "It got so fantastic," Adrian said later, "some of us were beginning to wonder if all this wasn't imagination."[10]

They were reaching the heights of their bohemian period. On any given evening, Fine Arts people might be in the press room, clanking away on Jacob Sloan's book for the Untide Press, the next *Illiterati,* or programs for plays and readings. Joe Gistirak had the cast and crew rehearsing *Ghosts,* Martin Ponch and his group were nearly ready with *Tennessee Justice,* the musicians practiced their concertos, and a new art exhibit was being prepared in the dining hall. During the winter storms, when the wind shook the very walls of the buildings and the rain rattled across the roof like gravel thrown by a giant hand, a gathering of a few or perhaps more might be relaxing around the crackling fireplace with the Dupres in the Jenny Wren, or cozy with the woodstove in one of the smaller cabins, talking of art, literature, philosophy, or the president's recent call for continued conscription after the war. Adrian related how they often talked of the poverty in America, a land of such material abundance. "Here in wartime America thousands of people have to live in medieval squalor," he wrote, "while millions are being blown up overseas." But it wasn't all doomsday and politics, he added. "For relief we usually get into sexuality, homosexuality, bisexuality, incest, and Henry Miller." They would then compare Miller to James Joyce, Proust, and D. H. Lawrence, throwing in a couple of dirty stories from Miller's letters or banned books. This might be followed by broader discussions on all aspects of art and media. "Eventually we get to mysticism and Clayton James."[11]

Sometimes the topic was abstract art. Bob Harvey was painting steadily, and the tiny cabin he and Joyce shared was like a mini-gallery with his paintings on the walls. One night Warren Downs asked if the abstraction was suggesting something that already exists, or if it was creating a whole new form. Joyce explained that the paintings weren't intended to represent any specific concrete *thing*, but rather meant to express a mood or the relationships of form and balance. Adrian studied each of the paintings on the wall and concluded that they must be good because he could understand them. "Maybe abstract painting isn't so obscure after all," he said. Harvey, for his part, remained aloof and focused on his work. One night, after a storm had washed through and a rare, bright moon illuminated the still-heavy waves, Harvey went for a walk on the beach and came back "raving about all the power and energy."[12]

Or they might talk of organizing as with a union. Each camper had made his individual stand by coming to CPS. But some occasions, they felt, might demand collective action. Adrian had continued his personal protest of staying in camp and choosing his own work of national importance, and Enoch Crumpton had simply reported him as RTW. But, unbeknownst to the campers, Forest Service supervisor Richman had written to agency headquarters in Portland that Adrian should be transferred because his ongoing refusal to work was hurting camp morale. When news of this spread, it had the opposite effect of what Richman had claimed. Jerry Rubin called for a full investigation. Everson said they should all go on a work slowdown. Others muttered their disgust at what they saw as Richman's underhanded manner. Adrian, while appreciative of the support, kept his opinion quiet. "But I suppose a little revolution," he wrote to his family, "say a work strike or mass walkout would be interesting."[13]

When the parties got going a little more in the cramped cabins, they might move their conversation to wherever was convenient. One night Vlad Dupre joined Everson and Clayton James sitting cross-legged under a table while the party swirled above them. The three sat there, talking, drinking and feeling more profound, but probably just getting drunk as they discussed, debated, and solved the world's problems. This could have been a beatnik happening in 1959 Greenwich Village or a crash-pad hangout in San Francisco. But it was 1945, in a tiny tourist cabin on a sliver of Oregon coastline hemmed in by the mountains and the sea, hours away from the nearest city of any size. Here at Camp Angel, their music was what they'd brought or made. Their books were what they'd borrowed or made. Their art was what they'd commissioned or made. It was primitive, but it was real.[14]

More and more, they talked about life after the war. The end was coming soon, everyone knew. Even President Roosevelt, reelected to an unprecedented fourth term, said in his January State of the Union address, "Nineteen hundred forty-five can see the final ending of the Nazi-fascist reign of terror in Europe. Nineteen hundred forty-five can see the closing in of the forces of retribution about the center of the malignant power of imperialist Japan." Then he added, "Most important of all—1945 can and must see the substantial beginning of the organization of world peace."[15]

World peace! Why, the men at Camp Angel had been working on that for years. Bud Hawkins, a Baptist CO and skilled boat builder from Maine, had been constructing boats for various Forest Service projects (including a rowboat for a Girl Scout camp). But Hawkins really wanted to build a schooner large enough for a group to live in and sail the oceans as citizens of the world. In fact, Hawkins said, he had ten thousand dollars he was prepared to invest in the project. Adrian and the Harveys loved the idea. "Think of it," Adrian wrote, "when a man leaves port he no longer owes allegiance to any government." Think of raising a family this way, he added. "The children would have a completely new perspective on the world. Instead of patriotism, they would love the world." As to survival, the ocean was full of food. They could also rent out the boat for cruises during the summer, or make a musical quartet of Erle, Harvey, Downs, and Adrian; when they stopped at coastal cities, they'd give concerts. "Bob, Joyce, and I are sold on it. And here we have a fellow with the skill and finances to work it for us," Adrian said. "So you see, the schooner is the salvation of the world."[16]

Cross-legged on the floor at a Camp Angel party. Everson at far left, talking to Bus Erle at right.

Another idea was closer to the current Fine Arts experience—a cooperative community grounded in the arts. If they could find people willing to band together and share the time and energy for basic necessities, they might create and foster an environment that allowed them time to do their art. With several families sharing a single car, refrigerator, laundry facilities, and even a common living room or library, the savings could be enormous, Eshelman explained in a letter to a prewar friend. "The qualification primarily required of a man is that he be able to contribute to the artistic output of the group." They could set up the press and maybe even get it to the point of making a profit; the crafts-oriented people could make and sell woodwork, pottery, and weaving. A number of campers were interested: Everson, Dupre, Eshelman, Kermit, and even Coffield over at Cascade Locks wanted the press to continue. Some of the painters were curious, and Kemper and Tom Polk Miller—both architects—were considering joining in and offering their talents to get the initial buildings constructed on a plot of land that would be bought by the group. "Our idea is to build a community that will enable us to avoid the usual economic pressures so we may create and also publish the work of other men less fortunate," Eshelman said. "Possibilities are, of course, endless."[17]

■ ■ ■

As January headed into its final week, Martin Ponch was ready with *Tennessee Justice,* the play constructed from a magazine article about the trial of nine African-American COs and their pastor in western Tennessee.[18] While Ponch's East Coast brusqueness had a way of irritating some of the more laid-back West Coast Fine Arts members, his direct approach to things often brought otherwise disparate groups together. His subject matter (conscientious objection to war, racial discrimination, and the rights of minorities), contemporaneity (the trial took place in early 1944), and approach to the presentation (mixing the article's text with a prewar peace sermon and Bible quotes) made it appealing to the more religiously oriented campers who might otherwise have avoided Fine Arts productions. He adapted a script from the published article and set the play in a courtroom. He then added a chorus—a standard element of classical Greek drama, in this case presented as a church choir. A number of Brethren camp members were competent singers who sometimes sang in the regional churches, and Ponch recruited them for his choir. He then asked them to also play jury members in the court scenes. "The scene changed from church to court, church to court," he explained later. "You'd hear the choir, then you'd hear the jury discussing, or listening to the evidence, and so forth."[19]

His casting choices may not always have been the best actors available, but they were certainly true to type. Ponch got two of the few

African-Americans at camp involved: James Williams played the preacher on trial, and Glenn Evans filled a speaking part as one of the CO defendants. Ponch recruited Charles Cooley, a Methodist from Ohio studying to become a minister, to play the district attorney, and Mark Rouch, a member of the Religious Interest Group (and also studying for the ministry) to play the judge. The Fine Arts were represented also, with Tom Polk Miller playing a witness, and Joe Gistirak as the defense lawyer (an appropriate casting for the Hedgerow actor, for he was a white man playing an African-American). The choir, as Ponch intended, was almost entirely Brethren, and an electrician in the backstage crew made sure Adrian—who oversaw set design and construction—knew how to run the stage lights using Francis Barr's saltwater dimmer switches. One scene required lights to flash alternately between the two sections of the stage, and Adrian practiced again and again, rushing from one tub of saltwater to another, so that the timing of action and illumination was correct. He compared the task to learning a new musical instrument. "The whole week was integrated (no time even for a shower until Friday evening), everything directed toward the set and lighting."[20]

Adrian poured his all into the play, working closely on stage design with Kermit, whose enthusiasm prompted Adrian to comment that he was seeing real possibility for socialized art, especially in cooperative theater. He even designed the program, initially going a bit overboard with the idea, folding the sheets of paper into the shape of a gavel. When his colleagues joked that he might as well make it a balled-up wad, or have homing pigeons deliver the notes into the laps of the audience, he printed a simple folder program and let the play promote itself.[21]

This was perhaps not the best thing. The play, it seemed, had more value in raising social consciousness than in presenting quality art. Even with Joe Gistirak and his Hedgerow experience, two performances at Camp Angel were panned by some in the Fine Arts. Eshelman called it "a retching staging." Warren Downs said it was "dramatic but not drama." Even Adrian admitted, "*Tennessee Justice* is a discouragingly bad play, but the transformation of the church into court and vice-versa may save it."[22]

That appeared to be what happened for a fair number of religious campers who previously had little interest in the Fine Arts or even theater. The Jehovah's Witnesses thought it was great, the best thing done so far, Adrian reported. And the Holy Joes, he said, began to wonder, "Maybe the Fine Arts has got some good in it after all."[23]

Ponch, who had witnessed the South's overt racism during his time at the Gatlinburg camp, set his sights on getting out the message and took the play on the road. A few weeks after doing the shows at Waldport, they packed up the stage equipment with the twenty-odd cast and crew members into the camp panel truck and three cars, and drove fifty miles down the coast and another fifty inland to Camp #59 at Elkton, in the Coast

Range hills. The audience there included a special contingent of young women from the University of Oregon, who dined with the Waldport and Elkton COs, curious about this statement on racism and religion. After dinner and conversation, the theater group retired to prepare themselves and the stage, and a bit later the audience was seated. Anticipation mounted as the room dropped into almost complete darkness and organ music played. Then the lights slowly came up to reveal the Tennessee reverend, kneeling in prayer as the choir began to sing.

The play itself wasn't particularly long, and its sense of forward action relied almost entirely on the four light-dimmer switches working correctly. At one point, the scene switched back and forth to both sides of the stage, the dialogue alternating between the district attorney in the courtroom and the reverend in the church—the scene that Adrian had practiced repeatedly that week before opening night. Chuck Cooley, who played the district attorney, remembered in particular a section from the closing arguments. The defense lawyer said in his deep Southern drawl that the reverend on trial

> . . . been preaching his religion for 30 years and never has given anybody any trouble. Long before this war started he planted the seeds of his religion in these boys' hearts. Now the war comes and the government says everybody got to fight. Do you think [the reverend] should say he has been preaching a lie all this time and for them to go ahead and fight?
>
> You know, this man was a heathen. His ancestors didn't have this religion when you brought them from the jungles of Africa. You white folks taught him your religion. You gave him your Bible to read. You told him about your Jesus. He believed in your Bible, he accepted your Jesus. You told him that it was a good religion, he believed it. Now are you going to say that this religion is wrong; that we are going to have to send you to jail because you believe it?[24]

"The response was exceptional," Cooley remembered, "communication between actors and audience was electric. The applause was prolonged." As soon as the play ended, he said, they cleared the space, scattered hay on the floor, and held a dance complete with polka music.[25]

The next night, they took it up to Eugene and played before one hundred people at the Methodist church downtown. Afterwards, it was more church youth activity, what Cooley called the "Three Fs . . . Fun, Food and Fellowship," and after that, a prayer circle, hymns and benediction.[26] Adrian recorded a slightly different perspective, noting that the gathering after the show featured cups of cocoa, tiny sandwiches, and games that seemed designed to exhaust youthful energy so that they'd be too tired to think of other activities. Later, some of the Waldport men went to spend the night at the home of Orval Etter, Fellowship of Reconciliation secretary for Oregon, whose family kept an open-door policy for traveling COs and peace workers, providing meals and bunk beds for whomever was there that night. It was all quite good, but there was an element of frustration as Adrian sat talking after dinner with Joe Gistirak and Bud Hawkins. "It is so stupid," Gistirak said, "these pure Christian Endeavor girls visiting camps, and F.O.R. people providing nice beds for you to sleep in when all you want is somebody to sleep with."[27]

Frustration showed itself on other levels. A January concert brought Donald Chamberlin, a bass vocalist from Cascade Locks, and Naomi Kirschner, wife of a CO there, who would play viola in a string quartet with Erle, Harvey, and Downs for a rendition of Matthew Arnold's "Dover Beach." Everyone got along well enough, but the practices were not promising. "Probably I'm just as much at fault," Downs wrote in his diary, "but it seems like Naomi doesn't play well enough (period) and Harvey doesn't play in time always or doesn't play softly enough at times."[28]

The performance was a flop, at least according to the musicians. After the show, Bus Erle stormed into the music room, threw the music sheets down and spat, "Jesus Christ!" No one challenged him. Downs wrote later that the group had nearly drowned out Erle's playing, that his own timing had been off, and that Naomi Kirschner had played a sharp note when she should have been flat. "Our Dover Beach was a Dover Bitch," he said. Plans to take the show to Portland—with expenses paid by the Fine Arts—were quietly shelved.

There was more talk about quality at the Fine Arts meeting a couple days later. Erle said they had to set standards for performances—and the first standard should be to accept nothing less than the highest quality. Others generally agreed, but on a less strict level. Joe Gistirak, perhaps thinking of his Hedgerow Theatre experience and current work in *Tennessee Justice*, felt that such restrictions amounted to censorship and would stifle creativity and experimentation. Erle retorted that experimentation was all fine and well—just don't have work of inconsistent quality sponsored by the Fine Arts. Downs thought this was not in keeping with the Fine Arts mission, which was to focus on critical analysis within the group rather than strive for recognition from outside. Where best to draw the line? It was a question that has long plagued artists everywhere.[29]

Other tensions grew as Camp Angel received transfers of more COs who had been difficult for other camps—such as the "permanent SQs," men who chronically reported to Sick Quarters as a way to protest or avoid work. The BSC also discontinued allowing transfers specifically for the Fine Arts, and perhaps the knowledge that the current group would be their final one exaggerated the personality conflicts. On top of that, nothing was definite—not the Fine Arts, not the camp leadership, not the CO enrollment, not even CPS itself. Nobody knew what orders might come down, when they might be changed, or even if the people giving the orders might be gone the next day. As a result, camp administration remained in flux; anything could change at any time. Enoch Crumpton continued as acting director, but with no real mandate or agenda beyond keeping the place from falling apart. Chuck Cooley stepped in as acting assistant director, but he was in no position to make substantial changes. The kitchen problems continued, this time with Kermit as dietician, whose hands-off approach to labor delegation grated on Eshelman after he found himself filling in for Cooley as acting assistant director. "Here we have our share of morons and farmers, grammar-school geniuses and twerps," the new administrator confided in a letter to a friend. "So the situation constantly arises: who is to take the responsibility of getting things done?"[30]

The Forest Service submitted its usual six-month plan for building and road maintenance, sign painting, firefighting, trail work, timber cruising, snag reduction, and campground improvements. The COs continued in their various responses—some doing the work, some doing it slowly, some doing it very slowly, and some refusing to work at all—resulting in paperwork, repeated consultation of the CPS rule book, ongoing questions and discussions, and general exasperation all around. According to camper Russell Eisenbise, a transferee from Pennsylvania was so upset about being at Waldport that he would just sit down when they reached the Project site. One time, they were returning from Mary's Peak and they ran out of gas a half mile from the crest of the last hill before Waldport. They figured if they could get to the top, they could coast all the way to a gas station in town. When the fifteen men got out to push the truck, the fellow who refused to work stayed inside, so they pushed the vehicle with his added weight, Eisenbise said. "I guess that was, ideally, showing the other cheek."[31]

Kemper developed his own work slow-down, carefully honing his technique to ride that fine line between refusing to work, which warranted punishment, and simply doing a very slow job, which was technically not breaking any rule. "He would move literally very slowly," Vlad Dupre remembered. "Working on the trail, those who were working hard would cut ten feet in thirty minutes." Kemper, though, took most of the day just to go ten feet, Dupre laughed. "He couldn't be accused of not working, but his level of accomplishment was minimal." Superintendent Richman was unimpressed; he barred Kemper from Project and reported that the CO was harming production, inciting rebellion, and damaging camp morale. The issue worked its way up the communications chain, involving Forest Service and NSBRO officials, leading to a threat that

Kemper would be transferred to Camp #135 in Germfask, Michigan, one of a handful of government-run camps that functioned as a kind of penal colony for misfits, insubordinates, and other problem campers. This prompted a group from Waldport to write Harold Row, urging the BSC to fight the transfer. They weren't condoning Nomland's actions, they said—a number of them actually disagreed with him—but Kemper *had not broken any rules.* The only thing he was guilty of, they insisted, was not fitting Richman's definition of completing the work "promptly and efficiently," as written in the regulations. Furthermore, they said, the question here was not the dictionary definition of "promptly and efficiently," but who interpreted that definition and how they arrived at that interpretation. They cited a recent case in Portland, in which Federal District Court Judge James A. Fee dismissed RTW charges against a CO, saying that the words "promptly and efficiently" were too ambiguous to define the law. "We agree," the Waldport group said. "The question becomes, who will determine?"[32]

There was still the opposite approach to the work issue—the "second mile" philosophy taken from the Sermon on the Mount—which at one point left the administrators stymied. Three members from the Church of the Firstborn, a sect of the Latter-Day Saints that among other things believed in taking the Bible literally, decided one day that they must not only double their workload from 51 to 102 hours per week, but that it must be Project work and not Overhead. Their reasoning was that the government administered Project work and the church administered Overhead. The government, they said, was the compelling force—and they must do their second mile for "whosoever shall compel thee." After two weeks of double time the men were stumbling around, dazed yet still trying to work. They were becoming a safety hazard, Orville Richman told Forest Service headquarters, to both themselves and their fellow workers. One of the men, whose job was driving a truck, voluntarily resigned his position after he noticed he was drifting off to sleep at the wheel. The other two were mechanics; they were relieved of their duties when it became clear they could no longer competently maintain and repair the vehicles. Yet all three insisted on working their 102 hours, even after they'd been ordered to take a two-day rest. They showed up for Project work but were told they couldn't go. When they said they'd go anyway, under their own power and on their own time, they were denied access to Forest Service tools and equipment. Undaunted, they pulled some broken shovels out of the scrap heap behind the camp garage and went off from dawn till midnight to work on roads they knew were scheduled for maintenance. This was unfortunate, Richman said, because until then they'd been excellent workers. "I feel that nothing remains but to refuse their services in any form and to turn the problem over to the B.S.C. and Selective Service."[33]

Enoch Crumpton fared no better. Laying out the sequence of events to Harold Row, offering as much background and sympathetic context as he could, the acting director told how the men had requested to take food on their voluntary excursions so that they might not waste time hiking back to eat. Crumpton allowed it because he believed they would choose not to eat at all rather than waste time coming back to camp for food. There was simply no reasoning with these men who were armed with the unshakable certainty that God was directing their every move. "I have no suggestions to make," Crumpton told Row. "I will anxiously be awaiting word from you."[34]

Up the command chain it went, until finally a letter from Colonel Kosch of Selective Service appeared. Even though the men were willing to work, he said, unless they work according to their assignments, they were technically refusing to work. The government agency, not the individual, decides what work is assigned and when it will be done, he said. Until the second-milers were ready to abide by these rules, he declared, they would be labeled RTW and denied furlough and other leave privileges—thus concluding perhaps the only case in which CPS enrollees were labeled as refusing to work because they wouldn't *stop* working.[35]

Walkouts also continued, as the peacetime conscription bill being debated in Congress and the obvious general knowledge that the war would soon end prompted more to leave camp and publicly post their statements of conviction—often with that disarming element of providing information on their whereabouts and how to contact them. When Henry Wolff (the same who had resurrected the *Untide* with Kemper the previous December) walked out and returned to his home in New York, he listed the usual complaints: CPS was not doing work of national importance, the program was the equivalent of slave labor, and those who resisted this were powerless to effect change from within the system. The peacetime conscription bill only made direct action more urgent, he said. "Therefore, my plans are to go home and work through some organization, such as the War Resisters League, to oppose such measures, which would take away the little freedom left the American people—measures which make machines out of men."[36]

Another problem was that not every man was capable of working like a machine. George Moyland, a thirty-nine-year-old accountant from Chicago, came to Waldport in the fall of 1944. He had been in three other camps over the course of two years, doing some outdoor jobs but also working as a cook and mental hospital attendant. When they put him on the snag-felling crew, he didn't complain although he was heavy-set, slow-moving, and more inclined to a life of the mind than spending his days building calluses on his hands. Jim Gallaghan, the welder who was quick on the job and mechanically inclined, remembered how difficult it was for Moyland to cut down a tree, needing to rest after just a minute of pulling on a two-man saw. The work just wasn't in him, Gallaghan said. "You had to tell him where to go; you had to watch out for him."

On a Wednesday in early March, Moyland's wife Muriel arrived, planning to find work and live in the area, as she had at previous camps where they'd been assigned. The next day, Moyland went out with the crew as usual, to cut snags on the beautiful and dangerous Cape Perpetua hillsides. But Gallaghan was sick in the infirmary, and Moyland was paired with someone who didn't know the portly accountant so well. "Nobody watched out for him," Gallaghan recalled. Around mid-morning, the working pair had a snag ready to fall over, and as the tree began to "talk," Moyland stepped aside while his partner drove a wedge to help guide the fall. But Moyland stepped only a few feet away and stood against another tree, perhaps thinking it would somehow protect him. As the snag fell, it hit a green spruce tree, breaking off a thick limb more than a dozen feet long that spun down end over end and caught Moyland in the back of the head, crushing his skull. The big man went down, bleeding from his ears and eyes. He was still breathing, and within twenty minutes the men managed to bring a doctor, who took one look and gave him almost no chance of survival. Three hours later, he died at the Waldport hospital.

All work was called off the next day as Forest Service and camp officials pieced together what had happened and discussed ways to implement greater safety measures. The more radical campers gathered that night at the Dupre cabin to consider direct action, determined not to be as quiet as they had been with the death of George Watkins five months earlier. Jerry Rubin wanted to call a strike unless some fundamental guarantees like insurance and proper training and equipment were immediately put in place. They wrote up a press release laying out what had happened and why it was so pointless, challenging the premise that felling snags in isolated areas—done by unfit men with little training and for no pay—was somehow nationally important. They wanted to take it beyond local news, aiming for the big-city dailies and weekly magazines, except that another story was sweeping the country right then—the iconic photo of six men raising the American flag at Iwo Jima.[37]

Martin Ponch was incensed, and he wrote a long statement to camp members. Anyone who accepted CPS in its current form was complicit in George Moyland's death, he said—including all of them at the Waldport camp. The work Moyland had been doing was *not* of national importance, Ponch said, and to call it that was a willful misinterpretation of the law. Very well, then, Ponch said, if they wanted him to follow the law, he would follow the law—to the letter. From now on, he would do work solely of national importance, which, as far as he had seen in his nearly three years in CPS, consisted of firefighting. Since the Oregon climate limited fire danger to only three or four months of the year, he said, he would spend the rest of his time doing whatever work he determined was of national importance. To quietly continue doing work of *unimportance* in this time of great need was no service but actually a disservice, he said — and he hoped that the church leaders might see the error of their ways, "lest they meet the moral equivalent of the fate of George Moyland."[38]

As the political tensions swirled, many of the artists focused on their particular medium. Everson had turned inward, revising and recasting the poems that completed the story of his incarceration and resulting marriage problems, which combined the *War Elegies* and *Waldport Poems* with two new sections of similar length under the rubric "Chronicle of Division." Another book brought together poems Everson had written before coming to Waldport and then published variously in the *Tide,* the *Illiterati,* and the *Compass.* A mimeographed edition of 330 signed copies, laid out by Eshelman and typed by David Jackson, came out in March as *The Residual Years* after months of waiting to acquire appropriate paper for the cover. At the letterpress, they were almost done with Jacob Sloan's book, *Generation of Journey,* although Eshelman reported difficulties printing one of Barbara James's illustrations, which ran across a two-page spread printed on separate sheets. "For one thing, the old press groans and grunts so much we are afraid to print both pages in one run," he said, "so late last night we tore off the chase [a frame that locks the type in place] and prepared to run the spread twice."[39] They had Kenneth Patchen's manuscript ready for typesetting, and they'd confirmed to George Woodcock, the anarchist poet and editor in London, that they intended to publish the collection of poems he'd sent them. Kermit was printing up his letterpress edition of *The Mikado in CPS,* excited about learning to set type. The next *Illiterati* was nearing completion, this one done entirely on the letterpress and featuring an excerpt from Henry Miller's *Air-Conditioned Nightmare,* due out later in the year. In between it all, Everson was printing up *another* book — completing a page here, a page there — which he called *poems: mcmxlii* and intended for private distribution.

The musicians quickly recovered from their embarrassment about the "Dover Beach" concert. Bus Erle and Warren Downs traveled up to Linfield College in McMinnville to help support a student concert — surely surprising a student when the seasoned and professional Erle joined him onstage to play a double violin concerto from Bach. In early March, Downs joined Erle and Bob Harvey, with Tom Polk Miller on piano and Adrian on clarinet, for a program featuring works by Beethoven and Haydn. They took on newer, experimental works also, when Adrian and Tom Polk Miller accompanied Wes DeCoursey as he sang a piece by Lauris Steere Guetzgow, a prize-winning composer and the wife of

Harold Guetzgow, a CO psychologist whom Adrian had known back at the Minnesota starvation experiment. The program even called for this piece to be performed twice because, as Adrian wrote in the introduction, "the atonality, the difficulty of the harmony and of the structure, make it impossible to appreciate on the first hearing." Perhaps to reward the listeners, the reception in Kimmel Hall featured further entertainment. Plates of homemade cookies were brought out (a rarity in these times of sugar rationing), they tacked a bed sheet to the wall and showed slides of the *Aria da Capo* performance from the previous fall, and later David Jackson read some sonnets he'd composed into a multitrack recorder—although on hearing the playback, he didn't care for the "tin edge" in his voice, especially when he was assured that this was how he actually sounded.[40]

Rehearsals for *Ghosts* were moving along, with Joe Gistirak pushing his actors to immerse themselves in their characters, maintaining the connection to the role outside of the rehearsal periods. Ibsen's tale of strict nineteenth-century morality and its consequences featured Joyce Harvey as Mrs. Alving, widow of a sea captain who'd had many affairs; Ibby Dupre as Regina Engstrand, Mrs. Alving's maid who doesn't know she is actually Captain Alving's illegitimate daughter; Kermit Sheets as Oswald, Mrs. Alving's son, who has inherited syphilis and falls in love with Regina; Martin Ponch as Jacob Engstrand, a carpenter who serves as Regina's surrogate father; and David Jackson as the local pastor. As with the other plays, Adrian was heavily involved with production. Here, he led construction of the set, which used as a backdrop a large abstract painting done by Bob Harvey; also featured was lighting designed by Joe Gistirak and costumes by Joyce Harvey. And it was here, in the shadows of late-night theater work, where emotional intensity and exhaustion walk a fine line, in the hours and days and weeks of rehearsal that create their own mixture of reality and desire, it was here in that mysterious, magical thing we call theater that a new world opened up for Joyce and Adrian.

To some degree it had begun back in February at a record hop held in camp as an alternative to the one down at Cap's Resort, where the "conscientious jitterbugs" on New Year's Eve had offended the American Legionnaires. The February event in the dining hall was poorly attended, and Adrian, who normally escaped the dance floor by playing in the band, this time had nowhere to go and found himself resignedly moving from partner to partner, dancing with Manche, Ibby, Jan Rubin, and others. Then he danced with Joyce. "When we danced together," he later said, "something awakened in Joyce as it did in me, something which had been dead in her relationship with Bob for a long time." Harvey had never been easy to live with; his mercurial nature, drinking, and infidelities had pushed Joyce further away over time. During the spring of 1945,

Adrian Wilson and
Joyce Harvey outside
Tillie the Whale
cabins, ca. 1945.

as Bob Harvey ignored the world, immersed in writing a novel and painting, Joyce and Adrian discovered each other—on the beach, in the workshop among the hanging costumes and background flats for the play, and
down on the old moss bed built the previous summer by Morris Graves
at his lean-to alongside the mouth of Big Creek. At first Adrian rational-
ized their affair in the context of the Ibsen play: Joyce, who was widowed
in the play and in real life had lost her husband to his art, was turning
to Adrian as a substitute for Bob. Or maybe she was trying to make Bob
jealous, Adrian surmised, for Mrs. Alving also had not been treated well
by her husband, and would have been justified—as far as the logic of
drama goes—in behaving this way. But that was all so much intellectual
claptrap; they were in love, and they had acted upon it. Their relationship
was dramatic, earthy, primal, Adrian said—the kind found in the poetry
of Robinson Jeffers. "The element of nature is all-powerful in it, the sea,
the great rocky headlands, the wind-flattened trees, the driving rain, and
brute clouds."[41]

Ghosts opened in May, a week late because Kermit had to attend
the funeral for his brother, who was killed in a lumber mill accident in
northern California—yet another cost of the war. Everything was ready
for opening night, so Adrian and Joyce decided to take a small boat Bud
Hawkins had recently completed out on the ocean that afternoon. But the
water became too rough for the young lovers armed only with paddles,
and when a large wave capsized the craft, they abandoned the adventure
and swam for shore. They made it to the beach, exhausted and thankful

as other campers rushed down and wrapped them in blankets, and Joe Gistirak berated them for taking such risks on opening day. But all worked out for the best, Joyce said: "Despite our dangerous adventure, the performance went well and the audience was impressed, even the Holy Joes who had never seen a live theater performance in their lives. One of them came up to me afterwards and expressed amazement that I could transform my usual self into the elderly impassioned Mrs. Alving, and experience such intense emotion on the stage *every night*."[42]

Joyce, who had little acting experience, was now hooked on theater. Adrian, who had little experience with women, was hooked on Joyce—and she reciprocated the feeling. When Harvey, who had been struggling not just with his writing but also with the decision of whether or not to walk out, learned that two of his paintings had sold for three hundred dollars at a New York gallery, he left for Portland to wait for the money and maybe go back East. Joyce had been giving him room to focus on his art, waiting for the appropriate time to tell him about Adrian and her. But careful timing no longer seemed necessary when she went to Portland and found Harvey drunk and with a woman in the studio of Wilfred Lang, an artist who had become friendly with the Fine Arts group. She returned to Waldport with word that Bob was heading to San Francisco.

Adrian was working steadily on the next *Compass,* an art and literary issue that was shaping up to be a "who's who" of the CPS art experience. One day he walked into the Untide Press room with a project in mind: he wanted to create a stationery logo for the *Compass* by setting type in a circle, running the name twice, coming together in two semi-circles. "How do I set 'COMPASS' in a circle?" he asked Bill Eshelman. "How do I make the letters work?"

"I don't think you can do it with our equipment," Eshelman replied. "You can't set type like Stonehenge."

"Well, what's our alternative?" Adrian asked.

Eshelman thought a minute and said maybe they could paste up the letter design on paper, send it to a company in Portland and have them make a linocut, which could then be printed on the press at Waldport.

"No, that would take too long," Adrian said, then took the pieces of type he needed and walked away, already deep in thought.

He came back a little later with a small plywood box filled with plaster of Paris. He had filled the block with plaster then set the letters in a circle, sunk uniformly to the proper height for printing, so that the block could then be locked into the press. It worked beautifully. "I can't put my hand in the press without revolutionizing the industry," he proudly wrote his parents. "The casting lasted through 3,000 impressions and begins to appear indestructible. In fact I am beginning to wonder how I am going to rescue the type."[43]

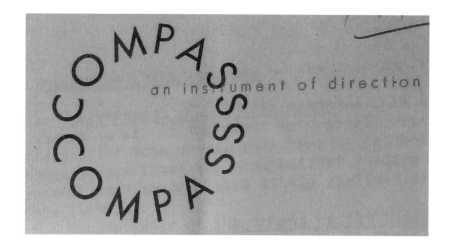

He was certainly on a roll. With the success of *Ghosts,* his ever-increasing expertise in the print shop, and discovering the love of his life, it seemed nothing could cloud his mood—not even when he dropped an entire case of italic type, which would consume a full days' labor to sort, and also discovered he'd forgotten to print forty-six pages for the *Compass,* after he'd already finished cleaning the press for the day. "But," he said, "that is what happens when all you think about is making love."[44]

■ ■ ■

It was the end of May 1945. The war in Europe was over, and the grim task of occupation and rebuilding had begun. Franklin Roosevelt had died; the nation mourned, then went back to the business of ending the war with Japan. At Camp Angel, Enoch Crumpton carried on as acting director, waiting for a replacement to take on the headaches. Eshelman continued as assistant director, fielding the political volleys as best he could, telling a friend, "I can imagine no place on earth more disillusioning to an idealist than a place supposedly filled with his ilk."[45] Chuck Cooley wrote of his smorgasbord of jobs: hauling firewood, sorting potatoes in the root cellar, building picnic spaces at the top of Cape Perpetua, cutting shingles, clearing brush from telephone lines, and replacing outhouse floors. On Overhead he did kitchen duty, was night watchman, handled transfer requests, and filled in for whomever was on furlough. "One day I was infirmarian, properties man and assistant director," he said, "all three."[46]

Everson had gone south on furlough, visiting Larry Powell in Los Angeles and then Edwa in Berkeley, where he confirmed what he already knew: they might still be legally married, but their relationship was ended. Back in the camp he learned of the point system Selective Service was proposing for someone to be released from CPS: "50 points for discharge. 1 point per month of service, 3 points for a wife. 13 points for a child. I have 31 points. So. Stick it out, man."[47]

In the cabins across the highway, talk was lively. What to do? When to do it? And where? They considered moving the Untide Press after the war to Eugene, home to the University of Oregon and what Eshelman termed "probably as cultured a city as there is in Oregon." Talk of a cooperative theater, probably in San Francisco, continued. Daily life went on, the work punctuated by games to relieve the stress. They fashioned a basketball court at one end of camp, between the laundry room and Dorm 4. "Playing is o.k.," Eshelman reported, "except for the wind, which sometimes causes considerable difficulty."[48]

Bus Erle had been joined by his wife, Hildegarde, and their young daughter, Robin, and they all moved into a cabin just behind the Tillie the Whale skeleton at the entrance to the court. Bus and Hildegarde were East Coast intellectuals, and a favorite pastime of theirs, which they called simply "The Game," quickly caught on. It was a kind of charades, with someone acting out the parts of a song or book title—which could get quite complicated for items like the collection of essays written about James Joyce's *Finnegan's Wake*, titled "Our Exgamination Round his Factifaction for Incamination of Work in Progress," or the Glenn Miller hit, "It Must Be Jelly ('Cause Jam Don't Shake Like That)"—accompanied by much laughing and shouting as little Robin slept soundly in the other room. One night in the Harvey cabin, as the radio played and the wine no doubt flowed, the group heard a thumping in the kitchen, where the Rubins were dancing—heavy-set Jerry and the much lighter Jan—prompting Kermit to quip, "It must be Jerry 'cause Jan don't shake like that!"[49]

Imagination works both ways, though, and apparently in the camp there were still some who were bothered by Manche's presence nearby. She had resigned her position with the Fine Arts, she'd moved out of Kimmel Hall, she'd agreed to stop taking meals in the dining hall, and she even honored the Brethren Service Committee request—sent directly by Harold Row from Elgin—that she no longer set foot in camp. But she was not prepared to leave the area. She had friendships and cultural advantages here that she couldn't find elsewhere, she told Enoch Crumpton—relationships and activities that were helping her to develop her sense of conscience and social justice, relationships she felt she couldn't take lightly. Crumpton said he could understand her perspective, but that didn't change the fact that some people in camp, and some in Waldport, were upset with her presence there—upset enough to create public relations problems. Manche understood all this yet maintained that she would stay, prompting Crumpton to write Harold Row with a message becoming depressingly familiar in regards to camp issues. "I must admit I am completely stumped for an answer to this problem and would appreciate your comments and recommendations."[50]

Whether it was direct action, finances, or the general wearing of the will when faced with a collective disapproval, the objective record doesn't reveal. A BSC letter sent after Crumpton's report to Elgin is but a single-sentence request from Row, dated May 12, 1945: "Will you please give me a report on the presence or absence of Miss Langley at the Waldport camp and the immediate community."[51] The final word appears to be a single-page blast by Everson, titled "A Personal Statement" and apparently read at a camp meeting. "Today, June 5, 1945, the campaign to evict Manche Langley from the Camp Angel community was successfully concluded," he said. "She departed on the three o'clock bus." This eviction was a concerted, mean-spirited group effort, Everson said. "Prejudice, moral censure, ostracism, slander, and finally downright lies—all these forms of social coercion were used against her." The administration was complicit, he charged; they'd agreed to deny her access to camp facilities, even to walk on the camp grounds. She came to Camp Angel and gave her sincerity, loyalty, and hard work to the Fine Arts, Everson said. Now she'd been driven away—and by Christians, who were supposedly known for their commitment to conscience, he added with contempt. "Shall we look to the Christians for tolerance and forbearance? Let them live with their conscience—if they can."[52]

Then there was Elwin Shank. One morning in May, the nineteen-year-old Brethren farmer from Idaho was at the wood yard, an area about five miles from camp where logs were hauled from the forest to be gathered for cutting into firewood. Shank was working as a "choker-setter"—placing metal cable in a noose around one end of large logs that could then be "skidded" or dragged on a tractor to the wood yard. As with most such accidents, it happened quickly and no one was exactly sure how. Apparently, the nose of a log being dragged by the tractor dug hard into the ground and caught under another log that suddenly popped up and whipped around, catching Shank across the waist and pinning him to the ground. These were big logs—the one that caught Shank was a thirty-foot section of Douglas fir—and it was nearly an hour before the campers could free the injured man, carry him to a truck and drive him down the bumpy roads to the highway and then up to the hospital in Toledo, where the doctors found his pelvis and hip bone horribly broken. But he seemed to have no internal injuries, and everyone was surprised when he died three days later. Wes DeCoursey, who had known the Shank family in Idaho, wished that the doctors had not been so optimistic, for otherwise Shank's parents might have traveled to see their son. In his capacity as Religious Interest Group secretary, DeCoursey sent a letter of condolence to the Shanks, then sent another as a personal note. "Having known Elwin and you for so long I feel deep regret," he said. "May God give you courage and may He forgive us if in any way we at camp might be at fault."[53]

Three deaths in eight months, five total for the camp—more than anywhere else in CPS. "The recent death of Edwin L. Shank [sic] at Camp Waldport, which is the third death as a result of project activities, has been the occasion for considerable discussion by various interested groups," NSBRO official J. N. Weaver wrote to Colonel Kosch at Selective Service. Since the tree-planting project ended, many had questioned the importance of the current work at Camp Angel, Weaver said. He suggested they close the camp, change the type of work being assigned, or at the very least increase safety precautions and training.[54]

The Forest Service people were not insensitive although they apparently felt compelled to defend themselves. "It would seem that the recent death that occurred in the wood yard has little if any connection with the work program," Supervisor F. V. Horton wrote to the Siuslaw Forest staff. "In fact the deaths that have occurred can be attributed to individual negligence and lack of assignee interest in the safety program rather than the hazards of the work."[55] Regional Forester H. J. Andrews was even more blunt in his report to the Forest Service chief regarding the NSBRO letter. "We can make this camp safer in two ways," he said, "either through the assignees themselves waking up and using their heads or by doing little or no work. Some of the assignees would probably favor the latter."[56]

Into all this walked Harold Cessna, the new camp director appointed by Harold Row. Thirty-seven years old, in CPS for barely a year but already having directed another camp back East, he was, Eshelman said, "two hundred thirty pounds of jouncing optimism with a Brethren bias." Perhaps the Waldport COs could be excused for sounding somewhat jaded; the camp was feeling the effects of time and the war's approaching end. For some time now, the various campers had weighed, discussed, debated, and in many cases already made their decisions about what they should, could, and eventually would do regarding their position in CPS.

Word trickled in of those who'd already left; rumors circulated about who might go. Jim Harman had gone to live with Henry Miller and the bohemian crowd at Big Sur and was picked up one day crossing the highway as he headed for the water to pry up some abalone, barefoot and bearded, looking suspicious with a tire iron in his hand; they tossed him in the local jail, then sent him up to await trial in Oregon. Larry Siemons was drifting around Portland, occasionally visiting a house friendly to COs, where, when he saw someone from the Waldport camp, he would sneak up from behind, stick his finger in their ribs and mutter out of the side of his mouth in a tough-guy detective voice, "Identify yourself!"[57]

Kemper, barred from Project work due to his slowdown tactics, was on the verge of being ordered to a government camp or being arrested for refusing to go; no one was quite sure which it would be. Coffield had left Cascade Locks and was now at Camp #115, a tiny unit at the University of Michigan, where he had volunteered as a subject for experiments on the body's ability to withstand heat and humidity in tropical climates. Hackett was long gone, working at a mental hospital in Chicago. Warren Downs was up in Montana, having joined the smoke-jumping crews there. Bob Harvey was somewhere, maybe back East in his familiar territory of New York. Clayton James had walked out, he and Barbara heading for the simple life on Puget Sound with Morris Graves and the burgeoning art colony there. Bud Hawkins headed back to Maine, leaving his Waldport boats behind. Ponch, Gistirak, Everson, and Eshelman were thinking of walking out. Adrian was getting closer to leaving although he wanted to stay with Joyce. Manche was gone, maybe back East. Vlad Dupre resigned as Fine Arts executive secretary, expecting a transfer to the Midwest and hoping to reunite with Ibby, who had left to visit her family there; Tom Polk Miller stepped into his post.

A new group of transfers arrived from Camp #42 in Wellston, Michigan, and volunteered *en masse* for the Hebo side camp, showing no interest in joining the Waldport base. Another group chose to stay together and go to Woahink, a side camp just south of Florence. Within the main camp there was a small but intense debate about a new tool of warfare: incendiary balloons launched by Japan and floated across the Pacific Ocean in an attempt to set western American forests on fire. Some COs felt the intent behind a fire could affect a pacifist's decision on whether or not to fight it. But such important discussion was lost on the majority in camp, Eshelman fumed in a letter to a friend. Mostly they were complaining about how CPS was changing, and ignoring the larger, more complicated questions. He summed it up in one word: "Stagnation!"[58]

Harold Cessna looked about his new camp and chose to take a positive approach. He placed a purple sign in his office that read: BE CHEERFUL. KEEP SMILING.

CHAPTER 11

What Now?

"TWO WONDERS OF GOD'S CREATION captured my attention," Chuck Cooley wrote on a calm July day. "The ocean and the beautiful birds." That summer, the Oregon coast had exceptionally low tides, opening the beach far beyond normal and offering a bonanza of crabs and clams for residents up and down the coast. The other marvel was the myriad swallows that had built their mud nests beneath the eaves of the camp buildings. After the fledglings spent their month or so of feeding and growing, it was a joy to see them, Cooley said, "joined with their parent-birds to dip and swoop in the brilliant rays of the sun."[1]

Cooley had reason to see things in a positive light. While visiting at Orval Etter's home near the University of Oregon in Eugene, he'd learned how he might finish the final year of his bachelor's degree in the liberal arts, which he had been working toward at Kent State University in Ohio when he was drafted. He set up an individual study schedule with a sociology professor at the university, in which he attended one-third of the class meetings and borrowed notes from fellow students for the others. He earned a 3.6 grade average for his senior year, and later recalled that to the best of his knowledge he was the only person to earn a college degree while in CPS.[2]

While his wife Louise sent money from her job at an insurance office back in Ohio, Cooley asked for and got the night watchman position at Camp Angel. He worked extra weekend hours to save up furlough days in which he could attend classes; he hitchhiked to Eugene and back. He even used his experiences in getting rides as college course material, when his anthropology professor asked him to survey the attitudes about CPS from drivers who had picked him up. Cooley said he found that half were interested in learning more about the camp, 20 percent were ready for a civilized debate, and another 20 percent glad to hear that people were questioning the war. At the extremes were 5 percent flatly against the COs and another 5 percent fully supporting them.[3]

Not everyone in camp chose such institutional paths. In late June, Adrian took his remaining furlough days, and with Joyce hitchhiked down to San Francisco for a sightseeing vacation. All the romance of the city was theirs, which made parting all the more unpalatable when Joyce boarded a train for New York, her mission to meet one more time with Harvey and finalize their separation. She and Adrian decided that he would hitchhike back to Waldport, wrap up his affairs there, then "walk out"—heading cross-country to Bud Hawkins's home on the coast of Maine, where he would meet up with Joyce.

Up in Washington State, Clayton and Barbara James had already walked out and were now in the world they'd longed for, a life of simple subsistence and art. They joined Morris Graves at his home—the Rock—outside Anacortes, on an island in the heart of Puget Sound. They helped clear land for Graves, and in return he helped them build a house beside the lake down from the Rock, in the lean-to style he had constructed at Waldport. Clayton summed up his feelings succinctly with a painting on the opening page of a letter he sent to Everson. It was reminiscent of the *sumi* style, with a minimum of watercolor strokes representing what was likely the view from their new home site: water stretching away from the shore, tall evergreen trees framing the scene, and the snow-peaked mountains beyond. Underneath it in Clayton's large penmanship: "Bill, we are in that land again—of great rest." In the following pages, he spoke of privacy and freedom, of his plans to quietly paint and garden—taking pleasure in how strange that would seem to the FBI agents who would almost certainly one day come for him. He wrote of the clarity coming to his mind now that he was away from the repression and chaos of CPS. His message was not new in itself, but it was new for him—and an important step in his development as an artist. The key was simplicity, he said, living close to nature and therefore close to oneself. He wanted to view the mountains in the distance or the light on the water or the geese flying across the moon not as spectacular exceptions but as ongoing marvelous experiences, part of his daily consciousness. The result, he hoped, would be greater awareness.[4]

Barbara also was smitten by the land. The mountains and forests with the eagles soaring overhead were "majestic and sublime," she wrote, "awe-inspiring, sweeping." Even the rocks were symbolic, reminiscent of Stonehenge, she said. "Everything is here, its mystery, the inspiration, the presence to understand well—that is our purpose."[5]

Come to this place, Clayton told Everson. They could build him a shelter on the land, close enough for companionship yet far enough away for complete privacy if he chose. Give up the Untide Press, Clayton urged, it wasn't that important. Come to Anacortes and get away from CPS. "Be free, man . . . I need you to be free."[6]

Everson wanted to be free, but his was a careful, analytical nature. He watched the labor problems continue in camp, in particular as Kemper's work slowdown earned him first a daily report of RTW—refused to work—and then ROP, refused on Project. It became a morning pantomime: Kemper walked up to the trucks where others were loading and raised his eyebrows at Orville Richman, the Forest Service superintendent. Richman looked back, silently signaling a negative. The trucks then left, and Kemper had the day free to paint or otherwise spend his time.[7]

Everson finally acted in July, by returning from Project one day and simply telling the authorities he couldn't go out again. He also knew that the grand jury in Portland handling such cases was recessed until September, so he figured he had at least a month to focus on his creative work. He spent his days writing in the morning, working the press through the afternoon, and socializing or returning to writing in the evening.[8]

Over the next few weeks he finished the printing on *poems: mcmxlii*, the collection of fourteen poems written before his arrival at Waldport. But this was not an Untide Press production, Everson insisted. None of the five hundred copies were for sale; they would simply be handed around to friends and acquaintances and offered to libraries. A somewhat quirky booklet, the design was not so much planned as it simply grew over the time it was printed in between other projects on the press. This was, the colophon read, "a practice resulting in the blemishes of haste, so that the venerable adage has come home to roost on the printer's head, a disquieting reminder." Problems included a late addition of titles in red ink that bled through the thin paper, and five lines missing from one poem so that an errata slip was inserted with a small woodcut done by Clayton James. The cover was also a Clayton woodcut—a sparse representation of water, mountains, and moon, not dissimilar to the sumi painting letter he'd sent to Everson some months back. But the printing was completed before the cover was done, so Clayton was not acknowledged in the book.[9]

Once Everson had this project completed, his next move was a typical startling yet matter-of-fact decision. After eighteen days of RTW, he announced over his morning coffee in the dining hall, "There is no reason for my not going out on Project today."

The others at the table turned to him in surprise.

Everson explained with an almost Lincolnesque gravity that he had taken his stand for practical as much as moral reasons. He'd chosen the RTW route, he said, because he had work he considered more important than the Forest Service jobs. Now that this work was completed, he no longer had any objections to going on Project and saw no benefit in suffering punishment simply for the sake of appearing immovable in his beliefs. He finished his coffee and joined the crews.[10]

This kind of practical reasoning factored into another decision, one with further-reaching implications: he would not continue with the Untide Press after the war ended and the camps emptied. He needed to regain his full writer's perspective, he wrote to Larry Powell. "Perhaps I'll have a small press for my own uses, but no publishing venture. Two years of that is enough.[11]

In some ways it made sense. Everson had published five books in a little over two years, covering virtually all of his writing leading up to and during the war. He'd seen some success and had reason to move on to bigger things. In other ways, though, the Waldport printing operation was poised to truly break out—and the contents alone of two publications released in the summer of 1945 packed enough energy and creativity for twice that number. The *Compass* art and literary issue came out; with financial assistance from the Fellowship of Reconciliation, they were able to print three thousand copies with generous photo layouts by having the pages sent to Portland for offset printing. This issue was perhaps a swan song for the Waldport internees and associates. Adrian was listed on the masthead as "Associate Editor, Layout and Printing." Prose included comments and essays by Ponch, Kermit, and George Woodcock. Poetry was well represented through Everson, Woodcock, Adrian, Ponch, Hackett, and others. Jim Harman, awaiting trial in Portland for his walkout, contributed a review of Henry Miller's antiwar tract, *Murder the Murderer;* a two-page spread from Jacob Sloan's *Generation of Journey* reproduced a poem from the book, along with one of the drawings by Barbara Straker James. A six-page foldout insert reproduced music for voice and piano by Allan Bunt and David Newton, and a piece by Lauris Steere Guetzkow, the composer whose work they'd performed earlier at one of the music shows. And, stuck inside an essay titled "On not listening to music" was Glen Coffield's poem "The Peewee's Note," accompanied by a bar of notes transcribed from a recording of Coffield's musical chants.

But it was the visual pieces that really stood out: a woodcut by Clayton James, titled "The Other Side" and done on blue paper; an abstract painting by Bob Harvey; cubist-influenced paintings by Wilfred Lang and Howard Sewall; photographs from Europe by Julius Boehm; paintings from Windsor Utley; a photo of a mobile installation by Kemper; a dark, full-page, close-up photograph of a violin player by Bus Erle; and representations of two paintings by Morris Graves—"Moon-Mad Crow in the Surf" and "In the Air," part of what was called the Journey Series. The fine print was dense in both design and meaning.

Like the last *Compass*, this issue featured somewhat irreverent author and artist bios accompanied by photos, drawings, or paintings of the persons; editorial comments included statements on aesthetic

THE ILLITERATI

PROPOSES:
CREATION, EXPERIMENT, AND REVOLUTION

TO BUILD A WARLESS, FREE SOCIETY;

SUSPECTS: TRADITION AS A STANDARD AND ECLECTICISM AS A TECHNIQUE;

REJECTS: WAR AND ANY OTHER FORM OF COERCION BY PHYSICAL VIOLENCE IN HUMAN ASSOCIATIONS.

NUMBER **4** SUMMER 1945

Title page of Illiterati #4. Done in 1945, a radical forerunner of the messages that would sweep the country a generation later.

intention, the shortcomings of CPS, a "Brief Blueprint for a Theatre Cooperative," and some particulars of the publishing process, even a mention of the "clam-action monster" press at the camp. An inserted leaflet—part errata slip, part subscription blank and part editorial message—included explanations for delays and problems, and a call for interested subscribers to continue their support. "With help, we may do more," the message concluded. "We may even become the peoples' international peace magazine we have dreamed may be the proper post-war future for COMPASS."[12]

The *Illiterati* put out its fourth edition that summer as well. Printed entirely on the letterpress, it opened with a proclamation, using large, bold type:

> The Illiterati proposes: Creation, experiment and revolution to build a warless, free society;
>
> Suspects: tradition as a standard and eclecticism as a technique;
>
> Rejects: war and any other form of coercion by physical violence in human associations.[13]

Along with the Henry Miller piece from the soon-to-be-published *Air-Conditioned Nightmare,* the *Illiterati* featured four-color graphics accompanying three poems from Kenneth Patchen's forthcoming Untide Press book; a selection from Everson's *poems: mcmxlii* with a linocut by the author; three poems by New York City schoolteacher and *Pacifica Views* contributor Irwin Stark, with a critical essay on his approach written by Coffield; four poems by George Woodcock—another preview of a forthcoming Untide book; and a poem called "Of a Woman Screaming in the Street" by a former CPS assignee named Lewis Hill, who also dreamed of founding a pacifist-oriented radio station where wide-ranging discussions could serve as an alternative to military conflict.[14]

With its more professional-quality production and inclusion of recognized names like Miller and Patchen, the *Illiterati* was moving into the tier of notable alternative journals like *Partisan Review* and *Twice a Year.* It was also articulating ideas that were being embraced by a new generation of college students and radical artists in places like New York and San Francisco. As a kind of bookend to its bold announcement on the opening page, the editors closed the issue with a less visually striking but no less radical statement: "The Illiterati is a magazine of directed pattern in creative expression and includes anyone who attempts genuinely to speak as a writer, artist, composer, etc., and whose ideology is of a more or less revolutionary pacifism. Its editors hold to the thesis that all organisms form an interconnected whole, that separation is possible only on the mental or verbal levels, and that war and all forms of physical coercion are always destructive of man."[15]

Then there was the Patchen book. This had been their most ambitious project from the beginning—and their most problematic. They'd been warned that Patchen was an author who killed small presses with his endless specific requirements and penchant for micromanaging the process—and this seemed to be confirmed to the Untide Press crew as technical complications dogged them at every step. First, there was Patchen announcing that he had added the book to his titles-in-print listed on the dust jackets of his other publications, and then asking after the fact when it would be out. There was the back-and-forth about design, for the author had insisted he have a strong voice in the process—although he had also specifically requested Kemper as designer, based on his work with the *Illiterati*.

The page design was unlike anything they'd ever done, a truly experimental combination of contrasting colors and shades making up the typography and background. The thirty-four poems were both numbered and titled—numbers in red, titles in black. The text was in red, superimposed over a gray "tint block" that ran top to bottom in a wide vertical column coloring about 80 percent of the page, leaving thinner strips of white on each side. Superimposed on every page—or rather reversed out—was the book's title, *An Astonished Eye Looks Out of the Air*. This was Patchen the eccentric; he was already well known for mixing text and graphics, using different-sized typefaces, and combining narratives so that a reader in some cases was following two or more stories simultaneously. It was certainly interesting to look at, Larry Powell told Everson, but it could be difficult to read.[16]

The cover, though, was striking in a simple and practical way; it took Kemper's use of solid rectangular blocks of color and stripped it down to its most fundamental property: contrast. The cover stock was black cardboard (called "stiff wraps" in bookbinder parlance) folded once and stapled at the spine. Then a smaller white rectangular sheet, perhaps three-quarters as wide and tall, was wrapped around the spine so that it covered the staples. This was then glued to the front and back in a way that created a white block surrounded on three margins by the larger black cover. Inside the white block was the title and author's name in bold type. The front cover showed the title in black and author in red; the back cover repeated the same in opposite colors. It was without a doubt the strongest design of the Untide books, perhaps even iconic. And with Patchen's name and dedicated fans, they aimed for their largest press run ever—two thousand copies, double the size of anything they'd done before.

As the summer wore on, however, one calamity after another struck. The press broke down and sat idle for two weeks. At one point the Untide crew misplaced the typescript of Patchen's introduction and asked if he could write another; luckily, it turned out that Kemper had taken it with him when he'd been assigned to a side camp. The tint blocks were a disaster: done by a Corvallis printer, they came back so dark that the text was nearly impossible to read. They decided to try a larger font size, which meant ordering new type from the foundry and adding further delays. "I am a cursing man, and heartily glad of it," Everson wrote to Patchen, "for I should not care to have a principle of that kind strained in the way it would surely have been."[17]

Cover design of Patchen's *Astonished Eye* would become internationally known when copied by City Lights Books.

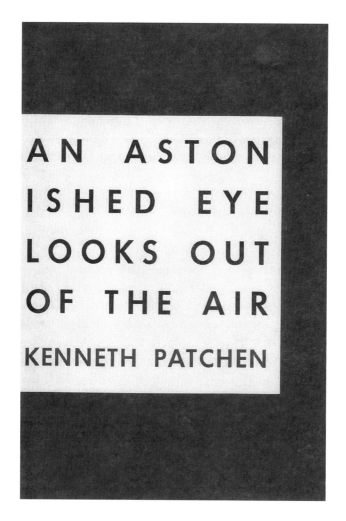

AN ASTON ISHED EYE LOOKS OUT OF THE AIR

KENNETH PATCHEN

22. I FEEL DRUNK
ALL THE TIME

Jesus it's beautiful!
Great mother of big apples it is a pretty
World!

You're a bastard Mr Death
And I wish you didn't have no look-in here.

O I don't know how the rest of you feel
But I feel drunk all the time

And I wish to hell we didn't have to die.

O you're a nervy bastard Mr Death
And I wish you didn't have no hand in this game

Because it's too damn beautiful for anybody to die.

23. SCIENCE TALKED TO

"the finest
lad of all is Mr
Natures (sp. b'kw'ds) who stands bravely by
to give the angels a bloodtest"

    BUT
damn my britches it'll be a long nose
that hasn't got a face back of it

(and and and AND
the muskrat you take for Christ's sake
the lowly rastmuk

Page from *An Astonished Eye Looks out of the Air* by Kenneth Patchen. The numbers and poem text are in red, titles in black. Vertical "tint block" is gray.

Meanwhile, the war ended. American forces had steadily landed on and taken island after island in the Pacific, moving ever closer to mainland Japan. The casualties were terrific—on Okinawa, the tiny island at Japan's southernmost tip, more than 12,000 Americans and 180,000 Japanese died—and there was no indication that Japan was inclined to surrender. On August 6, the United States dropped its brand-new atomic bomb on the port city of Hiroshima, incinerating 100,000 people and wreaking destruction on a level that surprised even the weapon's inventors. Three days later, America drove the point home with a similar obliteration at Nagasaki. Shortly thereafter, Japan surrendered.[18]

While the celebrations were huge, and America looked forward to the shift from a wartime to a peacetime society, this didn't mean everyone suddenly went home. It would take months, even years, to demobilize millions of military personnel, and the powerful forces of veterans' organizations and public opinion would not tolerate even the perception of COs being released into the workforce at rates faster than the military men. Political struggles in Congress, exacerbated by discrimination against COs and the inevitable administrative lags, left many in the camps with the feeling that not only would they be held indefinitely but that their time in CPS had been largely worthless. Walkouts became almost commonplace at Waldport, even as word came that some earlier AWOLs had received stiff punishment—such as Jim Harman, who'd finally been taken to court and sentenced to a year in prison at McNeil Island outside Seattle.

Floyd Merrill, a secular objector from Santa Monica, one day suddenly told his bunkmate, Chuck Cooley, that he was leaving and Cooley could have whatever he left behind. Mark Rouch, the ministry student who had been active in the Religious Interest Group and played the district attorney in *Tennessee Justice*, walked out to do social work at a community center in Portland. For more and more men, it was becoming increasingly difficult to stay in CPS. "Those who remain are the compromisers," Everson wrote to Powell. "While every other week some man leaves. He states his reasons and goes. And every time, your own position is thrown up, subtly but poignantly, against you. But still you hang on, out of many complex motives."[19]

Martin Ponch held fast to his declaration that he would only do work he considered nationally important, which resulted in a daily ritual similar to what had happened with Kemper's work slowdown. Each morning, Ponch approached supervisor Orville Richman and said he was ready to work but only if it were of national importance, which Ponch said must be related to firefighting needs.

"We consider all the work nationally important," Richman replied. "I can't tell you in advance what kind of work we are going to do." Then he asked, "Are you refusing to go out to work?"

Ponch said he would go if it supported fighting fires.

"Well, we haven't got it, so it amounts to the same thing," Richman said.

Ponch was reported as RTW. He laid out his version of the story in a tightly spaced six-page letter to camp director Harold Cessna, giving detailed descriptions of and reasons for his actions. Civilian Public Service had done a great disservice to humanity by endorsing forced, unpaid labor and denying sincere men the opportunity to serve their country to the best of their abilities, he declared, and the churches behind it had, with their appearance of religious sanction of military control over civilian activities, furnished a kind of American fascism. He concluded that CPS violated both the U.S. Constitution and the Selective Training and Service Act of 1940. No honest person could collaborate with such a system, he said, and he would continue resisting it in every way he could.[20]

One interesting twist came in late July when Clayton and Barbara James *returned* to camp. They'd had to leave Morris Graves when the painter insisted on absolute privacy, and they had spent some time in the mountains living on rice and beans. Now they were flat broke, with nowhere else to go. But Clayton had walked out, was AWOL, and he wasn't planning to return to work. They built a shelter on the beach, took their meals at the dining hall in camp, and returned to painting and other activities with the Fine Arts. This was a new one to Harold Cessna—should the camp be paying to feed a walkout who refused to live in the barracks or do work? Should they feed his wife as well? Since Clayton had originally come for the Fine Arts, Cessna called on Everson and current Fine Arts director Tom Polk Miller, who in turn brought in three non-Fine Arts campers to help assess the situation. The ad hoc committee concluded that Clayton was no different than other RTW campers who continued to take their room and board at camp—this member simply did not sleep in the barracks. He was prepared to be arrested and was not causing any trouble. The group decided to refer the matter to BSC headquarters—but added that they would not feel bound to act on its decision.[21]

When the FBI finally did come, they found Clayton and Barbara at their lean-to on the beach; they took Clayton away in handcuffs, apologizing as they did so, and sent him up to jail in Portland. With the war over, Clayton was given a suspended sentence by a lenient judge. "Barbara said it was because she sat in the court and had a long face," Clayton recalled years later. "It was stupid anyway because the war was over and there was no reason for sending us to jail." Clayton and Barbara were done with CPS.[22]

There certainly was a case to be made that sending COs to prison no longer served any purpose. But, as with the draft boards at the beginning of the war, interpretation of the law varied with the individual judge. Also, a single judge's decision might change from one case to another. Walking out of camp continued to be a crap shoot.

Those who remained in camp held out hope that the "duration of the war plus six months" edict would be honored and not turned into an extended punishment. For many, this was simply part of their over-all condition, and they would bear the burden until the time came for their release. The Fine Arts, although weakened in number, forged ahead with their projects. In the fall of 1945, the theater group put on George Bernard Shaw's *Candida*, a comic satire of Victorian England—and also historically significant in that it had been the first play produced at Jasper Deeter's Hedgerow Theatre when it opened in the 1920s. Hedgerow alum Joe Gistirak had walked out after his work with *Ghosts*, and David Jackson, the other Hedgerow man, preferred to work this time behind the scenes, assisting with production. So Kermit Sheets stepped up as director of *Candida*, also playing one of the six character roles. He put together a cast including Ibby Dupre as Candida, the wife of a power-ful clergyman; Enoch Crumpton as her husband; and Bill Eshelman as Marchebanks, a young poet who is in love with Candida and wants to free her from what he sees as her mundane life. Kermit cast Tom Polk Miller, Hildegarde Erle, and himself in the supporting roles. Miller and Erle also joined David Jackson in production, along with Martin Ponch, Francis Barr (of the saltwater dimmer switches), and others. Eshelman also set the type for and printed the programs.

Kermit applied what he'd learned from working with David Jackson in *Aria da Capo* and Joe Gistirak in *Ghosts*, keeping the actors focused as a holistic ensemble rather than individuals, and encouraging them to integrate their personal experiences into their characters. They rehearsed as a group every aspect of the entire play, every single line, prompting Eshelman to call Kermit's direction "a revelation." Tom Polk Miller, who had come to Waldport as a musician and writer, not an actor, said that his entire outlook on theater was changed by his deepened understanding of the relationship between actor and audience.[23]

After the weeks of rehearsal, set design, and stage construction, the curtain went up on a Thursday and Friday in early October. Chuck Cooley remembered the actors using Shaw's ambiguous references to great effect—and evoking diverse reactions. One conservative camper didn't like seeing a young poet kissing a minister's wife. The double entendres were loved by some, disdained by others. Most of all, people were impressed by one clear fact: there were some real actors on the stage; this was real theater.[24]

Emotional intensity in the theater is naturally more extroverted. Kermit was beside himself with his admiration for Ibby and her dramatic abilities; Hildegarde Erle was a surprising talent; and Martin Ponch, for all his New York directness and brusque manner, was a committed and effective team member. Despite the fragmentation and uncertainty of the camp and CPS, Kermit began to see the type of group dynamic he wanted to assemble into a cooperative theater now that the war was over and it was possible to imagine a realistic future.

The future, however, was anything but certain. Much of the group had already scattered, and nobody knew when someone might be released from CPS, picked up and thrown in jail, or set free. Joyce and Adrian had made it back to Maine and met up with Manche, who joined them and Bud Hawkins to set sail down the coast. They quickly realized the sloop was not equipped for the open sea, and the group split up at Marblehead just north of Boston. Manche and Joyce had become close friends at Waldport, and they'd come to an understanding that perhaps Manche was a better fit for Bob Harvey; she took off to check on him at his old farm in the Catskills. Joyce and Adrian went down to Philadelphia where Joyce had applied to study at the Hedgerow Theatre. As talk of an amorphous postwar "community" continued—maybe a co-op theater, maybe centered around the Untide Press—Joyce told Kermit that if they were set on continuing the group and they wanted her to be part of it, she would come. She felt she was caught between two worlds, though—this new world of peacetime and the responsibility of making a living, and the vital but receding Waldport community focused on being true to oneself through art. "With the end of the war, I can imagine the sense of eventual dispersal and readjustment invading you all," she said. "What now?"[25]

Ibby and Vlad Dupre, on furlough and visiting family in the Midwest, were also uncertain. Writing from Chicago, Ibby told Kermit she preferred the Bay Area over the Windy City, but the necessity of earning a living would probably put Vlad and her back in college. Complicating matters was the likelihood that Waldport would close before everyone was released from CPS, adding further uncertainty about where men would be sent. Vlad had been told he had a choice of being assigned to a mental hospital or a government camp, Ibby said, so they picked three names at random and sent them in. Ibby also made clear that while she liked the idea of joining the theater group, she wanted more to embark on her married life and raise a family—wherever that may take her.[26]

Ibby Dupre and
Enoch Crumpton in
Candida, 1945.

Uncertainty or not, the desire to create and build a cooperative theater was there. Kermit, Ponch, Adrian, and Joyce were definitely interested. If they could decide on a location, perhaps others would come on
board. Seattle and Portland were mentioned; Los Angeles was briefly considered but then rejected because Hollywood dominated the region. San
Francisco was probably the best place. Unlike the Pacific Northwest cities,
which were still somewhat undeveloped in regards to a fine arts presence,
the Bay Area had enough of an established culture yet remained open to
fresh ideas. The more they thought about it, the more it made sense: San
Francisco, it was. All they had to do was go down there, find a building,
buy it, and get to work. Granted, there was that problem of money—and
there would not be a Brethren Service Committee camp with barracks, a
dining room, and laundry service. But they would be free.

San Francisco in 1945 was a bustling city but decidedly not the cultural equal of the East Coast metropolitan centers. Less than a hundred years had passed since the 1849 gold rush changed the landscape of California, not even forty years earlier the great earthquake and fire of 1906 had devastated the city, and not much before that the notorious Barbary Coast district had offered its nightly array of drink, drugs, prostitution, graft, and just about every type of debauchery known to humankind. While on a fundamental level this was not really different from any other sizeable city, the difference between San Francisco and, say, New York was that the East Coast city had a more hierarchical class consciousness, with its financial and cultural institutions, whereas San Francisco was steeped in labor organization and had a strong connection to maritime and outdoor working-class politics. Kenneth Rexroth, a combination poet-radical-organizer-outdoorsman who came to San Francisco in 1927, remembered the city of the 1930s as a "backwater town" that was socially and spiritually as well as geographically removed from the publishing and tastemaker centers of New York and Boston. "There were people in San Francisco who were writing and not publishing anything when I came," he said. "The interesting thing is that most of them became practical labor organizers, rather than Bohemians sitting around in Union Square arguing about proletarian literature."[27]

Born in Indiana in 1905 and orphaned at a young age, Rexroth grew up through a hardscrabble life, hitting the road and working across the country as a newspaper reporter, bookstore clerk, restaurant owner, and later as a trail hand in the Pacific Northwest woods. Largely self-educated, he devoured books (including a complete reading of the *Encyclopaedia Britannica*) and spent time in Chicago as an art student, where he was introduced to leftist politics and circulated at the edges of the Chicago Renaissance, the literary movement of the 1910s driven by names like Sherwood Anderson, Vachel Lindsay, Edgar Lee Masters, and Carl Sandburg. In the 1920s Rexroth visited Taos, New Mexico, and met D. H. Lawrence; lived in Greenwich Village in a room beneath Hart Crane; and hitchhiked to Mexico City, hanging out in cafés with Diego Rivera and José Orozco. He shipped out on a steamer for Europe and visited expatriate Paris just long enough to confirm that the American West was where he belonged.

Back home during the Depression, he worked for the Works Progress Administration (WPA) and also supervised the night shift at the San Francisco City and County Psychiatric Hospital. He joined the Industrial Workers of the World and the Fellowship of Reconciliation; he lived, spoke, and wrote as a pacifist anarchist. When he tried to join the Communist Party, his application was returned with a note that he was too much an anarchist for the party. When war came, he registered as a conscientious objector and decided that he'd be an "absolute" objector, refusing even service in a CPS camp, but he passed the age limit of thirty-eight before his number was called. He also managed to learn that the FBI had a file on him filled with accusatory letters and statements from communists he had considered friends—but who apparently had succumbed to fear of being prosecuted themselves and so provided information deemed helpful by the authorities.

During the war, Rexroth continued his organizing and openly antiwar activities, involving himself with the National Committee for Conscientious Objectors, the Fellowship of Reconciliation, and the American Friends Service Committee—all the while cultivating his relationships with literary and arts figures, largely through the mail, for gasoline rationing made travel difficult. He founded an anarchist-thinker group called the Randolph Bourne Council (named after the World War I–era radical writer), and hosted regular poetry readings with his wife at their home on Potrero Hill south of downtown. The Rexroth house, like the Etter home up in Eugene, was a kind of haven for COs traveling in the region. "Many of these boys had little or no theoretical, ideological, or even religious basis for their conscientious objecting. They had simply gone on doing what their Sunday school teachers had told them to do," Rexroth remembered. "Many of them came down specifically to see me for counsel. Some of them were considerably distressed."[28]

Rexroth heard of Bill Everson through Henry Miller and James Laughlin, the New Directions publisher; he read Everson's early poetry and wrote to him in Waldport, asking for more. After receiving some samples of Untide Press material, the San Francisco radical invited the San Joaquin poet to visit anytime. Everson got down there during an October 1945 furlough, and immediately hit it off with the man some were calling the preeminent artistic and dissident force in the city. Everson, at thirty-three years old in camps largely populated by men in their twenties, was used to acting and being treated as the elder member of a group. But Rexroth, nearly seven years older, well traveled and with strong memories of the First World War, was the mentor here. Everson spent the night at Rexroth's, he later told Powell. "We sat late, drinking wine, myself listening. He has proclaimed me the most consequential poet to emerge during the war!! Well, well!"[29]

Everson returned to camp and the Untide Press, where they hoped to finish the Patchen book in time for Christmas. They'd completed the runs in black ink and were now set up to print the red-ink parts—whereupon they discovered that one of the black titles had been printed backwards, making eight of the forty pages in each copy unusable. They sent for more paper and learned from the supplier that the style they were using was no longer available and they'd have to wait until the mill began manufacturing it again. "I know what a blow this will be to you," Everson wrote Patchen. "For us, it is crushing." They'd been working at full power, with Kemper devoting literally all his time to it, Everson said. "We would have finished by December. We're all sorry."[30]

Go ahead with it anyway, said Patchen, who wanted the book out for Christmas. Explain the mistake in the colophon, including the paper delay, and release it to an interested and forgiving public. You can blame it on the author, he added—write that he insisted it come out in this imperfect form rather than waiting uncertain months. The pre-Christmas publication would make it all worthwhile, he said.[31]

Sorry, Everson replied, but that's impossible. Citing technical difficulties and the typographical chaos that would result from superimposing words of the poem literally over some of the titles, he made his stand for quality over all other considerations. This had been their rule from the beginning, and with this book they'd stretched perhaps beyond their abilities. Even so, he felt it was the best of all they'd done at Waldport, and he didn't want to compromise that just in the hope of catching a burst of seasonal buying. They would go ahead as originally planned, he said. The book would come out as soon as possible, but it would be no less than the best they were capable of doing.[32]

A few weeks later, he was able to offer some slightly better news. Not all the sheets had been printed backwards, and the crew was able to salvage about fifty sets intact. They bound up twenty-three copies and sent them as a Christmas gift to Patchen (who in turn made eleven handwritten, numbered limitation sheets explaining the printing error, then signed each and inserted them in selected copies as a "Rare Feather for Collectors"). That was as far as they got in Waldport. In his letter full of profuse apologies to Patchen, Everson added this note: "Then, too, Camp Waldport is closing." Most of the men were going to Cascade Locks, and they expected to move the press there, he said. "We will let you know when our address changes—probably before Christmas."[33]

Waldport didn't close without a struggle, however. It wasn't that the men wanted to stay; rather, it was a protest against the conditions of their ongoing internment. The agreement between the peace churches and the government defined the term as the war plus six months, which would be March 2, 1946—exactly six months after the Japanese surrendered. By that date, the COs figured, the churches would close down the camps and send everyone home. But when the Brethren Service Committee announced that they would close the camps yet continue supporting "detached service" in places such as psychiatric hospitals, church offices, medical experiment programs, and relief agencies, the COs argued that this went beyond the original purpose of CPS. The program had been created to provide an alternative to military service, they said; now that the war was ended, there was no reason for CPS to continue. Further support of the camps by the churches amounted to complicity in peacetime conscription, and the no-pay element was nothing short of slave labor. The men formed a Camp Waldport Committee for Co-ordinating Protest and drafted a letter to Harold Row, summarizing their renunciation of peacetime conscription and demanding that the BSC withdraw completely from CPS by the March 2 deadline. Eleven men in the camp took it a step further, commencing a hunger strike on November 20, two days before Thanksgiving. They sent out press releases announcing the strike's purpose: as a protest of the Brethren Service Committee's continued participation in Civilian Public Service, as well as what they saw as discrimination against conscientious objectors in general, noting that according to current timetables, 55 percent of military personnel would be released from service by January 1946, while less than 15 percent of COs would be freed. Never mind the ongoing privations of forced work with no pay, no insurance, or provision for dependents. As one striker put it, "We have served the government for more than four years under conditions that would not be countenanced by criminals." While they could hardly have expected much sympathy from the general public, they were astute enough to add one compelling point. During the war and its attendant labor shortage, it had made sense for the COs to pick up the necessary work even at their rate of no pay beyond subsistence costs. But now the market was flooded with workers, and to force the COs—again, with no pay—into jobs that could be filled by returning veterans and now-unemployed war workers amounted to not only slave labor but a serious threat to fair labor standards, they said. "Conscientious objectors do not wish to be a party to any movement that will depress wage and working conditions."[34]

Solidarity in the protest was short-lived. It was simply too much in a camp of so many with such different perspectives to agree on a single specific action. After fifteen days the number of strikers was down to three, and the final one ended after twenty. By that time, the camp had essentially collapsed. "Groups form and re-form, argue, discuss, rage, protest," Everson wrote Powell. The atmosphere was tight, the pressure increasing, he said. "Moral problem against moral problem: the terrible choices, the compulsion to act, the inability to act, the need and the fear; everything pulled to a stringency, a tension, and the inability to ever *know* what is right." Beneath this tension and uncertainty was the place itself,

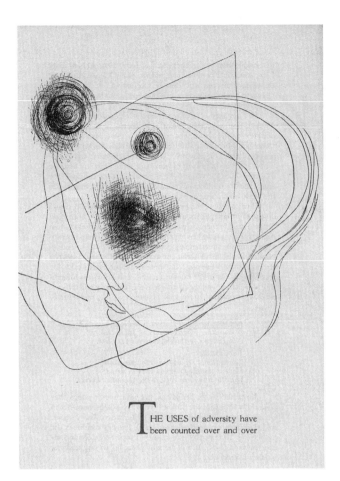

Illustration by
Barbara Straker James
for Jacob Sloan's
*Generation of
Journey*, 1945.

THE USES of adversity have
been counted over and over

the ocean, the mountains, the isolation: "immense, terrible, terribly beautiful, terribly remote, the forever sea, grinding, grinding, immense and beautiful and real, a great sense of terrible godliness, of reality beyond the human reality . . . the flashing face of non-human God." He could see the next war already coming, he said, with its unthinkable destruction of the atom bomb, and little tolerance for people like him. There was only one way to combat this hopelessness, he said, and it was to remember that there was still magnificence and wonder in the world. "The smoke that drifts from the toppling wave: or the dawn spread-eagled on its bloody east: all are testament to that serene face, that eye that looks and does not weep, at what we are."[35]

As the month of December, the year 1945, and Camp Waldport all came to a close, the men built a trailer to haul the Fine Arts materials to Cascade Locks. Everson and Bill Jadiker loaded it up and left on December 24, then spent Christmas Day in Portland at the home of artist friends Wilfred and Betty Lang, joined by Clayton and Barbara James. The next day they drove up the Columbia Gorge through a "howling storm," unloaded the books and papers, inks and other gear, then went back to Waldport for the monster press. Their little two-wheeled trailer barely held the heavy machine, which they balanced carefully across the axle, pulling out on New Year's Eve day, hoping the worn-out tires and groaning trailer frame would hold. They unloaded two days later at Cascade Locks; Jadiker went to work preparing a tiny cabin behind the barracks where he and his wife would live, and Everson collapsed in the infirmary with the flu.[36]

The Waldport camp emptied out over the holidays as if a blast of wind had come through and scattered everyone like so many leaves off a tree. Some went home on furlough, some walked out, most headed up to Cascade Locks or other camps. The Tillie the Whale cabin community dispersed. The Erles, Rubins, Jadikers, and Tom Miller and Isabel Mount went to the Locks; Eshelman and Kermit headed there as well. Vlad Dupre had returned from furlough in the Midwest; Ibby had remained there with family due to uncertainty about the future. So there Vlad was on Christmas Day, sitting in one of the lonely cabins. No doubt it was raining—maybe even sideways—and the constant wind and waves, which can be such comfort in good times, perhaps served as a mocking reminder of every human's ultimate solitary fate. At any rate, Dupre recalled years later, "It was miserable!"[37]

Civilian Public Service Camp #56 at Waldport officially shut down on December 31, 1945. Within the first two weeks of January just about everyone was gone—either assigned to other camps, folded into detached service, or disappeared over the hill. Don Fillmore, a nineteen-year-old Brethren drafted just a year earlier from northern California, remembered packing up and hauling away the final load with Harold Cessna. They took the church property to Camp Belden, not far from Fillmore's hometown in the Siskiyou Mountains, and later delivered surplus shoes, clothes, and medicine to the Church World Service, a multidenominational relief organization founded to provide food, clothing, and shelter to the millions suffering the war's aftermath in Europe and Asia.[38]

In the town of Waldport, news of the camp's closing was likely incidental to other matters. After a decade of economic depression followed by the war, the people could now get back to the business of their lives as working members of a peacetime society. "Conchie Camp at Waldport Closes; Projects Completed," announced the *Lincoln County Leader* weekly newspaper. A brief paragraph explaining why the COs had been there was followed by a more or less charitable summation of their work: "While accomplishment was not always up to expectation much forest work was completed which otherwise could not be attempted." They'd built roads and trails, the article said; they'd felled snags and constructed fire breaks, planted more than a million trees, fought forest fires, maintained and improved Forest Service structures, telephone lines, and recreational sites—and now that the region's young men were coming home, the COs were getting out of the way. "Fortunately," the article concluded, "closure of the camp comes at a time when labor to carry on is becoming more available and many veterans may be looking to the Forest Service for employment."[39]

The common-use name of the site reverted to its original Camp Angell designation; the Forest Service used the buildings for storage and turned the eastern end of camp at the foot of the bluff, beyond the dining hall and woodshed, into a dump.[40] The Tillie the Whale cabins and other rental lodgings readied themselves to welcome a new wave of tourists, perhaps even a business boom. Waldport and Yachats were gearing up for population increases; Cap's roadhouse, halfway between the towns, was no doubt preparing for some lively Saturday nights. The Waldport teetotalers and gossips must have been busy keeping an eye on the spirits dispenser's window at the town's liquor store as Doc Workman sat outside his secondhand shop, watching it all, amused and unperturbed. Dave Hall continued with his *Lincoln County Times,* but about the camp he didn't say a word. It had fulfilled its purpose—good, bad, and otherwise—and the community turned its attention elsewhere.

■ ■ ■

The Fine Arts as an official entity may have ended, but there was yet work to be done. Before they left Waldport, the theater group had begun work on another play. They'd wanted to do *The Glass Menagerie* by Tennessee Williams but couldn't acquire the production rights, so they went with *The Seagull,* Anton Chekhov's late-nineteenth-century drama about desire, love, and the search for happiness. The ensemble cast of thirteen characters was twice as large as any earlier production, and the stage crew alone numbered eleven. Adrian was out of the picture here, but Francis Barr remained with his ingenious light-dimmer system. Joyce and Ibby were gone, and the dependable seamstress Maude Gregory had returned to her family home, so Isabel Mount—who also acted in the play—oversaw the costume making. Joe Gistirak had walked out in June, but his fellow Hedgerow alum David Jackson stayed behind and directed the play—so committed that even after he was discharged from CPS in late December he came to Cascade Locks and saw the production through. Kermit also remained although he was discharged in January; he designed the set and played Trigorin, a writer and lover to Madame Arcadian, played by Hildegarde Erle. Tom Polk Miller was involved again, joined by a few new names from Waldport: John Land, David Vice, and Warren Kessler. A half-dozen Cascade Locks campers took part, along with some of their wives and partners. Bill Eshelman, engrossed in the press room with Everson as they slaved away on the

Tom Polk Miller
and Goldie Bock
in *The Seagull,* at
Cascade Locks
in 1946.

Patchen book, found time to print up a program featuring a summation of Chekhov's importance written by the famous actor and playwright Constantin Stanislavski. "Read him in the kitchen of life, and you will find nothing in him but the simple plot, mosquitoes, crickets, boredom, gray little people," the actor wrote. "But take him where art soars, and you will feel in the everyday plots of his plays the eternal longings of man for happiness, his strivings upwards."[41]

The Seagull opened on February 21, a Thursday, and ran through the weekend and beyond. A good crowd came for the shows, including some of the old Waldport gang. Joe Gistirak and Martin Ponch drove over from Portland. Manche came out from the city, as did Wilfred and Betty Lang. It was a remarkable time, Tom Miller wrote Vlad Dupre, particularly the way in which actors matured into their roles. "You'd hardly recognize John Land now, for instance—he blossomed out amazingly." Kermit also remembered the show as one of his favorites. "We wanted to get our teeth into plays that were written by the strongest writers of the early twentieth century and the end of the nineteenth"—and those were Ibsen, Shaw, and Chekhov, he said. "The favorite part I ever played was Trigorin, ever. I just loved that character and that play. I liked the sort of looseness of Chekhov."[42]

The music hadn't stopped, either. In November 1945, just weeks before Waldport closed, Bus and Hildegarde Erle had given a recital for violin and piano, featuring works by Bach, Paganini, and others. Of particular interest was Tartini's "The Devil's Trill"—an infamous piece that had purportedly come to the composer in a dream, played by Satan himself. Warren Downs called the program "almost defiant in scope and challenge, as if to claim a personal victory over conscripted camp life." It was so successful that they repeated the performance in April at Cascade Locks and in June at the public library in Portland.[43]

Meanwhile, release orders trickled in. Tom Polk Miller was set free in late January; he and Isabel Mount returned to Texas. After *The Seagull* was finished, Kermit took his release and went down to spend some time in Los Angeles. Bill Jadiker got the nod in March; he and Gertrude headed for New York. Word also came that Coffield was released in March from the Ann Arbor medical experiment unit. He, too, went to New York but couldn't find an affordable place to stay, so he headed south to live in a CPS unit outside Washington, DC, mopping floors at the University of Maryland. "If I should go to the West Coast, and we start a little theater," he wrote to Kermit, "I will be the house bum that annoys the customers; you know, by crawling under the seats and biting the ladies on the legs." Or, he said, "I may go to New York instead and sell pencils in front of the Empire State Building."[44]

Jim Harman got out of prison in March and headed down to Big Sur and the Bay Area. Vlad Dupre never made it to Cascade Locks. He was transferred to Camp #135, the government-run unit at Germfask, on Michigan's Upper Peninsula, but while he was en route, the BSC directed him to report to Elgin and step in as associate education secretary, replacing Bill Stafford, who had himself taken over the position vacated by Morris Keeton when he'd been released from CPS the previous November.[45]

After the Jadikers left their cabin at Cascade Locks, Everson moved in and commenced a kind of monastic existence, in keeping with his tendency toward self-reflection and simplicity in life. He was assigned night watchman duties and reveled in the solitude, all but completely retiring from social commerce with the rest of the camp. For the first time since he'd entered CPS, he was alone, and he wrote to Powell, describing his day. As the others awoke in the morning, he went to sleep. Waking in the afternoon, he brewed a cup of coffee on a tiny burner in his room, perhaps made a piece of toast or ate a handful of dried fruit, then sat and watched the early spring sun slanting through the budding trees. Long a vegetarian, he now excluded also milk and eggs from his diet, eating only a simple dinner in the dining hall before joining Eshelman in the press room to work on the Patchen book. Throughout the night, he made his rounds and performed his maintenance chores, spending the time in between with only his thoughts and the quiet world as company. The solitude suited him so well, in fact, that Everson eventually withdrew completely, dropping for a time even his work on the Untide Press. He ruminated instead on the purchase he'd made the previous fall while on furlough in San Francisco: Walking downtown, he'd seen an old hand press in a print shop window and bought it by cashing in an insurance policy his father had taken out years ago. He would print fine limited editions of his own work, he decided, and call it the Equinox Press, "after the seasons of balance and moderation, the equalizers, autumnal and vernal, the great suspension before the soar into summer and the plunge into fall."[46]

Eshelman carried on with the Patchen book, shipping the finished sheets down to Los Angeles, where Kemper completed the binding and distribution as he waited for his own court date to determine his status with CPS. When the book was finally released in May, they had orders for two hundred copies and another fifty ready for sustaining members of the Untide Press. It was anticlimactic as much as anything else, and Eshelman wrote to Patchen on a wry note, "We are happy someone is pleased with the book." The Untide Press had now completed its work begun in Waldport. There were more books planned, including the collection of poems sent by George Woodcock from London. The question now was: Who would do it? And where? The monster Challenge press sat quietly in its temporary headquarters, awaiting its next assignment—if there was going to be one.[47]

Simultaneously, somewhat incredibly, and no doubt through exertion of his tenacious personality, Martin Ponch shepherded out one more issue of the *Compass*—even though he was no longer part of the camp and now living in Portland, waiting to hear how his walkout case would be decided. With Adrian listed as associate editor and Wilfred Lang as art associate, and a couple other familiar names (Gertrude Jadiker on production, Manche on publicity) joined by a dozen others, the spring 1946 issue focused on peacetime conscription—making clear that the contents were not merely arguing what was wrong with conscription but what kind of world might be a functional alternative to a military-based economy. Sixteen contributors offered comments and criticism in four areas of society that the proponents of conscription had said would be improved by continued mandatory military service: international security, education, economic security, and health. Poems, illustrations, and the occasional editorial comment fleshed out the issue. But perhaps the most striking element (from the perspective of almost seventy years later) was the printing on the inside covers. They were facsimile newspapers projected twenty years into the future—dated May 15, 1966. Inside the front cover was *The Empire Builder*, reporting from a world in which military conscription was the norm. Headlines spoke of the United States and the Soviet Union at war, the president granted emergency unilateral powers, military guards protecting atomic energy plants, and university research labs developing secret weapons—in a world also featuring race riots, starvation in the Middle East, and strike-breaking squads at factories. The inside back cover was the opposite: *The World Citizen* featured headlines on the United States and the Soviet Union vacating military bases in the Pacific and granting independence to the Marshall Islands, atomic energy being dedicated to fighting cancer, a decrease in crime rates as home ownership increased, expanding individual freedoms in the Soviet bloc, and an annual Festival of Nations celebrating recognition of diverse ethnic groups.

Although the magazine listed Cascade Locks as its home, the masthead announced that this issue was likely the last to come from a CPS camp. "It is our hope, however," the statement concluded, "to see COMPASS continued as a literally *broad-minded* and widely circulated non-profit venture of peace-minded men and women in various parts of the world." In a society still a generation away from changing its use of the masculine pronoun when referring to both genders, the inclusion of those two words—"and women"—was truly subversive if not yet revolutionary.[48]

■ ■ ■

Back in Philadelphia, Joyce continued at the Hedgerow Theatre while Adrian did kitchen work and odd jobs for room and board at the Friends headquarters in Pendle Hill. But his heart was in cooperative theater on the West Coast, and, after meeting a husband-and-wife team who expressed desire to launch or help support such a project, Adrian and Joyce agreed that he should go to San Francisco and scout out the possibilities. He hitchhiked across the country in February, and through a CO connection landed work as a job printer in a commercial outfit, spending his spare time looking for a playhouse location in the city. Walking one day near a cable car crossing on Nob Hill, he saw a faded sign for Ferrier's French Theater of Art and learned that the owners wanted to sell it and retire. It was an old house with the classic San Francisco multiple floors; the theater was in the basement. It was perfect, Adrian said: an intimate theater with 150 cushioned seats, all the backstage equipment and gear. The house was for sale, too, and would make for a great cooperative living arrangement. All they needed was $25,000—or some kind of creative bank loan that might involve cooperative shares. Or they could rent just the theater space at $35 per show, maybe run a roof-top garden restaurant and serve dinners as well. The possibilities were endless, he wrote. "Such wonderful reveries!" The next day, the FBI walked into his workplace and picked him up.[49]

They took him to Portland, where he was lodged in the city jail, uncertain when he might be released. About a week later he was called to the visiting room and was shocked to see Joyce, who'd quit the Hedgerow Theatre, come west, and arranged for his bail. The reunited couple headed for a gathering with some of the Waldport crew, held at a room rented by Joe Gistirak, who was still waiting for his case to come before a judge. Martin Ponch joined them; Kermit, Tom Miller, and Bill Eshelman came; Manche showed up. It turned into a weekend of laughter and joy, with lots of talk and big ideas. They went out to restaurants: Chinese food one night, steaks another. They took in a comic opera, then settled down to talk serious theater. They were ready to start a production group, right there in Portland; they'd write friends immediately and ask them to come. Never mind that Kermit had to leave for San Francisco, Tom Miller was headed back to Houston, Eshelman back up to the Locks, and Adrian, Ponch, and Gistirak had no idea what their fates would be. Sure, everything was up in the air, Adrian said. "But we have the enthusiasm."[50]

It was the end of June when the three Waldport walkouts finally went before a Portland judge. All spring long the news had been varied, even contradictory. It seemed that a given judge might send one fellow to prison for a year and let the next one go free, perhaps citing some reference to sincerity. Adrian and the others obtained legal representation through the ACLU, and the lawyers worked to find loopholes or exceptions that could affect interpretation of the law. But it was the interpretation by District Court Judge James A. Fee that heralded change. In an earlier decision regarding a CO who'd walked out of the Friends camp at Elkton, Fee had ruled that transfer orders given by Colonel Kosch of the Selective Service, a military entity, did not follow the requirement that COs were to be under "civilian direction" as stated in Section 5(g) of the Selective Training and Service Act of 1940. Martin Ponch remembered his court appearance this way:

Judge Fee asked about his background, and Ponch told him.

Okay then, Fee said. "You were in a camp in Tennessee and you were transferred out here."

"Yes," Ponch confirmed.

"Why did you obey the transfer?" Fee asked.

"Well, I had really asked for it," Ponch replied.

"Yes," the judge said, "but who was it that was granting it?"

"Selective Service."

Fee ruled that Selective Service couldn't order transfers because they were military and not in charge of the camps, adding that Ponch had been a free man from the day he was ordered to Oregon. "Go away," he said.[51]

Adrian recalled his interaction somewhat more dryly. Judge Fee, he reported, heard the case then said, "The indictment is dismissed, the man is released, and his bail is exonerated." The same went for Joe Gistirak, and the men were free.[52]

Gistirak headed for San Francisco; Ponch stayed in Portland to see about starting up a theater with some people from Reed College, the private liberal arts school known for its creative approaches to education; and Adrian went with Joyce up to Washington's Olympic Peninsula, where they joined a loose communal-living group based around some land owned by Waldo Chase. There, outside Union, a tiny village on the Hood Canal waterway west of Tacoma, Chase had built a kind of lodge featuring all manner of idiosyncratic construction materials, ranging from wooden poles, rammed earth and hand-split cedar shakes to canvas and glazed chicken wire. Clayton and Barbara James were there, living in a teepee and plying the waters of the canal in Chase's wooden dugout canoe. Wilfred and Betty Lang came up from Portland, bringing their two young daughters and hauling a trailer of belongings, looking like the Depression-era migrant workers still fresh in the national memory. Joyce and Adrian moved into an old log cabin, furnished only with some built-in bunk beds with straw mattresses and a primitive brick stove in one corner. Water came from a bucket hung beneath the overflow drip from the village water tower; sanitation was a rudimentary outhouse a few yards beyond the cabin. They gardened and cooked with the others, living off subsistence farming and the plentiful oysters that grew along the water's edge, thinking up all manner of recipes to vary the presentation. The owner of a nearby tourist camp allowed them to strip the loose bark from cedar trees on his property, which they wove into table mats and sold to tourists at a nearby place called the Robin Hood Lodge. Waldo Chase had perfected a system of building wooden looms by hand, and he set up the community on an assembly line, building a dozen looms a week, which they sold to a Portland department store.

It was this simple, cooperative living attuned to the rhythms of manual work and nature that brought the kind of clarity and fulfillment sought by the group. They knew they couldn't do it forever; whatever they gained was more in the experience than monetary profit. But for now, it was summer in the woods and waterways of the Olympic Peninsula, one of the last truly wild places in America. The land was fertile and full of just about anything one might need, provided they knew how to look for it. "We took a marvelous canoe trip with the Jameses," Adrian wrote near the end of the season, "hearing the archaic cry of the blue heron, digging clams, picking berries and apples, watching the great mountains." It was, Clayton said, how you shed all the precepts and restrictions of your life, and therefore find yourself.[53]

Back at Cascade Locks, things were winding down but not always quietly. By May, the war had been over for nine months—three beyond the CPS term mandate of the war's duration plus six months—yet there were still some four thousand men in the camps. The discrepancy in release dates continued as well, with 77 percent of army draftees demobilized and only 44 percent of COs set free. Across CPS, protests such as the work slowdown had been perfected to an almost hilarious degree. At the government-run camp in Minersville, tucked away in the Trinity

National Forest of northern California, a CO ordered to toss out some leftover beans confounded his bosses by transferring the beans one at a time into the garbage pail. Word spread across camp and a crowd gathered, counting as he went along and taking guesses at what the total might be; finally, the exasperated director ordered the CO specifically to dump the beans together. Two other men consumed an entire day cleaning a single table and two pots, while another pair managed to use two days in moving a camp cot some one hundred yards. At the Big Flats camp in New York—from where Clayton James, Bus Erle, and Bob Harvey had come—the American Friends Service Committee relinquished administration to the federal government, prompting the remaining COs to raise a flag bearing the legend "U.S. Slave Camp." The local American Legion rattled their sabers, but the COs outflanked them by staging a parade through the nearby town of Elmira—but not in regards to themselves. Instead, they paraded for sending food to Europe, joined by townspeople and even a recently returned veteran, handing out pre-addressed boxes that donors could fill with canned and dried foods and mail to relief centers.[54]

But it was a work strike down in Glendora, the camp east of Los Angeles, that brought direct action to a critical mass. It began in April when the camp director ordered two men transferred to Minersville, which had opened in the summer of 1945, replacing Germfask as the unofficial penal colony of CPS where the radicals and troublemakers were sent. Forty men at Glendora went on strike to protest the transfer; two weeks later the number was eighty. Support strikes were planned for other western camps, including Minersville and Three Rivers in California, Mancos in Colorado, and Elkton and LaPine in Oregon. At Cascade Locks there was talk of a strike but not much action; a number of the men knew they were up for release, and they didn't want to jeopardize that. But one night in early May, Everson had an encounter that changed his thinking.

He was still doing the night watchman shift, quietly biding his time, expecting to receive his release orders any day. He knew about and supported the Glendora strike, but wasn't prepared to risk punishment. He'd been radical long enough, he said, and was done with idealism.

The night before the appointed date for a coordinated strike of the West Coast camps, Everson was visiting with Hildegarde Erle, still there with her husband and a handful of Waldport COs. They got to talking about Glendora, and Hildegarde wondered why Cascade Locks wasn't striking. Everson commented that, as the leader from Waldport, he could probably make a strike happen at the Locks.

"Why don't you do it?" Hildegarde asked.

"I don't want to," Everson replied.

She asked him why not.

"I would get my head lopped off," Everson said, referring to his impending release orders.

But the Selective Service office in Washington would have mailed his release on the first of the month, Hildegarde said; it would already be on its way. "You can expect it in a day or two."

"That is true," Everson admitted.

"Then what possible grounds could you have for not doing it?" Hildegarde said.

"Well . . . ," Everson said, then went on his rounds, thinking.

During the night he saw another CO, Lloyd Danzeisen, printing up posters in preparation for a strike all by himself. A twenty-nine-year-old Brethren from Ohio, Danzeisen was devoutly religious with a strong moral compass; he would do what he must do whether he was alone or joined by a hundred others. Between Hildegarde and Danzeisen, something clicked in Everson during the night. By daybreak he was making signs as well, and when it came time to ring the wake-up bell, he was striding through the dorms calling out, "Strike! Strike!"[55]

A dozen men—including Danzeisen, Wes DeCoursey, Warren Downs, Bus Erle, Jim Gallaghan, and Jerry Rubin from Waldport—joined a work and hunger strike. A press release went out, and the *Oregonian* reported that the "Cascade Locks Conchies" were on strike. The newspaper related the story from a tolerant perspective, noting in a short, six-inch column buried on page 9 that the strike had little effect on camp operations other than shutting down the laundry service. The point was to bring attention to the conditions in CPS, the strikers said; it was a demonstration more than an actual attempt to halt operations. Wes Smith, who'd been at Waldport and had a good enough relationship with the Fine Arts members, was then the Cascade Locks director, and his focus was on simply keeping the place from falling apart until it could close. The strikers were left alone and reported as RTW. Six of the fasters lasted a week; three of them went fifteen days. The final one, Danzeisen, held out for twenty, commenting with a touch of humor, "I am starving my body because I'm fed up with compulsory service."[56]

One thing, however, they hadn't anticipated. Their release orders weren't mailed out on May 1—or, if they were, they'd been somehow intercepted and revoked. None of the strikers from the Waldport group were released in May. Nor were they freed in June. As Cascade Locks prepared to shut down in July, six of the COs who had participated in the strike were sent to Minersville. Ironically, the two Glendora men who'd originally been ordered there never made the transfer—and now the men who'd acted on their behalf suffered this exile instead. "By such strange machinations do we progress," Everson wrote Powell. In one last Herculean effort, though, they managed to ship the Challenge press down to Kemper's parents in Pasadena, where it was stored in a shed behind their house.[57]

Minersville was in a state of perpetual work slowdown, and the Waldport refugees soon learned that if they simply did not cause trouble, they could apply for release and perhaps be out within a month. Most of them did so, and the wheels of bureaucracy finally turned in their direction. Besides, it was summer in northern California, and while Minersville was truly isolated, the forests were lovely, with clear, cold mountain streams and the literally breathtaking beauty of the nearby Trinity Alps. There were worse places to finish out one's time.

On July 23, a Tuesday evening, Everson returned from a firefighting work detail and was met by a camp officer who told him he was released. Everson stared at him for a few minutes, then shouted, "Jesus Christ!" and took off running. The next day, he was bound for Berkeley on the bus, dropping off a postcard to Powell: "July Twenty Four. THIS IS IT!!"[58]

Warren Downs got word a week later; he returned to Salem and, having been urged by Bus Erle, was thinking seriously about studying music back East. Eshelman got his release on August 12 and returned to Los Angeles with thoughts of finding a job and continuing the Untide Press with Kemper and Tom Polk Miller. Enoch Crumpton finally got out; Lloyd Dazeisen was released. In late September, Jerry Rubin wrote that there were eight men left at Minersville. But he apparently expected to be out soon, for he provided a San Francisco address. Although it wasn't until April 1947 that CPS officially closed, the program that had given birth to, nurtured, challenged, and shaped what happened at Waldport was essentially finished.

As the fall and winter of 1946 brought thousands upon thousands of men and women back home, brought families and friends back together—with the aching absence of so many others—one thing was certain: the world was very different. The Great Depression was over; World War II was ended. America was now the dominant political, military, and even cultural force on the planet. But America—and the world—had changed in ways deep and profound, both heartening and disturbing, terrifying yet exciting. For many, returning to their lives did not mean returning to the lives they had known. As much as they might wish, there was no going back. And for many across the land, a question came to mind, a question they perhaps hadn't anticipated, the same question Joyce Harvey had written from Philadelphia the previous August as hostilities were ending: *What now?*

CHAPTER 12

Unscrew the Locks from the Doors!

IN THE SUMMER OF 1947, an unassuming book appeared in stores, titled *On My Way Home*. A kind of diary-travelogue, it reported the cross-country journey of Richard Phenix, a twenty-nine-year-old former army captain who had spent his time in the war as a supply officer, most of it in the States. Now discharged from the service and recognizing that he had little experience as a civilian worker, he set out in his car to ease his way back into society, to see if he could not find his place in it, and perhaps somewhere along the way learn something of himself. He headed west from his army camp in Missouri, taking odd jobs and living in boarding houses, or, when necessary, sleeping in his car. He hauled junk in Salt Lake City, cut timber in the California Sierras, delivered laundry in San Diego, stocked shelves in a Hollywood grocery store. The book jacket blurb declared, "After all the self-consciously tough stories of returning soldiers, this quiet record of one man's way home comes as a relief. . . . The most exciting thing about this story is that nothing much happened to him. He just met a lot of Americans and slowly made up his mind what he wanted to do next. There must have been several million others somewhat like him, and they didn't, until now, seem to have got into books."[1]

The action is not only quiet but slow, the narrative honest but dull. Large sections are filled with filled with details concerning where and how the author would sleep on the road, or the step-by-step process of ordering and maintaining supplies of canned goods in his grocery store job. It is literally, perhaps too much so, real life. The reviewers trashed it, saying the story had little depth or point. The *New York Times* called it "somewhat inoffensive, vaguely readable, touched with the wistful charm of incompetence." And that seems largely to be the case.[2]

Still, there is one chapter, buried beneath the mundane reportage, that speaks of something larger than the author's pedestrian observations. After a few months of roaming the West, he finds himself walking at night on a beach in Carmel, facing the vast, dark ocean, the sharp night sky, the indifferent universe. "Suddenly I felt weary; my body lost its will to stay upright. I stopped where I was, pulled my coat tightly about me, and sat slowly down. There was a bank of soft, dry sand behind me and I lay back and looked at the stars. Wisps of gray and white clouds were gathering, and as I watched, the moon became obscured except for a luminous glow; I tasted the salt on my lips, relaxed in the warm folds of my coat and closed my eyes." He remembers where he has been, the people and places he has seen, the possibilities, the disappointments, the lessons, the dreams. He thinks about his army buddies, the hopes and dreams they had voiced, and the concessions they'd made to reality, what Phenix calls a "label." One fellow is a pipe-fitter, another a paint salesman. One is a short-order cook, another headed for factory work in Detroit. Phenix knows he's probably going in that direction soon enough, but he can't bring himself to do it yet. He imagines visiting his buddies, sitting down with a can of beer in the suburban backyards as they ask, "What are *you* doing, Cap'n?"

> How could I say, "I'm looking for something, Joe. I'm not satisfied with life as it is, and I don't know why, but I've got to find out before I can settle down.
>
> "People seem different to me, Joe. . . . They are full of distrust and unrest and fear; they no longer want freedom *to do* something, they want freedom *from* something. I can't see where to stand in this new world.
>
> "I'm looking for a label, Joe. A label that will tell me what I am and that will identify me to others. There are millions of labels, Joe, from those that say 'executive' to those that say 'bum,' and each of the million is shaded individually from black to white through every color of the spectrum. The colors mean 'Democrat' or 'Catholic' or 'Jew,' 'Communist,' 'Moralist,' or one of a thousand others. And the more subtle shadings of each color mean 'good' Democrat, 'bad' Catholic,' 'indifferent' Communist, 'political' Moralist, and so on. And the faint streaks in the shades are for the different interpretations of the meanings of 'good' and 'bad' and 'political.' But all the elements must be there for people to see, Joe; you have got to be labeled."

He goes on, questioning his values, the values of others, looking for that reconciliation between society's and the individual's needs. He doesn't mention it by name—he may not even be aware of it—but he's touching on Thoreau's quiet desperation, Sinclair Lewis's *Main Street*, and a phrase not yet known but that would become synonymous with the 1950s: *The Man in the Gray Flannel Suit*. He questions, but not too deeply. He pushes, but not too far. He knows he needs to figure things out, and he has no doubt that he will. He finishes his meditation with, "I knew I was rich. I had my eyes and ears, legs and arms, and good health.

I had a will to do something; all I needed was something to do and the faith that it was right."[3]

With these eleven pages of candid soul-searching planted among the other 256 of prosaic journaling, Phenix had written in effect a manifesto for the "several million" that would come to be known as the Silent Majority. The GI Joe who came home and turned into Joe Blow, the regular guy, the company man who went to work at the container factory or sold insurance. Who got married and raised a family, earned wages or a salary and bought station wagons, vacuum cleaners, electric toasters, and washing machines. The men and women who brought up a generation that would later rebel against them for that very acceptance of tract housing, television sets, and frozen vegetables.

All Phenix was saying, really, was that he simply wanted his piece of the pie. His generation had been through a decade of economic depression; they'd been through a world war. They'd seen plenty in their short time on this planet; they didn't need any more excitement. Now they just wanted to live.

■ ■ ■

About the same time, another young man was driving around the country. This fellow was also searching for something. But unlike Phenix, he wasn't searching for a label that would identify him to others. This young man, along with his friends, was after something less concrete but no less substantial. He was after the meaning of life. And, like so many young people who have their childhood behind them and their decades of adulthood to come, he knew the only thing to do was to move, to "take off" and hit the road. Out there, he believed, would be the answers, the experience, the stuff that makes life real. And, he wrote in recalling his adventures, "somewhere along the line I knew there'd be girls, visions, everything; somewhere along the line the pearl would be handed to me."[4] His name was Jack Kerouac, and his book would be called *On the Road,* a headlong narrative that was nearly the opposite of Phenix's careful accounting and methodical plan. Kerouac's seekers wanted nothing to do with labels; they smashed all conventions, lived for "kicks" and "highs" with exuberance, energy, excitement. They were, as Kerouac described in this oft-quoted passage, "the mad ones, the ones who are mad to live, mad to talk, mad to be saved, desirous of everything at the same time, the ones who never yawn or say a commonplace thing but burn, burn, burn like fabulous yellow roman candles exploding like spiders across the stars and in the middle you see the blue centerlight pop and everybody goes 'Awww!'"[5]

On the Road would become the bible of the 1960s generation, the baby boomers, who need no further defining here. But in 1947, America wasn't quite ready to embrace the "mad ones" as Kerouac did. It would be a decade before his book was even published. First, some ground needed to be plowed.

According to Kenneth Rexroth, the place for this to happen was San Francisco. Its combination of cosmopolitan and proletarian made for a rich mix of tolerance and skepticism, of libertarianism and anarchism, laissez-faire and radicalism. There was that West Coast sensibility, too, a climate of change. This was a land of earthquakes and gold rushes, of high risk and high reward, a place that looked to the future, not the past. Unlike the East Coast, where the sun rose out of the ocean and set comfortably into the woods and mountains beyond, here on the edge of the Pacific rim the sun came up from the land left behind and set into a fiery sea, as if daring one to follow. Here, you could almost see tomorrow.

Rexroth and his group continued their poetry readings and anarchist meetings after the war, reaching out to include even the old Workmen's Circle of Italian and Jewish radicals with their long mustaches and rumpled caps, the real revolutionaries from before the First World War. They started up a monthly dance evening, bringing in local jazz groups for the younger crowd or accordion and fiddle players for the old guard. Talk at their well-attended meetings ranged across the spectrum of philosophy, politics, and culture, with topics on Emma Goldman, Bakunin, Wilhelm Reich, Marx and Engels, Lao-tzu, Plato, Aristotle, and Francis Bacon. One meeting, titled "Sex and Anarchy," was so full that people climbed on each other's shoulders, and a twin meeting convened downstairs to handle the overflow. In the summer months they motored across the still-young Golden Gate Bridge for picnics up in Marin County, where they leavened their political talk and music with a more relaxed attitude in the natural environment. The intellectual climate in San Francisco was utterly different from New York, Rexroth said. They had more in common with the European anarchists, with Gandhi in India, and the anti-colonial movements in Southeast Asia. Besides, he added, they knew how to throw better parties.[6]

Across the bay in Berkeley, University of California English professor Josephine Miles and doctoral student Thomas Parkinson were nurturing the careers of young poets Robert Duncan, Jack Spicer, and Robin Blaser by inviting them to teach noncredit writing workshops and carrying on the tradition of public poetry readings there dating back to the First World War.[7] Duncan, then in his late twenties and studying medieval history part-time at the university, had already stirred the waters somewhat with his poetry and other writings. Born and raised in the Bay Area, he'd gone to New York at twenty, where he moved among the avant-garde groups in that city and the artist colonies upstate in Woodstock. There, while helping to edit a literary and pacifist journal, the *Phoenix,* he first encountered the work of Bill Everson, and the two commenced a correspondence. Drafted into the army, Duncan received a psychiatric discharge in 1941; four years later he published a magazine article titled "The Homosexual in Society," groundbreaking not only in its candid treatment of the topic but also in that Duncan identified himself as such. Now back in Berkeley, he and the other young poets organized events at a run-down boardinghouse on Telegraph Avenue, called Throckmorton Manor, where they read and discussed the work of the modern poets who had not yet cracked the academic canon. "There we had discussions of Stevens, Eliot, Pound, Williams, Yeats," Parkinson recalled. "There was a vitality in those discussions that grew from our conviction that these were *our* poets on whom there was no official word."[8]

Down in Big Sur near Henry Miller but also connected to Berkeley, an energetic editor named George Leite was putting out *Circle*, an occasional avant-garde journal that paid more attention than anyone else to the West Coast poets. Along with work by Miller and William Carlos Williams, the mimeographed second issue of *Circle* included poems by Everson and Coffield as well as two poems by Philip Lamantia, a teenage poet whose surrealist vision brought him comparisons to Rimbaud.[9]

Back in the city, down at the western edge of the Tenderloin district, Rexroth's anarchist friends had formed a group called the Libertarian Circle and were slowly printing up a literary journal called the *Ark*, done on an old letterpress on an entirely voluntary basis. This was true pacifist anarchy: ideas and action with no leaders—but perhaps a few strong personalities.

Into this mix came the various members of the Waldport group, with their ideas and experience regarding public poetry, independent printing, and cooperative theater. Everson lived first on a friend's apple farm set up as an artists' commune near Sebastopol in Sonoma County north of the city, installing himself in a remodeled shed behind the farmhouse, rooming for a while with the hand-operated press he'd bought in the city during his final furlough. He moved to Berkeley soon after, landing a job as night janitor at the University of California Press. It was there, he said, as his work of sweeping floors and emptying wastebaskets took him to every corner of the operation, that he learned the foundations of true book publishing.[10]

Soon, he was attending Rexroth's readings and discussion groups, joined by Duncan and Lamantia along with poets and writers Thomas Parkinson, Muriel Rukeyser, Sanders Russell, and Jack Spicer. Rexroth saw his opportunity here to forge the kind of literary movement he'd been cultivating for years, using the triumvirate of Duncan, Everson, and Lamantia. It would be a kind of "collective surge" of pacifism, eroticism, and anarchism, Everson recalled. "I was to be his Lincolnesque populist pacifist—the 'pome-splitter,' Duncan a celebrative dionysian aesthetic . . . Lamantia a dionysian surrealist."[11]

Rexroth lobbed his first volley in a "Letter from America" addressed to readers of George Woodcock's *Now* magazine, published in London. America, drunk on postwar excess, was culturally exhausted and morally bankrupt, Rexroth said. Its cities were a "madhouse" of alcohol and drugs, juvenile delinquency, gambling, and venereal disease. "The U.S.A. after dark has come to look like 4th century Rome, or late Weimar Germany. The eve of the Goth, the eve of Hitler, the eve of the bomb." The economy was shot, the workers with their factory jobs were now placated by bread and circuses, the artists also silenced in the security of their government positions in the War Information Department or the academic propaganda machines. A few voices survived here and there, Rexroth noted. But the future, he said, was of necessity in youth. He offered his list that included Sanders Russell, Robert Duncan, Rosalie Moore, Thomas Parkinson, and others. Philip Lamantia got two full sentences, but Everson was hailed in a separate paragraph as the most notable American poet to emerge from the war years: "literate, articulate, honest, and locked up for his beliefs." The comparisons to "Honest Abe" were inevitable, Rexroth continued, but there was more to Everson than that. "Because, in small letters, and in the most general sense, he is a conscientious objector, who is out to do something about it with his own hands."

So there you have it, Rexroth said. America today didn't make much sense, and he wasn't sure how much sense he had made of what was happening in San Francisco. But he did know this: "We have the young. When I was a kid after the first war, it was assumed that a college professor was, by definition, a whore and a liar. It was assumed that the world was divided into those who knew that society was a monstrous, evil lie, and those, the scissorbills, who didn't . . . the hip and square, as they say today."

And the hip, Rexroth said, were not paying attention to the squares. They'd turned away from the ossified East Coast intellectual cocktail parties that had made a fetish of Marx and Rimbaud. The young today are reading D. H. Lawrence, Henry Miller, Kropotkin, Randolph Bourne, Albert Schweitzer, and Kenneth Patchen, he said. "At least the young I know do."[12]

A month later, the squares fired a shot of their own. The April 1947 *Harper's* magazine featured an eleven-page exposé of the Bay Area scene, titled "The New Cult of Sex and Anarchy." Written by Mildred Edie Brady, a Berkeley "economist and free-lance writer," purportedly familiar with the scene, the article took a generally dismissive and somewhat bemused view of the young bohemians in San Francisco, Berkeley, and Big Sur. They were calling their home "the new Paris," Brady said, and themselves its artists and intellectuals. The region's mild climate and long history of tolerance for individualists, eccentrics, and oddballs made it easy for these self-styled anarchists and emancipators of civilization to live here, Brady said—and that was okay as long as they kept their silliness to themselves. After all, she noted, this business about anarchy and overthrowing the state was just a throwback to the 1920s, nothing to be concerned about. And they really had only one thing on their minds, she said: sex. Sex as the savior of humanity, sex as free expression, sex with midwestern girls come West seeking excitement and creative geniuses to nurture.

The movement's philosophical underpinnings were a mix of anarchism, mysticism, eroticism, and psychoanalysis, Brady said. Its bible was Wilhelm Reich's *Function of the Orgasm,* which espoused sexual potency as the antidote to society's ills; its prophet was Henry Miller; and its general, Kenneth Rexroth. Brady denounced them collectively: Miller was a dirty old man living in a shack, caught up in astrology and his own mythology as the heir to D. H. Lawrence; Rexroth was a 1920s anarchist living in the 1940s; George Leite with his *Circle* magazine was a literary pretender with more energy than coherence.

Then there were those pacifists, she said, the conscientious objectors who'd been disproportionately seeded into the West Coast work camps, who'd taken pilgrimages to Miller's Big Sur cabin after reading his pamphlet, *Murder the Murderer,* a blistering condemnation of war, and who now settled in the Bay Area with their strange mixture of nonviolence, anarchism, and sexual promiscuity.

And, of course, art. For it was through art, Brady said, that these radicals and revolutionaries believed they could blaze a trail out from this mechanized, homogenized, dying modern world. "So they write poetry. They paint. They write philosophy. They go to galleries and concerts." They believed, Brady said, "Only through art is it any longer possible to reach that all but buried spark of natural life dying under the intolerable weight of modern man's sadistic super-ego. And only through art will man find his way back to his spontaneous, natural creativeness."

Just in case her tone might be mistaken, Brady made clear her assessment of those artists' mystical and visionary poems:

> Lines about drinking "our father's blood or strangling our mother with her hair," or "chopping up the blood like dice of onions," or "quietly the mothers are killing their sons; quietly the fathers are raping their daughters" are far more frequent . . . than references to "trees flowing within me," or "this act of vision is an act of love"—lines, that is, promising green growth out of decay. . . . Some few of them are written with enough lucidity for ordinary mortals to understand them, but most of them are incomprehensible.[13]

In 1947, neither Brady nor America was ready for a new Paris. Rexroth's letter in *Now* didn't draw much attention beyond the eccentric margin, and the *Harper's* article certainly didn't draw the kind of attention Rexroth wanted. But it did draw some attention—and curious minds in New York and Boston and the other bastions of civilization back East glanced toward San Francisco and wondered, if only for a moment, if something might be going on out there.

Something *was* going on out there—and not just centered around Rexroth and Miller. After the Waldport group members had scattered to their various destinations, Kermit kept a round-robin correspondence going for those interested in starting up a theater, and in early 1947 he, Adrian, Joyce, and Martin Ponch sat down together in San Francisco and made the decision. Yes, they would do it, and they would do it here. It was indeed Paris in America, Adrian said, an ideal center of cultural activity—but also desperately in need of a bold, independent theater.[14]

They recruited friends and acquaintances, gathering about a dozen members, including Si Miller from Waldport days, and Don Kirschner and Bill Webb from Cascade Locks. Then who should appear from the East Coast but Glen Coffield—now with a less-tangled head of hair but as full of wit and ideas as ever. They put together a one-act show of George Bernard Shaw's *Great Catharine,* performing it for invited friends in the front parlor of a rented house. Adrian noted a "very responsive audience," which apparently gave them enough enthusiasm to launch their independent, cooperative repertory theater—even though they had no money, no sustaining membership, and no home. They didn't even have a name. So they called a meeting and decided people would write names on sheets of paper, then they'd share and choose a winner. They went around once and came up empty. They tried it again: nothing. Just as they were about to settle for something pedestrian like San Francisco Theater Company, Chris Rambo (whom Joyce described as "our company wit") took a large sheet of paper, lettered out a single word and held it up: INTERPLAYERS. "That's it!" the group cried. It was everything they were about—the interplay of the script and performance, the actors and audience; the interplay within the group itself. Kermit rushed off to put together a press release he could take to the *San Francisco Chronicle* theater columnist, with whom he'd been cultivating a relationship, while Adrian sat silent to the side, envisioning the name in all the theater programs he could print.

The story of the Interplayers is the story of any truly independent creative endeavor. They were driven by energy, passion, commitment, and a fair amount of talent. They were hobbled by financial limitations, creative and personality conflicts, and that recurring gremlin that seems to shadow so many start-up performing groups: the inability to secure a permanent home.

They started that spring at the Friends' Center on Sutter Street, in space charitably made available by the Quakers, doing one-act comedies by Chekhov, with Adrian running the lights using the saltwater dimmer switches he'd learned about at Waldport. David Jackson came from back East and directed Shaw's *Heartbreak House*, reinvigorating the sense that they were continuing their work from Waldport and not just starting anew. They thought about repeating the shows they'd produced there — *Ghosts* and *The Seagull*. "Add to these a couple of Strindberg or Lorca or Synge or Joyce or Cocteau or another Ibsen," Adrian wrote his family, "and San Francisco will have a season like it has never had before."[15]

But their decision to do Jean-Paul Sartre's *No Exit*, a bleak tale of three people in hell, caused enough discomfort with the administration at the Friends' Center that they were compelled to vacate the space and search for six months until they found room at the Legion of Honor theater, out past the Presidio in the northwest corner of the city. Despite this distant location, the Sartre play was their first sustained success, originally slated for just two performances but selling out half a dozen, and putting them on the map as a pioneer force in the resurgence of San Francisco theater.

Successes and challenges followed. Building on the positive response to *No Exit*, they produced the first American showing of *Under Way*, written by Norwegian playwright Hedge Krog, a Nobel Prize winner

A linocut by Adrian Wilson, depicting his printing space at the Interplayers' theater.

then unknown in the United States. In the fall of 1949, they found a home in an abandoned warehouse at Hyde and Beach streets, a cable-car crossing near the water at the foot of Russian Hill, where they pooled nearly all their resources and splurged three hundred dollars to buy an advertisement on a Hyde Street cable car, announcing their first production at the new site, Federico Garcia Lorca's *The Shoemaker's Prodigious Wife*. But problems with fire codes, public-gathering permits, and unpredictable landlords sent them from one place to another. They were shut down at the Hyde and Beach location; they tracked down permits and opened up again. They did a show at the San Francisco Museum of Art; they performed in the rain at the annual San Francisco Art Festival; they moved to a crumbling mansion further up Russian Hill, selling out thirteen straight weeks of Jean Giradoux's *The Madwoman of Chaillot*. But the landlady there, perhaps hoping to cash in on what she perceived as their financial success, sued for alleged damages to the ancient building, and they were homeless again.

Throughout the late 1940s and into the early 1950s, they never lost sight of their guiding principles—the same principles they'd conceived when launching their theater at Waldport. The commitment was to the show, the art, the group; everything was directed toward their ability to choose and produce works that challenged and rewarded audiences and performers alike. By 1954, when they settled into a relatively stable home in the old Bella Union Theater on Kearny Street between North Beach and Chinatown, they were recognized as one of the groundbreaking theaters of the 1950s San Francisco creative scene. It may have been their persistence as much as their vision that made the true difference in helping others to follow. When they'd been shut down at Hyde and Beach due to building code requirements, they were rehearsing a drama adaptation of Franz Kafka's novel, *The Castle*. As they negotiated the literal and figurative catacombs of the San Francisco building code system in their own Kafkaesque journey, a series of serendipitous personal conversations and relationships resulted in the Interplayers getting past the Class A permit requirement (rumored to have been engineered by proprietors of the large theaters in town to stifle competition). On recommendation from a building contractor with connections to the fire department commissioner, they appealed the initial permit decision and were cleared to run their theater. This opened the door for other theaters such as the now-legendary Actor's Workshop, Adrian recalled twenty years later. "It cracked an impossible barrier," he said. "Ever since then no one has bothered the theaters that came after we did."[16]

Nor was the theater evolving independently from the other arts movements in the city. Martin Ponch recalled bringing in some of the more extroverted poets from the North Beach jazz clubs when the Interplayers needed actors to fill out their casts. And Adrian, printing up programs for the theater performances, came closer to Rexroth's poetry renaissance than he may have initially realized. Word of mouth brought him to a tool shed behind an old mansion on O'Farrell Street, where he shared a rickety Challenge Gordon press with a group of anarchists—the Libertarian Circle—slowly putting together their literary magazine, the *Ark*. The shed was dark and unheated, so they set their type in a tiny walk-up kitchen a few blocks away on Ellis Street. It was pure bohemia, Adrian said, "the new Lost Generation in the making"—complete with dope smoking, sexual depravity, and self-absorbed poetry all in one. But it was apparently tolerable enough to Adrian that he brought his clarinet along and would join in a jam session after the typesetting was done: "The major poet played trumpet and dreamed of a renaissance in New Orleans; a minor poet pounded a cardboard box; the neighbors pounded the ceiling, and eventually the police arrived to restore quiet." Adrian fled the scene with his typesetting form to the tool-shed printing room—except the Challenge had no motor, and he couldn't run it alone. So he was joined by Coffield, who pumped the roller carriage while Adrian fed the sheets. It was a dance, like two men operating a railroad hand-car, Adrian recalled, "one of the great unseen pantomimes of the theater."[17]

A chance meeting with the Grabhorn brothers, long respected as top-level fine printers, provided Adrian with access to their "trimmings" pile of discarded sheets and scraps of handmade and other fine papers, which Adrian used to create unique and innovative programs for the Interplayers shows, which in turn brought him attention and contracts from businesses for items such as restaurant menus, advertising cards, and annual reports. A semester of architecture school in 1947 at the university over in Berkeley brought him back in touch with Everson, still working his janitor job, and together they explored the library's rare book room and saw some of the most impressive works of printing ever done. Another chance meeting the following year—pure happenstance as Adrian was out at Golden Gate Park, sketching the Japanese Tea Garden gate for a class assignment—had him conversing with Jack Stauffacher of the Greenwood Press, another fine-printing establishment in town. Shortly thereafter, Adrian was working with Stauffacher, printing commissioned books and papers during the day and producing a small, unique volume by night. Earlier, when they'd been printing Interplayers programs in the tool shed of the *Ark* press, Adrian and Coffield had been employed briefly loading scrap metal into boxcars. At the time, Coffield proposed that the young printer someday publish a volume of his poems, and handed over the bulk of his paychecks as advance payment. The result came in 1949, with *The Night Is Where You Fly*, a thirty-four-page collection featuring two-color abstract prints by painter Lee Mullican. It was the first hardcover edition in Coffield's prodigious string of publications, and the sixth book in Adrian's growing list.[18]

In these few years, Adrian established himself as a solid presence in the world of San Francisco printing, and no doubt his work helped spread the word about the Interplayers. For theater is that most ephemeral of arts—the performance is given and then is gone—and the only lasting identity of the work comes from reviews, announcements and programs. It was here, through the combination of working for pay and working for love, that Adrian developed the expertise and ethos that would guide his life as a professional printer. When visiting a prominent book collector one afternoon with Stauffacher, Adrian was overcome by the beauty and craftsmanship in the great breadth of works he saw. "Every word we uttered, he had a book for it—exquisite book after book, plus lots of original engravings," Adrian wrote. There is a danger in focusing solely on the physical book, he admitted, but he also believed good writing could stand the test of artistic treatment. He would rather, he said, that people read fewer books in a deep and meaningful way, than more books in a rapid and shallow manner.[19]

This integration of printing across the creative arts resonated with other Waldport alumni. In 1947, Everson moved his hand press from Sebastopol to his own tool shed behind a house in Berkeley, where over the next two years he put together his collection of post-Waldport poems, *A Privacy of Speech,* printing just one hundred copies as the first edition of his Equinox Press. In 1948, Joyce and Adrian left their small apartment next to Martin Ponch in a quiet neighborhood of old Victorian homes on Haight Street and moved into a flat on Baker Street in the Castro district, living beneath Kermit and his partner, James Broughton, a poet and filmmaker who had been connected to Rexroth's circle. Kermit and Broughton set up their own printing press in the basement and issued limited-edition poetry books under the Centaur Press imprint, with Kermit handling the design and typesetting. Although they put out only a handful of books, this, too, connected them to the growing scene. Two books by Broughton featured drawings by Lee Mullican and Dan Harris (who thereafter took the single-word moniker Zev), tying them in with the visual artist community; a collection of poems by Madeline Gleason, long active in San Francisco poetry circles, connected them to the writing crowd; and a book by poet and social justice activist Muriel Rukeyser brought them attention from the more politically minded groups. Plans for the first American publication of Anaïs Nin's *House of Incest* were stopped only by an effusively apologetic letter from the author, explaining that two New York publishing houses had suddenly offered her some much-needed money for rights to her books, and asking to break her contract with Centaur.[20]

The Untide Press was still around, also. In Los Angeles, Eshelman and Kemper—with Tom Polk Miller assisting from Texas—put out the George Woodcock book, *Imagine the South,* with illustrations by Wilfred Lang, in 1947. The following year they released issue number 5 of the *Illiterati,* featuring a healthy sampling of the San Francisco writers, including Rexroth, Broughton, Christopher Rambo, and Sanders Russell. The editors maintained their antiwar stance, but since there was no immediate war on the horizon of public consciousness, they stressed their view that all life is interrelated and the sum of its parts equal to a cooperative whole. "Individual responsibility is the aspect of our ethic most in need of development," they said, "and we submit that one way to do this is by the extension of art into all fields of activity."[21]

The *Ark:* Anarchy at work in 1947.

The *Ark* came out in spring 1947, declaring itself in "direct opposition to the debasement of human values made flauntingly evident by the war." Like any revolutionary-minded group, their aim was to change society, but they knew any real change must grow from individuals coming together. And the place for that to begin was in contemporary literature.[22]

The cast of contributors was a roll call of the San Francisco scene, along with some East Coast and international names. Joining Rexroth, Duncan, Everson, and Lamantia were Kenneth Patchen, George Woodcock, William Carlos Williams, and e. e. cummings. The journal did bring together somewhat those various forces in the Bay Area working for change, and represented the new approaches taking place in American writing and art. But conflicts between the editors resulted in a less-than-energetic release, and the *Ark* drew attention largely only within its bohemian circles.[23]

Other magazines came out: *Contour Quarterly* and *Berkeley Miscellany,* both short lived. Madeline Gleason, who'd come to the city in 1935 and worked with Rexroth on the WPA book, *American Stuff,* organized readings in art galleries, founded the San Francisco Poetry Guild, and in 1947 launched the Festival of Modern Poetry, a series of readings at a local art gallery that brought together the core quartet of Everson, Duncan, Rexroth, and Lamantia, along with a dozen others, including Josephine Miles, Sanders Russell, Thomas Parkinson, and Yvor Winters (who had made a name for himself as an individually minded critic and professor at Stanford University). A selection of their poems, edited and introduced by Muriel Rukeyser, appeared in the *Pacific Spectator,* with a generic reference to the recent *Harper's* article as "some nonsense . . . written recently about writing and painting in California." But people dedicated to their writing and painting were precisely what was needed in these confusing and complicated times, Rukeyser said. "Here are ten poets who speak from this latitude."[24]

The tensions between creative personalities are almost universal, often inevitable, and the consequences at best merely delayed. By 1949, Rexroth's Libertarian Circle was breaking up and its spiritual leader was off to Europe, courtesy of a grant from the Guggenheim Foundation. Almost incredibly, Everson the same year secured his own Guggenheim (for $2,400, the amount of his yearly janitor's salary), which would allow him a twelve-month period to write. His peregrinations and spiritual searching, though, took him to Catholicism, and in 1951 he joined the Dominican Order as a lay brother, taking the name Brother Antoninus and living as a priest while not ordained as one. Robert Duncan had gone back East to visit the aging Ezra Pound and follow his own star in Europe. *Circle* put out its tenth and final issue in 1948, with Leite in a single-page editorial slamming everyone from *Partisan Review* and *Now* to the *Harper's* article on the "Cult of Sex and Anarchy." Such a cult, he said, never existed: Henry Miller was married and raising a daughter on a steep mountain in Big Sur; Rexroth was a Guggenheim fellow with no connection to *Circle;* and he, Leite, was doing research in criminal psychopathology and was married with two children.[25]

The revolution would have to wait. "It took Korea and the second Eisenhower administration to make the country ready," Everson recalled later. "It took the man in the gray flannel suit as the national image and the crew cut as the prevailing college mode. The tranquilized fifties."[26]

■ ■ ■

When war broke out on the Korean peninsula in June 1950, the draft was still in effect, and U.S. forces were fighting as part of the United Nations. In the American public mind, communism had replaced fascism as the dark force of evil; Stalin had replaced Hitler as its face. Senator Joseph McCarthy of Wisconsin had the same year launched his campaign against the "Reds" he claimed were infiltrating the government, and suspicion was high. Conscientious objection was still recognized by the Selective Service, but CPS had closed down in 1947. While the program had been an important step in the acceptance of conscience as a viable element of society, as well as having been a milestone in public-private cooperation, CPS had also been an expensive effort for the churches and an unwieldy experience for the government. Few were interested in bringing it back. As with the run-up to World War II, intensive congressional lobbying, compromise, and deal making were the order of the day. The result was a change in the "work of national importance" language to "such civilian work contributing to the maintenance of the national health, safety and interest as the local board may deem appropriate," and the creation of the I-W (pronounced *one-w*) designation, in which COs would perform civilian work—this time for pay.[27] There were no camps, only the Brethren and Mennonites participated, and some 80 percent of the 10,000 men classified I-W between 1952 and 1955 served in hospitals, mostly mental institutions. As before, the significant majority of COs were devoutly religious farm boys with little experience outside their rural communities. For many, it was life changing. As one religious young man put it: "Working in a mental hospital has been a new experience to all of us and it has opened our eyes to the needs of the mentally ill and to the sinful and lost condition of the world."[28]

There was indeed a sense that something was being lost. Americans had been through the Depression, had fought a horrific global war, then picked up their lives and dutifully bent their backs, working to provide for their children a better life than the one they'd known. Yet here they were at war again, building machines to destroy machines that build machines that destroy. Here they were, with their young men and women dying again. And for what? It was almost too terrible to comprehend, too fearful to question. They turned to the World War II hero, Dwight D. Eisenhower, and elected him president. Under the benevolent leadership of "Ike," America moved into the shank of the 1950s, a period of mass conformity and standardization. "Life in the USA is ready-made," wrote social scientists Scott and Helen Nearing after three years of traveling and studying the country. "From the houses and cars that people buy, to the clothes they wear, to the foods they eat and the products they drink, the Americans have their wants canned, built up and satisfied according to plans of business organizations." But uneasiness accompanied the conformity, they said. "We found ourselves among a people obsessed by anxieties and fears, gripped by tensions, baffled by confusions and contradictions, plagued by uncertainty, and by a pervasive sense of insecurity."[29]

Even the reassuring Ike fed the fears. "We sense with all our faculties that forces of good and evil are massed and armed and opposed as rarely before in history," he said in his 1953 inaugural address. "Freedom is pitted against slavery; lightness against the dark."[30]

The "good" was, of course, America. The "evil" could be found in Korea, the Soviet Union, China, Eastern Europe, and a narrow region in Southeast Asia referred to as Indo-China but also known as Vietnam. But even here at home the differences between light and dark were not always clear. Even here, there was communism, the atom bomb, segregation, pollution, the ironies of obscene wealth and brutal poverty. This land of plenty, it seemed, came with a sword of Damocles. Something had to change.

By the mid-1950s, the Korean War had reached a kind of stalemated peace, Joe McCarthy had come and gone, and there was talk of sending rockets into space. Railroad passenger service was giving way to airlines and the automobile, television sets were replacing radio consoles as the centerpiece of American living rooms, and the young baby boomers were listening to a new loud and fast electric music called rock and roll. *The Man in the Gray Flannel Suit,* a novel by war veteran Sloan Wilson, became a bestseller and then a hit movie starring Gregory Peck. A small paperback called *New World Writing* came out with its seventh annual edition in 1955. It included a chapter from a work-in-progress, a satire on World War II titled *Catch-18,* by a young New York copywriter named Joseph Heller; also appearing was something called "Jazz of the Beat Generation," from an unpublished stream-of-consciousness novel by a young writer working under the pseudonym Jean-Louis, whose friends knew him as Jack Kerouac.

Rexroth was back in San Francisco, again hosting his Friday night discussions, writing newspaper and magazine columns, and presenting a weekly book review and poetry program on a new kind of radio station based in Berkeley: listener-supported KPFA, founded by Lewis Hill, the former CPS assignee who had been published in the *Illiterati.* Jim Harman was in town, working on a successor to the *Ark,* this one to be called *Ark II–Moby I,* joined by Lamantia and Michael McClure, a poet who'd come from the young yet already influential Black Mountain College back in North Carolina. Bill Everson, as Brother Antoninus, the monk-in-training, managed to continue writing and printing to some extent, occasionally giving readings in his intense, pensive, deep-voiced style. Adrian was making a name for himself as a printer, gaining attention from the Book Club of California and the Limited Editions Club, which subsidized fine-press publications of usually classic works, sold on subscription to their members. He continued working with the Interplayers, as did Joyce, Martin Ponch, and others. Kermit and James Broughton returned from Europe, where they'd been making films and had received a special award at the 1954 Cannes Film Festival, and now plugged back into the scene. Bob Harvey and Manche, now married, had come West with their two young children in the early 1950s, living in a tent down at Big Sur, where Harvey befriended Henry Miller, engaging in long discussions about writing and art. "If ever I spotted a born writer, this fellow Harvey was certainly it," Miller wrote in his memoir of life in Big Sur. Harvey talked as if reading from a book, Miller said. "Everything he related had form, structure, clarity and meaning." But Harvey seemed unable to reconcile his gifts as a painter, musician, and writer, Miller said.[31] He eventually left the artist community, haunted by his unrealized talent and increasing alcoholism. Manche also eventually split with Harvey and moved up to Marin County, heading into the city on occasion to work with Kermit and Joyce as part of the Interplayers and later the Playhouse Theatre after the original group split over creative differences.[32]

Things were also happening beyond San Francisco. Up in Washington State, Clayton and Barbara James had settled at the edge of the Skagit Valley, a stretch of coastline north of Seattle where mountains, fields, rivers, and ocean all come together under the notoriously overcast Northwest skies—and occasionally the sun cuts through the clouds and mist to create an intensely refracted light that attracts a particular type of artistic eye. There, in the Puget Sound territory, they established themselves among artists such as Morris Graves, Mark Tobey, Kenneth Callahan, and Guy Anderson—all of whom were featured in a 1953 *Life* magazine presentation titled "Mystic Painters of the Northwest."

In the Oregon Cascades foothills east of Portland, Glen Coffield once again struck out on his own. Like Thoreau at Walden Pond, Coffield literally went to the woods—for seven years. There, from 1947 to 1954, he lived the most basic existence, providing his food, shelter, and recreation with his own hands and ingenuity, growing beans and root vegetables and gathering berries from the woods; during harvest season he worked in the local farmers' fields to earn what little money he needed. He explored the woods and waters and skies; he studied agriculture,

William Stafford (L) and his family visit Glen Coffield (R) at his Grundtvig Folk School, ca. 1950.

architecture, literature, philosophy, psychology, soil and water conservation—and tried his hand at them all. He churned out literally hundreds of poems, booklets, journals, educational plans, and tracts on subsistence living. Among his projects was the Grundtvig Folk School, modeled after the rural educational programs developed by the nineteenth-century Danish educator and poet, Nikolai Grundtvig. Coffield offered two-week summer sessions combining outdoor skills and intellectual discussions, inviting—and often getting—guest speakers accomplished in their fields. Weekends brought visitors from the city, come for a taste of the mountain life that featured berry picking, trout fishing, communal cooking, and campfire songs. This balance of manual labor, creative work, and intellectual exercise in a primitive environment was a tonic for many, while a simple matter of self-sufficiency for Coffield. "If I did not ultimately solve all of the problems of the universe, including that of what is man," he wrote in retrospect, "I at least discovered some of the advantages of being a man in the universe."[33]

Back in San Francisco, the North Beach neighborhood around Telegraph Hill was becoming a counterculture center, with coffeehouses and jazz clubs like the Black Cat, the Cellar, Cafe Trieste, and Vesuvio attracting all manner of artists, musicians, and writers carving an alternative path to the homogeneity that had assumed its dominant role in American society. In 1953, across tiny Adler Alley from Vesuvio, at the edge of Chinatown and where Columbus Avenue slopes down toward the financial district, Sorbonne graduate and poet Lawrence Ferlinghetti with his friend Peter Martin opened a corner store that exclusively sold paperback books; they called it the Pocket Bookshop, later changing the name to City Lights Bookstore.

Ferlinghetti joined the Rexroth gatherings, becoming acquainted with the poets in the area—among them Kenneth Patchen, who had moved out West. Ferlinghetti wanted to publish his own books, and when Patchen gave him a copy of *Astonished Eye*, he was so taken by the cover design that he copied it exactly, down to the separate-color rectangular wrapper that covered the staples on the spine. Using this model, he launched the Pocket Poets Series, beginning with his own *Pictures of the Gone World* in 1955, followed the next year by a Rexroth translation titled *Thirty Spanish Poems of Love and Exile*, and Patchen's *Poems of Humor and Protest*. The books featured different color combinations but always the same block-on-block design.[34]

The scene around City Lights and Vesuvio started heating up as writers and artists arrived from around the country—particularly a group from New York calling themselves the Beat Generation, a term coined by Jack Kerouac, whose *On the Road* manuscript was confounding editors at the publishing houses back East and earning a reputation as the best unpublished novel in America. And a couple blocks over on Montgomery Street just off Broadway, a young New Jersey poet named Allen Ginsberg rented a third-floor apartment and began writing a long free-verse poem about his contemporaries on the margins of American society.

Also in 1955, the sixth number of the *Illiterati* appeared, produced again from Los Angeles by Bill Eshelman, Kemper Nomland, and Tom Polk Miller. The editors reiterated that the timing of publication was purely a matter of circumstance; each issue would come out only after they had gathered enough material and carved out the time to print it. Nor did there seem to be any conscious attempt to match content with emerging artistic or societal trends. No specific group of poets was presented, no particular type of commentary. But there was one poem, by Bill Stafford, who was now teaching at Lewis and Clark College in Portland and signing his work as William Stafford. He titled it "Report from an Unappointed Committee," and from the perspective of more than half a century later, it reads as a legitimate heir to William Butler Yeats's "The Second Coming," a meditation on revolution:

> The uncounted are counting
> and the unseen are looking around.
> In a room of northernmost light
> a sculptor is making some ugly beauty.
> In some university a strict experiment
> has indicated a need for more
> strict experiments.
> A wild confusion of order claws thru
> the system of our most reliable wires.
> Flowers have begun to lean
> toward all the torn places.
> In the farthest province a comet
> has flamed in the gaze of
> an unofficial watcher.
> In the back country a random raindrop
> has broken a dam.
> And a new river is out feeling for a valley
> somewhere under our world.

In October, the first wave broke. At the now-infamous Six Gallery reading on Fillmore Street, Ginsberg unleashed his long poem, "Howl," and he, along with Kerouac and the other Beats, commenced to make their mark on the San Francisco scene. Ferlinghetti was at the reading; he went home that night and typed out a telegram to Ginsberg, asking for the manuscript. It became Number Four in the Pocket Poets Series, the biggest seller of them all, with the white-against-black cover identical to

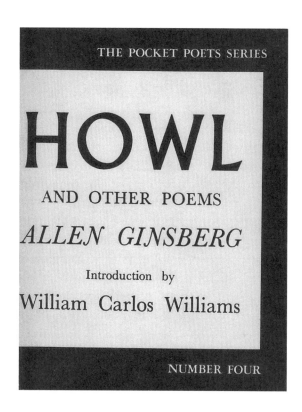

THE POCKET POETS SERIES

HOWL

AND OTHER POEMS

ALLEN GINSBERG

Introduction by

William Carlos Williams

NUMBER FOUR

Patchen's *Astonished Eye*—and announced to the world that a new river
had indeed broken free, a new generation harking to the call of Walt
Whitman's lines, from the epigram on the title page of *Howl and Other
Poems:* "Unscrew the locks from the doors! Unscrew the doors themselves from their jambs!"

Rexroth had his renaissance. He was the emcee at the Six Gallery;
he saw the audience reaction. He knew the time had come. City Lights
published *Howl* in 1956, it was declared obscene for its sexual references, and Ferlinghetti was taken to court—drawing further attention
to these strange "angelheaded hipsters," as Ginsberg called them, and
their quirky San Francisco lives.[35] The watershed year was 1957. Rexroth
published a spate of articles in which he made the same points he had ten
years earlier, but this time for a national audience, with pieces written for
the *Nation* and the new quarterly journal, *Evergreen Review,* published
by Grove Press of New York. He reiterated the CO connection, singled
out Everson, Duncan, and Lamantia, and declared that Ginsberg had
been a conventional academic poet until he'd come to San Francisco and
met people who were knowledgeable in the new music, writing, and art—
people who were so cool they didn't even bother to smoke marijuana. It
allowed Ginsberg to cut loose, Rexroth said. He then added this warning

to those who might view the poem as inconsequential: "*Howl* is the confession of faith of the generation that is going to be running the world in 1965 and 1975—if it's still there to run."[36]

There was indeed a generation coming up that would turn the country on its head. They would do it, however, not in government and business but on college campuses and in the streets, out on the highways with backpacks and their thumbs. They would do it in music and mass protest, political activism and huge festival gatherings. They would do it with sheer numbers, driven by a few fundamental ideas, so basic and simple they could not be cut down: Freedom. Love. Equality. Peace.

Rexroth knew this; he sensed it. He knew that the place where it all begins is in art. He knew that more often than not, revolutions are born far from the centers of power, far from the arbiters of taste and popularity—which in this case was New York. He knew that this time, the place to be was San Francisco. "Anyway," he wrote in the spring of 1957, "as an old war horse of the word, things have never looked better from where I sit. The avant garde has not only not ceased to exist. It's jumping all over the place. Something's happening, man."[37]

That September, Kerouac's *On the Road* was published. The *New York Times* called it "an historic occasion," comparing the book to Ernest Hemingway's *The Sun Also Rises* as the voice of a generation.[38] Over the next few years, *Howl* went into multiple printings, and a record album was made of Ginsberg reading it. City Lights became a destination, and North Beach a hotspot for tourists who were driven through the neighborhood in buses to watch the "beatniks" in action. Over in the Haight district, small groups of alternative-minded "flower children" began to question society's expectations about how people should behave and what they might do with their lives. Back in New York, the young copywriter, Joseph Heller, published his absurdist World War II novel under the revised title, *Catch-22*. As the baby boomers entered their teen years and tuned their AM radio dials to their favorite stations, rock and roll became the undisputed voice of rebellion against conformity and the past. In Minnesota, a young musician named Robert Zimmerman took his guitar and unique songwriting abilities to New York City and transformed the Greenwich Village folk music scene as Bob Dylan. Down in Alabama, a charismatic African-American preacher named Martin Luther King Jr. was drawing attention to the injustices and horrors of racial segregation with his "Letter from a Birmingham Jail" and nonviolent protest actions. Journalist and author Betty Friedan published *The Feminine Mystique*, a groundbreaking work that questioned the role of women as merely housewives and mothers, while a young freelance writer named Gloria Steinem went undercover to record the unvarnished realities of life as a

Allen Ginsberg dancing to the Grateful Dead at the Human Be-In, San Francisco, 1967. © Lisa Law.

Playboy Bunny. And in the hills outside Palo Alto, some twenty-five miles south of San Francisco, a young college wrestler from Oregon named Ken Kesey, who had also studied creative writing at Stanford University and volunteered as a guinea pig in government experiments with halluci-nogenic drugs, began to envision the possibilities of this new thing called LSD while working on a novel about rebellion against power in an insane asylum, which he called *One Flew over the Cuckoo's Nest*.

The revolution was on.

Let Us at Least Salute It

LOOKING BACK FROM THE PERSPECTIVE of seventy years, it may seem that the story of Camp #56 and the Fine Arts at Waldport can never be told completely. The story of the Beat Generation and its effects on society has taken its rightful place in our nation's cultural history, and the record of how the baby boomer generation changed the shape and scope of America has been examined and evaluated enough to satisfy even the most obsessive interest. Very little attention has been given, however, to the role conscientious objectors played in preparing the ground for these changes to occur. When the group at Waldport chose art over war, chose creation over destruction, they set in motion a chain of events that no one could have predicted. When they brought their energy and experience to San Francisco, their main intention was simply to carry on the work they had begun, to forge some direction for the path they had chosen. Whether it was fate or circumstance or something else that brought together Rexroth, Miller, Patchen, the Fine Arts COs and the East Coast Beats is impossible to say. But it does seem possible that the individuals would not have flourished as they did without the context of the larger group. San Francisco had been mixing the ingredients of social change for some years before the Beats arrived; Kerouac and Ginsberg and their friends had been searching for a place where their catalytic energy could take hold. It was that conjunction of opposites, of the East and West Coasts, that sparked the change, Everson said. "They came to San Francisco and found themselves, and it was *their* finding that sparked *us*."[1]

One could conceivably make the case that without this spark the 1960s scene in San Francisco would have been very different: that the great gatherings in the Haight-Ashbury district wouldn't have happened without Ken Kesey's "acid tests" in which participants drank Kool-Aid laced with LSD while psychedelic images were projected onto a giant screen and music was played by a band calling themselves the Grateful Dead. And one could say that Kesey might never have left his home in Oregon for San Francisco if he hadn't read *On the Road,* and that Kerouac's novel wouldn't have had the reception it did if Ginsberg's *Howl* hadn't already drawn attention, and that Ginsberg wouldn't have written his poem without the liberating experience of Rexroth's San Francisco renaissance, and that Rexroth's dream would have gone nowhere without the influx of COs from the West Coast camps after the war, and that their pacifist ideals wouldn't have achieved full articulation without the cohesion and purpose of the Fine Arts at Waldport. But this is only speculation—and can never be anything more.

What we do know is that these things did happen. And it wasn't only in San Francisco. Across the country—and other parts of the world—throughout the 1960s and beyond, as ideas of peace and nonviolence were manifested in action, the individual choices made by Waldport COs in those dark days of World War II were being repeated by others on a larger scale. John Lennon, the iconic leader of the Beatles, in 1969 spent a week in a Montreal hotel room, playing music and telling young people through the news cameras to do something nonviolent in protest, such as staying in bed or growing their hair for peace—as Glen Coffield had done in 1943. The civil rights and feminist movements of the 1960s and 1970s were already reality at Camp Angel in the 1940s—where blacks and whites sat together at meals, and generic references to human beings in writing were not always made with the "he" or "men" commonly used at the time, but also the more inclusive "he or she" and "men and women." The first national wave of environmental awareness, called "ecology" in the 1970s, aimed to point out that humans too often ignore the continuum of life, death, and regeneration on the planet—as Larry Siemons did in his short rumination for the *Untide* about the so-called "dead stump" in the forest. Restaurants and other public places in the 1970s began providing space for their patrons free of cigarette smoke—as the Waldport group had done in their dining hall thirty years earlier. A look through copies of the *Compass,* the *Illiterati,* and the Untide Press books is like walking through a young garden full of the seedlings of social change. Nearly all of the great issues of the 1960s and 1970s are there: education, conservation, environmentalism, equality, religion, conscription, incarceration, nutrition, mental health, social health, communal living, art in society—and, of course, peace.

The Waldport COs were hardly the only ones in America addressing these things, and they weren't necessarily the first, even if they did come up with some of the ideas on their own. But there was a concentration of energy, a convergence of thought and action, a creative intensity at Waldport that was rare and perhaps unique.

When Everson wrote in the *Untide* back in 1943—there on the edge of the continent, on the edge of society, on what must have seemed like the very edge of existence itself—that they could only watch and wait and bide their time, he was but partially correct. They were not merely biding time. They were conceiving ideas, creating shapes and forms for them to fill, and building an environment where this could occur. For that is how revolutions are born—when those who uphold the ideals go underground yet refuse to give up, when they care for and nurture and find a way to pass on those simple things in which they believe: Freedom, Love, Equality, Peace.

Along with the social and cultural legacy, there are more concrete examples. The million-plus trees that the COs planted on the blasted landscape in 1943–44 have become a forest, and if you're willing to drive a bit off the beaten path, you can see them today. Heading inland past the camp on Blodgett Road (the old Quarry Drive), you travel up a small rise and then along a chilly creek choked with ferns and birches and vine maple, the north sides of the trunks covered in moss. Then you head up again, up a washboard road and past a brown and white Forest Service sign that says Residence Ahead 500 Ft. No Shooting—with the corner blown away by a shotgun blast. Then you pass the residence and enter the woods, go through a couple miles of trees, up and around a hairpin curve, and there it is: an old "dead stump" just like in the *Untide* story—about six feet high from where the loggers cut it off, now with ridges and cracks and crevices and ferns and lichens and mosses and new young trees growing right up out of it. And if you look carefully, you can see more "dead stumps"—all of them slowly, inexorably, feeding and giving way to the next generation of growth, a silent reminder that in nature nothing is wasted. Then you go up and around another hairpin or two, bumping along the road, the old gravel showing through, gravel that maybe was crushed on that conveyor-belt contraption at the quarry beyond the camp. Finally, enough hairpins take you to what might be the top of the ridge, and when you stop and cut your engine, it's quiet and dark under the trees some sixty or seventy feet tall. You can hear a far-off rush—maybe the ocean, maybe a jet plane high overhead, maybe a light breeze, or maybe the sound of time passing. It's a quiet sound, a patient sound, the sound of a forest that grew and was cut down to fight a war and then was planted again by men who refused to fight the next war. And here the trees are, still around after nearly everyone who knew that particular war is gone.

Perhaps the most telling legacy is back at the camp itself. Camp Angell exists today as one of twenty-eight Job Corps Civilian Conservation Centers across the United States. Run by the Forest Service and Department of Labor, the residential camps serve young people from largely low-income and other challenging backgrounds, teaching them career, technical, academic, and related skills, very much in the vein of a domestic Peace Corps or the original Civilian Conservation Corps.

At today's Angell Job Corps Center, some two hundred young men and women live in dormitories on the bluff overlooking the old camp. The original space below still has a kind of quadrangle with a ballfield in the center, and in the buildings arranged around it, the students take courses and develop skills in culinary arts, masonry, carpentry, painting, plumbing, urban forestry, and welding. They work and live and study at the camp and through its satellite projects; they practice technical trades and prepare for professions. They learn personal responsibility and how to live in cooperative social structures; they function as individuals and as members of a group. They benefit from certain gifts of society, and they give back. Just like the COs in the 1940s, the campers today work on hiking trails and parks around the state. They may be trained for disaster relief and firefighting work. They volunteer for beach and highway cleanups, do work with Habitat for Humanity and the Red Cross. They choose to better themselves and their condition, and, knowingly or not, thereby better the state of society.

The personal is always the political when we recognize that we can affect as much as be affected by our environment. When Everson wrote that the men in CPS must wait until the principles they believed in could become "tangent again to the world," he could certainly be excused for feeling isolated. But in quiet, fundamental ways, the spirit of individual liberty through peaceful action had always been there and always would be. Every time a young person enrolls in the Angell Job Corps, every time they choose to turn away from the conditions that made their world and move toward creating a better life, a better environment for opportunity, a better chance for dignity, decency, and respect; every time they choose potential over resignation, possibility over surrender, creation over destruction, the values and principles for which the men and women of Camp #56 made their sacrifices and contributions—for which all those in CPS made their stand—remain always tangent to the world.

No, the story of Camp #56 and the Fine Arts can never be completely told. There are too many subplots and variations, too many strands in the pattern contributing to the whole. We must content ourselves with witnessing moments, listening to the words and seeing through the eyes of those who were there as they attempted to sort through the experience and make sense of the things that had happened because of the one thing they had refused to do.

"Tonight I sit in the pressroom, or what will someday be a pressroom, alone, the rain on the roof, the litter about me of all the Untide books and equipment," Everson wrote on a dark night in January 1946 after they'd just hauled the operation through the muck and gloom from the coast to Cascade Locks, "and I nurse inside me a song for Waldport, a dirge, a lamentation, for would I were there . . . on the beach, where the breakers are grinding their immemorial wheels upon the sand."[2]

It is when you leave the special places that you realize how special they are, he said. Other CPS camps were no doubt important, each with their own contribution. Others had art and music, some had theater and writing, creative activity, but it was more in the manner of hobby or diversion. Others were liberal. But Waldport, he said—Waldport was radical.

> There were men there. And they saw to the heart of the pure creative substance, the rock, and they began cutting to it, and they hewed off layer after layer of incidentals, and they got to the heart of it, stripped it down, made it shine. They made it shine in painting, in music, in drama, and in writing, and nothing else really mattered. . . . We called it the Fine Arts at Waldport. And it is dead. And the great years of my life lie there with it. And I'm proud. Proud of my part in it. Proud to be of those clean men. And to have done what I did, and built, not be satisfied with sitting on my ass.

Time can't be stopped or reversed, Everson said, no matter how one might yearn to have done something better or more complete. The only honest way to move forward is not to forget the past but to accept it— with all its challenges, triumphs, disappointments, and richness. "You can't go back," he concluded. "You create out of the inexplicable substance of experience, as it's loaded into your lap by the guy who operates the celestial garbage wagon. There are poems to be written. Books to be printed. And there's no weeping over the past, but let us at least salute it. *Waldport!*"

"Daddy, what did *you* do to help keep the peace?"

Lives after the Fine Arts

Glen Coffield ran his Grundtvig Folk School from 1947 to 1954 and later did graduate work at the University of Oregon, continuing to write and print his books of poetry, criticism, and commentary. Seriously injured by a hit-and-run driver while living in San Francisco in the mid-1960s, he was partially crippled and bothered by health problems for the rest of his life. He returned to Missouri in the early 1970s to care for his mother until her death; he died there in 1981 at age 64.

Warren Downs continued his music studies and graduated from the Oberlin Conservatory in Ohio. He played with the Denver, St. Louis, and Cleveland symphonies. In the early 1970s, he earned a master's degree in journalism and became a writer for the University of Wisconsin's Sea Grant program; he also was principal cellist for the Madison Symphony. He lives in Madison, occasionally teaching and playing chamber music.

Vladimir Dupre earned his Ph.D. at the University of Chicago, using his experience as a cook at Waldport when he and Ibby worked as housekeepers for linguistics professor S. I. Hayakawa and his family. Vlad became a psychology professor at Grinnell College and the University of Kansas, served as president of the National Training Laboratories in Washington, DC, and ran a private psychotherapy practice. He divides his time between the East and West coasts.

Ibby Dupre raised six children with her husband, earned a master's degree in social work, and worked as a nursery school teacher and addiction counselor. She died in 2007 at age 85.

Broadus Erle founded the New Music Quartet in 1948, a pioneering group that performed contemporary music. He joined the Japan Philharmonic Orchestra in Tokyo and later became professor of violin at Yale University. His marriage to **Hildegarde** did not last, and he twice married former students. He died in 1977 at age 59.

William Eshelman studied with Lawrence Clark Powell in Los Angeles and embarked on a long career as a university librarian and activist for peace, intellectual freedom, and desegregation. He was editor of the *Wilson Library Bulletin* and president of the Scarecrow Press. He retired to Oregon and died there in 2004 at age 82.

William Everson, whom *Time* magazine dubbed the "Beat Friar" in 1959 for his connection to the San Francisco scene, lived as Brother Antoninus for eighteen years then resigned from the church in 1969 to marry a woman thirty-five years his junior. He published many books and joined the faculty at the University of California, Santa Cruz, where he founded the Lime Kiln Press and lived north of the town in a rustic cabin he called Kingfisher Flat. He suffered from Parkinson's disease and died in 1994 at age 81.

Joe Gistirak (no photo available) was a cofounder of the Interplayers and presumably continued in theater and film. A "Joseph Gistirak" is listed as directing plays in the 1950s. Vlad Dupre recalls that he came to the National Training Laboratories in the 1970s and applied for a job, but it didn't work out. The 1996 CPS *Directory* lists Gistirak as dead but gives no date.

Harold Hackett became a teacher in the Congregational Church; one source indicates that he spent time teaching in Japan. He died in 1980 at age 59.

James Harman spent time as a salmon fisherman in Alaska, then was based in San Francisco, where he co-edited *Ark II/Moby I* with Michael McClure in 1956–57 and was sole editor of *Ark III* in 1957. His book of poems, *In Praise of Eponymous Iahu,* was published by Bern Porter in 1956. The 1996 CPS *Directory* lists him as dead but gives no date.

David Jackson was involved with the Interplayers and according to one source later became head proofreader at the *New Yorker* magazine. The 1947 edition of the CPS *Directory* lists him as a teacher. The 1996 edition states that he died in 1988.

Clayton James and **Barbara Straker James** (no photo available) settled in the Skagit valley north of Seattle, where they became integral members of the artists' community. Barbara was active in the local arts scene and was the first curator of the Northwest Museum of Modern Art. She suffered from Parkinson's disease and died in 2007. Clayton earned worldwide fame as a sculptor but found the publicity associated with gallery exhibits too restricting to his art, and he became more reclusive with the years. He still lives in the house he and Barbara bought in 1953 from the painter Richard Gilkey.

Manche Langley married **Bob Harvey** (no photo available) and settled in the San Francisco area. They had two daughters but separated a few years later, and Manche raised the children alone. She was involved with the Interplayers and the Playhouse Theatre, and engaged in peace and civil rights activities throughout the 1960s, also acting in James Broughton's 1968 film, *The Bed*. She died in 2010. Bob Harvey never escaped his alcoholism, dying in the San Francisco Tenderloin district, leaving behind a roomful of paintings.

Tom Polk Miller and **Isabel Mount** married in 1947 and founded Mount-Miller Architects in Denton, Texas. They designed residential and commercial buildings and were active in many civic organizations, jointly receiving the Community Arts Recognition Award in 1982. Tom died in 2000 at age 85; Isabel in 2007 at age 90.

Richard C. Mills was discharged from CPS in late 1945 and went to work as an advocate and educator for the American Friends Service Committee in Southern California. The 1996 edition of the CPS *Directory* lists his profession as a YMCA secretary. He died in 1964 at age 56.

Kemper Nomland, Jr. returned to Los Angeles and joined his father in the architecture firm Nomland and Nomland. In 1947, they designed a case study house in Pasadena as part of an experimental program to address postwar housing shortages. Kemper also designed a house for the actress Jane Russell. He died in 2009 at age 90.

Martin Ponch co-founded the Interplayers and later taught theater at San Francisco State College, also playing small parts in movies and television. He died in 2004 at age 93.

Bruce Reeves became an elementary school teacher in Washington State, and has been active in the Democratic Party, serving on various governors' committees and later as president of the Senior Citizens' Lobby, retiring from that position in his nineties. He lives in Olympia, Washington, where he and his wife, Margie, raised four children.

Jerry Rubin and Jan Rubin (no photos available) settled in the San Francisco area and continued not only their labor-related activities but also their weaving. Jan died in 1973, and Jerry died in 2001.

Kermit Sheets co-founded the Interplayers and Centaur Press, then went to Europe and worked with James Broughton on experimental movies, starring in *Looney Tom, the Happy Lover.* Returning to San Francisco, he managed the Playhouse Theatre and later became director of the Lighthouse for the Blind, an organization helping visually impaired people. He died in 2006 at age 90.

Larry Siemons is listed in the 1947 edition of the CPS *Directory* as a painter. The 1996 edition lists his whereabouts as unknown.

Adrian Wilson founded the Press in Tuscany Alley in San Francisco, where he continued printing fine books and ephemera for university presses, museums, and the Limited Editions Club. His work in the fields of printing and typography brought him international acclaim; among his many recognitions was a 1983 MacArthur "Genius Grant." His *The Design of Books* is considered a classic of the discipline. He suffered from heart problems and died in 1988 at age 64.

Joyce Lancaster Wilson collaborated with her husband on a number of projects, including *The Making of the Nuremberg Chronicle* and *A Medieval Mirror,* as well as writing and designing children's books and heading a nursery school for twenty years. She died in 1996 at age 81.

Fine Arts Group Members and Associates

ADMINISTRATION

William Everson, Director (1944–1946)
Vladimir Dupre, Executive Secretary (1944–1945)
Tom Polk Miller, Executive Secretary (1945–1946)
Manche Langley, Secretary (1945)

WRITING AND PRINTING

Glen Coffield*
Charles Davis
Vladimir Dupre
William Eshelman
William Everson
Harold Hackett
Manche Langley
Kemper Nomland
Martin Ponch
Kermit Sheets
Adrian Wilson
*Left before Fine Arts officially began.

MUSIC

Warren Downs (cello)
Broadus Erle (violin)
Hildegarde Erle (piano)
Bob Harvey (violin)
Victor McLane (piano)
Tom Polk Miller (piano)
Bob Scott (piano)
Adrian Wilson (clarinet)

THEATER

Enoch Crumpton
Wesley DeCoursey
Ibby Dupre
Vladimir Dupre
Hildegarde Erle
William Eshelman
James Harman
Joyce Harvey
Joe Gistirak
David Jackson
Gertrude Jadiker
William Jadiker
Ray Johnson
Manche Langley
Tom Polk Miller
Isabel Mount
Martin Ponch
Kermit Sheets
Adrian Wilson

VISUAL ARTS

Clayton James (painting, block printing)
Barbara Straker James (painting, illustration)
Bob Harvey (painting)
Kemper Nomland (painting, illustration)
Bruce Reeves (photography)
Larry Siemons (silk-screening)

CRAFTS

Glenn Evans
Barbara Straker James
Bruce Reeves
Jerry Rubin
Jan Rubin

VISITING ARTISTS

Waldo Chase (early 1944)
Morris Graves (Aug.–Sept. 1944)

Creative Works at Waldport

Adapted from "Bibliography of the Untide Press" by William Eshelman (*Imprint: Oregon*, Fall-Spring 1978–79) and examination of copies. Sale prices of books at publication are listed if known.

Ten War Elegies
Alternative title: *X War Elegies*. Poetry by William Everson. Designed and illustrated by Kemper Nomland, Jr. 20 pages, 6 x 9 inches, stapled with covers glued to the spine. First printing in April 1943, 100 typewritten copies mimeographed with silk-screened titling on blue construction paper cover. Five more printings ran through December 1943, for a total of approximately 1,000 copies, all done at Waldport. No distinction made between printings, although mimeograph stencils of each page were replaced as they wore out, leading to variations of quality. During the fifth printing, the yellow paint used on the cover ran out and was replaced temporarily by red. The paper used was highly acidic, and surviving copies are usually chipped, cracked, and very fragile. 10 cents.

Ultimatum (from the Unforgettable)
Poetry by Glen Coffield. Designed and illustrated by the author. 12 pages, 8½ x 5¾ inches, folded sheets loose inside cover. Released in July 1943 from Waldport, 50 typewritten copies mimeographed with line-drawing graphic of an eye on green construction paper cover. Highly acidic paper, with the attendant problems of chipping and cracking. Distributed by author; unknown if sold or as gifts.

The Horned Moon
Poetry by Glen Coffield. Designed by Charles Davis and William Everson in consultation with the author. Cover illustration by Charles Davis. 32 pages, 6 1/8 x 7½ inches, single signature pamphlet,

hand-sewn, with folded wrapper cover. Issued in February 1944, 520 copies (colophon states 600) on India Mountie Eggshell Book paper. Text pages done on 5 x 8 Kelsey Excelsior hand-operated press; wrapper printed on 14½ x 22 Challenge Gordon press at Waldport. Unknown number of copies sent out as gifts to subscribers of the *Illiterati* with mimeographed announcement laid in. 25 cents.

The Waldport Poems

Poetry by William Everson. Linoleum block illustrations by Clayton James, who also designed book in consultation with the author. 32 pages, 9 5/8 x 6½ inches, single signature pamphlet, 400 copies hand-sewn, remainder stapled, cover glued to spine. Total edition of 975, single printing on Ivory Linweave Text Antique laid paper, August 1944, printed on Challenge Gordon at Waldport. 25 cents.

War Elegies

Poetry by William Everson. Designed and illustrated by Kemper Nomland, Jr. 32 pages, 9 5/8 x 6½ inches, single signature pamphlet, stapled, cover glued to spine. Single printing of 982 copies (colophon states 975) on Linweave Early American paper, Gold Atlantic cover. Printed December 1944, on Challenge Gordon at Waldport. Second edition of these poems, first letterpress printing, with a different "War Elegy V" added. Typographical error in Elegy XI: "diminished" was printed "dimished." 35 cents.

Generation of Journey

Poetry by Jacob Sloan. Illustrated and designed by Barbara Straker James. 40 pages, 9 5/8 x 6½ inches, single signature pamphlet, stapled, cover glued to endpapers at spine. Single printing of 850 copies (colophon states 950) on Ivory Linweave Text paper, Antique Grey Hammermill cover. Printed March 1945, on Challenge Gordon at Waldport. Typographical error in "Walterville Valley" in less than 100 copies; typo in last line of "Waiting En Route" in entire run. Glue used for cover caused chemical reaction on paper, resulting in fading along spine. 25 cents.

The Residual Years

Poetry by William Everson. Designed by David Jackson, William Eshelman, and the author. 32 pages, 7¼ x 8¾ inches, single signature, hand-sewn pamphlet, cover of gray construction paper glued at spine. Mimeographed pages, edition of 330 copies signed by author with hand-corrected error on page 5. Some unsigned copies extant. Released in April 1945 from Waldport. Highly acidic paper with often severe chipping and cracking. 15 cents.

poems: mcmxlii
Poetry by William Everson. Illustrated by Clayton James, designed by the author. 40 pages, 9 5/8 x 6 3/8 inches, single signature pamphlet, stapled with cover glued to endpapers at spine. Single printing of 500 copies on White Mountie Eggshell Book paper, India Antique Atlantic cover. Printed on Challenge Gordon press at Waldport; released August 1945. Errata slip tipped in, featuring small linocut made for it by Clayton James. Intended as gifts distributed by author.

An Astonished Eye Looks Out of the Air
Poetry by Kenneth Patchen. Designed by Kemper Nomland, Jr. from an idea of the author. 40 pages, 9½ x 6 5/16 inches, single signature pamphlet, stapled, outside label glued around spine to cover staples. Gabardine Book paper, Black Antique Albermarle cover. Single printing of 1,950 copies on Challenge Gordon; 50 completed in December 1945 at Waldport, remainder completed in May 1946 at Cascade Locks, bound in Pasadena, California. Many difficulties attended the printing of this book, yet it is usually considered the most impressive production of the Untide Press (see pages 203–204 for details).

Imagine the South
Poetry by George Woodcock. Illustrated by Wilfred Lang, designed by Lang and the Untide Press. 40 pages, 9 5/8 x 6½ inches, single signature pamphlet, stapled with cover glued to heavy endpapers at spine. Single printing of 1,000 copies on White wove Strathmore text, Rhododendron cover. Completed November 1947 on Challenge Gordon at Pasadena, California. 50 cents.

Arma Virumque Cano
Poetry by John Walker. Illustrated and designed by Kemper Nomland, Jr. 40 pages, 9 5/8 x 6½ inches, single signature pamphlet, stapled with cover glued to endpapers at spine. Single printing of 500 copies begun in May 1949 and completed in April 1950 on Challenge Gordon at Pasadena, California.

OTHER WALDPORT PUBLICATIONS

From examination of original copies, committee and program records, and correspondence.

The Tide
Official Camp #56 newsletter; rotating editors from camp membership. Seven issues, irregular publication 1942–44, varied pagination and size. All issues mimeographed; vol. 2, nos. 4 and 5 with silkscreen covers. Circulation unknown.

The Untide
Unofficial satire of the *Tide;* edited by "The Mole" (Glen Coffield, Harold Hackett, Larry Siemons). Twelve weekly issues, January–March 1943. Generally four mimeographed pages, 8½ x 5½ inches, folded and unbound. Three numbers of a volume 2 showed up in April, May, and September 1943 (editors uncertain), and two more numbers in December 1944 (edited by Kemper Nomland, Jr. and Henry Wolff). Circulation unknown.

The Illiterati
Edited by Kemper Nomland and Kermit Sheets. "Poems, stories, musical compositions, informal sketches written by pacifists conscripted to do work of national importance" (*Untide* 1, no. 12). *Illiterati* issues 1 and 2 produced at Cascade Locks, both mimeographed; no. 3 at Cascade Locks and Waldport, combination mimeograph and letterpress; no. 4 at Waldport; nos. 5 and 6 at Pasadena (all done by letterpress). Circulation unknown. Issue 1 extremely rare after post office destroyed unknown number of copies due to a drawing of a nude female considered "of an obscene, lewd, lascivious and indecent character" (see page 79).

The Compass
A magazine of literary, artistic, political, and social expression, featuring professionally printed photography and graphics. Eight issues published from November 1942 to Spring 1946. First four issues edited by DeLisle Crawford at Camp #32 in West Campton, New Hampshire. Martin Ponch, associate editor, took over as editor and moved the journal first to Camp #108 at Gatlinburg, Tennessee, and then to Camp #56. Two issues were published at Waldport; the final issue was published from Portland, although it states Cascade Locks as its circulation address. Funding assistance came in part from the Fellowship of Reconciliation, and circulation went as high as three thousand copies.

The Fine Arts at Waldport
A single-issue publication introducing the Fine Arts program, written by William Everson and published in early 1944. Ten mimeographed pages, 8½ x 7 inches, folded and stapled. When asked about the fanciful graphic that resembled an upside-down and backwards numeral 4, Everson replied that he simply liked the image and had no idea that it meant anything further. Circulation unknown although it should be presumed that copies went to the 150-plus CPS camps and the various administrative agencies.

Good News

An occasional mimeographed 8½ x 11 sheet of inspirational messages and quotes from the Bible. Probably issued in 1943–44, and perhaps related to *Remember Now Thy Creator* (see below).

The Holy Apple and Others

Poetry by Glenn Miller. Twelve mimeographed pages, hand-drawn illustrations, 4½ x 5 inches. "Included are war poems, erotic poems and poems on social reconstruction" (*Untide* 1, no. 11). Published March 1943, unknown number. 5 cents.

The Idol of Nationalism

Booklet that "deals with whether or not a Christian should take part in war" (Religious Life Committee Report, Oct. 1942–Dec. 1944). No copies located; size, format, and number unknown although the Religious Life Committee report noted a "second edition" was printed.

Remember Now Thy Creator

Compiled by Robert Hyslop. "A devotional and guide book especially written for young people but applicable to all ages" (Religious Life Committee Report, Oct. 1942–Dec. 1944). Linoleum block cuts on cover by Adrian Wilson. 58 mimeographed pages, 8½ x 11 inches. Completed fall 1944. Rare copies in special collections at University of Oregon, Lewis and Clark College, and UCLA. Microfilm at Brethren Historical Library and Archives, Elgin, Illinois.

CPS Anthology

This anthology was never published, nor was it even close to publication. In his "Note" attached to the Fine Arts files organized for and sent to the Brethren archives, Everson wrote of the anthology from Cascade Locks on June 10, 1946:

> It was begun as a venture of the Untide Press, which hoped to put out a collection of CPS writing. It was subsequently taken up by the Writers Group of Fine Arts and officially sponsered [sic]. The material that came in voluntairly [sic] was not too good; the material that we really wanted had to be hunted out, sought after, begged for, and then often never came in. Gradually local creative efforts took up our attention. The Anthology never came off. And although a great heap of material was collected, the best CPS work is as yet scattered. Even the best work at Waldport never got into the collection. Perhaps someone with more patience and energy than any of us will in time assemble the really significant work done in the camps. I hope so.

The only evidence of the attempt is in the microfilmed records of Camp #56 housed at the BHLA. (The originals were photographed and then destroyed in 1948.) The files are incomplete, and some submissions are unsigned or unreadable due to the poor quality of carbon copies and blurriness in the microfilm. Also, much of the material was rejected by the editorial group, as indicated by the submission slips with multiple initials under the "reject" heading. Any attempt to resurrect this project will face significant and perhaps insurmountable challenges.

THEATER PRODUCTIONS

Compiled from programs, letters, and memoirs.

Aria da Capo, by Edna St. Vincent Millay. Directed by David Jackson. Cast: Manche Langley, Kermit Sheets, Vladimir Dupre, William Eshelman, Enoch Crumpton. Production by Kemper Nomland, Francis Barr, Don Godwin, Adrian Wilson, James Siple, Manche Langley, Kermit Sheets, Maude Gregory, Don Roberts, and Gerald Rubin. Performed at Waldport, September 22–23, 1944; at Cascade Locks, October 7.

Tennessee Justice, adapted from contemporary news article by Martin Ponch, who also directed. Main cast: James Williams, Charles Cooley, Glenn Evans, Joseph Gistirak, Tom Polk Miller, Mark Rouch, Linwood Flowers, and Arthur Snell; ten-member jury-choir. Production by U. Adrian Wilson, Arthur Snell, Francis Barr, Floyd Minear, Warren Kessler, Rudolph Cinco, Isabel Mount, and William Shank. Performed at Waldport, January 26 and February 3, 1945. Repeated at Elkton and Eugene, respectively, February 17 and 18.

Ghosts, by Henrik Ibsen. Directed by Joseph Gistirak. Cast: Elizabeth T. Dupre, Martin Ponch, David Jackson, Joyce Harvey, Kermit Sheets. Production by U. Adrian Wilson, Robert S. Harvey, Joyce Harvey, and Joseph Gistirak. The program adds, "The production wishes gratefully to acknowledge the valuable aid contributed by persons not directly affiliated with it and by members of the camp." Performed at Waldport, May 13–18, 1945.

Candida, by George Bernard Shaw. Directed by Kermit Sheets. Cast: Enoch A. Crumpton, Hildegarde Erle, Tom Polk Miller, Kermit Sheets, Elizabeth Dupre, William Eshelman. Production by Francis Barr, Marie Cessna, Hildegarde Erle, David Jackson, Tom Miller, Martin Ponch, and Karl Wennerberg. Performed at Waldport, October 11–13, 1945.

The Seagull, by Anton Chekhov. Directed by David Jackson. Cast: Hildegarde Erle, Tom Polk Miller, Robert Constable, Goldie Bock, Don Kirschner, Isabel Mount, Eunice Picone, Kermit Sheets, John E. Land, Charles Ghent, David Vice, Warren Kessler, Lila McCray. Production by Kermit Sheets, Francis Barr, Warren Kessler, Herbert Michael, and Isabel Mount. Performed at Cascade Locks, February 21–26, 1946.

DRAMATIC READINGS AND PERFORMANCES

Compiled from programs, letters and memoirs, and a chronological list in the Kermit Sheets Collection at Lewis and Clark College. All events at Waldport unless otherwise noted.

"Musicale," songs and readings. Glen Coffield, Norman Haskell, Charles Mahin, Hugh Merrick, Carl Rutledge, Keith Utterback. February 3 and 7, 1943.

"Conversation by Moonlight," from *Look Homeward, Angel* by Thomas Wolfe. Glen Coffield, reader; Warren F. Downs, cellist; Robert H. Scott, pianist; Harold Hackett, narrator; James Harman as Ben; William Everson as Eugene. March 18–19, 1944.

U.S.A., by John Dos Passos. Excerpts from the trilogy of novels, read by William Eshelman, William Everson, Harold Hackett, and James Harman. Norman Haskell read a poem by Pushkin, Art Snell performed a song, and Warren Downs played an obbligato on the cello. April 15, 1944.

The Masculine Dead, by William Everson. Set design by Glenn Evans and Larry Siemons. Cast: Cloe Wakefield, Millie Gardner, Florence Mason, Etta Spurling, Kay Rice, James Harman, Harold Hackett, William Everson. April 22, 1944.

"Men at Work: A Program of Material, with Explanatory Comments, by the Men who Wrote It." Martin Ponch, James Harman, Harold Hackett, William Everson. May 20, 1944.

"A Morality Play for the Leisure Class," by John Balderston. Read by James Harman and Martin Ponch. June 17, 1944.

The Mikado in CPS, by Kermit Sheets. A parody of Gilbert and Sullivan's *Mikado,* lyrics adapted to CPS subject matter. Waldport cast and production unknown. July 29, 1944. (Earlier version performed at Cascade Locks, February 27.)

The Fine Arts Reading Series ran July through November 1944, a more or less weekly performance of dramatic readings that enjoyed participation beyond the usual members of the Fine Arts. Presentations included: *Our Town* and *The Woman of Andros,* by Thornton Wilder; *Androcles and the Lion, Saint Joan,* and *Heartbreak House,* by George Bernard Shaw; *Petrouchka—a Ballet,* by Igor Stravinsky; *My Heart's in the Highlands,* by William Saroyan; *High Tor,* by Maxwell Anderson; works by fourteen contemporary authors in various CPS and literary publications; three short stories by Raymond J. Sender, Niccolo Tucci, and Dorothy Parker; *The Iliad,* by Homer; *The House of Atreus* and *Agamemnon,* by Aeschylus; *Electra,* by Sophocles; *Iphigenia in Aulis,* by Euripides; *Lilimon,* by Ferenc Molnar; and *Twelfth Night,* by William Shakespeare.

A reading series cooperatively sponsored by the Fine Arts and the Religious Interest Group, taken from *The Little Plays of Saint Francis,* by Laurence Housman, ran on five successive Sunday evenings in October 1944.

The Record Concert Series ran through much of 1944, usually presenting classical works and hosted by Bob Scott in the camp music room. Bill Everson also presented some jazz programs, and Warren Downs hosted at least two.

A movie series ran from June to November 1945, featuring films loaned from the Museum of Modern Art. Representative titles included *Four Horsemen of the Apocalypse, Fall of the House of Usher, Cabinet of Dr. Caligari, Mutiny in Odessa,* and *Potemkin.*

MUSIC PERFORMANCES

All performances at Waldport unless otherwise noted.

April 29, 1944[?]: Warren Downs, cello; Robert Scott, piano. Vivaldi, Kreisler, Burch, Beethoven.

October 21, 1944: Warren Downs, cello; Broadus Erle, violin; Robert Harvey, violin; Robert Scott, piano; Adrian Wilson, clarinet. Bach, Schumann, Ernest Bloch, Beethoven.

January 25, 1945: Broadus Erle, violin; Warren Downs, cello; Robert Harvey, violin; Naomi Kirschner, viola. (Works performed not named.)

January 28, 1945: Donald Chamberlin, bass; Wencil Prochazka, piano; Broadus Erle, Robert Harvey, Naomi Kirschner, Warren

Downs, string quartet. "Dover Beach," Handel, Mozart, Beethoven, Schubert, Brahms, Bach, Prochazka, Schneider, Munro, Huhn, Verdi.

March 3, 1945: Warren Downs, cello; Broadus Erle, violin; Robert Harvey, violin; Tom Polk Miller, piano; Adrian Wilson, clarinet. Pergolesi, Hindemith, Beethoven, Chausson, Haydn.

March 29, 1945: Wesley DeCoursey, Tom Polk Miller, Adrian Wilson. (Instruments and works performed not named.)

November 17, 1945: Broadus Erle, violin; Hildegarde Erle, piano. Bach, Franck, Persichetti, Delius, Paganini/Kreisler, Paganini/Spalding, Boulanger, DeFalla/Kochanski, DeFalla/Kreisler, Tartini/Kreisler. Repeated in Portland, April 6, 1946.

ART EXHIBITS

Little written record exists of art exhibits; there were apparently no catalogues printed. Mention is made of works exhibited by Kemper Nomland in 1943 and by Morris Graves in August–September 1944. Presumably, works done by visiting artist Waldo Chase were also shown, and efforts by various campers were exhibited in the dining and recreation halls.

The Birth of the Untide Press

Exactly how and when the Untide Press was born, and precisely who deserves credit for what, will probably never be ascertained beyond all doubt. But one source seems reasonably reliable: a poem Coffield sent to Everson in 1945, from his lodgings in the medical experiment unit at Ann Arbor, Michigan. The author's tendency toward wit and playfulness notwithstanding, here is an early record of the founding of the Untide Press.

The Birth of the Untide Press

I.

I think it had not been except for Larry,
Since other evil minds were also wary.

But one who lacks the potency of doubt
Can be more potent in impotent rout.

And so the three of us upon a heath
Were gathered to pull Wit's sword from Fun's sheath.

First, Larry with a hat that hid his face,
Both hiding and the hid a sore disgrace.

And Hackett that cool youngster slow and sly
Who had a devil's gleam in his blinked eye.

Myself, a dangling straw tied to a beard,
The emptiness of which was what crows feared.

When we three bumped our heads, you surely guess,
There sprang into the air the Untide Press.

Somewhat like Venus, or the birth of Buddha,
But more an ape that chewed on baricouda.

Above the cliffs, the rain came slowly down,
To bless the creature in its white nightgown;

That yawned and would have crept back into bed
Except that Larry charmed it when he said:

"I will release you from my evil eye
If you will teach me how to tell a lie!"

The ape said: "Sweetheart, conjure up a mole
By blowing duck's down in a rabbit hole,

And he will teach you all you need to know
Of how to bite a back or malice sow."

And Larry clapped his clammy hands in glee,
Whereat I gave a groan of misery.

II.

Hackett was the first one to discover
Wit can be a fair and tripping lover,

Or a tiny dagger for the back
That lets warm blood flow through a teensy crack,

No more a flood than little pin points make,
But just enough to cause a wince, or quake.

It was while dreaming of these things there came
The apparition called the Mole by name,

That said: "Who tries to liquidate my hide
Must catch the editor of the Untide,

For that is who I am I do declare!"
With which he vaporized into thin air.

"Well, well!" said Hackett, "What a quaint old fellow;
His wit is sharp, his brain is mild and mellow!"

While Larry sat there with his jaw dropped wide:
"So he's the editor of the Untide!"

Whereat we went to work with fierce sensations
Interpreting for man the Mole's vibrations.

III.

One day there came a fourth into the clan,
And he did bring a change to Mole and Man;

I think it was a chance and not an omen
That Everson was one born of a woman,

That soon a Buzzard flew into the picture,
To be at first a sign, and then a fixture;

But it will make poor Larry's tear drops start
To think back, how the Mole accepted art;

And soon a ragsheet went to livery,
And finally to books of poetry.

Thus seeds of valor when in lightness sowed,
Can by the brooding mind pay what they owed,

And visions of a culture find redress
For youthful rancor's biting eagerness.

Ah me! in time the legend reached a head,
And rumors started that the Mole was dead.

Just like the Buzzard's efficacious beak,
The Mole was someone's tongue in no one's cheek.

—Glen Coffield
Ann Arbor, Michigan
September 8, 1945

Copyrights and Illustration Credits

The author wishes to thank the copyright holders, publishers, and libraries listed below for their permission to reproduce materials included in this book. Every reasonable effort has been made to trace the ownership of copyrighted material and to make full acknowledgment of its use. If errors or omissions have occurred, they will be corrected in subsequent editions, provided that notification is submitted in writing to the publisher.

COPYRIGHTS

William Eshelman Papers. Courtesy of Pat Rom.

William Everson Papers, William Clark Memorial Library, University of California, Los Angeles. Courtesy of Jude Everson.

"Allen Ginsberg Dancing to the Grateful Dead. The Gathering of the Tribes for a Human Be-In, Golden Gate Park, 1967." © Lisa Law.

Allen Ginsberg, *Howl and Other Poems*. Copyright ©1956 by City Lights Books. Reprinted by permission of City Lights Books.

Morris Graves letters and paintings. "Sea, Fish and Constellation," Seattle Art Museum, gift of Mrs. Thomas D. Stimson. All items courtesy of the Morris Graves Foundation.

"Morris Graves, Painter, 1950." © 1950, 2013 The Imogen Cunningham Trust.

Kenneth Patchen, *An Astonished Eye Looks Out of the Air*. Copyright © 1944 by Kenneth Patchen. Courtesy of Special Collections, University Library, UC Santa Cruz.

William Stafford, "Report from an Unappointed Committee" from *The Way It Is: New and Selected Poems*. Copyright © 1998 by the Estate of William Stafford. Reprinted with the permission of The Permissions Company, Inc. on behalf of Graywolf Press, Minneapolis, Minnesota, www.graywolfpress. org.

Adrian Wilson Papers, Joyce Lancaster Wilson Papers, Bancroft Library, University of California, Berkeley; letters and photographs from *Two Against the Tide*. Courtesy of Melissa Marshall.

Most of the photographs of Camp #56 do not have a photographer named, although many were taken by Bruce Reeves while he was assigned there. Unless noted, the photographer is officially unknown. Photos are identified by page number after the permissions grantor or collection from which they came. If more than one image is on a page, each is further identified by short description.

Associated Press: Page 30.

Author's collection: Pages 76 (both), 78, 79 (both), 125, 150, 171, 201, 204, 205, 215, 239, 246, 253 (*Compass 2*, nos. 1 and 2), 257 (Harman: *Compass 2*, nos. 3 and 4).

Francis Barr CPS Collection, Manchester University Archives and Brethren Historical Collection: Page 257 (Jackson).

Brethren Historical Library and Archives: Pages 4, 7, 9 (both), 33 (top), 35, 38, 39, 40, 41 (right), 45, 58, 61 (both), 72, 94, 109 (top), 117 (both), 124, 152, 153 (both), 155, 210, 255 (Downs, Vlad Dupre, Ibby Dupre), 256 (Eshelman, Hackett), 258 (Reeves). Most of these photos were taken by Bruce Reeves.

Eliza E. Canty-Jones: Page 128, 257 (Langley).

Charles Cooley: Pages 31, 33 (bottom). Photos likely by Bruce Reeves.

Imogen Cunningham Trust: Page 140 (Morris Graves, Painter, 1950. © 1950, 2013 The Imogen Cunningham Trust.)

Vladimir Dupre: Pages 103, 109 (bottom), 129, 259 (Siemons, Joyce Wilson).

William Eshelman: Pages 6, 13, 80, 87, 96, 111, 159, 256 (Everson). Most of these photos were taken by Bruce Reeves.

Jude Everson: Page 3. Photographer possibly Waldo Chase.

William Everson Papers, Clark Memorial Library, University of California, Los Angeles: Cover (group portrait). Pages 56, 67, 192.

Lisa Law: Page 248 (Allen Ginsberg Dancing to the Grateful Dead. The Gathering of the Tribes for a Human Be-In, Golden Gate Park, 1967.) Copyright © by Lisa Law.

Melissa Marshall: Pages 135 and 190 (*Two Against the Tide*), 235 (*The Work and Play of Adrian Wilson*).

Kim Stafford: Page 243 (photo by Russ Hosking), 255 (Coffield).

Seattle Art Museum: Cover (detail at top). Page 141. Courtesy of the Morris Graves Foundation.

Siuslaw National Forest: Pages 41 (left), 50, 54. Photos likely by Bruce Reeves.

The *Untide*: Pages 5 (1, no. 5); 10 (2, no. 1); 42 (1, no. 5); 44 (1, no. 5); 62 (1, no. 11).

Aubrey Watzek Library Archives and Special Collections, Lewis and Clark College. Portland, OR: Pages 83, 107, 139, 145, 156 (photo by Henry Blocher), 179, 218 (photo by Bruce Dean), 256 (Erle photo by Henry Blocher), 257 (James), 258 (Miller, Mount, Mills, Nomland; Ponch photo by Henry Blocher), 259 (Sheets, Adrian Wilson). Most Camp #56 photos by Bruce Reeves.

Notes

NOTES TO CHAPTER 1

1   Sibley and Jacob, *Conscription of Conscience*, 83, 487.

2   Barber, Ogden, and Jones, *Camp 56: An Oral History Project*, Charles Davis, 30. Hereafter cited as *Oral History Project*, followed by the name of the interviewee and page numbers.

3   William Everson to Edwa Everson, January 21, 1943. William Everson Papers, 1937–71, William Andrews Clark Memorial Library, University of California, Los Angeles. Hereafter cited as Everson Papers, UCLA. All letters attributed to Everson are from this collection unless otherwise noted.

4   Everson, *The Residual Years*, 368.

5   Bartlett, *William Everson*, 37.

6   *Oral History Project:* Charles G. Jehnzen, 106. See also quote from Selective Service Director Lewis B. Hershey: "The conscientious objector, by my theory, is best handled if no one hears of him." (U.S. Senate, Committee on Military Affairs, *Conscientious Objectors' Benefits*, 78th Congress, 1st sess., Feb. 17, 1943, 17.)

7   Eshelman, "Everson and the Fine Arts at Waldport," in Hall, Hotchkiss, and Shears, *Perspectives on William Everson*, 10.

8   Mills, "History of the Founding and Organization of the Waldport Camp," in Camp Waldport Records, UO, 2.

9   Ibid., 5.

10 Ibid., 5.

11 Everson to Lawrence Clark Powell, Jan. 28, 1943, in Everson and Powell, *Take Hold*, 353.

12 *Oral History Project:* Jim Gallaghan, 75.

13 Sibley and Jacob, *Conscription of Conscience*, 216–17.

14 Murray Morgan, *Islands of the Smokey Sea: The Story of Alaska's Aleutian Chain* (Fairbanks: Alaskan Prospectors Publishing, 1981), 11–13.

15 Infrastructure Finance Authority, Waldport Community Profile, accessed Oct. 11, 2009, www.orinfrastructure.org/profiles/Waldport.

16 Mills, "History of the Founding," 2.

17 *Oral History Project:* Forrest Jackson, 95.

18 Mills, "History of the Founding," 3, 7.

19 Everson and Powell, *Take Hold,* 369; Assignment form, Center on Conscience and War Records (DG 025, Series F-1, Box 166, Part 1, Harold Hackett), Swarthmore College Peace Collection.

20 Coffield biography compiled from Everson to Edwa, Jan. 29, 1943 and Feb. 7, 1943; and Hackett to Edwa, Aug. 1, 1943, all from Everson Papers, UCLA; Everson and Powell, *Take Hold,,* 353; Glen Stemmons Coffield Papers, Coll. 217, Special Collections and University Archives, University of Oregon, Eugene, OR. (Hereafter cited as Coffield Papers, UO.)

21 *Tide,* Nov. 1942; Sibley and Jacob, *Conscription of Conscience,* 193.

22 All quotes in this and the following paragraphs are from *Untide* vol. 1, nos. 1–12 (Jan.–Mar. 1943). Unless otherwise noted, all *Untide* quotes are from Coffield Papers, UO. The identity of the Mole has been a topic of much conjecture over the years, with different sources claiming it was Coffield or Hackett. Upon full review of the Untide Press records, Everson papers, and Coffield papers, the author's conclusion is that the Mole was a joint identity: Coffield and Hackett the main writers, with Everson and Siemons contributing to varying degrees. See appendix 4 for Coffield's explanation in verse.

23 Palandri, "Waldport," 16.

NOTES TO CHAPTER 2

1 Milne, *Peace with Honour,* 4, 49.

2 Ibid., 107.

3 Ibid., 209–11.

4 Ibid., v.

5 Milne, *War with Honour,* 12.

6 Jacob, *Origins of Civilian Public Service,* 9–10.

7 Hershberger, *War, Peace, and Nonresistance,* 382–83.

8 Schlissel, *Conscience in America,* 29.

9 Ibid., 30.

10 Hershberger, *War, Peace, and Nonresistance,* 93.

11 As cited in Schlissel, *Conscience in America,* 47.

12 As cited in Selective Service System, *Conscientious Objection,* 1:38.

13 Ibid., 1:39–40.

14 Henry D. Thoreau, "Civil Disobedience and Non-Violent Resistance," in Sibley, *The Quiet Battle,* 26–27.

15 Schlissel, *Conscience in America,* 88.

16 Ibid., 89, 110–12.

17 Thomas, *Conscientious Objector,* 62; Schlissel, *Conscience in America,* 90.

18 Pringle, *Record of a Quaker Conscience,* 44, 77.

19 Schlissel, *Conscience in America,* 124.

20 Ibid., 119.

21 Thomas, *Conscientious Objector,* 65.

22 Carnegie Endowment for International Peace, "Endowment History," accessed July 20, 2010, www.carnegieendowment.org/about/index.cfm?fa=history.

23 Bernays, *Propaganda*, 9. Bernays provides an illuminating note on how he created the term "public relations," in the 2002 BBC documentary, *Century of the Self*. "I decided that if you could use propaganda for war, you could certainly use it for peace. And 'propaganda' got to be a bad word because of the Germans using it, so what I did was to try to find some other words. So we found the words 'counsel on public relations.'"

24 Thomas, *Conscientious Objector*, 66.

25 Section 4, Selective Service Act, as quoted in Sibley and Jacob, *Conscription of Conscience*, 11.

26 Sibley and Jacob, *Conscription of Conscience*, 13.

27 Thomas, *Conscientious Objector*, 143–44.

28 Meyer, *Hey! Yellowbacks!*, 45–46, 118, 150–51, 201; Thomas, *Conscientious Objector*, 201.

29 Meyer, *Hey! Yellowbacks!*, 203–4.

30 War Resisters International, accessed July 23, 2010, www.warresisters.org/wri.

31 O'Sullivan and Meeker, *The Draft and Its Enemies*, 153–55.

32 Hershberger, *War, Peace, and Nonresistance*, 162.

33 Bowman, *Church of the Brethren*, 268.

34 Hershberger, *War, Peace, and Nonresistance*, 383. Members of the group were Rufus M. Jones and Walter C. Woodward of the Society of Friends; E. L. Harshbarger, Harold S. Bender, and P. C. Hiebert of the Mennonite Church; and Rufus D. Bowman and Paul H. Bowman of the Church of the Brethren.

35 "The Civilian Conservation Corps," *American Experience*, accessed Oct. 19, 2010, www-tc.pbs.org/wgbh/americanexperience/media/uploads/special_features/download_files/ccc_transcript.pdf.

36 Minutes of the Brethren Service Committee, Oct. 27, 1940, as cited in Jacob, *Origins of Civilian Public Service*, 13.

37 Bowman, *Church of the Brethren*, 279.

38 Sibley and Jacob, *Conscription of Conscience*, 116–18

39 Ibid., 122–23.

40 Ibid., 121.

41 Frazier and O'Sullivan, *We Have Just Begun*, 10.

NOTES TO CHAPTER 3

1 Thompson, "Onward Christian Soldiers," 27. See also Freeman, "In the Beginning," 8–9, 52–53.

2 Rufus M. Jones, ed., *George Fox: An Autobiography*, (Philadelphia: Ferris & Leach, 1919), 125.

3 Sibley and Jacob, *Conscription of Conscience*, 28.

4 Ibid., 30–31.

5 Selective Service System, *Conscientious Objection*, 1:14–19, 24.

6 Ibid., 3–4.

7 Kovac, *Refusing War, Affirming Peace*, 54.

8 Hurwitz and Simpson, *Against the Tide*. In 1948, Thomas Banyacya was named one of the four Hopi "messengers" appointed by tribal elders to reveal the ancient prophecies warning of threats to the natural balance of the earth. He spent the rest of his life fulfilling that duty. See also Thomas, "Thomas Banyacya."

9 Sibley and Jacob, *Conscription of Conscience*, 60, 64.

10 Palandri, "Waldport," 5.

11 Selective Service System, *Quotas, Calls and Inductions*, Special Monograph No. 12, vol. 2 (Washington, DC: Government Printing Office, 1948), 43, 46–47; Selective Service System, History and Records, www.sss.gov:80/induct.htm (accessed Dec. 24, 2011); Sibley and Jacob, *Conscription of Conscience*, 229.

12 "Californians Get Warning," *Oregonian*, Dec. 10, 1941, 4.

13 Earl Pomeroy, "City Takes Firm Hold," *Oregonian*, December 8, 1941, 1, 10; "Life on the Home Front."

14 *Yaquina Bay News*, Apr. 23, 1942, as cited in G. Thomas Edwards, "The Oregon Coast and Three of Its Guerrilla Organizations, 1942," in *The Pacific Northwest in World War II*, ed. Carlos A. Schwantes (Manhattan, KS: Sunflower University Press, 1986), 33.

15 "Portland Soon to Be Cleared of All Japs," *Oregon Daily Journal*, Apr. 29, 1944, 1.

16 "Jitterbug Zoot Now 'Unzooted,'" *Oregonian*, Sept. 4, 1942, 1.

17 "Untouchable," *Oregonian*, Oct. 4, 1942, 1.

18 Lewis, "World War II Mystery," 61.

19 "Why Summertime Is Sabotage Time," *Civilian Front*, July 17, 1943, 12. As cited in "Life on the Home Front."

20 "Northern Security District Counter Fifth Column Plan," 1944, 3, as cited in "Life on the Home Front." The term "fifth column" stems from the Spanish Civil War (1936–39), when General Emilio Mola Vidal, as his four columns of troops converged on Madrid, referred to the sympathizers and supporters within the city as his "fifth column."

21 Martin, "Beach Patrol," 74; Webber, *Retaliation*, 89.

22 Mills, "History of the Founding," 1; *Oral History Project*: Charles Cooley, 24.

23 Key members of the crew were: Rodney Lehman, office manager; Harold Kleiner, foreman of the Overhead staff; William McReynolds and Bob Carlson, dieticians; and Norman Haskell, head of laundry service. The Forest Service supervisor was Ursis F. McLaughlin (Mills, "History of the Founding," 1–2).

24 Palandri, "Waldport," 10–11.

25 Robert C. Hyslop, "Wellston," *Tide* 1, no. 1 (Nov. 1942): 5; Education Report, Feb. 1943, Camp Waldport Records, UO.

26 Elizabeth Meeks, "CO Wife Goes West, Relates Experiences," *Tide* 1, no. 1 (Nov. 1942): 9.

27 Everett Groff, "Waldport, Oregon, October 24, 1942," *Tide* 1, no. 1 (Nov. 1942): 3.

28 Hyslop, "Wellston," 5.

29 It was not unusual for CPS camps to have informal, and sometimes numerous, names. In this case, Camp Waldport was an obvious geographical nod. Numerous references in camp records and communications identify Camp Angell as a continuation of the CCC camp name, honoring Albert G. Angell, who worked almost thirty years for the Forest Service until his death in 1941. William Everson in his 1977 interview with Guido Palandri claims the Camp Angel version with one "l" was coined as a subtle protest. If so, it caught on, for that spelling appears often in communications at many administrative levels.

30 C. R. Bunyan, "Presenting Camp Angel"; F. V. Flaska, "Walhalla," *Tide* 1, no. 1 (Nov. 1942): 2, 6.

31 Bunyan, "Presenting Camp Angel," 2, 5.

32 "Dan West Speaks," *Tide* 1, no. 1 (Nov. 1942): 6.

33 "Camp Govt. Organized," *Tide* 1, no. 1 (Nov. 1942): 7. Camp president was Jim Ragland and secretary was Rodney Lehman. Chairs of committees were: Earl Kosbab, Workers; Don Kimmel, Public Relations; Frank Allen, Religious; Calvin Kiracofe, Health; Bob Carlson, Recreation. See also Mills, "History of the Founding," 3; and Camp Waldport Constitution, Camp Waldport Records, UO.

34 Mills, "History of the Founding," 3; Palandri, "Waldport," 10.

35 Everson to Edwa, Jan. 22, 1943, Everson Papers, UCLA.

36 Education Report, Feb. 1943; Religious Life Committee Report, 1942–44, Camp Waldport Records, UO.

37 Education Report, Feb. 1943, Camp Waldport Records, UO.

38 Everson to Edwa, Feb. 3, 1943. Everson Papers, UCLA.

39 Everson to Powell, Mar. 15, 1943, Everson and Powell, *Take Hold*, 365. No records have been found of others making the same choice, although comments about privacy do occur in the oral histories. It is not unthinkable that those with heightened sensitivities found solutions similar to Everson's.

40 "Conchies Doing Forestry Work," *Lincoln County Leader*, Feb. 4, 1943: 1.

41 Finucane, *History of the Blodgett Tract*, 8, 13, 28.

42 One camper noted that the milk began turning to butter after being carried through the rugged woods in their packs. *Oral History Project:* Harold Zimmerman, 252. See also Everson to Edwa, Mar. 10, 1943, Everson Papers, UCLA.

43 Everson to Edwa, Feb. 3, 1943, Everson Papers, UCLA.

44 Cooley, *Obeying the Commandment*, 180.

45 *Oral History Project:* Merle Hoover, 92; "What makes a good adequate recreational program?" Camp Waldport: Dinner Table Skits, Camp Waldport Records, UO.

46 Everson to Edwa, Feb. 3, 1943, Everson Papers, UCLA.

47 "Govt. Project Complete," *Untide* 1, no. 5 (Feb. 6, 1943): 19.

48 "Trees—4F," *Untide* 1, no. 7 (Feb. 20, 1943): 33.

49 "What Makes a Good Adequate Recreational Program?" Camp Waldport Records, UO; *Tide* 2, no. 4 (Apr. 1943): 17.

50 Compiled from the *Tide* 2, no. 2 (Feb. 1943): 12; *Untide* 1, no. 7 (Feb. 20, 1943): 35; *Oral History Project:* Harold Zimmerman, 252; Everson to Edwa, Oct. 13, 1943, Everson Papers, UCLA.

51 Everson to Edwa, Feb. 3, 1943, Everson Papers, UCLA.

52 *Untide* 1, no. 5 (Feb. 6, 1943): 24.

53 Larry Siemons, "A Question of Life and Death," *Untide* 1, no. 5 (Feb. 6, 1943): 22; reprinted in the *Tide* 2, no. 3 (Mar. 1943): 20.

54 D. Kimmel and C. Bunyan, "Lagro," *Tide* 1, no. 1 (Nov. 1942): 7.

NOTES TO CHAPTER 4

1 "Our Prayer," *Tide* 2, no. 1 (Jan. 1943): 1.

2 J. K. U., "Birthdayites Revel," *Tide* 2, no. 1 (Jan. 1943): 5.

3 "Navy Plane Crashes in Sea," *Newport Journal,* Jan. 6, 1943.

4 "Joint Rites Held for Darrow," *Tide* 2, no. 1 (Jan. 1943): 2.

5 J. N. Weaver, typed note after "ACCIDENTS—Serious accidents, death, Adverse Community Relations," *Civilian Public Service Handbook,* Camp Waldport Records, UO.

6 *Tide,* vol. 2, no. 1 (Jan. 1943), 11.

7 Religious Life Committee Report, 1942–44, Camp Waldport Records, UO, 4–5.

8 Ibid., 7–8.

9 Activities Coordinator Report, Spring 1943; Glenn Evans and Bob Stevens to Cedric Scholberg, July 26, 1944; Education Report, Mar. 1943, Camp Waldport Records, UO.

10 Education Report, May 1943, Camp Waldport Records, UO.

11 Ralph Borsodi, "Postulates for Decentralization. Normal Living: The Concept of Normal Individual, Community and Social Living," typescript proposal, Brethren Historical Library and Archives, Elgin, IL (hereafter BHLA).

12 Education Report, Feb. 1943, Camp Waldport Records, UO; Everson to Edwa, Feb. 9, 1943, Everson Papers, UCLA; Bruce Reeves, interview with author, May 11, 2013.

13 Education Report, Feb. 1943, Camp Waldport Records, UO.

14 Everson to Edwa, Jan. 22, Feb. 7, and Mar. 23, 1943, Everson Papers, UCLA.

15 C. Ludwig and D. Salstrom, "Community Living Tried, Experiment Under Way," *Tide* 2, no. 1 (Jan. 1943): 4.

16 *Oral History Project:* Robert Wood, 249; "A Plan for Fellowship," *Tide* 2, no. 2 (Feb. 1943): 13; Education Report, April 1943, Camp Waldport Records, UO.

17 Adrian Wilson, *Two against the Tide*, 83. The cabin memories were written by Joyce Lancaster Wilson, editor of Adrian's letters. The background of Tillie the Whale is from an unsigned, typed story compiled from various sources on file at the Waldport Heritage Museum, Waldport, OR.

18 *Oral History Project:* Mary Kessler, 120.

19 Marion Stern to Business Manager, CPS Camp 56, Feb. 2, [1943], Camp Waldport Records, UO.

20 Don Redfield, "Culinary Comments," *Tide* 2, no. 2 (Feb. 1943): 7.

21 *Oral History Project:* Clayton James, 100; *The Reporter*, Feb. 15, 1943, Everson Papers, UCLA.

22 "Brown Builds 'Friendship,'" *Tide* 2, no. 3 (Mar. 1943): 11.

23 Everson to Edwa, May 14, 1943, Everson Papers, UCLA.

24 Education Report, May 1943, Camp Waldport Records, UO.

25 Ibid.

26 Ibid.

27 Don Brumbaugh, "Coordinations," *Tide* 2, no. 3 (Mar. 1943): 9.

28 Education Report, June 1943, Camp Waldport Records, UO.

29 Ibid.

30 Ibid.

31 Ibid.

32 Ibid.

33 Everson to Edwa, Feb. 25, 1943, Everson Papers, UCLA; Earl Kosbab, "Under the New Agreement," *Untide* 1, no. 6 (Feb. 13, 1943): 29.

34 "A.W.S.," *Tide* 2, no. 3 (Mar. 1943): 5; Everson to Edwa, Mar. 19, 1943, Everson Papers, UCLA; "The Bull by the Horns," *Untide* 1, no. 11 (Mar. 20, 1943): 53–54.

35 Palandri, "Waldport," 17; Everson to Edwa, Mar. 24, 1943, Everson Papers, UCLA.

36 Reeves, interview with author, May 11, 2013. Reeves noted that some camp members would check into the infirmary on Saturdays—a CPS work day—when there was a particularly good football game scheduled on the radio.

37 "Men Walk Out," *Tide* 2, no. 3 (Mar. 1943): 14.

38 Everson to Edwa, Apr. 2–8, 1943, Everson Papers, UCLA.

39 Ibid., Mar. 12, 1943, Everson Papers, UCLA.

40 Education Report, Apr. 1943, Camp Waldport Records, UO.

41 Everson to Edwa, Jan. 31 and Feb. 9, 1943, Everson Papers, UCLA.

42 Exchanges compiled from: Everson to Edwa, Apr. 4 and May 9, 1943; Edwa to Everson, May 12, 1943, Everson Papers, UCLA. Comment about sharing the bed is from Bartlett, *William Everson*, 52.

43 Everson to Edwa, May 30, 1943, Everson Papers, UCLA.

44 Everson to Powell, Aug. 2, 1943, Everson and Powell, *Take Hold*, 382–85.

45 Pyle, *Here Is Your War*, 297.

46 President's State of the Union Address, 1943, as quoted in the *Portland Oregonian*, Jan. 8, 1943.

47 Sibley and Jacob, *Conscription of Conscience,* 143–49.

48 *Oral History Project:* Bruce Reeves, 203.

NOTES TO CHAPTER 5

1 Everson and Powell, *Take Hold,* 357.

2 Ibid., 373.

3 "Words on the Origin of the Untide Press," Camp Waldport Records, UO, 1.

4 Once the Camp Angel name was coined by the men there, and used in correspondence, it functioned as the official name, in practice if not in policy. See note 29 in chapter 3.

5 "Creative Work in CPS," *Pacifica Views* 1, no. 1 (June 11, 1943): 2.

6 "War Elegies," *Pacifica Views* 1, no. 6 (July 16, 1943): 3

7 Everson to Edwa, Aug. 16, 1943. Everson Papers, UCLA.

8 Schlesinger, *Almanac of American History,* 493–95.

9 "The Fine Arts at Waldport," *Compass* 2, nos. 1 and 2 (Summer–Fall 1944): 26.

10 "Glenn Miller Announces," *Untide* 1, no. 12 (n.d. [Mar. 27, 1943]): 56.

11 The machines used for publications were shared by different groups, with quite separate purposes and goals. Bill Eshelman emphatically stated that *Remember Now Thy Creator,* compiled by Robert Hyslop, "is definitely *not* an Untide Press publication." Eshelman to Martin Schmitt, Aug. 31, 1948, Camp Waldport Records, UO.

12 Coffield to Keeton, June 15, 1943, Camp Waldport Records, UO.

13 Coffield, *Ultimatum,* unpaginated.

14 Coffield to Sheets, Oct. 26, 1943, Untide Press Records, BANC MSS 72/213 c, The Bancroft Library, University of California, Berkeley; hereafter cited as Untide Press Records, Bancroft.

15 *Oral History Project:* Charles Davis, 31.

16 The title comes from *A Midsummer Night's Dream,* act 5, scene 1, in which the "rustic" performer, Starveling the Tailor, playing the role of Moonshine, holds up a lantern and says, "This lantern doth the hornéd moon present." Bill Eshelman said that Coffield's book was printed without an accent on the word "Hornéd" because the press did not possess any accent marks in their type collection (interview with author, Mar. 31, 2001).

17 K. Stafford, "Our Man of the Mountain," 31–35. Stafford wrote the author that his father, William Stafford, who knew Coffield for many years, told him the story of the fire and family loss.

18 Announcement for the *Illiterati,* ca. 1943, the Kermit Sheets Collection OLPb006SHE, Lewis and Clark College Aubrey Watzek Library Archives and Special Collections, Portland, OR, 6.17; hereafter cited as Sheets Collection, L&C.

19 Kemper Nomland later recalled a particular response to the image on the *Illiterati* cover: "It had a hand, and a circle on the hand. So someone

decided that circle represented Japan, our enemy. It was just a circle as far as I knew." (Werner and Campbell, "Art in a Time of War.")

20 Kermit Sheets, interview with author.

21 Post Office Department Solicitor to Kemper Nomland, June 10, 1943, Untide Press Records, Bancroft.

22 Cascade Locks postmaster to Don Baker, July 9, 1943, Untide Press Records, Bancroft.

23 *Illiterati,* no. 2 (Summer 1943): 36.

24 Coffield to Morris Keeton, June 25, 1943, Camp Waldport Records, UO.

25 Eshelman, *No Silence!,* 32–33.

26 Everson and Powell, *Take Hold,* 413–14.

27 Keeton to Coffield, June 18, 1943, Camp Waldport Records, UO.

28 Educational Report, July and Aug., 1943, Camp Waldport Records, UO. The origin of Brumbaugh's word "gestopoic" is unknown.

29 Everson to Edwa, July 31 and Aug. 3, 1943, Everson Papers, UCLA; Palandri, "Waldport," 8.

30 Sheets to Keeton, July 7, 1943; Keeton to Sheets, July 29, 1943, Untide Press Records, Bancroft.

31 Tom Polk Miller to Kermit Sheets, Sept. 27, 1943, Untide Press Records, Bancroft.

32 Everson to Sheets, Sept. 24, 1943, Untide Press Records, Bancroft.

33 Ibid., Sept. 26, 1943.

34 Sheets to Keeton, Oct. 5, 1943, Untide Press Records, Bancroft.

35 Everson to Sheets and Nomland, Oct. 16, 1943, Untide Press Records, Bancroft.

36 Keeton, Memo #342-E, n.d., Keeton to Nomland, Oct. 13, 1943 and Keeton to Sheets, Oct. 18, 1943, Untide Press Records, Bancroft; Palandri, "Waldport," 8; Eshelman, interview with author, Mar. 31, 2001.

37 Everson to Sheets and Nomland, Oct. 16, 1943, Untide Press Records, Bancroft.

38 Meltzer, *Golden Gate,* 71.

39 Everson and Powell, *Take Hold,* 396–97. A somewhat embellished version of this story exists in Meltzer's *Golden Gate,* with Everson recalling the event through a prism of twenty-six years. The version sent to Powell, written directly after the trip, is likely more accurate and hence the one reproduced here.

40 Everson to Edwa, Nov. 9, 1943, Everson Papers, UCLA.

41 Ibid., Nov. 28, 1943.

42 Ibid.

43 Ibid., Dec. 12, 1943.

44 Ibid., Nov. 30, 1943.

45 Fine Arts School Committee minutes, Dec. 26, 1943, BHLA.

46 Henry Miller, *The Air-Conditioned Nightmare,* 20, 24–25.

47 Everson and Powell, *Take Hold,* 407–9.

48 Miller to Everson, Jan. 3, 1944, Everson Papers, UCLA.

49 Palandri, "Waldport," 22; Everson to Edwa, Aug. 30, 1943, Everson Papers, UCLA; Reeves, interview with author.

NOTES TO CHAPTER 6

1 Everson to Morris Keeton, Jan. 20, 1944, Everson Papers, UCLA; Downs diary, Jan. 30, 1944. The Winchell quote is from Everson's letter; it is very likely an approximation of the literal text.

2 Dave Hall, "Ramblin' Around," *Lincoln County Times,* Jan. 27, 1944, 1; Mar. 9, 1944, 1.

3 "Waldport Director Explains Attacks," *Fellowship of Reconciliation Oregon Newsletter,* Feb. 1944, Camp Waldport Records, UO, 4.

4 Civilian Public Service Camp #56 Public Relations Committee, "To Our Friends and Neighbors," Mar. 1944, BHLA.

5 Mills to camp members, Apr. 8, 1944, Camp Waldport Records; Everson and Powell, *Take Hold,* 418.

6 Downs diary, Feb. 27, 1944.

7 Winslow Ames, an art professor at Antioch College in Ohio, upon receiving a copy of the prospectus, commented on Everson's choice to flip "the old guild symbol (the 'perfect' number four) upside down." Some guilds used variations of the number to signify their relationship to "the four corners of the world, the four winds, the gospels, etc.," Ames said. Everson replied that he wasn't aware of the reference when he did it. "It just seemed interesting that way and I put it together." Ames to Everson, Feb. 22 and Mar. 20, 1944; Everson to Ames, Mar. 4, 1944, Everson Papers, UCLA.

8 "The Fine Arts at Waldport," pamphlet, BHLA, 2.

9 Ibid., 4, 6.

10 Ibid., 6, 8.

11 Everson to Sheets, Jan. 13, 1944, Eshelman letters; Downs, "From the Pulpit to the Stage," Sheets collection, L&C, 3; Downs diary, Jan. 6, 1944.

12 Everson to Sheets, Jan. 13, 1944, Eshelman letters.

13 Martin Ponch, open letter to "Anyone Concerned about Him," May 5, 1944, Camp Waldport Records, UO.

14 Dupre, interview with author, Nov. 18, 2010.

15 Eshelman to James and Steers, Feb. 22, 1944, Camp Waldport Records, UO.

16 Eshelman to Fran, Apr. 2, 1944, Eshelman letters.

17 Downs diary, Jan. 31, 1944; Reeves, interview with author, May 11, 2013.

18 Downs diary, Jan. 19, Feb. 28, Mar. 2 and 7, 1944. Regarding the note about travel: bus, train, and hitchhiking were standard modes of transportation. When Paul Weaver, a pastor from Yakima, Washington, requested directions for hitchhiking from Cascade Locks to Waldport, the camp education directors replied that it would be easiest to hitch the seventy-five miles from Portland to Hebo, the side camp on the northern Oregon

coast. (Evans and Stevens to Weaver, July 5, 1944, Camp Waldport Records, UO.)

19 Mills to camp members, Apr. 8, 1944, Camp Waldport Records, UO; Downs diary, Mar. 1, 1944.

20 Downs diary, Mar. 15, 1944.

21 Ibid., Mar. 16, 1944.

22 Schlesinger, *Almanac of American History,* 495–96.

23 Sibley and Jacob, *Conscription of Conscience,* 189. In what appears to have been one of the more cynical political manipulations of the time, Congressman Joseph Starnes of Alabama inserted an amendment to the Army Appropriation Bill of June 30, 1943, forbidding CPS assignees to do relief work outside the United States, effectively stopping them from helping the people suffering in war-devastated countries. Layers of legislative interpretation obscured this detail when the bill passed, but Sibley and Jacob report that the congressman "knew full well what he was doing, and would make it his business to see that the prohibition stayed. He had no wish to see c.o.'s glamorized by overseas service" (*Conscription of Conscience,* 228). Starnes had earlier earned a measure of infamy as a member of the House Unamerican Activities Committee (HUAC) when, in 1938, theater director Hallie Flanagan, testifying in her defense, made reference to the Renaissance playwright Christopher Marlowe. "You are quoting from this Marlowe," Starnes said to Flanagan. "Is he a communist?" (Eric Bentley, ed., *Thirty Years of Treason: Excerpts from Hearings before the House Committee on Un-American Activities, 1938–1968* [New York: Viking Press, 1971], 24–25.)

24 Sibley and Jacob, *Conscription of Conscience,* 337.

25 Downs diary, Feb. 23 and 25, 1944. The "Smith" here, while not specifically identified, is almost certainly Wes Smith (J. Wesley Smith), a member of the more liberal Community Church from Portland, Oregon, and who later corresponded with Eshelman. The CPS *Directory* lists only two others with this surname at Waldport: Gay W. Smith, a Jehovah's Witness, and Robert D. Smith, a Brethren—neither of whom would be a likely candidate for a walkout, due to their religious beliefs.

26 Dupre, interview with author, Nov. 18, 2010.

27 Everson to Keeton, May 16, 1944, BHLA.

28 Keeton to Everson, May 20, 1944, BHLA.

29 Everson to Keeton, May [illegible], 1944, BHLA. Correspondence over the ensuing decades, particularly in personal letters, refers to the group in various ways, including the acronym "FAG" After Bill Eshelman and Tom Polk Miller launched the Waldport Project in the 1990s, they began to use the acronym FAW, for Fine Arts at Waldport.

30 Gallaghan, interview with author, Jan. 17, 2011; interview with Dave Wershkul.

31 Everson to Edwa, Dec. 12, 1943, Everson Papers, UCLA.

32 Downs diary, Feb. 3, 1944.

33 It may also have been something that was decades away from being identified by the medical community: Seasonal Affective Disorder (SAD). After
moving to the somewhat brighter and drier environment at Cascade Locks,
Coffield wrote to Everson on Apr. 3, 1944, about his mood: "It may be the
climate and the setting. My mind feels lifted of a terrific weight of depression; it is partly green grass, tops on the trees, and snow on the mountains—to say nothing of the direction of a river rather than the finality of
an ocean" (Everson Papers, UCLA).

34 Keeton to Everson, Mar. 3, 1944, BHLA.

NOTES TO CHAPTER 7

1 Don Brumbaugh to Morris Keeton, Apr. 26, 1944, Camp Waldport
Records, UO; Bruce Reeves, "Sketching Class," *Tide* 3, no. 1 (May 1944):
6.

2 "The Fine Arts at Waldport: First Showing" program, Mar. 18–19, 1944,
BHLA; "Fine Arts," *Tide* 3, no. 1 (May 1944): 5.

3 Downs diary, Mar. 18, 1944.

4 "Fine Arts," *Tide* 3, no. 1 (May 1944); Everson to Coffield, May 17, 1944,
Everson Papers, UCLA.

5 Downs diary, Apr. 15, 1944.

6 Downs diary, Apr. 22, 1944; *Tide* 3, no. 1 (May 1944): 5.

7 Downs diary, Apr. 14 and 28, 1944. Review of concert is from "Fine Arts,"
Tide 3, no. 1 (May 1944): 5-6.

8 Everson to Keeton, May 16, 1944; Keeton to Everson, May 15, 1944,
BHLA.

9 Grayland, "Wartime Journey," 3–4.

10 Halper, *Clayton James,* 11.

11 *Oral History Project:* Clayton and Barbara Straker James, 99–100.

12 Everson to Sheets, Apr. 25, 1944, Eshelman letters; Everson to Keeton,
May 16, 1944, BHLA.

13 Everson to Keeton, May 16, 1944, BHLA.

14 Martin Ponch, "Towards a Legitimate Theatre," *Compass* (Spring 1944):
35–37.

15 Downs diary, June 17, 1944; Downs, "From the Pulpit to the Stage," 5.

16 *Our Town* reading sign-up sheet, BHLA; Eshelman to Fran, July 14, 1944,
Eshelman letters.

17 Everson to Sheets, June 6, 1944, Eshelman letters.

18 War Resisters League: Frances Rose Ransom to "Dear Representative,"
Apr. 27, 1944, BHLA.

19 "An Indelicate Commission," broadside, Waldport, OR: CPS 56, May 6,
1944, BHLA.

20 Keeton to Everson, May 18, 1944, BHLA.

21 Alan Harvey to Everson, May 22, 1944, BHLA.

22 "An Importunate Proposition," broadside, Waldport, OR: CPS Camp 56,
n.d. [1944], BHLA. For further comment on the anthology project, see
appendix 3.

23 Anne Kiley and Joseph Fairbanks, "Whittier College," in *Founded by Friends: The Quaker Heritage of Fifteen American Colleges and Universities,* eds. John W. Oliver Jr., Charles L. Cherry, and Caroline L. Cherry (Lanham, MD: Scarecrow Press, 2007), 195; Downs diary, Apr. 12 and 13, 1944; William Everson, "Evaluation of Ruth Suckow's Visit, June 13–20," Camp Waldport Records, UO.

24 Glenn L. Evans, "Strange Fruit," *Tide* 3, no. 1 (May 1944): 4.

25 Eshelman to Wes Smith, May 12, 1944, Eshelman letters.

26 Eshelman to Bob Carey, May 26, 1944; Eshelman to [unknown], May 14, 1944, Eshelman letters.

27 Education Report for June–July 1944, Camp Waldport Records, UO.

28 Ibid; Reeves, interview with author, May 11, 2013.

29 Education Report for June–July 1944, Camp Waldport Records, UO.

30 Ibid.

31 Everson to Keeton, May 16, 1944, BHLA; Eshelman to Bob Carey, Apr. 8, 1944, Eshelman letters.

32 Miller's responses to the invitation and rejection compiled from: Miller to Everson, Jan. 20, Mar. 23, and Mar. 31, 1944, Everson Papers, UCLA.

33 Everson and Powell, *Take Hold,* 451–54.

34 Miller to Everson, Sept. 6, 1944, Everson Papers, UCLA.

35 Everson to Keeton, July 3, 1944, BHLA.

36 Dupre, interview with author, Nov. 18, 2010.

37 Ibid.

38 Everson to Keeton, July 3, 1944, BHLA.

39 Dupre to Keeton, June 30, 1944, BHLA.

40 Downs diary, June 7, 1944. While the case at CPS camps was overwhelmingly in favor of pacifism, it's worth a reminder that not all conscientious objectors were pacifists, as Warren Downs notes in his diary for June 11, 1944: "Learned from Roger that one of the men at Mapleton (John Welch, a JW) got in an argument apparently and socked Vic [McLane]. Vic refused to hit back, even though everyone thought he should. Somewhere in the course of all this, Welch pulled a knife and cut Floyd Sexton's hand, and seemed on the verge of stabbing him more fatally. A Forestry man who was present is quite incensed at all this, and is going to 'do something about it,' according to Roger. The Mapleton bunch has a few good kids like Martin, [McLane], Armentrout, but on the whole they're a motley bickering crew."

41 Everson and Powell, *Take Hold,* 466.

42 Halper, *Clayton James,* 12.

43 "Poems of Conscription," *Pacifica Views* 2, no. 13 (Sept. 1, 1944): 3; J. F. Powers, "William Everson: *War Elegies* and *Waldport Poems,*" *Accent* 3, no. 5 (Spring 1945): 191; Donald F. Drummond, "Minority Report," *Poetry* (Feb. 1945): 281; Coffield to Everson, Aug. 10, 1944, BHLA. In the same letter, Coffield voiced his enthusiasm for another young poet: "I would like to put in a popular request for a collection of Bill Stafford's poems after the *War Elegies.* Stafford is ripe. He has had poems in *Retort* and *Motive* and is generally in the light. Not only that, it would be an expression of good faith to publish the works of a C.P.S. man who is not

actually at the school. Such an expression is much needed to counter a lot of criticism, and I do not think there is much question but what Stafford's work would hold up."

44 Everson and Powell, *Take Hold,* 466.

45 Del Vaniman, "Contemplation of My Navel on the Slope of Mt. Hood," *Illiterati* 3 (Summer 1944): unpaginated.

46 Bill Stafford, "So Long, Chimes," *Illiterati* 3 (Summer 1944): unpaginated.

47 Kermit Sheets, "Pilgrimage to Henry Miller," *Illiterati* 3 (Summer 1944): unpaginated.

48 Glen Coffield, "The Only Truths Are Those Men Dream About," *Illiterati* 3 (Summer 1944): unpaginated. Also, Coffield to Everson, Mar. 27, 1944, BHLA. In this letter, Coffield revisits the topic from that day on Project (noted by Warren Downs in his January 31, 1944 diary entry). "There is a discussion in January *Ethics* relative to our prolonged discussion of relativity and absolutism. He [the author] carries to the logical conclusion, the relativity of the definitions of all works and traditional nature of language, in addition to the obvious relativity of the accuracy of the senses, so that if any man ever dreams that he can state an absolute, his dream is absolutely ridiculous."

49 "The Fine Arts at Waldport," *Compass* 2, nos. 1–2 (Summer–Fall 1944): 20–27.

NOTES TO CHAPTER 8

1 Mary Manche Langley was born February 9, 1918, to Lotus Lee Langley and Eva Grace Allen. Her aunt was Manche Irene Langley (Jones, "All Done," 21, 33).

2 Manche Langley, interview with Eliza Jones, 2004, Manche Harvey Langley Collection, OLPb019LAN, Lewis and Clark College Aubrey Watzek Library Archives & Special Collections, Portland, OR (hereafter cited as Langley Collection, L&C), tape 9; Jones, "All Done," 47. On Saroyan and Steinbeck, see Ellingham and Killian, *Poet Be Like God,* 41.

3 Manche Langley, interview, tape 4, Langley Collection, L&C.

4 Ibid.

5 Langley to [Sheets?] ca. June 1944, Sheets Collection, L&C.

6 Ibid., July 10, 1944.

7 Manche Langley, interview, tape 9, Langley Collection, L&C.

8 Ibid.

9 Ibid., tape 5.

10 Ibid., tape 13.

11 Ibid., tape 5.

12 Erle and Harvey to Keeton, June 3, 1944, BHLA. The spelling of Erle's surname is inconsistent. A letter dated June 3, 1944, is signed "Broadus Earl" (BHLA), and it is spelled as such in his CPS files (Swarthmore) as well as the CPS *Directory* editions of 1947 and 1996. However, references to him

in Camp Angel records and correspondence from 1944 and later, as well as his *New York Times* obituary, spell his name "Erle." It may be possible that he chose to change the spelling while at Waldport.

13 Rarey and Falorni, *Fools and Heroes.*

14 Dupre to Erle and Harvey, June 27, 1944, BHLA.

15 Hammond to Gory, June 27, 1944, BHLA.

16 Harvey to James, n.d. [July 1944], Everson Papers, UCLA.

17 Everson to Hammond, July 3, 1944, BHLA.

18 Downs diary, July 6, 1944.

19 Kermit Sheets, *The Mikado in CPS.* A full examination of the February performance at Cascade Locks is given in Kovac, *Refusing War, Affirming Peace,* 123–26.

20 Sheets, interview with author, Aug. 5, 2004. He insisted that the booklet was not important, merely a lark, although he did admit that he must have felt it possessed enough value to commit it to print.

21 "Brief Report on the Theatre Group of the Fine Arts at Waldport," n.d. [Jan. 1946], BHLA..

22 Adrian Wilson, *Two against the Tide,* 37–38.

23 Ibid., 47.

24 Ibid., 70.

25 Ibid., 82.

26 Ibid.

27 Ibid., 83–84.

28 Ibid., 85–86.

29 Ibid., 88.

30 Ibid., 87. Adrian also wrote here of how they traversed the thick woods by walking on giant felled tree trunks left behind by the early loggers, the lengths being too heavy to lift or drag out. While hitchhiking, Adrian met a driver who said that he had worked in logging for some time, but he couldn't abide the company cutting down fourteen-foot-diameter trees and then leaving them where they lay because they were too big to move, so he quit.

31 Vladimir Dupre summed it up succinctly: "I was never the director. . . . Everson was always the director, no matter what" (interview with author, Nov. 18, 2010).

32 Wight, Baur, and Phillips, *Morris Graves,* 32; Halper, *Clayton James,* 10.

33 Palandri, "Waldport," 26.

34 Graves to Everson, June 22, 1944, Everson Papers, UCLA.

35 Everson to Graves, July 3, 1944, Everson Papers, UCLA.

36 Everson, interview by Teiser, "Brother Antoninus," 32–33; Eshelman to [unknown], Aug. 8, 1944, Eshelman letters. Big Creek is also identified as such on Forest Service maps of the time. Interestingly, it is not mentioned in any edition of *Oregon Geographic Names,* the definitive reference work on Oregon names, published in multiple editions since 1928.

37 Vladimir Dupre, interview with author, Nov. 18, 2010; Manche Langley, interview, tape 5, Langley Collection, L&C.

38 Eshelman to Jim, Aug. 18, 1944; Eshelman to Fran, Sept. 13, 1944.

39 Everson, interview by Teiser, "Brother Antoninus," 32–33.

40 Adrian Wilson, *Two against the Tide,* 34; Vladimir Dupre, interview with author, Nov. 18, 2010.

41 Everson, interview by Teiser, "Brother Antoninus," 32–33.

42 This incident is reconstructed from two interviews: Palandri, "Waldport," 27, and Everson, interview by Teiser, "Brother Antoninus," 34–36. The dialogue from both sources is nearly identical, reinforcing the accuracy of these accounts.

43 Victor McLane interview, Faulconer, L&C.

44 *Oral History Project:* William Eshelman, 53; Eshelman, *No Silence!,* 25. In both publications, Eshelman names Jim Gallaghan as the person planting the trees roots-up. Also, the March 13, 1943, *Untide* printed a cartoon of a tree with two dozen trunks sprouting out, dated "2500 A.D." and with a sign identifying "The Famous Gallahan [*sic*] spruce." However, when the author interviewed Gallaghan in 2011 and asked directly if he had done it, the ninety-two-year-old retired mill worker said, "No. . . . I would have told them to shove the trees up their ass, first."

45 Fine Arts Group meeting minutes, Aug. 19, 1944, BHLA.

46 Monday Night Meeting minutes, September 4 and 11, 1944, BHLA.

47 Jerry Rubin interview, Faulconer, L&C. This is Gerald Rubin, not the Jerry Rubin of 1960s political activism fame.

48 Palandri, "Waldport," 21.

49 Ibid., 21–22. Some called him "Pope Bill," said Jim Gallaghan in a 1996 interview. "There was an Irishman, a drunken Irishman, who lived up the hill, across the road from us, and he's the one who nicknamed him Pope Bill" (Faulconer, L&C).

50 Eshelman to Norm, Aug. 3, 1944, Eshelman letters.

51 "Memo to the Camp from Dick Mills," Aug. 16, 1944, Camp Waldport Records; J. N. Weaver to Harold Row, Nov. 8, 1944, Center on Conscience and War Records (DG 025, Series C-1, Box 89, General Material), Swarthmore College Peace Collection.

52 Compiled from Monday Night Meeting minutes, Sept. 4 and 11, 1944, and Minutes of the Fine Arts Meeting, Aug. 25, 1944, BHLA.

NOTES TO CHAPTER 9

1 Adrian Wilson, *Two against the Tide,* 92.

2 Eshelman to Jim, Sept. 20, 1944, Eshelman letters.

3 Patchen to Nomland, Aug. 13, 1944, Untide Press Records, Bancroft.

4 "Minutes of Fine Arts Meeting," Aug. 25, 1944, BHLA.

5 Glenn Evans, "CPS and the Race Problem," *Compass* 2, nos. 1 and 2 (Summer–Fall, 1944): 19.

6 "Men Who Made this Compass," *Compass* 2, nos. 1 and 2 (Summer–Fall, 1944): 43–44.

7 "The Fine Arts at Waldport," *Compass* 2, nos. 1 and 2 (Summer–Fall, 1944): 21.

8 Ibid., 22.

9 Adrian Wilson, *Two against the Tide,* 96, 99; *Aria da Capo* program, BHLA.

10 *Oral History Project:* Barr, 19–20; interview with author.

11 Dupre to Everson, Sept. 24, 1944, Everson Papers, UCLA.

12 Eshelman to John, Earl, Jim, Oct. 9, 1944, Eshelman letters.

13 Kovac, *Refusing War, Affirming Peace,* 133.

14 Eshelman to John, Earl, and Jim, Oct. 9, 1944; Eshelman to Jim, Oct. 9, 1944, Eshelman letters.

15 Dupre to Everson, Sept. 29, 1944, Everson Papers, UCLA.

16 Downs diary, Sept. 20, 1944.

17 Adrian Wilson, *Two against the Tide,* 97.

18 Ibid., 97.

19 Dupre to Everson, Sept. 29, 1944, Everson Papers, UCLA.

20 Downs diary, Sept. 25 and 26, 1944.

21 Adrian Wilson, *Two against the Tide,* 100.

22 Ibid., 101–2.

23 Ibid., 102.

24 Downs diary, Oct. 5 and 18, 1944.

25 Ibid., Oct. 21, 1944; Adrian Wilson, *Two against the Tide,* 102–3.

26 Adrian Wilson, *Two against the Tide,* 103.

27 Schlesinger, *Almanac of American History,* 498.

28 *Oral History Project:* Eisenbise, 50–51.

29 *Tide* 3, no. 1 (May 1944): 3.

30 Adrian Wilson, *Two against the Tide,* 99.

31 Downs diary, Oct. 15, 1944; *BCPS Bulletin,* Oct. 20, 1944; *CPS Directory,* rev. 1996, 422. In that curious manner of coincidence (or fate, depending on one's perspective), another Waldport-related death had occurred in August but was barely noted. According to the September 1, 1944, *BCPS Bulletin,* Jerry H. Bell, a twenty-four-year-old Brethren church member who'd changed his mind and decided to enroll in military service, had been granted furlough in May to await his induction. Living with his in-laws at Newberg, west of Portland, he was driving home from his preinduction physical exam when he was hit head-on by a logging truck whose driver had lost control of his rig. Bell died of his injuries three days later. In a further twist to the story, the *Bulletin* noted his hometown: Accident, Maryland.

32 Adrian Wilson, *Two against the Tide,* 103.

33 Richard C. Mills, "The Impact of the Resentful Individual upon CPS Camps," 3.

34 Ibid., 5–6.

35 Compiled from Everson to Sheets, Oct. 29, 1944, Sheets, L&C; Eshelman to "guys," Nov. 2, 1944, Eshelman letters; Fine Arts Group meeting minutes, Nov. 8, 1944, BHLA.

36 Story of the kitchen fire compiled from Everson to Sheets, Oct. [30], 1944, Sheets, L&C; Eshelman, "7:00 a.m.," mimeographed letter, Oct. 30, 1944, Eshelman letters; *Oral History Project:* Pottenger, 192–93; Clayton James, interview with author; Orville Richman to Forest Supervisor, Nov. 4, 1944, and Richard C. Mills, "Report of Fire Occurring in North End of the Dining Hall on the Early Morning of October 30, 1944, C.P.S. Camp #56, Waldport, Oregon," Box 20, CPS Camp 56, National Archives and Records Administration—Pacific Alaska Region, Seattle (hereafter cited as NARA).

37 Everson to Kermit, Oct. 29, 1944, Eshelman letters.

38 Eshelman to "Kermer," Nov. 2, 1944; Eshelman to "guys," Nov. 2, 1944, Eshelman letters.

39 Fine Arts Group meeting minutes, Nov. 8, 1944, BHLA.

40 Ibid.

41 Ibid.

42 Adrian Wilson, *Two against the Tide,* 105.

43 Ibid., 107–8.

44 Ibid., 104, 107, 109.

45 "Christian Service," *Tide* 3, no. 1 (May 1944): 2. While the Christian Service Group was a self-styled loose confederation of individuals, the implied association with other religious groups was inevitable—in the same way that some camp members did not differentiate between the Fine Arts and the various publishing operations that used the same press.

46 Religious Life Committee Report: "10/42–12/44," BHLA.

47 Education Report, Oct. 1944, Camp Waldport Records, UO.

48 Martin Ponch, interview, Faulconer, L&C. As cited in Ryder, "Here on the Edge," 28.

49 Fine Arts meeting minutes, Nov. 3, 1944, BHLA.

50 Adrian Wilson, *Two against the Tide,* 108.

51 Ibid., 108. Regarding the vote on the Fine Arts, reports of the exact count are inconsistent. "Evaluation of Fine Arts Program" [Nov. 1944], from the main camp and Hebo side camp, shows a 45 to 20 vote that the Fine Arts be continued (BHLA). Morris Keeton, in a Nov. 28, 1944, letter to Everson, mentions a "52 to 13 vote of confidence" (BHLA). Adrian Wilson quotes a 46 to 13 result (Adrian Wilson, *Two against the Tide,* 108).

52 Robert Scott, "To Whom It May Concern," Nov. 14, 1944, BHLA.

53 Eshelman, *No Silence!,* 43.

54 Downs diary, Nov. 14, 1944.

55 Everson to Keeton, Nov. 21, 1944, BHLA.

56 "Evaluation of Fine Arts Program," [Nov. 1944], BHLA.

57 Adrian Wilson, *Two against the Tide,* 117.

58 The author has found enough references and names noted in letters and interviews to substantiate the veracity of these general statements. To list the details seems unnecessary.

59 Adrian Wilson, *Two against the Tide,* 110–12, 114–15. John Welch at Waldport is listed in the 1947 edition of the CPS *Directory* as well as in

NSBRO personnel files, Center on Conscience and War Records (DG 025, Series C-1, Box 89, Director), Swarthmore Peace Collection. He is not listed in the 1996 *Directory* or on Web sites that used this edition.

60 Downs diary, Dec. 7, 1944.

61 Everson to Keeton, Dec. 14, 1944, BHLA.

62 Adrian Wilson, *Two against the Tide,* 111. The CPS *Directory* appears to have inverted the order of camps attended by Miller; it lists that he was at Cascade Locks before Waldport and at Tallahassee afterwards. However, letters in the BHLA between Miller and Everson in July and August 1944 confirm that Miller came to Waldport from the Florida camp.

63 Adrian Wilson, *Two against the Tide,* 113.

64 Ibid., 110, 116–17.

65 Ibid., 118.

66 Everson and Powell, *Take Hold,* 404–6.

NOTES TO CHAPTER 10

1 "New Year's Dance Saturday Night," *Lincoln County Times,* Dec. 28, 1944, 1.

2 "The Act Has a Nasty Odor!!!" *Lincoln County Times,* Jan. 4, 1945, 2.

3 Jadiker interview, Faulconer, L&C.

4 Crumpton to Row, Feb. 13, 1945, BHLA.

5 F. W. Furst to "Operation," Mar. 2, 1945, NARA, Box 20, CPS Camp 56.

6 "Geo. B. Williamson" to Col. Wooten, Jan. 20, 1945, BHLA.

7 Lewis F. Kosch to George B. Williamson, Feb. 2, 1945, BHLA.

8 Eshelman to Haskell, Feb. 16, 1945, Eshelman letters.

9 Compiled from Eshelman to Haskell, Feb. 16, 1945; Huston to Row, Mar. 24, 1945, and Dupre to Row, Mar. 27, 1945, BHLA.

10 Adrian Wilson, *Two against the Tide,* 120.

11 Ibid., 122.

12 Adrian Wilson, *Two against the Tide,* 120, 122; Downs diary, Jan. 13, 1945.

13 Adrian Wilson, *Two against the Tide,* 123.

14 Dupre, interview with author, Nov. 18, 2010.

15 President Franklin D. Roosevelt, State of the Union Address, Jan. 6, 1945, in the *Oregonian,* Jan. 7, 1945, 7.

16 Adrian Wilson, *Two against the Tide,* 123–24.

17 Compiled from Eshelman to Fran, Jan. 22, 1945; Eshelman to JRM, Sept. 9, 1944; and Eshelman to Jim, Nov. 2, 1944, Eshelman letters.

18 "Trial in Tennessee," 92. This Fellowship of Reconciliation publication made no secret of its editorial leanings. The article introduction notes, "The following report of testimony of defendants and arguments of the lawyers before the jury reveals vividly the sincerity of the defendants and the prejudice of the prosecution. It is not a verbatim record, but was based on careful notes. The words may not agree exactly with the court record, but they do preserve the meaning of the essential points."

19 Ponch interview, Faulconer, L&C.

20 Adrian Wilson, *Two against the Tide*, 121.

21 Ibid., 119, 121.

22 Eshelman to Norm, Jan. 22, 1945; Downs diary, Feb. 3, 1945; Adrian Wilson, *Two against the Tide*, 119.

23 Adrian Wilson, *Two against the Tide*, 121.

24 "Trial in Tennessee," 97. As quoted in Cooley, *Obeying the Commandment*, 215.

25 Cooley, *Obeying the Commandment*, 215.

26 Ibid., 216.

27 Adrian Wilson, *Two against the Tide*, 125.

28 Downs diary, Jan. 25, 1945.

29 Ibid., Jan. 29 and Feb. 1, 1945.

30 Eshelman to Haskell, Feb. 16, 1945; Eshelman to "Jn," Feb. 21, 1945, Eshelman letters.

31 *Oral History:* Russell Eisenbise, 49.

32 Dupre, interview with author, Nov. 18, 2010; Sibley and Jacob, *Conscription of Conscience*, 242, 249; *1944 Supplement to the Code of Federal Regulations of the United States of America*, Washington, DC: Division of the Federal Register, the National Archives, 1945, 2608; unsigned letter, Waldport campers to Row, Feb. 23, 1945, Camp Waldport Records, UO.

33 Richman to Forest Supervisor, May 11, 1945, NARA, Box 20, CPS Camp 56.

34 Crumpton to Row, May 10, 1945, NARA, Box 20, CPS Camp 56.

35 Kosch to J. N. Weaver, July 17, 1945, NARA, Box 20, CPS Camp 56. Chuck Cooley wrote that Selective Service demanded these men be transferred to three different camps, obviously to isolate them. "Some among us wondered if this might not have been a miscalculation, for in their evangelistic zeal, each of the three might not encourage protests in their new locations" (Cooley, *Obeying the Commandment*, 252).

36 Henry Wolff, "Why I Can No Longer Remain in Civilian Public Service Camp #56," Jan. 22, 1945, NARA, Box 20, CPS Camps. Chuck Cooley, who had known Wolff at Camp Kane in Pennsylvania, noted years later, "It had been my privilege to see his conviction mature greatly from what I interpreted as impetuousness to something that was both serious and firm" (Cooley, *Obeying the Commandment*, 212).

37 Paragraphs on the death of George Moyland are compiled from *Oral History:* Eshelman, 54, Gallaghan, 95, Johnson, 111 and Verbeck, 240; Cooley, *Obeying the Commandment*, 218; Downs diary, Mar. 9, 1945; Adrian Wilson, *Two against the Tide*, 127; Camp #56 News Release, Mar. 13, 1945, and Simon Jarvi, Siuslaw National Forest, report dated Mar. 8, 1945, NARA, Box 20, CPS Camp 56.

38 Martin Ponch letter to "Fellow CPSmen and Administrators," Mar. 12, 1945, Camp Waldport Records, UO.

39 Eshelman to Jim, Mar. 6, 1945, Eshelman letters.

40 Warren Downs, chapter on music in the Fine Arts, [ca. 1995], author collection; Adrian Wilson, *Two against the Tide*, 131–32.

41 Adrian Wilson, *Two against the Tide*, 126, 132–33.

42 Ibid., 136.

43 Compiled from Adrian Wilson, *Two against the Tide*, 134; Eshelman, *No Silence!*, 34; *Adrian Wilson, July 1923–February 1988*, pamphlet; and Eshelman, interview with author, Mar. 31, 2001.

44 Adrian Wilson, *Two against the Tide*, 137.

45 Eshelman to "Geez, guy!," Apr. 22, 1945, Eshelman letters.

46 Cooley, *Obeying the Commandment*, 208–10.

47 Everson and Powell, *Take Hold*, 478.

48 Eshelman to Linden, May 12, 1945; Eshelman to John, May 6, 1945, Eshelman letters.

49 Adrian Wilson, *Two against the Tide*, 130; Eshelman to Jim, June 15, 1945, Eshelman letters.

50 Crumpton to Row, Apr. 4, 1945, BHLA.

51 Row to Crumpton, May 12, 1945, BHLA.

52 William Everson, "A Personal Statement," June 5, 1945, Sheets Papers, L&C.

53 DeCoursey to "Mr. and Mrs. Shank," May 27, 1945; DeCoursey to "Dear Folks," May 28, 1945, Camp Waldport Records, UO.

54 Weaver to Kosch, May 31, 1945, NARA, Box 20, CPS Camps. Regarding Shank's name, the *CPS Directory* and Forest Service correspondence identify him as "Edwin." But personal letters written at the time by COs who knew and lived with him—as well as the camp roster—spell his name "Elwin" (Camp Waldport Records, UO).

55 Horton to Staff, June 18, 1945, NARA, Box 20, CPS Camp 56.

56 Andrews to "Chief, Forest Service," June 29, 1945, NARA, Box 20, Camp 56.

57 Martin Ponch, interview, Faulconer, L&C.

58 Eshelman to Mills, May 30, 1945; Eshelman to Jim, May 15, 1945, Eshelman letters.

NOTES TO CHAPTER 11

1 Cooley, *Obeying the Commandment*, 233.

2 *Oral History:* Cooley, 25–26; Cooley, *Obeying the Commandment*, 205–6, 233, 244.

3 Cooley, *Obeying the Commandment*, 272.

4 C. James to Everson, May [21?], 1945, Everson Papers, UCLA.

5 B. James to Everson, July 13, 1945, Everson Papers, UCLA.

6 C. James to Everson, May 5 and June 8, 1945, Everson Papers, UCLA.

7 Cooley, *Obeying the Commandment*, 249.

8 Everson and Powell, *Take Hold*, 482.

9 Ibid., 483, 491.

10 Cooley, *Obeying the Commandment*, 249–50.

11 Everson and Powell, *Take Hold*, 483.

12 *Compass* 2, nos. 3 and 4 (1945).

13 *Illiterati*, no. 4 (Summer 1945): unpaginated.

14 Lasar, *Pacifica Radio*, 6, 24.

15 *Illiterati*, no. 4 (Summer 1945): unpaginated.

16 Everson and Powell, *Take Hold*, 532.

17 Everson to Patchen, July 13, 1945, Untide Press Records, Bancroft.

18 Schlesinger, *Almanac of American History*, 501.

19 Sibley and Jacob, *Conscription of Conscience*, 237–41; Cooley, *Obeying the Commandment*, 247–48; Everson and Powell, *Take Hold*, 484–85.

20 Ponch to Harold Cessna, June 12, 1945, Camp Waldport Records, UO.

21 Cooley, *Obeying the Commandment*, 235.

22 *Oral History:* Clayton James, 101–2; Clayton James, interview with author.

23 Eshelman, *No Silence!*, 31; Tom Polk Miller, "Civilian Island," 15.

24 Cooley, *Obeying the Commandment*, 305.

25 Joyce Lancaster to Kermit, Aug. 22, 1945, Sheets Collection, L&C.

26 Ibby Dupre to Kermit, Nov. 11, 1945, Sheets Collection, L&C.

27 Meltzer, *Golden Gate*, 19–20.

28 Rexroth, *Autobiographical Novel*, 500; Hamalian, *Life of Kenneth Rexroth*, 20–40; and Rexroth to Everson, Sept. [n.d.] 1945, Everson Papers, UCLA.

29 Everson and Powell, *Take Hold*, 495.

30 Everson to Patchen, Nov. 14, 1945, Untide Press Records, Bancroft.

31 Patchen to Everson, Nov. 16, 1945, Untide Press Records, Bancroft.

32 Everson to Patchen, Nov. 21, 1945, Untide Press Records, Bancroft.

33 Everson to Patchen, Dec. 11, 1945; Eshelman, *Bibliography of the Untide Press*, 38; Patchen, handwritten limitation sheet from *Astonished Eye* copy, courtesy of betweenthecovers.com. There is a slight discrepancy between the two sources of this story. Patchen's account says "about 70" copies were saved in December 1945, and "23 of these" were sent to him; *Bibliography* notes say fifty were completed and twenty-five sent to the author. It seems plausible that the Untide Press version is the more accurate one. A possible distinguishing mark in the so-called first printing could be that one sheet of eight pages was printed on Hadley Deckle rather than Gabardine Book paper, but the record does not make this certain.

34 Compiled from Eisan, *Pathways of Peace*, 190–91; press release, Nov. 30, 1945; "For Sunday Papers," Dec. 2, 1945 and Camp Waldport Committee for Co-ordinating Protest to Harold Row, Nov. 21, 1945, Camp Waldport Records, UO; and "The Waldport Hunger Strike," *Pacifica Views* 3, no. 28 (Dec. 14, 1945): 4.

35 Everson and Powell, *Take Hold*, 502–3.

36 Ibid., 507, 511.

37 Dupre, interview with author, Nov. 19, 2010.

38 *Oral History:* Fillmore, 60; Church World Service, www.churchworld service.org/site/PageServer?pagename=action_who_history (accessed Oct. 11, 2011).

39 "Conchie Camp at Waldport Closes; Projects Completed," *Lincoln County Leader,* Jan. 10, 1946.

40 Beckham, *Building No. 1381,* 14.

41 *The Seagull* program notes, BHLA.

42 Tom Polk Miller to Vlad Dupre, Mar. 13, 1946, BHLA; Kermit Sheets, interview with Katrine Barber, as cited in Ryder, "To the Heart of It," 27–46.

43 Downs, chapter on music from the Waldport Project, author collection.

44 Coffield to Sheets, Mar. 14, 1946, Sheets Collection, L&C.

45 Dupre, interview with author, Nov. 18, 2010.

46 Everson and Powell, *Take Hold,* 528–29, 531.

47 Eshelman to Patchen, Apr. 10, 1946, Untide Press Records, Bancroft.

48 *Compass* 2, nos. 5 and 6 (Spring 1946).

49 Adrian Wilson, *Two against the Tide,* 162.

50 Ibid., 163–64.

51 *Oral History:* Martin Ponch, 188.

52 Adrian Wilson, *Two against the Tide,* 167.

53 Ibid., 165–68.

54 "Roaring at the Flats," *Pacifica Views* 3, no. 48 (May 3, 1946): 3.

55 Everson, interview by Teiser, "Brother Antoninus," 26–27.

56 The stories of the Cascade Locks strike and the subsequent transfers to Minersville are compiled from: "The C.P.S. Strikes," *Politics,* July 1946, 177–80; "Roaring at the Flats," *Pacifica Views* 3, no. 48 (May 3, 1946): 3, and "Revolt at Glendora," ibid., no. 49 (May 10, 1946): 3; "Cascade Locks Conchies Strike against Draft Act," *Oregonian,* May 15, 1946, 9; Kovac, *Refusing War, Affirming Peace,* 148–49; Eshelman, *No Silence!,* 37–40; and Cooley, *Obeying the Commandment,* 316–31. Cooley also names "Bowers," "Evans," Clayton and Barbara James, Ray Johnson, and Martin Ponch as strike participants—although none of them are listed on the Camp #21 roster (Kovac, 159–72) or in the *CPS Directory* as having been enrolled at Camp #21.

57 Everson and Powell, *Take Hold,* 547–48.

58 Ibid., 552–53. Everson suspected his release was delayed due to his participation in the Cascade Locks strike. He said his papers were stamped in red ink, stating that the delay was due to the RTW reports on his record (*Pacifica Views,* Aug. 23, 1946, 2). In his NSBRO personnel files, the single word "STRIKER" is written in red pencil at the top of his discharge papers (Center on Conscience and War Records, DG 025, Series F-1, Box 119, William Everson, Swarthmore College Peace Collection).

NOTES TO CHAPTER 12

1 Richard Phenix, *On My Way Home,* dust jacket blurb quoted from Lewis Gannett.

2 Charles Poore, "Books of the Times," *New York Times,* Aug. 24, 1947, sec. 7, p. 9.

3 Phenix, *On My Way Home,* 215–25.

4   Kerouac, *On the Road*, 11.

5   Ibid., 8.

6   Rexroth, *An Autobiographical Novel*. 518–20.

7   Hamalian, "Genesis of the San Francisco Poetry Renaissance," 5.

8   Parkinson, "The Poets Take Over," 19.

9   *Circle* 1, no. 2 (1944): unpaginated

10   Everson, "Latter-Day Handpress," 35.

11   William Everson, "Dionysus & the Beat."

12   Rexroth, "Letter from America": 59–65.

13   Brady, "New Cult," 312–22.

14   Wilson, *Printing for Theater*.

15   Adrian Wilson, *Two against the Tide*, 178.

16   The Interplayers story is compiled from Adrian Wilson, *Two against the Tide*, 169–88; Wilson, *Printing for Theater;* Adrian Wilson interview with Teiser; Bennett, "Adrian Wilson," 66–72; William R. Eshelman, "Adrian Wilson," inserted between 136 and 137; and J. Wilson, "Adrian Wilson," 27–30. The treatment given here is but a brief acknowledgment of the Interplayers' role in the San Francisco renaissance. A complete history of this pioneering group awaits research and publication.

17   Wilson, *Printing for Theater*, 12.

18   Adrian Wilson, *Work & Play*, 30–31; Jane Wilson, "An Adrian Wilson Checklist," 32.

19   Adrian Wilson, *Two against the Tide*, 187.

20   Nin to Broughton and Sheets, n.d., Sheets Collection, L&C.

21   *Illiterati* 5 (1948): 1.

22   *Ark* (1947): 1–2.

23   Tovey, *Guide to New American Poetry*, 28.

24   Rukeyser, "Group of Region Poets," 42–43.

25   *Circle* 10 (Summer 1948): 1.

26   Meltzer, *Golden Gate*, 91.

27   Keim and Stoltzfus, *Politics of Conscience*, 139.

28   Ibid., 145.

29   Nearing, *USA Today*, 4–9.

30   *Inaugural Addresses of the Presidents of the United States* (Washington, DC: Government Printing Office, 1965): 257–59, as cited in Nearing, 239.

31   Miller, *Big Sur and the Oranges*, 52–56.

32   Jones, "All Done."

33   Coffield, *The Grundtvig Experiment*, 10.

34   Lawrence Ferlinghetti, e-mail to author, Nov. 17, 2010.

35   Ginsberg, *Howl*, 9.

36   Rexroth, "San Francisco Letter," 5; Rexroth, "San Francisco's Mature Bohemians," 16.

37   Rexroth, "Disengagement," 41.

38   Millstein, "Books of the Times," 27.

1 Meltzer, *Golden Gate*, 91–92.

2 Everson and Powell, *Take Hold*, 511–12.

Bibliography

BOOKS AND MONOGRAPHS

Anderson, Richard C. *Peace Was in Their Hearts: Conscientious Objectors in World War II.* Scottsdale, PA: Herald Press, 1994.

Baker, John H. *Camp Adair: The Story of a World War II Cantonment.* Newport, OR: John H. Baker, 2004.

Bartlett, Lee. *William Everson: The Life of Brother Antoninus.* New York: New Directions, 1988.

Beckham, Stephen Dow. *The Resource Center, Building No. 1381, Angell Job Corps Center, Waldport, Oregon: A Historical Assessment.* Boston: USA Research, 1986.

Bernays, Edward. *Propaganda.* New York: Liveright, 1928.

Bowman, Rufus D. *The Church of the Brethren and War: 1708–1941.* Elgin, IL: Brethren Publishing House, 1944.

Brock, Peter, ed. *Liberty and Conscience: A Documentary History of the Experiences of Conscientious Objectors in America through the Civil War.* New York: Oxford University Press, 2002.

Camus, Albert. *Neither Victims Nor Executioners.* New York: Liberation, 1960.

Cantor, Margery, William Eshelman, Deanna LaBonge, and Zahid Sardar. *Adrian Wilson, July 1923–February 1988.* San Francisco: Press in Tuscany Alley, [1988].

Clay, Steven, and Rodney Phillips. *A Secret Location on the Lower East Side: Adventures in Writing, 1960–1980.* New York: The New York Public Library and Granary Books, 1998.

Coffield, Glen. *The Grundtvig Experiment.* Portland, OR: Glen Coffield, 1957.

Cooley, Charles F. *Obeying the Commandment, Trusting the Beatitude.* Columbus: Charles F. Cooley, 2000.

Cortright, David. *Peace: A History of Movements and Ideas.* Cambridge: Cambridge University Press, 2008.

Eisan, Leslie. *Pathways of Peace: A History of the Civilian Public Service Program Administered by the Brethren Service Committee.* Elgin, IL: Brethren Publishing House, 1948.

Ellingham, Lewis, and Kevin Killian. *Poet Be Like God: Jack Spicer and the San Francisco Renaissance.* Hanover, NH: Wesleyan University Press, University Press of New England, 1998.

Erickson, Doug, Paul Merchant, and Jeremy Skinner. *Footprints of Pacifism: The Creative Lives of Kemper Nomland and Kermit Sheets.* Portland, OR: The Berberis Press, 2007.

Eshelman, William R. *No Silence! A Library Life.* Lanham, MD: The Scarecrow Press, 1997.

Everson, William. *The Residual Years: Poems, 1934–1948.* Santa Rosa, CA: Black Sparrow Press, 1997.

Everson, William, and Lawrence Clark Powell. *Take Hold Upon the Future: Letters on Writers and Writing by William Everson and Lawrence Clark Powell, 1938–1946.* Edited by William R. Eshelman. Metuchen, NJ: The Scarecrow Press, 1994.

Finucane, Stephanie. A *History of the Blodgett Tract: 1890 to 1946.* Waldport, OR: Siuslaw National Forest, 1980.

Frazier, Heather T., and John O'Sullivan. *We Have Just Begun to Not Fight: An Oral History of Conscientious Objectors in Civilian Public Service during World War II.* New York: Twayne, 1996.

French, Paul Comly. *We Won't Murder: Being the Story of Men Who Followed Their Conscientious Scruples and Helped Give Life to Democracy.* New York: Hastings House, 1940.

Gara, Larry, and Lenna Mae Gara, eds. *A Few Small Candles: War Resisters of World War II Tell Their Stories.* Kent, OH: Kent State University Press, 1999.

Gingerich, Melvin. *Service for Peace: A History of Mennonite Civilian Public Service.* Akron, PA: Mennonite Central Committee, 1949.

Ginsberg, Alan. *Howl and Other Poems.* San Francisco: City Lights Books, 1956.

Goossen, Rachel Waltner. *Women Against the Good War.* Chapel Hill, NC: University of North Carolina Press, 1997.

Guetzkow, Harold Steere, and Paul Hoover Bowman. *Men and Hunger: A Psychological Manual for Relief Workers.* Elgin, IL: Brethren Publishing House, 1946.

Hall, James B., Bill Hotchkiss, and Judith Shears, eds. *Perspectives on William Everson.* Grants Pass, OR: Castle Peak Editions, 1992.

Halper, Vicki. *Clayton James.* La Conner, WA: Museum of Northwest Art, 2002.

Hamalian, Linda. *A Life of Kenneth Rexroth.* New York: W. W. Norton, 1991.

Hershberger, Guy Franklin. *The Mennonite Church in the Second World War.* Scottsdale, PA: Mennonite Publishing House, 1951.

——. *War, Peace, and Nonresistance.* Scottsdale, PA: Herald Press, 1946.

Hurwitz, Deena, and Craig Simpson, eds. *Against the Tide: Pacifist Resistance in the Second World War: An Oral History.* 1984 War Resisters League Calendar. New York: War Resisters League, 1983.

Jacob, Philip. *The Origins of Civilian Public Service.* Washington, DC: National Service Board for Religious Objectors, [1940?].

Kass, Ray. *Morris Graves: Visions of the Inner Eye.* New York: George Braziller, 1983.

Keim, Albert N. *The CPS Story: An Illustrated History of Civilian Public Service.* Intercourse, PA: Good Books, 1990.

Keim, Albert N., and Grant M. Stoltzfus. *The Politics of Conscience: The Historic Peace Churches and America at War, 1917–1955.* Scottsdale, PA: Herald Press, 1988.

Kerouac, Jack. *On the Road.* New York: Viking, 1957.

Kovac, Jeffrey. *Refusing War, Affirming Peace: A History of Civilian Public Service Camp No. 21 at Cascade Locks.* Corvallis, OR: Oregon State University Press, 2009.

Lasar, Matthew. *Pacifica Radio: The Rise of an Alternative Network.* Philadelphia: Temple University Press, 1999.

Laughlin, James, ed. *New Directions 9.* Norfolk, CT: New Directions, 1946.

Matthews, Mark. *Smoke Jumping on the Western Fire Line: Conscientious Objectors during World War II.* Norman, OK: University of Oklahoma Press, 2006.

Meltzer, David. *Golden Gate: Interviews with Five San Francisco Poets.* Berkeley, CA: Wingbow Press, 1976.

Metres, Philip. *Behind the Lines: War Resistance Poetry on the American Homefront since 1941.* Iowa City: University of Iowa Press, 2007.

Meyer, Ernest L. *Hey! Yellowbacks!* New York: John Day, 1930.

Miller, Henry. *The Air-Conditioned Nightmare.* New York: New Directions, 1945.

———. *Big Sur and the Oranges of Hieronymus Bosch.* New York: New Directions, 1957.

Milne, A. A. *Peace with Honour: An Enquiry into the War Convention.* 4th ed. London: Methuen, 1935.

———. *War with Honour.* London: Macmillan, 1940.

National Interreligious Service Board for Conscientious Objectors. *Directory of Civilian Public Service, Revised 1996.* Washington, DC: NISBCO, 1996.

Nearing, Helen, and Scott Nearing. *USA Today.* Harborside, ME: Social Science Institute, 1955.

Nunnally, Joe. *I Was a Conscientious Objector.* Berkeley, CA: Sooner Publishing, 1948.

O'Sullivan, John, and Alan M. Meeker, eds. *The Draft and Its Enemies: A Documentary History.* Chicago: University of Illinois Press, 1974.

Peck, Jim. *We Who Would Not Kill.* New York: Lyle Stuart, 1958.

Phenix, Richard. *On My Way Home.* New York: William Sloane, 1947.

Pringle, Cyrus. *The Record of a Quaker Conscience: Cyrus Pringle's Diary.* New York: Macmillan, 1918.

Pyle, Ernie. *Here Is Your War.* New York: Henry Holt, 1943.

Rexroth, Kenneth. *An Autobiographical Novel.* New York: New Directions, 1991.

Schlesinger, Arthur M., Jr., ed. *The Almanac of American History.* New York: G. P. Putnam's Sons, 1983.

Schlissel, Lillian, ed. *Conscience in America: A Documentary History of Conscientious Objection in America, 1757–1967.* New York: Dutton, 1968.

Selective Service System. *Conscientious Objection.* Special Monograph No. 11. 2 vols. Washington, DC: Government Printing Office, 1950.

Sibley, Mulford Q., ed. *The Quiet Battle: Writings on the Theory and Practice of Non-violent Resistance.* Boston: Beacon Press, 1963.

Sibley, Mulford Q., and Philip E. Jacob. *Conscription of Conscience: The American State and the Conscientious Objector, 1940–1947.* Ithaca, NY: Cornell University Press, 1952.

Stafford, William E. *Down in My Heart.* Elgin, IL: Brethren Publishing House, 1947.

Tatum, Arlo, ed. *Handbook for Conscientious Objectors.* 9th ed. Philadelphia: Central Committee for Conscientious Objectors, 1968.

Taylor, Steven J. *Acts of Conscience: World War II, Mental Institutions, and Religious Objectors.* Syracuse, NY: Syracuse University Press, 2009.

Thomas, Norman. *The Conscientious Objector in America.* New York: B. W. Huebsch, 1923.

Tucker, Todd. *The Great Starvation Experiment: The Heroic Men Who Starved So That Millions Could Live.* New York: Free Press, 2006.

Walker, Charles C., ed. *Quakers and the Draft: A Workbook Following the Friends National Conference on the Draft and Conscription, at Richmond, Indiana, October 11–13, 1968.* Philadelphia: Friends Coordinating Committee on Peace, 1968.

Wilhelm, Paul A. *Civilian Public Servants: A Report on 210 World War II Conscientious Objectors.* Washington, DC: National Interreligious Service Board for Conscientious Objectors, 1994.

Webber, Bert. *Retaliation: Japanese Attacks and Allied Countermeasures on the Pacific Coast in World War II.* Corvallis, OR: Oregon State University Press, 1975.

Wight, Frederick S., John I. H. Baur, and Duncan Phillips. *Morris Graves.* Berkeley, CA: University of California Press, 1956.

Wilson, Adrian. *Printing for Theater.* San Francisco: Adrian Wilson, 1957.

——. *Two Against the Tide: Selected Letters, 1941–1948.* Edited by Joyce Lancaster Wilson. Austin: W. Thomas Taylor, 1990.

——. *The Work and Play of Adrian Wilson: A Bibliography with Commentary.* Austin: W. Thomas Taylor, 1983.

Wittner, Lawrence S. *Rebels Against War: The American Peace Movement, 1933–1983.* Philadelphia: Temple University Press, 1984.

Zinn, Howard. *Artists in Times of War.* New York: Seven Stories Press, 2003.

ARTICLES AND BOOK CHAPTERS

Barber, Katrine, and Eliza Elkins Jones. "The Utmost Human Consequence: Art and Peace on the Oregon Coast, 1942–1946." *Oregon Historical Quarterly* 107 (2006): 510–35.

"The Beat Friar," *Time,* May 25, 1959, 58–59.

Bennett, Paul A. "Adrian Wilson: Designer-Printer at Tuscany Alley." *Publishers' Weekly,* 185, no. 15 (April 6, 1964): 66–72.

Bone, Ida Mae. "A Taste of War at Fort Stevens." *Oregon Coast* (Dec. 1987/Jan. 1988): 26–28.

Brady, Mildred Edie. "The New Cult of Sex and Anarchy." *Harper's* (Apr. 1947): 312–22.

Edwards, G. Thomas. "The Oregon Coast and Three of Its Guerilla Organizations, 1942." In *The Pacific Northwest in World War II*, ed. Carlos A. Schwantes, 20–34. Manhattan, KS: Sunflower University Press, 1986.

Eshelman, William R. "Adrian Wilson: Book Designer, Printer and Publisher." *California Librarian* 22, no. 1 (Jan. 1961).

Etter, Orval, ed. *Fellowship of Reconciliation Oregon Newsletter*, 1943–45.

[Everson, William] Brother Antoninus. "Dionysius [*sic*] and the Beat Generation." *Fresco, The University of Detroit Quarterly* 9 (Summer 1959): 2–8.

Everson, William. "Dionysus and the Beat: Four Letters on the Archetype." *Sparrow* 63 (Dec. 1977): unpaginated.

———. "Latter-Day Handpress: A Venture in Joy, Knowledge, and Tribulation." *Book Club of California Quarterly News-Letter* 15, no. 2 (Spring 1950): 31–39.

———. "Of Robert Duncan." *Credences*, nos. 8/9 (Mar. 1980): 147–51.

Freeman, Russell. "In the Beginning: The Story of the First C.P.S. Camp." *Compass* 1, no. 3 (Spring 1943): 8–9, 52–53.

Grayland, Vicki. "Wartime Journey." *Inkfish* (Aug. 1995): 3–4.

Hallett, Elizabeth V. "Civilian Public Service Camp #56." *Oregon Heritage* (Winter–Spring 1995): 24–28.

Hamalian, Linda. "The Genesis of the San Francisco Poetry Renaissance: Literary and Political Currents, 1945–1955." *Literary Review* 32, no. 1 (Fall 1988): 5–8.

Hesseldahl, Norm. "The New Deal on the Oregon Coast." *Oregon Coast* (May–June 1990): 50–52.

Justice, Joyce. "World War II Civilian Public Service: Conscientious Objector Camps in Oregon." *Prologue* 23 (Fall 1991): 266–73.

Lamantia, Philip. "Letter from San Francisco." *Horizon* (Oct. 1947): 118–23.

Lewis, William B. "World War II Mystery Solved." *Oregon Coast* (Jan./Feb. 2009): 59–61.

Maclaine, Christopher. "We and They: The Artist in California." *Poetry* (Aug. 1948): 256–61.

Marshall, Don. "The Cowboy Coast Guard." *Oregon Coast* (Jan./Feb. 1997): 39–41.

Martin, Tom, Sr. "Beach Patrol." *Oregon Coast* (Nov./Dec. 1997): 73–75.

Miles, Josephine. "Pacific Coast Poetry: 1947." *Pacific Spectator* 2 (Spring 1948): 134–50.

Millstein, Gilbert. "Books of the Times." *New York Times,* September 5, 1957.

O'Neil, Paul. "The Only Rebellion Around." *Life* (Nov. 30, 1959): 115–30.

Palandri, Guido. "Waldport: An Interview with William Everson." *Imprint: Oregon* 5, nos. 1–2 (Fall–Spring 1978–79): 2–27.

Parkinson, Thomas. "Phenomenon or Generation." In *A Casebook on the Beat*, ed. Thomas Parkinson, 276–90. New York: Thomas Y. Crowell, 1961.

———. "The Poets Take Over." *Literary Review* 32, no. 1 (Fall 1988): 66–72.

Rexroth, Kenneth. "Disengagement: The Art of the Beat Generation." *New World Writing*, no. 11 (1957): 28–41.

———. "Letter from America." *Now* #7 (Feb.–Mar. [1947]): 59–65.

———. "San Francisco Letter." *Evergreen Review*, no. 2 (1957): 5–14.

———. "San Francisco's Mature Bohemians." *The Nation* (Feb. 23, 1957): 159–62.

Rukeyser, Muriel, ed. "A Group of Region Poets." *Pacific Spectator* 2 (Winter 1948): 42–55.

Ryder, Andrew. "Here on the Edge: Community-Building Theatre during World War II." *Platform* 5 (Spring 2011): 19–39. London: Royal Holloway, University of London.

———. "Living from Moment to Moment: Kermit Sheets, Theatre, and the Fine Arts at Waldport, 1942–1946. *Western States Theatre Review* 16 (2010): 40–54.

———. "To the Heart of It: American Theatre from Hedgerow to the Oregon Coast." *Theatre Annual* (2010): 27.

Stafford, Kim. "Our Man of the Mountain: Oregon's Glen Coffield and the Grundtvig Folk School." *Oregon Quarterly* (Summer 2008): 31–36.

Thompson, Robert E. S. "Onward, Christian Soldiers." *Saturday Evening Post*, Aug. 16, 1941, 27, 53–54, 56.

"Trial in Tennessee." *Fellowship* 10, no. 5 (May 1944): 92, 97.

Wilson, Jane. "Adrian Wilson: The Book Designer in Tuscany Alley." *Book Club of California Quarterly News-Letter* 33, no. 2 (Spring 1968): 27–30.

———. "An Adrian Wilson Checklist." *Book Club of California Quarterly News-Letter* 33, no. 2 (Spring 1968): 31–36.

CIVILIAN PUBLIC SERVICE PUBLICATIONS

Brethren Civilian Public Service (BCPS) Bulletin (Elgin, IL), 1944–45.

The Compass (West Campton, NH; Gatlinburg, TN; Waldport, OR; Cascade Locks, OR), 1942–46.

The Fine Arts at Waldport (Waldport, OR), 1944.

The Illiterati (Cascade Locks, OR; Waldport, OR; Pasadena, CA), 1942–55.

Pacifica Views (Glendora, CA; San Francisco; Chicago), 1943–47.

The Reporter (Washington, DC), 1942–46.

The Tide (Waldport, OR), 1942–44.

The Untide (Waldport, OR), 1943–44.

NEWSPAPERS

Eugene (OR) Register-Guard
Lincoln County (OR) Leader
Lincoln County (OR) Times
Newport (OR) Journal
Portland Oregon Daily Journal
Portland Oregonian

INTERVIEWS

Barr, Francis. Interview by author, telephone, May 27, 2013.

Cooley, Charles. Interview by author, telephone, Mar. 19, 2010.

Davis, Charles, William Eshelman, James Gallaghan, William Jadiker, Manche Harvey, Kemper Nomland, Martin Ponch, Bruce Reeves, Jerry Rubin, Kermit Sheets, Victor McLane. Interviews by Dave Wershkul, videocassette, 1995–96. Tracy Faulconer Collection, Special Collections, Lewis and Clark College, Portland, OR.

Downs, Warren. Interview by author, telephone, May 1, 2010.

Dupre, Vladimir. Interview by author, Davis, CA. Nov. 18 and 19, 2010.

Eshelman, William, and Pat Rom. Interview by author, Portland, OR. Mar. 31, 2001.

Etter, Orval. Interview by author, Eugene, OR, Mar. 21, 2010 and Jan. 8, 2011.

Everson, William. *Brother Antoninus: Poet, Printer, and Religious.* Interview by Ruth Teiser, University of California Bancroft Library/Berkeley Regional Oral History Office, 1966. www.archive.org/stream/brotherantoninu-sooeverrich/brotherantoninusooeverrich_djvu.txt (accessed Mar. 29, 2011).

Gallaghan, James. Interview by author, Monroe, OR. Jan. 17, 2011.

James, Clayton. Interview by author, La Conner, WA. Sept. 13, 2011.

Reeves, Bruce. Interview by author, telephone, May 11, 2013.

Sheets, Kermit. Interview by author, Novato, CA. Aug. 5, 2004.

Wilson, Adrian. *Adrian Wilson: Printing and Book Designing.* Interview by Ruth Teiser, University of California Bancroft Library/Berkeley Regional Oral History Office, 1966. www.archive.org/stream/printingbookoowilsrich/printingbookoowilsrich_djvu.txt (accessed Sept. 14, 2010).

SPECIAL COLLECTIONS AND ARCHIVES

Angell Civilian Public Service Camp No. 56 Collection. Waldport Heritage Museum. Waldport, OR.

Archives. Angell Job Corps Center. Yachats, OR.

Bruce Reeves Collection. Aubrey Watzek Library Archives and Special Collections, Lewis and Clark College. Portland, OR.

Camp No. 56 Records. Brethren Historical Library and Archives. Elgin, IL.

Camp Waldport Records. Special Collections and University Archives, University of Oregon Libraries. Eugene, OR.

Center on Conscience and War Records. Swarthmore College Peace Collection. Swarthmore, PA.

Civilian Public Service Camp No. 56 photographs. Siuslaw National Forest Waldport Ranger District. Waldport, OR.

CPS Camp #56 files. National Archives and Records Administration—Pacific Alaska Region. Seattle.

Francis Barr CPS Collection. Archives and Brethren Historical Collection, Funderburg Library, Manchester University. North Manchester, IN.

Glen Stemmons Coffield Papers. Special Collections and University Archives, University of Oregon Libraries. Eugene, OR.

Henry and Mary Blocher Collection of Civilian Public Service Photographs. Aubrey Watzek Library Archives and Special Collections, Lewis and Clark College. Portland, OR.

Kemper Nomland Collection of CPS Artwork. Aubrey Watzek Library Archives and Special Collections, Lewis and Clark College. Portland, OR.

Kermit Sheets Papers. Aubrey Watzek Library Archives and Special Collections, Lewis and Clark College. Portland, OR.

Manche Langley Harvey Oral History Collection. Aubrey Watzek Library Archives and Special Collections, Lewis and Clark College. Portland, OR.

Oregon CPS Oral History Collection. Aubrey Watzek Library Archives and Special Collections, Lewis and Clark College. Portland, OR.

Untide Press Records. The Bancroft Library, University of California, Berkeley.

Waldport, OR, files. Oregon Historical Society. Portland, OR.

William Everson Papers. William Andrews Clark Memorial Library, University of California, Los Angeles.

World War II files. Oregon Coast History Center. Newport, OR.

UNPUBLISHED WORKS, THESES, DISSERTATIONS

Downs, Warren. "The Spoken Word: From the Pulpit to the Stage." [1998]. Author's collection.

———. Typescript selections from diary for 1944. SFM 239, Special Collections and University Archives, University of Oregon Libraries. Eugene, OR.

———. Holograph diary for 1945. Author's collection.

Eshelman, William. Letters. From the collection of Pat Rom.

Eshelman, William, and Warren Downs. Manuscript chapters from The Waldport Project, an unfinished collaboration by Camp #56 members. Author's collection.

Jones, Eliza Elkins. "All Done as a Real Pacifist: Manche Langley's Recollections of Peace and Art in America's Mid-Twentieth Century Far West." Master's thesis, Portland State University, 2005.

Miller, Tom Polk. "Civilian Island: Some Aspects of Alternative Service for Conscientious Objectors, 1941 to 1946." Paper presented at the Denton Forum, Feb. 16, 1985. SFM 237, Special Collections and University Archives, University of Oregon Libraries. Eugene, OR.

Mills, Richard C. "History of the Founding and Organization of the Waldport Camp." Camp Waldport Records, Bx 034, Special Collections and University Archives, University of Oregon Libraries. Eugene, OR.

———. "The Impact of the Resentful Individual upon CPS Camps." [Oct. 1944]. Earl Garver Papers. Archives and Brethren Historical Collection, Funderburg Library, Manchester University. North Manchester, IN.

Ritter, Marilynn Alper. "Hard Time: The Effects of Internment on Political Prisoners of Conscience." Master's thesis, University of Oregon, 1982.

Robinson, Mitchell Lee. "Civilian Public Service during World War II: The Dilemmas of Conscience and Conscription in a Free Society." Ph.D. diss., Cornell University, 1990.

Taylor, Jacqueline A. "Civilian Public Service in Waldport, Oregon 1941–1945: The State Faces Religion, Art and Pacifism." Master's thesis, University of Oregon, 1966.

Tovey, Eloyde. "A Guide to the New American Poetry: San Francisco Bay Scene 1918–1960." Eloyde Tovey, 1984.

Walker, R[obert]. S. "An Introduction to CPS 56, Waldport, Oregon, 1942–45," Paper for Juvenile Deliquency, Soc. 122. William Stafford Archive, Lewis and Clark College, Portland, OR, May 22, 1947.

Wallach, Glenn. "The CO Link: Conscientious Objection to World War II and the San Francisco Renaissance." Senior essay, Yale University, 1981.

VIDEO RECORDINGS

Ehrlich, Judith, and Rick Tejada-Flores. *The Good War and Those Who Refused to Fight It.* Paradigm Productions in association with the Independent Television Service, 2000.

Rarey, Ondine, and Luigi Falorni. *Fools and Heroes.* Munich University of Television and Film in association with Bayerischer Rundfunk, 1998.

Werner, Michael, and Katie Campbell. *Art in a Time of War.* The Oregon Documentary Project and the University of Oregon School of Journalism and Communication, 2009.

WEB SITES

Barber, Katrine, Jo Ogden, and Eliza Jones, eds. *Camp 56: An Oral History Project, World War II Conscientious Objectors and the Waldport, Oregon Civilian Public Service Camp.* www.ccrh.org/oral/co.pdf (accessed Feb. 28, 2008).

Carnegie Endowment for International Peace: Endowment History. www.carnegieendowment.org/about/index.cfm?fa=history (accessed July 20, 2010).

"The Civilian Conservation Corps." *American Experience.* www-tc.pbs.org /wgbh/americanexperience/media/uploads/special_features/download_files /ccc_transcript.pdf (accessed Oct. 19, 2010).

The Civilian Public Service Story: Living Peace in a Time of War. civilianpublicservice.org (accessed Aug. 2, 2011).

Global Anabaptist Mennonite Encyclopedia Online. www.gameo.org/encyclopedia/contents/C52.html (accessed Apr. 21, 2010).

"Life on the Home Front: Oregon Responds to World War II." arcweb.sos.state .or.us/exhibits/ww2/index.htm (accessed Nov. 5, 2010).

Swarthmore College Peace Collection. www.swarthmore.edu/Library/peace (accessed July 5, 2009).

Thomas, Robert McG. Jr. "Thomas Banyacya, 89, Teller of Hopi Prophecy to World." Feb. 15, 1999. www.nytimes.com/1999/02/15/us/thomas -banyacya-89-teller-of-hopi-prophecy-to-world.html (accessed March 28, 2011).

War Resisters International. www.warresisters.org/wri (accessed July 23, 2010).

Index

Freud, Sigmund, 20
Friends. *See* Society of Friends

Gallaghan, James (Jim), 58, 67, 103–4,
    186–87, 225, 294n44
Gandhi, Mahatma, 23, 230
Gardner, Millie, 269
Generation of Journey. See under Sloan,
    Jacob
George, Keith, 46
Germfask, MI. *See* Civilian Public Service
    camps: #135
Ghent, Charles, 269
Ghosts (Ibsen), 172, 177, 189–91, 268
Gibble, Pius, 49
Ginsberg, Allen, 245–50: *Howl and Other
    Poems,* 245–47
Giradoux, Jean: *Madwoman of Chaillot,
    The,* 236
Gistirak, Joe, 171, 177, 181, 183, 189–90,
    196, 217–18, 221–22, 256, 262, 268
Gleason, Madeline, 238–39
Glendora, CA. *See* Civilian Public Service
    camps: #76
Godwin, Don, 268
goldbricking, 11, 42, 100
Good News (broadsheet), 74, 267
Gotham Book Mart, 148
Gounod, Charles, 44
Goya, Francisco: *Disasters of War, The,*
    15, 77
Grabhorns (printers), 237
"Gras-Tips" (dried grass food), 56
Grateful Dead, The, 248–49
Graves, Morris, 137–142, 147, 190, 196,
    198, 200, 207, 243, 262, 271
Greenwood Press, 237
Gregory, Maude, 33, 112, 128, 134, 152,
    217, 268
Groff, Everett, 283n27
Grundtvig Folk School, 243–44. *See also*
    Coffield, Glen
guerrillas (Oregon coast), 29–31
Guetzkow, Harold, 188
Guetzkow, Lauris Steere, 188–89, 200

Habitat for Humanity, 252
Hackett, Harold, 8, 66–68, 70, 96, 99,
    113, 153, 170, 200, 256: Fine Arts, 104,
    107–9, 261, 269; protest/goldbricking,

41, 44, 64–65; *Untide,* 9, 11, 62–63,
    266; Untide Press, 76, 88, 121, 273–74
Hall, Dave, 91–93, 116, 174–75, 217
Hammond, W. M., 131
Handel, George, 106, 271
Harman, James (Jim), 67, 85, 88, 96,
    104–9 passim, 112, 121–22, 135–36,
    143, 146, 153–54, 160, 195, 200, 206,
    219, 242, 257, 262, 269: *In Praise of
    Eponymous Iahu,* 257
Harshbarger, E. L., 281n34
Harvey, Alan, 114–15
Harvey, Joyce. *See* Wilson, Joyce Lancaster
Harvey, Robert (Bob), 130–31, 170, 179,
    196, 198, 257: with Manche Langley,
    209, 242–43; music, 155–57, 173, 183,
    188, 261, 270–71; painting, 178, 189,
    191, 200, 262, 268; writing, 190, 242
Haskell, Norman, 33, 107–8, 113, 269,
    282n23
Hawkins, Bud (Havilah), 179, 183, 196,
    198, 209
Hayakawa, S. I., 255
Haydn, Joseph, 60, 188, 271
Hebo (side camp), 99, 113, 159, 169
Hedgerow Theatre, 111–12, 171, 209, 221
Heller, Joseph: *Catch-18,* 242; *Catch-22,*
    247
Hemingway, Ernest: *Farewell to Arms, A,*
    15; *Sun Also Rises, The,* 247
Henderson, William, 124
Hershey, Lewis B., 24–25, 175, 179n6
Hiebert, P. C., 281n34
Higgins, Jimmy, 145
Hill, Lewis, 202, 242
Hindemith, Paul, 271
Hirabayashi, Gordon, 50
historic peace churches, 16, 23, 25, 93
hitchhiking, 110, 197, 221, 288n18
Hitler, Adolph, 15, 240
Hockett, Himelius M., 18–19
Homer: *Iliad, The,* 270
Homig, Charles, 46
homosexuality, 66, 78, 90, 177, 231
Hood Canal, 223
Hopi Nation, 28
Horned Moon, The. See under Coffield,
    Glen
House Unamerican Activities Committee
    (HUAC), 289n23

printing presses, 85: Challenge Gordon, 80–81, 92, 113, 123, 177, 188, 220, 226, 264–65; Kelsey, 75–76, 264

Prochaska, Harry, 77, 124

Prochazka, Wencil, 271

propaganda, 20–21, 73, 81, 91, 232. *See also* public relations

protests, 43, 64–65, 101–2, 165, 178, 184–88, 199, 213–14, 224–26. *See also* strikes; walkouts

Proust, Marcel, 177

Provincetown Players, 112, 133

Public Information, Committee on, 20. *See also* public relations

Public Law 135 (pay for COs), 149

public relations, 20: origin of term, 281n23. *See also* Bernays, Edward; propaganda

Pushkin, Alexander, 107, 269

Pyle, Ernie, 68, 73

Quakers. *See* Society of Friends

Quarry Drive, 4, 251

race relations, 99, 115–16, 151, 180–83

radar, 31

Ragland, Jim, 43, 283n33

rain. *See* weather

Rambo, Christopher (Chris), 234, 239

Randolph Bourne Council, 212

Ransom, Frances Rose, 113

Read, Herbert, 148

record concerts, 52, 99, 270

Recreation Committee, 36

Red Cross, 29, 252

Redfield, Don, 285n20

Reed College (Portland, OR), 222

Reeves, Bruce, 64, 117, 122, 149, 258, 262, 290n1

Reich, Wilhelm, 230: *Function of the Orgasm*, 233

Religious Life Committee (later Religious Interest Group), 48, 74, 149, 166, 172, 181, 194–95, 267, 270

Remember Now Thy Creator, 74, 166, 267, 286n11

Rexroth, Kenneth, 211–12, 230–34, 239–41, 246–47, 249: *Thirty Spanish Poems of Love and Exile*, 244

Rhode Island School of Design, 110

Rice (Forest Service employee), 42

Rice, Kay, 269

Richman, Orville, 108, 160, 162–64, 168, 178, 184–85, 199, 206–7

Rimbaud, Arthur, 231–32

Rivera, Diego, 211

Roberts, Don, 268

Robin Hood Lodge, 223

Roosevelt, Eleanor, 29, 150

Roosevelt, Franklin D., 16, 23–24, 28, 30–31, 68–69, 101, 179, 192

Rouch, Mark, 181, 206, 268

Row, Harold, 32, 82, 147, 162, 164, 170, 175, 193–94

Royal Order of the Descendents [*sic*] of the Mole, 82

Rubin, Gerald (Jerry), 145–46, 149, 161–63, 172, 178, 187, 193, 216, 225–26, 259, 262, 268

Rubin, Jan, 145, 172, 193, 216, 259, 262

Rukeyser, Muriel, 231, 238–39

Russell, Bertrand, 23

Russell, Jane, 258

Russell, Sanders, 231–32, 239

Rutledge, Carl, 46, 51, 269

sabotage, 31–32

Salstrom, D., 284n15

San Francisco, 211: Art Festival, 236; Haight-Ashbury, 238, 247, 249; Museum of Art, 236; North Beach, 244

San Francisco Chronicle, 234

San Francisco Poetry Guild, 239

San Francisco Renaissance, 230–34, 246, 250, 287n39

San Joaquin valley, 2

Saroyan, William, 127: *My Heart's in the Highlands*, 270

Sartre, Jean-Paul: *No Exit*, 235

Scarecrow Press, 256

School of Fine Arts. *See* Fine Arts Group

School of Living, 51

Schools in CPS: School of Co-operative Living, 69; School of Foods Management, 69; School of Pacifist Living, 69, 97, 104–5; School of Race Relations, 69

Schubert, Franz, 271